THE DSM-5 SURVIVAL GUIDE:
A Navigational Tool for Mental Health Professionals

Joan D. Atwood, Ph.D., LCSW, LMFT#
Kathryn Busch, M.A., LMFT*

Joan D. Atwood, Ph.D. Professor of Marriage and Family Therapy, Hofstra University. President and CEO, New York Marriage and Family Therapists (www.NYMFT.Com)
*Kathryn Busch, M.A., LMFT. Behavior Intervention Specialist at ARHC (Association for Habilitation and Residential Care). Licensed Marriage and Family Therapist in private practice.

% A special thanks to Dominique Saint Amand, Dr. Atwood's graduate assistant, for her help with the references.

The DSM-5 Survival Guide:

A Navigational Tool for Mental Health Professionals

JOAN D. ATWOOD, PH.D.
KATHRYN BUSCH, M.A., LMFT

 iUniverse

THE DSM-5 SURVIVAL GUIDE: A NAVIGATIONAL TOOL FOR MENTAL HEALTH PROFESSIONALS

iUniverse books may be ordered through booksellers or by contacting:

iUniverse
1663 Liberty Drive
Bloomington, IN 47403
www.iuniverse.com
1-800-Authors (1-800-288-4677)

Because of the dynamic nature of the Internet, any web addresses or links contained in this book may have changed since publication and may no longer be valid. The views expressed in this work are solely those of the author and do not necessarily reflect the views of the publisher, and the publisher hereby disclaims any responsibility for them.

Any people depicted in stock imagery provided by Thinkstock are models, and such images are being used for illustrative purposes only.
Certain stock imagery © Thinkstock.

ISBN: 978-1-4917-6697-2 (sc)
ISBN: 978-1-4917-6698-9 (e)

Print information available on the last page.

iUniverse rev. date: 04/30/2015

Contents

Preface

Joan D. Atwood, Ph.D.

You have graduated with a Bachelor's Degree in Psychology or one of the other social sciences. You understand individual, psychological theory, diagnoses and philosophy very well because you have been through an excellent and thorough program. Then you enter a graduate program in Mental Health Counseling, Systemic Therapy or Marriage and Family Therapy and you are introduced to systemic thinking. Your world goes topsy-turvy. Everything you once thought about psychology, the way you thought about human behavior-- goes out the window. But after a while and several courses, you finally get it--you see the system; you understand the structure; you are finally able to apply your theory into practice. You see the socially constructed world through systemic lenses.

So you graduate and get your first job in an agency. You are very excited. But wait! You are thrown back into the psychological way of diagnosing and thinking! Topsy-Turvy again. You have case presentations with psychiatrists, psychologists and other mental health personnel--most of whom use individual psychological diagnoses and do not see through the lenses of the system. But, now it's worse because you have to do a balancing act--keep your systemic hat intact but every now and again, switch back into your individual, psychological hat. How will you ever manage this?

This is a dilemma experienced by marriage and family therapists and other systemic thinkers when they enter the world of private practice and/ or the agencies. This book is geared to that person--one who is attempting to see the world through both lenses. The book will help you learn the diagnoses as they are required by the agency and the insurance companies in order to obtain reimbursement for services, as well as help you stay grounded in systemic theory.

Each chapter presents the more common disorders as they are typically encountered in agencies. It is a book for mental health and human service professionals--graduate students in social work, counseling, psychology, clinical sociology, psychiatric nursing, and personnel in the criminal justice system. It is also a book for the experienced practitioner, psychiatrists, psychologists and other mental health professionals who want to stay grounded in systems theory but often are required to present cases or diagnose from an individual or psychodynamic point of view.

The book imparts technical knowledge in a non-technical view. It is based on many years of clinical practice by the primary author (Joan D. Atwood, Ph.D.); it is based on the feedback from graduated students as they enter the mental health fields, and based on discussions with experienced professionals who, by virtue of their agency responsibilities, have to wear two hats. It bridges the gap between the more individually, diagnosable disorders and the systemic perspective, which does not locate pathology within the individual. Looking through two different lenses allows the practitioner to see the individual within a framework or context and to free them from a mutually exclusive outlook.

Each chapter is separated into the following format: (1) a presentation of the disorder, along with the symptoms as they are typically presented, (2) a case history of someone who exhibits the disorder, (3) a description of how a therapist can recognize the disorder- for example, what does a depressed person look like, (4) a description of how the client feels, (5) The client's dilemma, (6) A brief explanation of the theories used to describe the etiology of the disorder, (7) An assessment from an individual lens, (8) An assessment from a systemic lens, (9) A list of individually based therapeutic strategies, (10) and a list of systemic strategies that could be used for treating the client.

The systemic perspective provides a practical concrete approach to clients that in many ways helps to alleviate painful symptoms. Sometimes, though, it can lack a view of the client's internal and affective experiences, which would enhance our understanding of how they experience themselves and their world. The deeper understanding of the client's emotional base increases the capacity for empathy and understanding of the client's difficulties and emotionally focused life tasks. The systemic perspective broadens this view and explores with the client their families and environment, which might be supporting their stress. Additionally, the systemic approach to therapy in terms of therapeutic outcome research is supported by many years of studies.

In some ways, this is a how to book--a survival guide so to speak for Marriage and Family Therapists and other systemic thinkers on how to manage DSM-V world. It is also a book for mental health professionals for it explores the categories they use in the agencies in order to receive insurance reimbursement. Although the book by no means covers all the disorders in the DSM-V, it is a start, a beginning. The chapters include the more common and frequently seen disorders: (1) Marriage and Family Therapists, Systemic Thinkers and the DSM-V, (2) The Developmental Disorders, (3) Oppositional Disorders, (4) Anxiety, (5) Depression, (6) Obsessive Compulsive Disorder, (7) Phobias, (8) Post Traumatic Stress, (9) Eating Disorders, (10) Sexual Dysfunctions, (11) Substance Abuse Disorders and (12) Schizophrenia, (13) Psychopharmacology.

Chapter 1

Marriage and Family Therapists, Systemic Thinkers, and the DSM-V

Joan D. Atwood, Ph.D.
Michelle Parisano, M.A., MFT

Thomas Kuhn (1962), in *The Structure of Scientific Revolutions*, set out to scientifically study and challenge commonly held assumptions about the way in which sciences change. He stated that most theorists believe that science advances in a cumulative manner, each advance building on all that preceded it-- by slow and steady increments. Kuhn, however, believed that important changes in science occur from revolution. He believed there were five stages in paradigmatic revolution. They were (1) paradigm, (2) normal science, (3) anomalies, (4) crisis stage, and (5) revolution.

A paradigm, according to Kuhn, is a fundamental image of the science's subject matter. Normal science requires a period of accumulation of knowledge in which scientists work and expand the reigning paradigm. Eventually, such research and data accumulation creates anomalies, discrepancies in the paradigm that eventually may produce a scientific revolution. When the discrepancies in the reigning paradigm increase to the point that the paradigm is no longer supported by the existing research, etc., a revolution occurs and the reigning paradigm is overthrown and a new one is born.

This chapter focuses on the three waves of family therapy and explores the notion that they represented paradigm shifts from the more psychologically based theories and therapies. It includes a brief section on the beginnings, the adolescence, and the current state of family therapy. In this way, the reader explores the different levels of analyses as one proceeds from the more traditional psychological linear models, to the more circular models, and finally into post modernism. The basic premise is that the theorists presented are examining different levels of analysis, using different lenses to "see," assess and diagnose their clients. From these frameworks, different therapeutic models flow.

Traditional Psychological Perspectives

In the twentieth century, the two most influential approaches to psychotherapy were Freud's psychoanalysis and Carl Rogers' person-centered therapy, which were both predicated on the assumption that psychological problems arose from unhealthy interactions with others and could best be alleviated in a private relationship between the therapist and patient. Psychological conflict has traditionally been approached from an individual psychological perspective. Historically, traditional psychotherapeutic approaches have focused mainly on the influence of early parent-child interactions on adult behavior, emphasizing how these interactions determine the ways we perceive reality as adults. Therapy involves regression to those early experiences, reliving the emotionality associated with them, and then working forward to the next stage or area of conflict. The role of the therapist in this model is to direct and guide the client and to help the client discover how early conflicts are relived in present interactions with others.

This view of the person came to be known as the medical model. The medical model of psychotherapy assumed that individuals exhibiting a mental disorder were "sick," and needed "medical help." The individual became a "patient" and went to a "medical doctor" where they were "diagnosed." After diagnosis, they were either given "medication" or psychotherapy or both. If this worked, they were said to be "cured."

PARADIGM SHIFT I: FROM THE INDIVIDUAL TO SYSTEMS

As previously discussed, traditionally mental illness has been explained in linear terms, either medical or psychological. In both paradigms, emotional distress is treated as a "symptom of internal dysfunction with historical causes" (Nichols, 2013, 6). Systems theory represents a paradigm shift in terms of how we understand human behavior, focusing on relationships and relationship issues between individuals, rather than the individual and individual problems viewed in isolation (Becvar & Becvar, 1999, 2006). General systems theory was the result of efforts by biologist Ludwig von Bertalanffy (1968) and sociologist Walter Buckley (1967) to investigate the principles common to all complex entities. Von Bertalanffy and Buckley hypothesized that an observer could formulate the rules that account for the functioning of interconnected parts. "This thinking represents a fundamental change from focusing on content, material substance, and the distribution of physical energy to considering pattern, process, and communication as being the essential elements of description and explanation" (Guttman, 1991, 42).

Systems are defined as open organization, which are in continuous interaction with their environments. A family can be thought of as a system, its parts being the individual members who create a whole by virtue of their interaction. From a systems theory lens, a family system is viewed as a network of interactions between family members, rather than as a collection of individual member's characteristics. Von Bertalanffy (1968) argued that the way that the parts of a system are organized determines the system's identity, which is independent of the characteristics of each individual member of the system. A system's identity is therefore created by the interaction of its parts rather than their individual content. In other words, the whole is greater than the sum of its parts.

It is important to note that systems do not exist in a vacuum. Therefore, families must be viewed in relation to other larger systems, such as the local community, educational system, legal system, and the state. Like all systems, families have boundaries that protect them from being disrupted or destroyed. Boundaries, defined by family rules, determine who is a part of the family system and who is not.

Each family member's behavior cannot be studied and treated in isolation, since the components of a family system are interrelated. All behavior and events in a family system must be considered simultaneously, relative to context, as both antecedent and subsequent to the behaviors of the other family members. Therefore, systems theory directs us away from linear cause-effect thinking (A influences B, but B does not influence A), toward a reciprocal or circular notion of causality (A influences B and B influences A), "where A and B exist in the context of a relationship in which each influences the other and both are equally cause and effect of each other's behavior" (Becvar & Becvar, 2006, 10).

Each family member is seen in relation to the other members of the family, as each affects and is affected by the other members. According to systems theory, to understand each member of a family, one must observe how each member is in relation to each of the other family members; it makes no sense to study each person independently. To study an individual member out of the context of the family relationships, is to understand that member relative to a new context, the one in which he or she is studied, rather than in the context of his or her family (Becvar & Becvar, 1999).

The Pioneers: Family Therapy Beginnings

Cybernetics

The seeds of the family therapy movement were sown by a disparate group of researchers and theorists from a variety of disciplines. Some were early explorers in the field of cybernetics. Included in this group were mathematicians Norbert Wiener, John Von Neumann, and Walter Pitts; physician Julian Bigelow; physiologists Warren McCulloch and Lorente de No; psychologist Kurt Lewin; anthropologists Gregory Bateson and Margaret Mead; economist Oskar Morgenstern; as well as others from the fields of anatomy, engineering, neurophysiology, psychology, and sociology (Wiener, 1948).

In what has since been recognized as a major departure in the way we study and come to know our world, the science of cybernetics concerned itself with organization, pattern, and process rather than with matter, material, and content. In the words of Ashby (1956), another pioneer, cybernetics "treats, not things but ways of behaving. It does not ask 'what does it do'.... It is thus essential functional and behavioristic" (p. 1). The field of cybernetics dates from approximately 1942 and Norbert Wiener is usually given credit for naming the science.

Norbert Wiener

Norbert Wiener (1948, 1954), an M.I.T. mathematician who had worked on computer technology during the war, wrote about the "Second Industrial Revolution." He coined the term "cybernetics." meaning circular and reflexive system of information flow in which information and control are linked together. This is an important forerunner of the way some systems therapists later began to look at human communication and systems interactions. More recently, Watzlawick's *How Real is Real?* (1977) delineates some of the same issues in anecdotal form. Cybernetics, known as systems theory in the United States, is the basic underlying theory of most major schools of family therapy.

Gregory Bateson

Gregory Bateson is considered to be one of the most important figures in the development of systemic family therapy, especially in the delineation of the philosophical framework underlying this movement. Bateson played a vital role in the process of bridging the worlds of the physical and behavioral sciences. His translation of the concepts of mathematics and engineering into the language of the behavioral sciences was crucial. For Bateson, cybernetics resolved the ancient problem posed by dichotomous thinking about mind and body. Rather than being considered transcendent, mind could not be described as immanent in systems.

Bateson was a leading figure in the schizophrenic research project in Palo Alto, which helped to shape the course of family therapy. Bateson, along with Jay Haley, John Weakland, William Fry, and Don Jackson, developed a theory of communication that explained the development of schizophrenic behavior within the family system. The theory was that schizophrenic symptoms function to maintain homeostasis in the family system, and therefore must be the result of interactions among family members.

Bateson and his colleagues (1956) introduced the concept of the "double bind" to describe how schizophrenic symptoms could be explained in the context of the family system. Although many of their assumptions regarding the role of the family in schizophrenia later proved to be incorrect, the research was a springboard for the developing field of family therapy. The Palo Alto group research project resulted in some of the earliest observations of organization and communication among family members.

Cybernetics of Cybernetics

With Einstein's theory of relativity (in Capra, 1983; Zukav, 1989) and Heisenberg's (1958) uncertainty principle, the certain, predictable, reductionist universe was pulled out from under us. The finding that human observations at the quantum level could actually change what was being observed moved us into a new way of understanding and *seeing*. The resulting paradigmatic shift (Kuhn, 1970) infiltrated the social sciences in the 1960s, and supported by Maturana's (1980) research and Gergen's (1985) theory, has made its way into the family therapy literature as constructivism and social constructionism the new epistemology or second-order cybernetics, holding profound implications for not only family therapy theory, but also for family therapy practice.

For example, Hoffman (1987) describes a therapeutic approach that respects a second-order cybernetic epistemology and Epston and White (1990) elaborate on its application. In Hoffman's view, the therapist initially assists the couple in learning processes that help them to amplify (be aware of) their couple processes, provides techniques that the couple can use to generate new possibilities, and is someone who creates a safe environment where the couple can explore their process, generate new possibilities, consider the implications of the possibilities, and negotiate a shared agreement around the chosen change. These ways of learning can be used by the couple outside therapy. In the sense that the therapist provides opportunities for the couple, there is initially some "therapist residue"; however, over time as the couple learns to rely on their own self-healing processes, they become more confident in the processes and their own abilities to generate growth and change.

The therapist assists clients to become aware of their present frame through an exploration of the issue. In doing so, clients decide, what, where, and how to change. In a second-order cybernetic stance, the therapist does not prescribe specifically, but instead works with clients to establish mechanisms for seeing and creating alternative points of view. The therapist helps clients to develop abilities to determine for themselves when change is necessary, and then through questioning and exploring, assists them in implementing the change. With second-order cybernetics, clients become experts on their process, their own diagnosticians, and their own generators of possibilities.

Second-order cybernetics tends to incorporate constructivism or social constructionist perspectives. Constructivism can be traced back to philosophers Kant (in Atwood, 1992), Hume (1934), Wittgenstein (in Atwood, 1992), and Husserl (in Nathanson, 1963). Piaget (1951) and Kelly (1969) represent proponents from psychology. Biologists Maturana (1980, 1987, 1988) and Varela (1979, 1981), cybernetician and biophysicists Heisenberg (1958) and Prigogine and Stengers (1984); constructivist von

Glaserfeld (1984); and anthropologist Bateson (1972, 1978, 1980, 1991) also share this perspective. Social psychologists, Cooley (1902), Mead (1934), Berger and Luckmann (1966), Reiss (1981), Gergen and Gergen (1983) and Gergen (1985) taking into account the larger sociocultural environment, contributed to the notion that our knowledge about the world is constructed by the observer and laid the groundwork for social construction theory. The proponents of the new epistemology in family therapy included Dell (1982), Keeney (1983, 1985), Tomm (1987), Anderson and Goolishian (1988), and Hoffman (1987, 1990). Social constructionism and constructivism offer new epistemological explanations of how we know what we know and are representative of second-order cybernetics.

Both constructivists and social constructionists believe that how we know what we know is *not* through an exact pictorial duplication of the world; the map is not the territory. Rather, reality is seen experientially, in terms of how we subjectively interpret the constructions (von Glasserfeld, 1984). In a sense, we are responsible for what we believe, feel, and see. What this means is that our story of the world and how it works is not the world, although we behave as though it is. Our experiencing of the world is limited to our description of it. Von Foerster (1981a, 1981b, 1984a, 1984b) states, "If you desire to see, learn how to act [take action]." Using language ("languaging") is action and it's through language that people define and experience reality. It is therefore through languaging in therapy that an environment conducive to change is created.

The Family Therapy Movement

The family therapy movement, as we know it today, grew primarily out of the field of cybernetics and psychiatry. It first appeared as a separate discipline with a series of paper emphasizing the importance of family in the etiology and management of serious emotional difficulties. In 1921 Flugel published the *Psychoanalytic Study of the Family*. In the 1930s and 1940s, Moreno's work with group psychodrama included work with married couples and other family members. In 1939 Ackerman published an article entitled "The Unity of the Family." In 1945 Richardson's book, *Patients Have Families*, was published. In 1949 in England, John Bowlby published an article, "The Study and Reduction of Group Tension in the

Family," in which he describes the idea of conjoint family interviews used as an adjunct to individual interviews at the Tavistock Child Guidance Clinic. In 1949 and 1951 in the United States, Rudolf Dreikurs of the Community Child Guidance Center of Chicago developed a similar program to the one at Tavistock.

Family therapy was founded between 1952 and 1961. It began simultaneously, among independent therapists and researchers, in many parts of the United States. By the end of the 1950s, it emerged as a connected movement whose members exchanged correspondence and visits and began to cite one another in footnotes. In 1952 a number of pioneers took major steps toward establishing conjoint family therapy as an approach to treatment. Then, in 1961 nearly all of them met to prepare the way for the first state-of-the-art joint handout and to found a common journal, *Family Process*, which first appeared in 1962 (Gurman and Kniskern, 1981, 1991).

As the field of marital and family therapy expanded and scientific research accumulated variations on systems theory emerged. MRI's communication theory (1959), Bowen's multigenerational theory (1961), Haley's strategic theory (1963), and Minuchin's structural theory (1974) provided various orientations that continue to expand the field from the more traditional individual therapies to encompass the family. These diversified theoretical orientations offered the premise that dysfunction within the marital or family system is represented by one (or more) member(s) as symptomatic behavior. In other words, using this approach, the locus of pathology and the focus of intervention are on the family system, or the context within which the individual is embedded, rather than on the individual him/herself. This, of course, represents what most theoreticians call a paradigm shift, a la Kuhn.

Some Founding Members:

Murray Bowen

Trained as a psychoanalyst, Murray Bowen's theory clearly illustrates the psychodynamic approach to family therapy. Bowen joined the staff at the Menninger Clinic in Topeka, Kansas, in 1946, and remained until

1954. Originally trained in neurosurgery, he switched to psychiatry and was among those influenced by Joseph Rosen's work with schizophrenics and their families. However, by 1950 Bowen had begun to focus on mother/child symbiosis, assuming "schizophrenia was the result of an unresolved tie with the mother" (Hoffman, 1981, 29). In 1951 he instituted a treatment plan at Menninger in which mothers and their schizophrenic children resided together for several months in cottages on the clinic grounds. In 1954 Bowen went to National Institute of Mental Health (NIMH), where he instituted and directed the classic study in which whole families of schizophrenic patients were hospitalized for observation and research. Bowen presented reports of his research in the spring of 1957, at two national professional meetings that some family therapists regard as the symbolic beginning of the family therapy movement.

In that same year, Bowen was part of a panel on family research at the meeting of the American Orthopsychiatric Association. This significant event marked the first public acknowledgment at the national level of studies previously unrecognized and somewhat underground. The panel, organized by John Spiegel, included Theodore Lidz of Yale University and David Mendel of Houston, Texas. Bowen, along with Lidz and Don Jackson, was part of the family research panel for which Nathan Ackerman served as secretary at the 1957 APA meeting in Chicago. At the time of these meetings, Bowen, who had left NIMH in 1956, was a faculty member in the department of Psychiatry at Georgetown University Medical School. His plans to take the family research project with him did not materialize, for the department chairperson who had hired him died shortly after Bowen arrived.

However, at Georgetown, Bowen developed his comprehensive theory of family therapy. Bowen (1976) viewed families as open natural systems whose members enter and exit over time, altering the boundaries of the family. Therefore, families were understood from an intergenerational perspective of interlocking, reciprocal, and repetitive relationships. Inspired by an entire generation of students, he became an internationally renowned leader of the family therapy movement. Indeed, Bowenian family therapy has made many important contributions in terms of such concepts as triangulation, intergenerational transmission, differentiation of self, and undifferentiated family ego mass.

Nathan Ackerman and Psychodynamic Family Therapy

Throughout its early years, the family therapy movement was divided along ideological lines between those who leaned toward an intrapsychic approach and those who espoused a systemic orientation. Nathan Ackerman, a child psychoanalyst, was the outstanding proponent of the former position. He combined psychodynamics with the notion of an individual's social role to understand the ongoing interaction between heredity and environment to maintain homeostasis within and between the person, the family, and ultimately, society. However, he emphasized the intrapsychic effects of families on individuals more than the effects of behavioral sequences, communication, and interaction that later systems-oriented family therapists stressed.

In the early 1950s, Nathan Ackerman began to use family interviews in his work with families, seeing the family as the proper unit of diagnosis and treatment. He believed that not only did a symptomatic family member reflect an underlying issue in the family system, but also that intrapsychic conflict was being manifested in the family system (Rasheed et al., 2011). While much other work with families was an outgrowth of research into schizophrenia, Ackerman believed that undue emphasis on this obscured family therapy's true origins "in the study of nonpsychotic disorders in children as related to the family environment" (Ackerman, 1967). For the clinical world, he provided the primary bridge between the intrapsychic and the systemic approaches to therapy. His article "The Family as a Social Unit" appeared in 1937 and is credited as the earliest publication in the field. Indeed, Ackerman is considered by some to be the "Grandfather of Family Therapy" (Nichols, 1984).

In 1955 he organized and led the first session of family diagnosis and treatment at the American Orthopsychiatry Association meeting in New York City (Nichols, 1984). Two years later he opened the Family Mental Health Clinic at Jewish Family Services in New York City, which led to the founding of the Family Institute. In 1962, two years after he opened the Family Institute, he joined Don Jackson of Palo Alto and began publishing what is today one of the most influential journals in the field, *Family Process*, with Jay Haley as the first editor. Soon after his death in 1971, the Family Institute was renamed the Ackerman Family Institute in his honor.

Carl Whitaker and the Symbolic Experiential Approach

Carl Whitaker was originally trained in obstetrics and gynecology, before moving to psychiatry and psychoanalysis. Noted for his pioneering work with schizophrenic patients and their families, he also worked with children in a child guidance format and with delinquent adolescents in a residential facility in Louisville, Kentucky. In the early 1940s, he moved to Oak Ridge, Tennessee, where, with John Warkentin, he began introducing family members into therapeutic sessions for co-therapy. Whitaker and Warkentin moved to Emory University in Atlanta, Georgia, in 1946, and Thomas Malone joined them in 1948. From 1945 to 1965, Whitaker treated schizophrenics with aggressive play therapy. He and his group experimented with various ways to treat such patients and their families.

Exposed to Rankian influences during his Louisville years, he developed an approach known as Existential Psychotherapy or Symbolic Experiential Therapy. His approach has been widely demonstrated in workshops and conferences around the United States and elsewhere. Whitaker's contributions are reflected in *From Psyche to System* (Neill and Kniskern, 1982). Whitaker also published one of the first significant papers on conjoint marital therapy (1958), and was among the first to team-teach with others and begin sharing techniques and discoveries in the growing family therapy field (Guerin, 1976).

Whitaker believes that theories are only useful for beginners; when therapists develop courage based on their abilities, they can give up theories. His model is hard to understand and almost impossible to duplicate because of his a theoretical approach. He believes that therapy is an art and recommends substituting faith in one's own abilities for theory. In this sense, therapy is a growth process from which both therapist and client share and benefit. It is an intimate, interactive, parallel experience in which each becomes equally vulnerable and neither takes responsibility for the other. It is experiential, intrapsychic, and paradoxical. The aim of Whitaker's approach is to help individuals grow in the context of their families. The family is an integrated whole, and from a sense of belonging to the whole comes the freedom to individuate and separate. The family is the key to individual growth and development.

Virginia Satir and Humanistic Family Therapy

Virginia Satir, one of the original members of the MRI group, merged communication theory with a human growth perspective. She termed her approach a "process model" in which the therapist and the family join forces to promote wellness. This model's premise is that families are balanced, rule-governed systems through which the basic components of communication and self-esteem provide a context for growth and development. Through her therapeutic interventions she reinforced the family's central and critical function of increasing the self-esteem of its members.

Satir believed that individuals are innately good and have the capacity to develop to their full potential, and that all individuals possess all the resources necessary for positive growth and development. In her model, there is mutual influence and shared responsibility--everything and everyone has an impact on and responds to the impact of everything and everyone else. Therefore, there can be no blame, only multiple stimuli and multiple effects. Therapy for Satir is a process of interaction between clients and therapist. The therapist may take the lead in helping to facilitate growth, but each individual is in charge of him/herself. In Satir's approach the goal of therapy is the facilitation of clear, direct, and honest communication within the family system (Rasheed et al., 2011).

The Milan Group

Systemic family therapy as practiced by the Milan Associates (Selvini-Palazzoli et al., 1978) was influenced by the work of Gregory Bateson. Bateson's *Steps to an Ecology of the Mind* helped them view systems as always evolving, even while appearing to be stuck. The process of the Milan Group builds on systems theory/cybernetics and information theory. They see the world primarily in terms of patterns and information, rather than of mass and energy. Theirs is a recursive approach in that theory and clinical practice respond to feedback derived from the therapy. They participate in and are a part of the families they see.

They believe that mental health problems reflect problems in social interaction. Therapy is directed toward inferred patterns of interaction, rather than toward individuals or intrapsychic problems. Their model is built on a circular epistemology in which the observer focuses on recursiveness in the interactions of the family and on holistic patterns. The members of a family seem caught in this recursive pattern and are viewed more with compassion than with condemnation.

The Milan Group focused on overcoming the tyranny of linguistics, which they believe keeps therapists and clients thinking in an intrapsychic linear manner. They forced a different language on themselves, in order to understand families in different ways, in the process substituting the verbs "to seem" and "to show" for the verb "to be." Families were described as paradoxical, in the sense that they came to therapy to change, yet each member of the system sought to prevent change. The group devised interventions to break the impasse imposed by the family's paradoxical request for both stability and change. Such interventions took the form of the *counter paradox*, which effectively overwhelmed the paradox posed by the family; "We think that you should not change, because it is a good thing that...." They would give a positive connotation to all behaviors in the homeostatic pattern and prescribe no change in the context of change (therapy), putting the family in a therapeutic double bind.

The Milan Associates explain their in-session behavior in terms of three themes: *hypothesizing, circularity,* and *neutrality* (Selvini-Palazzoli et al., 1980). The therapist is constantly generating hypotheses about why the family behaves as it does. These hypotheses create a map from which questions can be directed to the family and interventions made. All hypotheses, including those developed by the family, are considered equally valid. Circularity describes the way the therapist conducts the session. Throughout, she/he uses triadic or circular questions in which one family member is asked to comment on the interactional behaviors of two others. In this way the therapist develops a systemic picture of the family's behavior (Penn, 1982) and new information is introduced allowing family members to experience themselves in a new context. Palazzoli et al. (1980) contend that sometimes simply conducting a session using circular questions will introduce enough new information to produce change.

PARADIGM SHIFT II: THE ADOLESCENT STAGE: FAMILY THERAPY DIGS IN

Object Relations Theory

Many object relation's theorists have developed their own idiosyncratic object-relations theories that stem basically from Freudian psychoanalysis. However, from the perspective of psychoanalysis, there is greater emphasis on the internal world of fantasized objects, while in the case of family therapy, there is a greater emphasis on the external world and on the objects about which such fantasies are created.

Psychodynamic/psychoanalytic family therapy assumes that resolving problems in relationships in the clients' current families or in their current lives calls for intrapsychic exploration and resolution of problematic unconscious object relationships internalized from early parent-child relationships. These early influences affect and explain the nature of present interpersonal difficulties.

Object relations theory can be applied to relationships across generations. For example, children may be unconsciously perceived by a parent as projections of that parent's own split-off traits. Children, in turn, may subtly conform to these projections and act out the parent's introjects. For example, one child may be unconsciously chosen as the "promiscuous one," to act out the impulsive sexual behavior that his or her parent has internalized as a bad object and then projected onto the child. Another child may act as "feelings" of a highly rational parent. The role of each family member, according to Brody (1959), "allows the internal conflict of each member to be acted out within the family, rather than within the self…" (p. 392). For a detailed explanation of contemporary object relation's family therapy, see Scharf and Scharf (1987); and Slipp (1991).

Strategic Family Therapy

Strategic family therapy and structural family therapy were born on opposite coasts of the United States. Strategic family therapy is rooted in the Palo Alto research group of the early 1950s. As part of his research on family communication, Gregory Bateson began to look at schizophrenia has a discrepancy between levels of communication. When the Bateson project published "Toward a Theory of Schizophrenia," they helped therapists throughout the country examine the double-binding communications of family members. In so doing, strategic family therapy came of age.

Strategic family therapy is characterized by its use of specific strategies for addressing family problems (Madanes and Haley, 1977). Therapy is geared toward changing the presenting complaint and is typically accomplished by the therapist first assessing the cycle of family interaction, then breaking that cycle through straightforward or paradoxical directives. Therapy is not growth- but change-oriented, and the therapist is responsible for successful therapeutic outcomes. The therapist focuses on present interaction; she/he does not interpret family members' behavior or explore the past. Therapy is terminated when the presenting problems have ceased. Strategic Family Therapy is represented by Jay Haley and the Milan Group.

Jay Haley

Jay Haley is acknowledged as a pioneer in the field of family therapy. He began his career by studying schizophrenia with Gregory Bateson. In 1967 he became director of family therapy research at the Philadelphia Child Guidance Clinic, where he worked with Salvador Minuchin, Braulio Montalvo, and Bernice Rosman until 1976. In 1976, Haley founded the Family Therapy Institute of Washington, D.C., with his wife, Cloe Madanes.

Haley focuses on sequences of behavior, communication patterns, and the here-and-now. He uses directives and action plans to change behavior and creates strategies to fit the uniqueness of the family. His approach to therapy is method-oriented and problem-focused, with little or no attempt to instill insight. He also uses the concepts of power and control in his description of family patterns, for he sees communication sequences and symptoms as attempts to control or influence. According to Haley, people inevitably engage in reciprocal attempts, through digital and analogic communication, to control the nature of their relationships. Symptoms are behaviors beyond one's control. They are, on the other hand, very controlling in terms of the alternatives available to anyone who has a relationship with the symptom bearer. The non-symptomatic person in the relationship is relatively powerless since it is not appropriate to try to make someone stop doing what she/he cannot help doing. Haley therefore defines certain symptoms as tactics to maintain a particular arrangement in a relationship or a family.

Haley agrees with Minuchin that a faulty family hierarchy maintains problems. One goal of therapy, therefore, is to alter the family's interactions, thereby changing the hierarchical structure. Also, he contends that the presenting problem is often a metaphor for the actual problem (Haley, 1976; Madanes, 1981).

Haley often aligns himself with the parental generation in dealing with child-focused problems (Haley, 1980). Bringing parents together to work on a child's problem can realign problematic hierarchies and strengthen the couple's relationship. Haley and Madanes alter malfunctioning triangles (Haley, 1976, 1980) and incongruent hierarchies (Madanes, 1980, 1981) through such diverse interventions as paradox, reframing, ordeals, "pretending," and unbalancing through creating alternative coalitions.

In his therapy, Haley does not believe that asking why a problem exists is useful. They key question is, what is maintaining the problem? Telling people what they are doing wrong is not only not useful, it often initiates resistance. Further, like the behaviorists, Haley believes that changing behavior leads to changes in feelings and not vice versa, as the object relations theorists believe.

His general therapy strategy is to intervene so that the covert hierarchical structure reflected in repeated sequences of behavior cannot be maintained. In addition he seeks to change symptomatic metaphors to allow more adaptive ones to emerge. Directives are very important. While directives are generally viewed as assignments for the family to perform outside therapy, Haley suggests that all therapist behavior in the session is a directive. Directives serve three purposes: (1) they facilitate change; (2) they involve the therapist in the therapy by keeping him/her figuratively in the family during the week; and (3) they offer a stimulus, reactions which give the therapist information about family structure, rules, boundaries, and interactions.

Going beyond the behavior paradox that one cannot not behave and the communication paradox that one cannot not communicate, Haley adds that one cannot *not* attempt to influence the definition or nature of relationships. He is convinced that whole families should be treated. Only one therapist is to see the family, in order to direct the therapy more immediately and to establish control. A second therapist or team observes the family from behind a one-way mirror. There may be flexibility about the first interview. It should accomplish (1) the social engagement of the family, (2) the definition of the problem, (3) the interaction stage at which the family members discuss the problem among themselves, (4) the definition of the desired changes in terms of solving the presenting problem as specified in behavioral terms, and (5) the ending of the interview with directives and the scheduling of the next appointment.

According to Haley some, but not all, directives are paradoxical in the sense of prescribing the symptom or prescribing resistance. In either case the therapist maintains control by anticipating family members' responses to therapy. Another form of directive is the *metaphoric task*. During the session the therapist might use a metaphor to symbolize a problem or issue that the family does not discuss. The therapist thus indirectly plants the seeds of possible change. Another directive used by Haley (1984) is *ordeal therapy*. Here the therapist prescribes an ordeal equal to or greater than the distress of the symptom itself, so the symptom becomes harder to keep up than to abandon. It is essential to select an ordeal that is good for the client, such as dieting or exercise. The ordeal must also be something the client can do and cannot legitimately object to doing. Further, it cannot harm the person or anyone else. For example, for people who suffer from insomnia, Haley might prescribe that they scrub the kitchen floor with a toothbrush whenever they wake up in the middle of the night.

Haley feels that in order for change to occur in the client, the style of interaction in the social unit of which the client is a member must also change.

Structural Family Therapy

While communication theorists tend to emphasize the "how" of family interaction, the "bits and pieces" of communication, structural theorists tend to emphasize the dynamic orderings of the system itself, the actual structure within which elements of communication take place.

Salvador Minuchin

Salvador Minuchin is the person most frequently associated with the development of the structural school. In the 1960s he and his colleagues were working at the Wiltwyck School for boys, serving a population primarily from New York's inner city. They found long-term psychoanalytic, passive, growth-oriented therapy extremely ineffective with these children, whose issues were immediate and survival-based. These therapists experimented with a more active approach to therapy in which they worked with the boys and their families together (Aponte and VanDeusen, 1981). *Families of the Slums* (Minuchin et al., 1967) was written about the Wiltwyck School experiences and is the first book to present the structural approach in therapy. The other theorists who contributed to its development are Montalvo, Umbarger, Aponte, Walters, Fishman, and Greenstein.

Minuchin has since broadened his theoretical base and applied this approach to patients of varying socioeconomic classes with a variety of presenting problems (Minuchin and Fishman, 1981). In this sense Minuchin is one of the first family therapists who considered the larger sociopolitical system as a major influence on family organization and structure (see also Elizur and Minuchin, 1989).

He believes that the structure of the family is "an open sociocultural system in transformation" (Minuchin, 1974, 14). Family structure is sociocultural in that it integrates the demands of society with those of the internal family system to shape the individual. Because Minuchin was one of the first family therapists to recognize and examine larger sociocultural influences on the family system, it would be most illuminating to read an analysis by him of the organizing role of gender. Minuchin is well aware of the gender inequities in contemporary society, and this, combined with his knowledge of macro-sociological theory, makes him the natural theorist to integrate the role of gender into structural family therapy theory.

Minuchin describes four types of stress: (1) stressful contact of one family member with extra-familial forces, (2) stressful contact of the whole family with extra-familial forces, (3) stress at transition points in a family, and (4) stress around idiosyncratic problems. In each of these situations, the key to successful adaptation is the transformation of structure through boundary negotiation.

Structural family therapy focuses on patterns of interaction which give clue to the basic structure and organization of the system. For Minuchin (1974) structure refers to the invisible set of demands that organizes the way the family interacts, or the consistent, repetitive, organized, and predictable modes of family behavior that allow us to consider the family as "structured" in a functional sense. Thus, observations of patterns of family interactions provide information about how the family is organized to maintain itself. A family operates through repeated transactional patterns, which regulate the behavior of its members. These patterns include how, when, and to whom family members relate. The concepts of *patterns* and *structure* imply a set of covert rules of which family members may not be consciously aware, but which consistently characterize and define their interactions.

For structural theorists, diagnosis is directed toward, and treatment is predicated upon, a system's organizational dynamics. They believe that *boundaries* are critically important. Boundaries are the rules and regulations that separate the system from its environment. They may be a manifestation of the system's rules and regulations. A boundary can be highly permeable, so that thoughts and feelings are easily exchanged, or highly impermeable, so that thoughts and feelings are either not exchanged at all or are exchanged only with difficulty. The clarity of the boundaries is determined by how well lines of responsibility have been thought out and how clearly designation of authority has been defined. Minuchin postulates three types of boundaries: (1) enmeshed boundaries, where relationships are diffuse and close; (2) disengaged boundaries, where relationships are inappropriately rigid and distant; and (3) clear boundaries, where relationships are within the "normal" range. The extremes of disengagement and enmeshment indicate the potential for symptom formation.

Structural theory defines three subsystems: the spouse subsystem, the parental subsystem, and the sibling subsystem. The rule among these subsystems in the functional family is hierarchy. Structural theory insists on appropriate boundaries between generations.

Minuchin charges the therapist with three major tasks: (1) To join the family as a leader; (2) to unearth and evaluate the underlying family structure; (3) to create circumstances to allow the transformation of this structure. The therapist's tasks are to form the therapeutic system and to restructure the family system. There are at least seven strategies for facilitating change: actualizing transactional patterns; marking boundaries; escalating stress; assigning tasks; utilizing symptoms; manipulating moods; and providing support, education, and guidance.

The family developmental tasks in this process require modification of the family structure. This structural modification is accomplished through boundary negotiation and modification. Minuchin believes that there are generic and idiosyncratic constraints on this process. The generic constraints are so called because they are "universal rules governing family organization" (Minuchin, 1974, 52). For example, in any family system with children, there must be a power hierarchy. The idiosyncratic constraints are composed of unique individual expectations and intentions of each family member. Through universal rules the patterns are explicitly or implicitly formed.

The goals of structural therapy are somewhat idiosyncratic, although some general patterns and structures do recur within a given cultural context. These general goals therefore guide the structural therapist:

1. There must be effective hierarchical structure. The parent(s) must be in charge. There must be a generation gap based on parental/ executive authority.
2. There must be a parental/executive coalition. The parents must support and accommodate each other, to provide a united front to their children.
3. As the parental/executive coalition forms, the sibling subsystem becomes a system of peers.
4. If the family is disengaged, the goal is to increase frequency of interaction and moved toward clear, rather than rigid, boundaries. This shift brings an increase in nurture and support to complement the previous independence and autonomy characteristic of families with rigid boundaries.
5. If the family is enmeshed, the general goal is to foster differentiation of individuals and subsystems. This reflects a respect for differences in developmental stages of the children and permission for age-appropriate experimentation with independent activity.
6. There must be a spouse subsystem established as an entity distinct from the parental subsystem.

Structural family therapy focuses on two kinds of live, here-and-now activities: *enactments* and *spontaneous behavioral consequences*. When a therapist asks for an enactment, she/he seeks a demonstration of the way a family deals with a specific kind of problem in order to observe the sequence. This gives the therapist clues to the family structure. Spontaneous behavior sequences are transactions in the family as natural parts of its pattern. If the therapist successfully joins the family, the family will begin to reveal pieces of its structure through transactions.

Solution Focused Therapy

The solution-focused therapies appeared in response to the traditional psychological and family therapy deficit approach and in an attempt to respond to the developing postmodernist milieu (deShazer, 1991; Dolan, 1991; Lipchik & deShazer, 1986; O'Hanlon & Weiner-Davis, 1989; Walter & Peller, 1992). Solution-focused therapists replace the deficit story with one of success by addressing and focusing on the competencies and strengths of the clients. In the solution-focused approach, active participation in the solution by the client is required as the more positive aspect of the client's life become foreground, via finding exceptions, and the trauma or the problem fades into the background.

Steve DeShazer and Insoo Berg

DeShazer (1985) was one of the first theorists responsible for solution-focused therapy. His work led him away from a focus on the problem in therapy toward a focus on finding a solution that a client deemed helpful. He stated that often the solution a client constructed had very little to do with the problems he saw, but that it "fit" with the client's definition of the problem. Consequently, the therapy moved away from the therapist trying to understand the client's problem and design a solution to it to a focus on questioning the client about personal goals and encouraging self-exploration as a potential resource for problem solving.

The following table compares traditional/modernist and solution-focused/postmodernist therapy assumptions.

Comparison of Problem/Deficit Models of Therapy with Solution-Focused Models

Traditional Approaches	Solution Focused Therapy
• Therapist is an expert--has special knowledge regarding the problem to which the client needs to submit (colonization/ missionary model)	• Client and therapist both have particular areas of expertise (collaborative model)
• Client is viewed as damaged by the abuse (deficit model)	• Client is viewed as influenced by not determined by abuse history, having strengths and abilities (resource model)
• Remembering abuse and the expression of repressed affect (catharsis) are treatment	• Goals are individualized for each client, but do not necessarily involve goals of catharsis or remembering
• Interpretation	• Acknowledgment, valuing, and opening possibilities
• Past oriented	• Present/future oriented
• Problem/pathology oriented	• Solution focused
• Must be long-term treatment	• Variable/individualized length of treatment
• Invites conversations for insight and working through	• Invites conversations for accountability and action and declines invitations to blame and invalidation

From O'Hanlon, W. (1993). In J. Atwood & F. Genovese (Eds.). *Counseling the single parent family* Alexandria, VA: American Counseling Association.

At this point, we can present some of the major differences between individual psychotherapeutic approaches to human behavior and the more systemically oriented therapies.

Comparison of the Assumptions of Individual Psychology with Systemic Family Therapy

Individual Psychology	Systemic Family Therapy
• Asks, Why?	• Asks, What?
• Linear cause/effect	• Reciprocal causality
• Subject/object dualism	• Holistic
• Either/or dichotomies	• Dialectical
• Value-free science	• Subjective/perceptual
• Deterministic/reactive	• Freedom of choice/proactive
• Laws and law like external reality	• Patterns
• Historical focus	• Here-and-now focus
• Individualistic	• Relational
• Reductionistic	• Contextual
Absolutistic	Relativistic

From Becvar D. S. and Becvar R. J. (2006). *Family therapy: A systemic integration* (6th ed.). Boston: Pearson Education.

Paradigm Shift III: Second-Order Cybernetics, Postmodernism, And Social Constructionism

Postmodernism is philosophically rooted in Nietzsche's views that there are no facts, only "interpretations." that each perspective originates from a "lust to rule," and that claims to "truth" mask the workings of the "will to power." The postmodernists of the quantum world assume that our relations with the world do not always correspond with the world; the way we explain the world arises from active cooperation of person in relationship; whether or not knowledge is maintained depends on social exchanges; and constructed meanings are social activities and are no separate from the rest of our social life (Gergen, 1988).

Social Constructionism

Berger and Luckmann (1966) in their classic work, The Social Constructionism of Reality, described social constructions as the consensual recognition of the realness and rightness of a constructed reality, plus the socialization process by which people acquire this reality. A social construction includes not only the routines and the mechanisms for socializing the children of the system, but also the means for maintaining the definition of reality on which the system is based. They see the human origin of social realities very simply as a process by which individuals who repeatedly confront a task or situation relevant to their lives develop habitual ways of dealing with it. A situation once typified this way often leads to the development of roles or functions which cooperating partners perform in connection with the task involved. Thus, a social construction includes not only the routines and scripts for educating and socializing the young in the system, but also the means for maintaining the definition of reality on which the system is based and the subjective loyalty of the family members.

Social construction theory and therapy are based on a second order therapeutic stance. Although Narrative therapy is based in Social Construction assumptions, our approach to therapy in more socially based, taking socially defined meanings and scripts as the target for restorying.

The Narrative Therapies

There are two strands of narrative therapies: one represented by a problem-determined or collaborative language systems approach (Anderson & Goolishian, 1988; Andersen, 1987; Hoffman, 1990) and the other by the externalization approach (Epston, 1989; Tomm, 1987; White, 1989). White (1986, 1989), building on Bateson's (1972) notion of restraints, proposed a similar model of "alternative descriptions." As defined by Bateson (1972), restraints are the limitations placed on people by their beliefs and values that make them less likely to notice other aspects of their problem-saturated life. White termed these other aspects "subjugated knowledge" and developed a narrative therapy through which people explore their ongoing story. Therapy in this case involves exploring the process by which individuals tell themselves stories, give themselves meanings, interpret their behaviors, and then assisting individuals to re-author their lives.

Epston and White (1990) believe that, "When persons are established as consultants to themselves, to others, and to the therapist, they experience themselves as more of an authority on their own lives, their problems and the solution to these problems." (p. 28). White's work in terms of subjugated knowledge clearly puts him into a second-order cybernetic stance and a therapy of expanding realities.

In sum, from the following chart, the reader can see the major differences between not only Traditional Assumptions and Modernist Family Therapy, but also, a comparison of the assumptions of the Post-Modernist views.

Comparison Of Traditional Psychotherapy Assumptions With Modernist Family Therapy Assumptions And Post Modernist Family Therapy Assumptions

Traditional Psychoanalytic Therapy Assumptions	Traditional Family Therapy/Modernist Assumptions	Social Construction/ Post Modern Assumptions
There is an objective reality and it is knowable.	There are multiple interpretations of one objective reality.	Reality is socially created through social interaction.
There ARE models of normalcy.	Models of normalcy should be adhered to.	The client defines what is normal.
The therapist is an expert.	The role of the therapist is to be an expert.	THE CLIENT IS THE EXPERT. The role of the therapist is to collaborate with client to co-construct new stories that hold new possibilities.

The therapist is a diagnostician who does assessment.	The therapist in a therapeutic tool, a lever intending to created change in the system.	The client is a diagnostician who does assessment.
The therapist is transparent, in that the therapist is a toneless sounding board.	The therapist is very visible AND CENTRAL TO INTERVENTIONS.	The therapist is transparent (attempts to keep all biases and assumptions out of the therapy arena).
The client has one self, not very malleable.	There are multiple aspects of self.	The client has many selves.
The symptom is caused by the pathology, which is located in the self.	Pathology is located in the family system and the symptom functions to maintain the system.	The client is having a problem in living. The problem persists because the client does not know how to fix it.
Change is an either/ or process.	Change is an either/ or process.	CHANGE IS A BOTH/AND PROCESS
A client is dependent on the therapist to fix future problems.	A client is dependent upon the therapist to fix future problems.	THE GOAL IS FOR THE CLIENT TO BE INDEPENDENT OF THE THERAPIST

Traditional therapies adhere to the following assumptions:

- There is an objective reality and it is knowable.
- There can be models of normalcy.
- The therapist is an expert.

- The therapist is a diagnostician who does diagnosing.
- The therapist is transparent in that the therapist is a toneless sounding board.
- The client has one self, not very malleable.
- The symptom is caused by the pathology that is located in the self.
- Change is an either/or perspective.
- A client is dependent on the therapist to fix future problems.

Traditional Family Therapies make the following assumptions:

- There are multiple interpretations of one objective reality.
- Modules of normalcy should be adhered to.
- The role of the therapist is to be an expert.
- The therapist is a therapeutic tool, a lever intending to create change in the system.
- The therapist is very visible.
- There are multiple aspects of self.
- Pathology is located in the family system.
- The system functions to maintain the system.
- Change is an either/or process.
- A client is dependent upon the therapist to fix future problems.

Post-Modernist Therapies make the following assumptions:

- Reality is socially created through interactions with others.
- The client defines what is normal.
- The role of the therapist is to collaborate with client to co-construct new stories that hold new possibilities.
- The client is a diagnostician who does assessment.
- The therapist is transparent (attempts to keep all biases and assumptions out of the therapy arena).
- The client has many selves.
- The client is having a problem in living. The problem persists because the client does not know how to fix it.

Compare the post-modernist language (co-create,-co-construct, social constructs, narrative, themes, story, scripts, audience, meaning systems, etc., with the language of the earlier models (pathology, sick, treatment, disturbed, dysfunctional, toxic communication, enmeshed, disengaged, etc.)

- The client has many selves.
- The symptoms is caused by problems in living.

In the next section, a presentation of Diagnosis from a Traditional Psychological Frame and Assessment from a Family Therapy frame is presented.

Diagnosis From a Traditional Psychological Frame and Assessment From A Family Therapy Frame

The DSM and its author, the American Psychiatric Association (APA), adhere to the traditional medical model. Practitioners from medical and traditional psychological approaches have historically seen "patients" and treated "mental illnesses," focusing on the pathological or dysfunctional approach.

The medical model of mental disorders is basically the model that is used today in individual psychological models. Over the years, a book of diagnoses was published, listing all the various diagnoses and their symptoms. When first published in 1952 it was called The Diagnostic and Statistical Manual of the Social Sciences. Since then, it has gone through six revisions and is now called the Diagnostic and Statistical Manual of Mental Disorders (DSM-V). According to Maddux (2002):

> With each revision, the DSM has had more and more to say about how people should live their lives and about what makes life worth living....As the boundaries of "mental disorder" have been expanded with each DSM revision, life has become increasingly pathologized, and the sheer numbers of people with diagnosable mental disorders has continued to grow. The framers of the DSM have been

gradually pathologizing almost every conceivable human
problem in living. (Maddux, 2002, 64).

At this time, the DSM has become the mainstay of mental health
professionals. Insurance companies require a diagnosis for each individual
requesting treatment and in order for the provider to be paid for services
or the client reimbursed, a code number from the DSM must be given for
the specific disorder.

Assumptions of the DSM-V

The *Diagnostic and Statistical Manual of Mental Disorders* (DSM)
provides the organizational structure for almost every textbook and
course on abnormal psychology and psychopathology for undergraduate
and graduate students, for psychologists, psychiatrists as well as almost
every professional book on the diagnosis and treatment of psychological
problems. It also forms the basis of the lens through which mental health
professionals "see" the client.

There is an intellectual foundation underlying the DSM, which
consists of a number of assumptions about human behavior and how we
understand it.

Assumption I: Categories Are Facts About the World

The diagnostic system of the DSM is based on the assumption that a
system of socially constructed categories of "mental illness" reflects a set
of "facts" about people struggling in the world. "Disorders" are created
based on reports of complaints and functional disturbances, with arbitrary
distinctions being drawn between the types of dysfunction. Once these
distinctions are made, the cluster of symptoms is given a name and thus
transformed into a real entity. Therefore, it can be said that illnesses are
created and do not necessarily reflect facts about individuals (Barone,
Maddux, & Snyder, 1997). With more and more disorders included in the
book, some everyday problems, which are not that serious, are considered
mental illnesses.

Assumption II: We Can Distinguish between Normal and Abnormal

The second assumption of the DSM is that clear criteria can be established for distinguishing between normal and abnormal thinking, feeling, and behaving; between healthy and unhealthy psychological functioning. The DSM "does not simply describe and classify characteristics of groups of individuals, but…actively 'constructs' a version of both normal and abnormal" (Parker, Georgaca, Harper, McLaughlin, & Stowell-Smith, 1995, 93).

Assumption III: Categories Facilitate Clinical Judgment

Proponents of diagnostic categories of dysfunction often argue that these categories facilitate understanding of patients or clients and serve as an aid to clinical judgment and decision-making. However, diagnostic categories can cloud clinician's judgments by setting into motion a "vicious cycle" in which error and bias are encouraged and maintained despite the clinician's good intentions

Underlying this "vicious cycle" are four beliefs that the clinician brings to the initial encounter with a client. The first belief is that there is a dichotomy between normal and abnormal or healthy and unhealthy psychological functioning. The second belief is that distinct syndromes known as "mental disorders" actually exist and have real properties. The third belief is that the clients who come to "clinics" must have a "clinical problem," which must fit one of these distinct syndromes. The fourth and final belief is that the clinician is an accurate observer of others, an objective gatherer and processor of information about others, and an unbiased decision maker.

Assumption IV: Categories Facilitate Intervention

The ultimate goal of any diagnostic system is to understand the person's needs and resources and facilitate the implementation of therapeutic interventions that alleviate suffering and enhance well-being. The diagnostic system, which focuses on negative categories, does not provide the insight necessary to identify interventions that enhance client adjustment and well-being. According to Maddux (2002), the validity of a diagnostic system for "mental disorders" is closely linked to its ability to lead to the development and selection of effective treatment. However, the *Diagnostic and Statistical Manual of Mental Disorders* (American Psychiatric Association, 2013) clearly states, that the "DSM-V does not provide treatment guidelines for any given disorder" (p. 25). The DSM is purely descriptive and a-theoretical, and therefore does not deal with the etiology.

Psychiatrist Allen Frances has been critical to the revised DSM-V and in a 2012 New York Times Editorial, he warned that the DSM-V version will "medicalize normality and result in a glut of unnecessary and harmful drug-prescription." (81) In a 2012 blog post in Psychology Today, Frances lists the ten most potentially harmful changes in the DSM-V: 5(82).

1. The category Disruptive Dysregulation Disorder is a category for temper tantrums.
2. Major Depressive Disorder includes normal grief responses.
3. Minor Neurocognitive Disorder for normal forgetting in old age.
4. Binge Eating Disorder for overeating.
5. Adult Attention Deficit Disorder that encourages psychiatric prescriptions of stimulants.
6. Autism, defining the disorder more specifically, possibly leading to decreased rates and the disruption of school services.
7. First time drug users are lumped in with addicts.
8. Behavioral Addictions making a "mental disorder of everything we like to do a lot."
9. Generalized anxiety disorder that includes everyday worries.
10. Post-traumatic stress disorder, opening the gate to even more to the already existing problem of misdiagnosing of PTSD in forensic settings.

Or as John M. Grohol states, "'The DSM simply reflects the belief system of a socially dominant group that has selectively chosen which knowledge to utilize in order to better understand the world" as they see it.

Assessment From A Systemic Framework

The concept of family therapy implies an assumption that a set of categories exist by which families can be assessed to be functional and healthy or dysfunctional and unhealthy. The early approaches to family therapy provide a framework for distinguishing between functional and dysfunctional, normal and abnormal, or healthy and unhealthy families. Therefore, the success of therapy is measured by the progress of the family toward what is defined as normal, healthy, and functional by the particular approach being used.

From the perspective of object relation's family therapy, family health and functioning is assessed relative to the ability of individuals to master appropriate developmental tasks and as adults to be successful in creating mature relationships. The degree to which the family is able to provide a context that supports such development on the part of its members is the measure of its functionality. Healthy family members are able to relate to one another fully, expressing understanding and compassion.

In Minuchin's structural approach to family therapy, the therapist observes the family structure, generational boundaries, hierarchy, degrees of enmeshment and disengagement, and provision for change over time. The promotion of both autonomy and interdependence are also important. In addition, assessment from this approach must consider cultural variations and the particular idiosyncrasies of the family and its circumstances.

In Satir's humanistic approach, feelings of self-worth as well as clear, direct, and honest communication are valued. This approach also calls for family rules that are clear, specific, and flexible as appropriate to various circumstances. In addition, healthy parents are considered to be essential to the development of healthy children.

However, there are some concerns related to assessment from the perspective of the traditional family therapy approaches. A major concern from the systemic perspective is whether the categories described by the models are treated as true, accurate descriptions of the family, rather than as categories we might use to understand families for therapeutic approaches. The metaphor of the categories often becomes the reality; for each assessment model describes a valuable framework, and therapists using any model to guide their interventions toward goals defined by the model necessarily impose values despite admonitions to respect cultural and situational contexts.

A related concern is that the family might adopt the framework of the therapist regardless of its appropriateness for them. In other words, assessment implicitly imposes a set of imperatives and prohibitions on the family. When a therapist reifies a description of a family, the assessment becomes an "is" rather than a label that is chosen from a great variety available. From a systemic perspective, the therapist must be aware that the assessment metaphors or labels or maps are not the territory.

Another important concern is that what is treated is largely what the therapist assessed to be the problem. Therefore, the conceptual model used defines the problems treated by the therapist, who imposes a theoretical or more general assessment model on the family unit. Although the family comes with its own assessment of the problem, generally focused on the identified patient or the individual who is the symptom-bearer, by asking the family to participate in therapy, the systems paradigm has already been imposed on the family unit. Thus, the problems treated in therapy are those invented to be treated, either by the therapist or by the family. In other words, "we choose the problems we treat by what we choose to call them" (Becvar & Becvar, 2006, 288). For example, if the label "depression" is given, then depression is what is treated. It is also important to be aware that in some cultures the concept of depression does not exist.

From a second-order cybernetics/postmodern perspective, the observer is part of the observed. Therefore, when faced with the challenge of assessing clients and their problems, therapists operate in a manner that is as respectful as possible and incorporates both the expertise of the therapist and of the clients. Additionally, from a postmodern perspective, reality is socially constructed through language. Therapists and clients are believed to have only stories, rather than an absolute truth, about what is going on. Therefore, they try avoid the use of labels or metaphors that pathologize or participate in the creation of problem-saturated stories which become a part of the client's reality. From this perspective, therapists do not see theories as universal standards about the way families should or should not be, but rather as general guidelines. The focus is holistic, considering the impact of internal system dynamics, as well as interactions with other systems in the larger context. Client input is sought throughout the course of therapy, and assessment is understood as an ongoing, shared process of feedback, reflection, and mutual influence.

An essential part of assessment from a postmodern perspective is to introduce the idea of multiple realities. The use of the term "story" can be used to cue therapists that their view is merely one of many views possible, and that they like family members, are part of a multiverse of multiple perspectives. Assessment is ongoing and therapists should continually request input from family members regarding their stories, goals, and reactions to therapeutic interventions. As with the clients, therapists are invited to recognize and reflect on the impact of their particular setting and its constraints on the therapy process, as well as on value and ethical issues that may emerge. Finally, consideration of the influence of the therapist's personal characteristics and theoretical orientation, as well as reflection on other approach that could have been taken is suggested.

Assessment from this perspective allows for the recognition of the uniqueness of each family system. It brings an awareness that assessment constitutes intervention that by the act of observing the system the observer influences that which they are attempting to understand.

The traditional models of family therapy implicitly held certain assumptions regarding what constituted family normality as well as those family structures, interactional patterns, and value orientations that were indicators of family emotional health. In many respects these assumptions were based on middle-class or work-class notions of the ideal family. Yet there was the undeniable fact that families do differ in how they structure their family lives. Due to variables of race, gender, and class, there were alternative family forms that deviated from the generally accepted assumptions about "ideal" families. There was also the increasing acceptance that many of the early models of family therapy were apolitical in that they ignored the broader sociopolitical context structuring the live of families. According to Fish (1993), although many family therapy models understood the dynamics of power in the helping relationship, the client's or family therapist's gender, class, ethnic, or racial location within the larger social order were not considered as having an impact on the therapeutic process. Without this understanding of the possible power differential association with a client's or therapist's social location, a salient aspect of a client's experience was felt to be ignored.

Is There Assessment From A Social Construction Frame?

From a Social Construction frame of reference, there is no assessment made by the therapist. The client is the expert; the client defines the issues and the goals; the therapist uses questions as interventions to assist the client in the process of accomplishing their goals.

Gender and Family Therapy

With regard to the issue of gender, early family therapy models were challenged for failing to consider the larger social, political, and ideological context when looking at family dysfunction (Hare-Mustin, 1978; Laird, 1989; Luepnitz 1988). In terms of gender, the early family therapies were viewed as biased in that they adhered to the notion that all family participants, regardless of gender, contribute equally and have shared responsibility for family problems. As a consequence of such biases, therapists assumed a neutral stance toward those inherent sexist and patriarchal practices that were unquestionably seen as part of "normal" family life. Those who challenged these sexist assumptions felt that those therapists were continuing to see mothers as the source of pathology in families. Furthermore, but not looking the differential power relationships as structure by traditional gender roles and expectations, these therapists were contributing to maintaining the sexist and patriarchal sexist status quo. As a consequence, they could not interrogate the role of women as being exploited, devalued, and oppressed, especially in families structured by more traditional and structural/functionalist ideas of gender roles and expectations.

Feminism and Multiculturalism and Family Therapy

Feminism is an area in family therapy that has changed over time. There is research that shows that while there are three different frameworks in the realm of feminism, most people think of the radical framework "holds that sexism is manifested primarily by the power men over women and that the oppression of women is the fundamental oppression" (Dankoski, Penn, Carlson & Hecker, 1998). This implies that people believe that feminism in therapy focuses on the woman's issues and that her "issues" are a result of men having the power and/or control. While initially this may have been the case, but now, males are generally included and treatment is considered to be fair and unbiased in terms of gender (Evans, Kincade, Marbley & Seem, 2005). Along with concern about gender biases, there was a greater recognition within the discipline of family therapy of the disparity in the social status of ethnic minorities. Furthermore, there was greater awareness that these disparities often reflected the realities of racism, poverty, and oppression. As family therapy practitioners became engaged with racial and ethnic minority families, questions emerged as to what extent these practice models take into account the following stressors that these families encounter (Ho et al., 2004). In addition to coping with racism, oppression, poverty, and societal constraints, there is the recognition that ethnic minority families encounter the following stressors that impact their engagement in family therapy. According to the research, "feminism and multiculturalism are actually a tight bond. Both aim to equalize power and privilege for marginalized groups" (Goodrich & Silverstein, 2005). Both look into various topics and can be intertwined.

Systemic Thinkers, Post Modern Thinkers and the DSM-V

According to Denton, Patterson, & Van Meir (1997), "Family therapy has had a history of ambivalence toward diagnosing individuals with mental illness." There are those who believe that diagnosis is simply a process of labeling illness and/or a means to a financial gain (Hohenshil, 1996). Some see it as a mechanism that distances clinicians from the client and overwhelms the client's voice with the language of the socially constructed diagnoses (Gergen, Hoffman, & Anderson, 1996). Others see diagnosis is an effective tool in creating effective treatment plans (Hohenshil, 1996). Although diagnosing client may be controversial for clinicians working with individuals, it can be accommodated with training and some philosophical flexibility. However, the same cannot be said of Marriage and Family Therapists and other Systemic Thinkers. Many Marriage and Family Therapists have expressed concerns "that they will be losing some of their hearts or possibly selling their souls by incorporating diagnosis into their practice" (Carlson, Hinkle, & Sperry, 1993, 308).

Many systemic thinkers are finding that their profession has been marginalized by the DSM-V and third-party payers who seldom, if ever, allow for relational diagnoses in their reimbursement plans (Christensen & Miller, 2001). The DSM-V does provide some relational diagnosis (the so called "V Codes"), yet although these diagnoses are arguably less stigmatizing and may be relationally based, they are not eligible for reimbursement by third-party payers. This creates an ethical dilemma of how to diagnose a family in a manner that creates the least harm to any one individual, but still makes it financially possible for therapy with the family to continue. In order for families to be reimbursed for services, Marriage and Family Therapists must "redefine the issue as individual mental health problems in order to obtain reimbursable services instead of being able to seek treatment for their primary complaint" (Shumway et al., 2004, 77). But as stated by Hamann (1994), "Under no circumstances should clinical professionals compromise they regarding the accuracy of a diagnosis to make it 'fit' acceptable insurance company [and third-party payer] criteria. To do so is clearly unethical and fraudulent" (p. 260). This creates an ethical double bind for the Marriage and Family Therapist and other systemic thinkers.

The goal of this chapter was to give the reader some insight into the development of systemically based therapies. The following chapters explore the more common issues as they are presented in therapy.

References

Ackerman, N. (1958). The emergence of family diagnosis and treatment: A personal view. *Psychotherapy, 4,* 125-29.

Aponte, H., & VanDeusen, J. (1981). Structural family therapy. In A. Gurman and D. Kniskern (Eds.), *Handbook of Family Therapy.* New York: Brunner/Mazel.

Ashby, W. (1960). *Design for the Brain.* London: Chapman Hall Science Paperbacks.

Atwood, J. D. (1992). *Family therapy: A systemic behavioral approach.* Chicago: Nelson-Hall.

Atwood, J. D. (1997). Social construction theory and therapy. In J. D. Atwood (Ed.), *Challenging family therapy situations: Perspectives in social construction* (pp. 1-40). New York: Springer Publishing.

Atwood, J., & Genovese, F. (Eds.). (1993).*Counseling the single parent family*. Alexandria, VA: American Counseling Association.

Becvar, D. S., & Becvar, R. J. (1999). *Systems Theory and Family Therapy: A Primer* (2nd ed.). Lanham, MD: University Press of America.

Becvar, D. S., & Becvar, R. J. (2006). *Family therapy: A systemic integration* (6th ed.). Boston: Pearson Education.

Bell, J. E. (1961). *Family Group Therapy*. Public Health Monograph No. 64. Washington, DC: U.S. Government Printing Office.

Bowen, M. (1978). *Family therapy in clinical practice*. New York: Jason Aronson.

Brody, W. (1959). Some family operations and schizophrenia. *Archives of General Psychiatry, 1,* 379-402.

Capra, F. (1983). *The tao of physics*. New York: Bantam.

Dankoski, M. E., Penn, C. D., Carlson, T. D., & Hecker, L. L. (1998). What's in a name? A study of family therapists' use and acceptance of the feminist perspective. *The American Journal of Family Therapy,* 26, 95-104.

Elizur, J., and Minuchin, S. (1989). *Institutionalizing madness: Families, therapy, and society*. New York: Basic Books.

Epston, D., & White, M. (1990). *Consulting your consultants: The documentation of alternative knowledges.* Dulwich Center Newsletter, p. 4.

Evans, K. M., Kincade, E. A., Marbley, A. F., & Seem, S. R. (2005). Feminism and feminist therapy: lessons from the past and hopes for the future. *Journal of Counseling & Development,* 83, 269-277.

Gergen, K. (1985). The social constructionist movement in modern psychology. *American Psychologist, 40,* 266-75.

Goodrich, T. J., & Silverstein, L. B. (2005). Now you see it, now you don't: feminist training in family therapy. *Family Process,* 44(3).

Guerin, P. J. (Ed.). (1976). *Family therapy: theory and practice.* New York: Gardner Press.

Gurman, A. S., & Kniskern, D. P. (1981). *Handbook of family therapy.* New York: Brunner-Mazel.

Gurman, A. S., & Kniskern, D. P. (1991). *Handbook of family therapy* (vol. 2). New York: Brunner-Mazel.

Haley, J. (1976). *Problem-solving therapy.* San Francisco: Jossey, Bass.

Haley, J. (1980). *Leaving home.* New York: McGraw-Hill.

Heisenberg, W. (1958). *Physics and philosophy.* New York: Harper Torchbooks.

Hoffman, L. (1981). *Foundations of family therapy.* New York: Guildford Press.

Hoffman, L. (1981). *Foundations of family therapy: A conceptual framework for systems change.* New York: Basic Books.

Hoffman, L. (1987). Toward a second order family systems therapy. *Family Systems Medicine, 3,* 381-86.

Hume, R. E. (1934). *The thirteen principal upanishads.* New York: Oxford University Press.

Kerr, M. (1981). Family systems and therapy. In A. Gurman and D. Kniskern (Eds.), *Handbook of Family Therapy.* New York: Brunner/Mazel.

Kuhn, T. (1962). *The structure of scientific revolutions.* Chicago: University of Chicago Press.

Kuhn, T. (1970). *The structure of scientific revolutions* (2nd ed.). Chicago: University of Chicago Press.

Lidz, R., & Lidz, T. (1949). The family environment of schizophrenic patients. *The American Journal of Psychiatry, 14,* 241-48.

Lidz, T., Cornelison, A., Fleck, S., & Terry, D. (1957). Intrafamilial environment of the schizophrenic patient: I. The father. *Psychiatry, 20,* 329-42.

Madanes, C. (1981). *Strategic family therapy.* San Francisco: Jossey-Bass.

Madanes, C., & Haley, J. (1977). Dimensions of family therapy. *Journal of Nervous and Mental Disorders, 165,* 88-98.

Maturana, H. (1980). Biology of cognition. In H. R. Mantura & F. Varela (Eds.), *Autopsies and cognition* (pp. 60-83). Boston: Reidel.

Minuchin, S. (1974). *Families and family therapy.* Cambridge, MA: Harvard University Press.

Minuchin, S., et al. (1967). *Families of the slums.* New York: Basic Books.

Minuchin, S. & Fishman, H. (1981). *Family therapy techniques.* Cambridge, MA: Harvard University Press.

Minuchin, S., Rosman, B., & Baker, L. (1978). *Psychosomatic families: Anorexia nervosa in context.* Cambridge, MA: Harvard University Press.

Nathanson, M. (1963). *The philosophy of the social sciences.* New York: Random House.

Neill, J., & Kniskern, D. (1982). *From psyche to system: The evolving therapy of carl whitaker.* New York: Guildford Press.

Nichols, M. (1984). *Family therapy: Concepts and methods.* New York: Gardner Press.

Nichols, M. P. (2013). The foundations of family therapy. In M. P. Nichols (Ed.), *Family therapy: Concepts and methods* (10th ed.) (pp. 1-8). Upper Saddle River, N.J.: Pearson Education.

Penn, P. (1982). Circular questioning. *Family Process, 21* (3), 267-80.

Scharf, D., & Scharf, J. (1987). *Object relations family therapy.* Northvale, N.J.: Jason Aronson.

Selvini-Palazzoli, M., et al. (1978). *Paradox and counterparadox.* New York: Jason Aronson.

Selvini-Palazzoli, M., et al. (1980). Hypothesizing-circularity-neutrality: Three guidelines for the conductor of the session. *Family Process, 19,* 3-12.

Singleton, G. (1982). Bowen family systems theory. In A. Horne and M. Ohlsen (Eds.), *Family counseling and therapy.* Itasca, IL: F. E. Peacock.

Slipp, S. (1988). *The technique and practice of object relations family therapy.* Northvale, N.J.: Jason Aronson.

Tomm, K. (1984). One perspective on the Milan systemic approach: Part II. *Journal of Marital and Family Therapy, 10,* 253-71.

Watzlawick, P. (1976). *How real is real?* New York: Random House.

Wiener, N. (1948). Cybernetics. *Scientific American, 179,* 14-18.

Wiener, N. (1954). *The human use of human beings.* New York: Anchor Press.

Zukav, D. (1989). *The dancing Wuli masters: An overview of the new physics.* New York: William Morrow.

Chapter 2

Developmental Disorders

Liat Rinat, M.A., MFT

The Neurodevelopmental disorders are a group of conditions with onset in the developmental period. The disorders typically manifest early in development, often before the child enters grade school, and are characterized by developmental deficits that produce impairments of personal, social, academic, or occupational functioning. These deficits include limitations of learning or control of executive functions to global impairments of social skills or intelligence.

The most common forms of these disorders include intellectual disability, autism, bipolar disorder, schizophrenia, attention-deficit/hyperactivity disorder, and learning and memory impairment. This chapter focuses on two common disorders Attention-Deficit/Hyperactivity Disorder (ADHD) and Autism.

Attention –Deficit/Hyperactivity Disorder (ADHD)

What is ADHD and How to Recognize It?

Attention deficit hyperactivity disorder (ADHD) is a collection of symptoms such as inattention, inability to focus, disorganization, distractibility, impulsivity, and over-activity. These symptoms usually begin early in childhood, and typically occur wherever the individual is. These symptoms can impact a child's functioning in any setting such as home or school, and cause significant problems. ADHD symptoms can persist throughout a person's lifetime, many children do not "grow out of it" and ADHD can continue to cause problems for an individual even in his/her adulthood.

Attention deficit hyperactivity disorder (ADHD) was first described in 1902. It is one of the most common conditions in childhood. Approximately, 5% of children have ADHD (American Psychiatric Association, 2013). It is very difficult for Children with ADHD to concentrate as other children of the same age. The attentional mechanisms in their brains are inefficient. They have great difficulty concentrating on schoolwork and their work often contains careless errors, and shows lack of precision and attention to detail. These difficulties of maintaining attention are usually greater in a setting of a classroom, where there are many distractions. Additionally, children with ADHD usually have greater difficulty concentrating on things they have to listen to, rather than things they have to look at. Children with severe ADHD may have difficulty staying on any task for very long and may be unable to sit and watch a movie or play a game they enjoy. Such children may constantly flit from one activity to another (Selikowitz, M. 2009).

ADHD and Hyperactivity and Impulsivity:

Diagnostic criteria: 314.01 (F90.2)

ADHD involves a persistent pattern of inattention and/or hyperactivity-impulsivity that interferes with functioning or development, as characterized whereby the individual often fails to give close attention to details or makes careless mistakes, does not seem to listen when spoken to directly, frequently does not follow through on instructions and fails to finish tasks, has difficulty organizing tasks and activities, often avoids, dislikes, or is reluctant to engage in tasks that require sustained mental effort, loses things necessary for tasks or activities, is easily distracted by extraneous stimuli and may include unrelated thoughts, and is often forgetful in daily activities.

Symptoms of hyperactivity and impulsivity involves an individual who often fidgets with or taps hands or feet or squirms in seat, who frequently leaves seat in situations when remaining seated is expected, who regularly runs about or climbs when it is inappropriate, who is often unable to play or engage in leisure activities quietly, is often "on the go", acting as if "driven by a motor," who often talks excessively, and blurts out an answer before a question has been completed, who frequently has difficulty waiting his or her turn, who often interrupts or intrudes on others and where there is clear evidence that the symptoms interfere with, or reduce the quality of social, academic, or occupational functioning.

Case Description

The following case is taken from Spitzer R.L.et al. (2002):

Noreen Hamilton, a 35-year-old clerk and mother of three small children, applied for treatment at a Montana mental health clinic with the complaint that "My mind wanders. It's hard for me to keep my attention on one task, and I get distracted so easily". She also described herself as disorganized, restless, irritable, and bad tempered. She tended to overreact emotionally and was often depressed for days at a time. Her relationship with her longtime lover had begun to unravel. The couple had frequent arguments, exacerbated by Noreen's temper. Her lover complained that "Problems just never get solved". She also found it difficult to handle her two boys, whom she described as "hyperactive".

The Psychiatrist asked the patient's mother to complete a questionnaire in which she was asked to recall Noreen's behavior as a child. The results placed Noreen in the 95th percentile of childhood "hyperactivity".

Although Noreen's memories of her own childhood were sketchy, she recalled being a disciplinary problem and often being sent to the principal's office in elementary school. She had no treatment as a child, but at age 20 and again at age 23 saw a counselor because she had difficulty "coping". Her marriage, which had been very stormy, terminated after the birth of the third child, at age 25, and she was again briefly in treatment. Finally, 2 years ago she went to the community mental health clinic and was given antidepressant medication, which she took for several months without any noticeable improvement.

What Does the Person Diagnosed with ADHD Look Like?

People with ADHD show significant signs of inattention, hyperactivity, and/or impulsivity. They seem to be in constant motion and they do not always seem to listen when being spoken to. Children with ADHD have trouble playing quietly, they talk excessively, interrupt or intrude others, are easily distracted, and do not finish tasks.

How Does the Person Feel?

Every person has a unique experience with ADHD. Some people with ADHD cannot tolerate loud noises, clutter, too many chores or too much sensory and over-stimulation. They may feel they are hurting others as they may zone out during conversations, which can make others, including partners, feel ignored and devalued. They may also disappoint others by being forgetful, for example forgetting a spouse's birthday. Being impulsive, they sometimes blurt things out without thinking, which may cause hurt feelings; and sometimes cause reckless behavior. And most of all they may feel constantly criticized, micromanaged and misunderstood.

The Client's Dilemma

Noreen stated she suffers from an inability to complete tasks at work. She was constantly distracted, restless and disorganized. She had troubles with her boyfriend and difficulties managing her sons. However, on some days she felt depressed. She thought all her symptoms indicate that she suffers from some kind of depression. She was even prescribed with antidepressant medicine, which did not improve her condition. In some aspect, she knew she might have ADHD, as she remembers having disciplinary problems as a child. She can even recognize the symptoms in her two boys. Nevertheless, she needs guidance to fully understand what she suffers from and receive the proper treatment.

Therapy

The clue to what is probably the correct diagnosis is in Noreen's chief complaint: "My mind wanders. It is hard for me to keep my attention on one task, and I get distracted so easily". This problem with attention and focusing is one of the cardinal symptoms of Attention-Deficit/Hyperactivity; and her mother confirms that as a child.

Noreen has the following typical feature of attention deficit: difficulty sustaining attention and organizing tasks, and distractibility. When an adult complains of inattentiveness, distractibility, affective lability, problems controlling temper, and impulsivity, the clinician should be alert to the possibility of the persistence of the childhood disorder. Such patients frequently also have an unusually high energy level, but this was apparently no true for Noreen.

Cognitive Behavioral Therapy

Cognitive Behavioral Therapy (CBT) has been found to improve adults with ADHD (Safren et al., 2005). CBT approaches for adult ADHD emphasize psych education, developing and implementing effective coping strategies (e.g., organization skills, time management, and planning), problem solving, cognitive restructuring, and environmental modifications to better manage the effects of ADHD on daily functioning (Ramsay, J.R.and Rostain, A.L., 2011).

The first CBT sessions should be focused on setting treatment goals and defining how progress will be evaluated. For example, one goal could be "breaking down the steps needed to complete a report at work and working on it a little every day". The steps of dividing different tasks into manageable steps, planning realistic time frames for follow through to allow time for completion by the deadline, and being able to engage in the scheduled task are all important in breaking down a projects steps, in this case a report. This can help Noreen to get organized, focused and less distracted.

By the use of psych education Noreen would be able to better understand the effects of ADHD. This will increase her self-awareness on how ADHD affects her daily functioning. Treatment would also include specific therapeutic tasks and homework assignments that will increase the likelihood of initial successful experiences. This will in turn promote self-efficacy, and decrease the likelihood of premature dropout.

Following sessions are used to track progress in the implementation of the coping skills needed to achieve treatment goals and to generalize these skills to other domains of life. Many adults with ADHD may develop maladaptive or challenging belief systems related to inadequacy, self-mistrust, and failure when approaching new situations with a sense of pessimism and in the case of Noreen - Depression.

Cognitive interventions are crucial for building and maintaining motivation for follow-through on important tasks. Motivation can be thought of as the ability to generate an emotion about a task that enhances the likelihood for follow-through in the absence of proximal reinforcement. The therapeutic process for engendering motivation involves generating a compelling rationale for the importance of personal goals and elaborating on the long-range benefits for completion of necessary component steps to maintain the salience of these steps (Barkley, R.A., 1997).

Although the current model of CBT for adult ADHD emphasized personalized treatment planning, it included standard behavioral coping strategies for managing the effects of ADHD that are commonly employed in the course of treatment. Organizational skills, planning and time management, problem management and decision making skills, implementation strategies, and environmental engineering are common coping domains that are addressed in the course of most psychosocial treatment programs for adult ADHD (Ramsay, J.R. 2010).

Family Therapy

Psychosocial approaches treat ADHD in its interpersonal context, recruiting the child's family and caretakers as partners and equipping the team with resources for managing a challenging and persistent disorder (Whalen & Henker, 1991).

Children with ADHD impact the entire family system. Parents will often experience greater stress and ongoing struggles. They will most likely display negative reactions around their children's behaviors that can result for a lower self-esteem. Therefore, coping with a child with ADHD may cause marital conflicts and create a complete focus on the behavioral issues of the child. In many cases, the parent's interactions are mostly about the child and this will affect their intimacy and couplehood. Siblings too can feel frustrated, angry and even embarrassed by the ADHD child. They may also feel rejected by their parents, who need to invest more attention and resources to the ADHD child.

Therapists can offer parents parenting skills training, where they will be given tools and techniques for managing their child's behavior. As part of the training, parents are encouraged to create a system of rewards and penalties that can be an effective way to modify a child's behavior. For example, parents can use a token chart or point system for immediately rewarding good behavior or work. For example, if the child completes all of his/her chores they may get a sticker to place on their chart. After receiving five stickers, the child may receive a prize that is meaningful to them. If the child does not complete the given chores, then they do not receive a sticker and a penalty is implemented. An example for penalty is the use of "timeout" or isolation to a chair or a bedroom, when the child becomes untamed. Parents may also want to give the child "quality time" each day, in which they share an enjoyable or relaxing activity together. The parent can take this "alone time" opportunity to notice and point out what the child does well, and praise his or her strengths and abilities.

Lastly, once the parents understand the implications of ADHD, the next step is to help develop appropriate strategies to cope with the associated difficulties that are present at home also in the school setting.

Autism Spectrum Disorder (ASD) 299.00 (F84.0)

What is Autism and How Do You Recognize It?

Autism spectrum disorder is a persistent impairment in reciprocal social communication and social interaction, and restricted, repetitive patterns of behavior, interests, or activities. These symptoms are present from early childhood and limit everyday functioning. Core diagnostic features are evident in the developmental period, but intervention, compensation, and current supports may mask difficulties in at least some contexts. In recent years, reported frequencies for Autism Spectrum Disorder (ASD) across U.S. and non-U.S. countries have approached 1% of the population. According to Bernier, R. and Gerdts, J. (2010) the average age of diagnosis for all autism spectrum disorders ranges from 3.5 to 5 years of age in the United States. However, parents of children with autism spectrum disorders often report symptom onset between 12 and 18 months of age. Males are more often affected than females and the sex ratio of males to females with a diagnosis of autism spectrum disorder is approximately 4:1.

Many individuals with autism spectrum disorder also have intellectual impairment and/or language impairment (such as slow talk, language comprehension). Even those with average or high intelligence have an uneven profile of abilities. Motor deficits are often present, including odd gait, clumsiness, and walking on tiptoes. Self-injury such as head banging or biting the wrist may occur.

The behavioral features of autism spectrum disorder first become evident in early childhood, when the child lacks an interest in social interaction in the first year of life. Some children experience developmental plateaus or regression, with deterioration in social behaviors or use of language.

Many options exist for providing treatment to individuals with autism spectrum disorder. Early intensive behavioral intervention is the recommended treatment approach to address the core symptoms and is the only treatment that has received positive research support to date. A behavioral intervention approach called Applied Behavior Analysis (ABA) has been studied extensively and has demonstrated promising results in improving outcomes for individuals with autism spectrum disorder.

Only a minority of individuals with autism spectrum disorder live and work independently in adulthood; those who do tend to have superior language and intellectual abilities.

Symptoms for Autism Spectrum Disorder

Diagnostic Criteria 299.00 (F84.0)

An autistic individual has deficits in social communication and social interaction across multiple contexts, has deficits in social-emotional reciprocity, ranging, for example, from abnormal social approach and failure of normal back-and forth conversation; to reduced sharing of interests, emotions, or affect; to failure to initiate or respond to social interactions, has deficits in nonverbal communicative behaviors used for social interactions, and deficits in developing, maintaining, and understanding relationships. The severity is based on social communication impairments and restricted, repetitive patterns of behavior. There may be stereotyped or repetitive motor movements, use of objects, or speech, an insistence on sameness, inflexible adherence to routines, or ritualized patterns of verbal or nonverbal behavior.

Case Description

The following case is taken from Spitzer R.L.et al. (2002):

> Twenty-two-year old Betsy was referred for evaluation by the staff of her group home. She had been placed in the group home some 3 months previously, following court ordered "deinstitutionalization" from a large residential facility for the retarded. The evaluation was requested because Betsy "didn't fit in" with other patients and had developed some problem behaviors, particularly aggression directed toward herself and, less commonly, toward others. Unlike other patients in the group home, she tended to "stay to herself" and had essentially no peer relations, although she did respond positively to some staff members. Her self-abusive and aggressive behaviors usually were triggered by changes made in her routine. Self-abusive behavior consisted of repeated pounding of her legs and biting of her hand.

> Betsy had been placed in a residential treatment when she was age 4 and had remained in some kind of residential setting ever since. Her parents had both died, and she had no contact with her only sibling. At the time of her transfer to the group home, she was reported to have had several abnormal electroencephalograms, but no seizures or other medical problems had been noted. When last given psychological tests, she achieved a full-scale IQ of 55, with comparable deficits in adaptive behaviors.

> During the evaluation, Betsy spends much of her time reading a children's book she discovered in the waiting room. Her voice is flat and monotonic. She is unable to respond to any questions about the book she is reading and reacts to interruptions of her ongoing activity by pounding her legs with her fist. She rocks back and forth continually during the interview. She makes eye contact with the examiner initially, but otherwise seems oblivious of everyone around her. She neither initiates activities, imitates the play of the examiner, nor responds to attempts to interest her in alternative activities, such as playing with a doll. From time to time she repeats a single phrase in a monotonic voice, "Blum, blum". Physical examination reveals extensive bruises covering most of her lower extremities.

Betsy was the product of a normal pregMichelle, labor, and delivery. She was noted to have been an unusually easy baby. Her parents had first become concerned when she failed to speak by age 2. Motor milestones were delayed. Her parents initially thought that she might be deaf, but this was obviously not the case, as she responded with panic to the "live in her own world". She had not formed attachments to her parents, had idiosyncratic responses to some sounds, and always became extremely upset when there were changes in her environment.

By age 4, Betsy was still not speaking, and placement in the state institution was recommended following a diagnosis of childhood Schizophrenia. In the year after her placement, Betsy began speaking. However, she did not typically use speech for communication; instead, she merely repeated phrases over and over. She had an unusual ability to memorize and became fascinated with reading, even though she appeared not to comprehend anything she read. She exhibited a variety of stereotyped behaviors, including body rocking and head banging, requiring a great deal of attention from the staff.

What Does Autism Spectrum Disorder Look Like?

The autistic child does not smile or has any joyful expressions by six months or after. They usually do not have facial expressions, or back-and-forth gestures such as pointing, showing, reaching or waving by 12 months. The autistic child is a late talker, and have delays in language development. He/she prefers solo play, and tend to play in the same way or the same toy over and over again. The child has no meaningful, and no social skills at any age. Individuals with an Autism Spectrum Disorder exhibit problems with communication and social behavior. It causes many difficulties in many areas of their life, such as their social and occupational aspects. In severe cases a person with Autism Spectrum Disorder will need full-time care for life. Those that are high-functioning autistic adults are able to work successfully in mainstream jobs, but they usually are do not have any social contact with other co-workers. They have difficulty understanding gestures, body language and facial expressions. They are unaware of what is socially appropriate and have difficulty choosing topics to talk about. They may not be socially motivated because they find communication difficult and as a result do not have many friends. They choose not to socialize very much and appear to be in their own closed world.

How Does the Autistic Person Feel?

Autism Spectrum Disorder includes many neurological conditions, with varying degrees of difficulties with language and communication, and rigid patterns of thought and behavior (Hu 2013). People with Autism Spectrum Disorder have difficulties in emotion recognition and difficulty recognizing facial expressions of emotion (Harms, et al. 2010).They are not even aware of other people around them. Additionally, people with autism can also be overwhelmed by stimuli such as bright lights, strong smells and loud sounds, all of which affects their behavior.

The Client's Dilemma

Betsy has behavioral problems since she was a very young child, including problems in social interactions and social awareness. She can communicate, but speaks in a monotonic form and repeats phrases again and again. She has limited interests and has the habit of hurting herself. When she was placed in the state institution, she was diagnosed as having a childhood Schizophrenia. However, all of the evidence show that she has an Autism Spectrum Disorder.

Theories and Explanations of Autism

Environmental

A variety of factors such as advance parental age, low birth weight, or fetal exposure to valproate, may contribute to risk of autism spectrum disorder. In addition to these factors, there has also been evidence that perhaps chemicals in a variety of everyday household items could be a risk factor for an individual to be diagnosed with an autism spectrum disorder. Two products that are often overlooked are perfume and cosmetics (Bagasra et al, 2013). Many women would never think twice about using these products, but as the article suggests, these could play a role in an autism spectrum diagnosis being given.

Genetics and Physiological

There is indisputable evidence for a genetic component in autism (Rodier, 2000). With identical twins, if one is autistic, the likelihood that the other twin will have some form of autism is 90% (Ratajczak, 2011). As many as 15% of cases of autism spectrum disorder appear to be associated with a known genetic mutation. According to Kellyn Betts, another factor that may play a role in a person being born with an Autism Spectrum Disorder is due to an endocrine disruption. Betts notes "the observation that males may be four times as likely to be diagnosed with ASDs as females suggests hormonal involvement" (Betts, 2014). In looking at the hormonal levels as a cause, this is also intertwined with the idea of different chemicals playing a contributing factor possibly as well.

Family Therapy

According to family systems theory, everything that happens to any family member has an impact on everyone else in the family (Goldenberg & Goldenberg, 2003). A family is considered one emotional and functional unit where individuals cannot be understood in isolation from one another. Instead, all parts of the family are interconnected and interdependent.

Families with an autistic child cope with struggles such as self-blame, guilt, anger, denial, grief and shame. Treatment has to include ways for coping, acceptance and techniques to redefine the family original system and its day-to-day functioning (Horn, 2009).

In therapy, roles of the parents needs to be addressed to the autistic child and his/her siblings. Therefore, boundaries should be formed and therapist can help the parents to create special attention to other subsystems of the family, such as siblings. The autistic child will inevitably cause stress on the parents and other siblings. In addition, siblings who know that their brother or sister is unusual should be included in the coping process so they will not be left out and will feel more compassionate, and tolerant about the autistic child's difficulties. It will also help them with any embarrassment they may feel. Acceptance is part of the adjustment process and it needs to include cooperative work of all family members to create a balance.

The autistic child affects the entire system, as autistic children need an intensive, comprehensive professional treatment. Some of the interventions a child with autism may need are speech and language therapy, occupational therapy as well as learning social skills. Parents must be educated about the disorder, and should have a support system. Parents and family should be taught different techniques to help the child develop. Example of such a technique is Floortime in which an adult can help a child expand his/her circles of communication by meeting him/her at their developmental level and building on his/her strengths. It is often incorporated into play activities on the floor. It should be at a level that the child currently enjoys and where the parent is instructed to later move the child toward more complex interactions.

Children diagnosed as having Asperger Syndrome very often have an area of special interest, which can dominate their attention and conversation. (Frith, 1991). From a systemic therapy perspective such a dynamic system can be treated as a resource to therapeutic conversation to the entire family. The therapist and family can communicate at times with each other through the area of this special interest and creating a shared and meaningful language for the family. This is another example for a treatment, which empowers the entire family and can help manage the children (Atwood 1998).

When to Refer

Early intervention is a key component when looking at individuals with an autism spectrum disorder. If one knows the early identification signs that there could be a problem, early intervention could improve the individual's quality of life (Falck-Ytter, Bolte, & Gredeback, 2013). With the rate of an individual being diagnosed with an autism spectrum disorder so high, studies suggest that pediatricians will have an advantage with identifying these early signs and referring for early intervention (Cangialose and Jackson Allen, 2014). It has been recommended that at a child's nine, 18 and 30 month well visits that there be a standard general screening performed and a more specific screening should be completed at the 18 and 24 month visits (Cangialose and Jackson Allen, 2014). Again, this would allow an individual to get the proper treatment they could benefit from early enough so that they may possess a long quality of life. Some areas with deficits that can be identified during the first year of life would include; motor skills, language skills, and cognitive functions (Falck-Ytter, et al, 2013).

In addition to the child's pediatrician performing these different screenings, it is also important for the parents of the child to know the early signs. While there are some skills (i.e.; social, preverbal gestures) that are seen as having a deficit prior to 18 months of age, the average age of an individual being diagnosed with autism is 5.7 years (Cangialose and Jackson Allen, 2014). This could be due to a lack of knowledge or training to a sense of denial a parent may face. Research reports that parents of individuals with an autism diagnosis had concerns during the child's first two years of life as well as even having concerns by 12 months (Cangialose and Jackson Allen, 2014). The best step a parent can take if they do have these concerns is to follow up and ask their primary care physician. They should not feel embarrassed or ashamed at what the outcome may bring. The primary care physician could then make a referral and if needed the child can get receive early intervention help.

References

American Psychiatric Association. (2013) Fifth Edition. *Diagnostic and Statistical Manual of Mental Disorders: DSM-V.* **American Psychiatric Press.**

Atwood, T. (1998). T*he Complete Guide to Asperger's Syndrome.* **Jessica Kingsley publishers**

Bagasra, O., Golkar, Z., Garcia, M., Rice, L.N., & Pace, D.G. (2013). Role of perfumes in pathogenesis of Autism. *Medical Hypotheses* **80.6, 795.**

Barkley, R. A. (1997). *ADHD and the nature of self-control.* **New York: Guilford Press.**

Bernier, R. and Gerdts, J. (2010). *Autism Spectrum Disorders: A Reference Handbook In Contemporary World Issues.*Santa Barbara, Calif: ABC-CLIO.

Betts, K. (2014). Clues to autistic behaviors: exploring the role of endocrine disruptors. *Environmental Health Perspectives,* **122.5,** A137.

Bradley-Klug, K. L. and Chesno Grier, J. E. Book Review Section Adolescents and Their Families: Coping with ADHD. *School Psychology Quarterly, Vol. 15, No. 4, 2000, pp. 480-485*

Cangialose, A., & Jackson Allen, P. (2014). Screening for autism spectrum disorders in infants before 18 months of age. *Pediatric Nursing,* **40.1, 33.**

Falck-Ytter, T., Bolte, S., & Gredeback, G. (2013). Eye tracking in early autism research. *Journal of Neurodevelopmental Disorders,* **5, 28.**

Frith, U. (Ed.) (1991) *Autism & Asperger Syndrome.* Cambridge: Cambridge University Press.

Goldenberg, I., & Goldenberg, H. (2003). *Family Therapy: An Overview (6th ed.).* Pacific Grove, CA: Brooks/Cole.

Harms, M.B., Martin, A., & Wallace, G.L. (2010). Facial emotion recognition in autism spectrum disorders: A review of behavioral and neuroimaging studies. *Neuropsychology Review, 20, 290–32.*

Horn M., Melanie. (2009). Systems Theory: Families and Autism. Retrieved February 5, 2014, from http://www.cccfcs.edu.

Hu, H. (2013). Breaking bounds. *Diverse Issues in Higher Education, 30(18), 11-12.*

Ramsay, J. R. (2010b). *Nonmedication treatments for adult ADHD: Evaluating impact on daily functioning and well-being.* Washington, DC: American Psychological Association.

Ramsay, J.R., & Rostain, A.L. (2011). CBT without medications for adult ADHD: An open pilot study of five patients. *Journal of Cognitive Psychotherapy: An International Quarterly. 25(4).*

Ratajczak, H.V. (2011). Theoretical aspects of autism: Causes—A review. *Journal of Immunotoxicology, 8(1), 68–79.*

Rodier, P. M. 2000. The early origins of autism. *Scientific American 282:56–63.*

Safren, S. A., Otto, M. W., Sprich, S., Winett, C. L., Wilens, T. E., & Biederman, J. (2005). Cognitive-behavior therapy for ADHD in medication-treated adults with continued symptoms. *Behaviour Research and Therapy, 43, 831–842.*

Selikowitz, M. (2009). *In Attention-deficit Hyperactivity Disorder.* Oxford: Oxford University Press. 2nd ed.

Spitzer, Robert L., Gibbon, Miriam, Skodol, Andrew E., Williams, Janet B. & Michael First, B. (2002) Fourth Edition. *DSM-IV-TR Case book: A Learning Companion to the Diagnostic and Statistical Manual of Mental Disorders.*

Whalen, C. K., & Henker, B. (1991). Therapies for hyperactive children: Comparisons, combinations, and compromises. *Journal of Consulting and Clinical Psychology, 59, 126-137.*

Chapter 3

Oppositional Disorders

Svetlana Popova, M.A., MFT

What is Oppositional Defiant Disorder and How Do We Recognize It?

Sometimes it may be difficult for parents to understand if a child is overly emotional or has symptoms of Oppositional Defiant Disorder. Parents may become stressed out or hurt by their children's uncooperative behavior. (Fitzgibbons, 2011). Unfortunately their anger and opposition towards parents may not be properly identified and their emotions may not be addressed at the right time. Many children may display defiant behavior and have temper tantrums but only some of them will develop symptoms of the disorder, which are associated with distress, and negatively impact important areas of functioning such as social, occupational, and educational environments.

Oppositional Defiant Disorder belongs to a group of behavioral disorders called disruptive, impulse-control, and conduct disorders. Children with Oppositional Defiant Disorder appear to disrupt those around them. Evidence suggests that Oppositional Defiant Disorder is common among children and occurs in 1-16 per cent of children and adolescents (Loeber et al, 2009). Oppositional Defiant Disorder usually develops in late preschool or early school-aged children. It is more common for boys in younger children. However, it is equally distributed between boys and girls in school-aged children and adolescents (Orr, 2008).

Oppositional Defiant Disorder is less severe and more common than Conduct Disorder. The defining feature of Oppositional Defiant Disorder is repeated defiant, disobedient, or hostile behavior towards authority figures whereas in Conduct Disorder it is persistent and overt aggression, and serious rules violations. In many cases, children with Oppositional Defiant Disorder grow up to have Conduct Disorder. In some cases, adults may develop Antisocial Personality Disorder when the treatment for Oppositional Defiant Disorder was not received or an individual with Oppositional Defiant Disorder did not respond well to the treatment.

Oppositional Defiant Disorder and Conduct Disorder are designated separately but the diagnoses are related. Some research suggests that Oppositional Defiant Disorder may be a developmental precursor to Conduct Disorder (Greene et al, 2002). Another view is that Oppositional Defiant Disorder may be a milder form of Conduct Disorder. However, most children with Oppositional Defiant Disorder do not develop Conduct Disorder. Conduct Disorder is a more serious behavioral disorder. Those children who did not develop Conduct Disorder symptoms in the first 3-4 years with Oppositional Defiant Disorder are not likely to develop it later.

Children with Oppositional Defiant Disorder are at risk for developing other problems besides Conduct Disorder such as anxieties and depressive disorders (Burke et al, 2002). There are also certain risk factors associated with development of Oppositional Defiant Disorder. Risk factors can be linked to a stressful family environment that a child is vulnerable to (Greene & Doyle, 1999). Risk factors include but not limited to: financial problems, lack of supervision, family instability such as occurs with divorce, multiple moves, or changing schools or child care providers, parents with a severely troubled marriage, neglect, rejection, physical or emotional abuse, and brutal discipline. These risk factors may increase the possibility of disruptive behavior. There are several factors, outside of family, that may be held accountable for Oppositional Defiant Behavior such as deviant peer involvement, community disadvantage, lack of social activities, and low academic involvement. Promotive factors include: positive peer relationships, family involvement, low parental stress, and good housing quality.

Symptoms: Oppositional Defiant Behavior (313.81)

Disruptive, impulse-control, and conduct disorders include conditions involving problems in the self-control of emotions and behaviors. These problems are demonstrated in behaviors that offend the rights of others (e.g., aggression, destruction of property) or that bring the individual into disturbance with societal norms and authority figures (APA, 2013).

The disorders include Oppositional Defiant Disorder, Intermittent Explosive Disorder, Conduct Disorder, Antisocial Personality Disorder, Pyromania, Kleptomania, and other specified and unspecified disruptive, impulse-control, and conduct disorders.

Diagnostic features include a frequent and persistent pattern of angry/irritable mood, argumentative/defiant behavior, or vindictiveness. Individuals with the disorder who display the angry/irritable mood symptoms frequently have the behavioral features as well. The symptoms may be only shown in one setting, such as home or school. However, in more severe cases, the symptoms of the disorder are present in multiple settings. Because these behaviors are common among siblings, they must be noticed during interactions with other individuals. There are several key considerations for determining if the behaviors are symptomatic of Oppositional Defiant Disorder. Criterion A includes a pattern of angry/ irritable mood, argumentative/defiant behavior, or vindictiveness lasting at least 6 months as evidences by at least 4 symptoms from any of the following categories, and manifested during interaction with at least one individual who is not a sibling.

Someone diagnosed with Oppositional Disorder often loses his or her temper, is often touchy or easily annoyed and is often angry or resentful. S/he often argues with authority figures or often actively defies or refuses to comply with requests from authority figures or with rules, or deliberately annoys others. S/he often blames others for his or her mistakes or misbehavior and can be vindictive.

The symptoms of the disorder are often are part of a pattern of problematic interactions with others. Individuals with this disorder do not think of themselves as angry, oppositional, or defiant. Instead, they often justify their behavior as a reaction to inconsistent demands or circumstances.

Two of the most common co-occurring conditions are ADHD and Conduct Disorder. Oppositional Defiant Disorder has also been connected with an increased risk of suicide attempts. The disorder appears to be somewhat prevalent in males than in females (4:1) prior to adolescents.

The first symptoms usually manifest during the preschool years and rarely later than early adolescence. Oppositional Defiant Disorder often precedes the development of Conduct Disorder, but not always. Oppositional Defiant Disorder also conveys risk for the development of anxiety disorders and Major Depressive Disorder, even in the absence of Conduct Disorder. The defiant, argumentative, and vindictive symptoms carry most of the risk for Conduct Disorder, whereas the angry-irritable mood can result in emotional disorders. Children and adolescents with Oppositional Defiant Disorder are at an increased risk for a number of problems in adjustment as adults, including antisocial behavior, impulse-control problems, substance abuse, anxiety, and depression.

ADHD is often comorbid with Oppositional Defiant Disorder. To make an additional diagnosis of Oppositional Defiant Disorder, it is important to determine that the individual's failure to conform to requests of others is not solely in situations that demand sustained effort or attention or demand that the individual sits still. Rates of Oppositional Defiant Disorder are much higher in individuals with ADHD, and this may be the result of shared temperamental risk factors.

High levels of emotional reactivity and poor frustration tolerance have been predictive of the disorder. Inconsistent or neglectful parenting techniques play a significant role in many causal theories of the disorder. When Oppositional Defiant Disorder is persistent throughout development, individuals with the disorder experience frequent conflicts with parents, peers, and romantic partners. Such problems often result in significant impairments in the individual's emotional, social, academic, and occupational adjustment.

The behaviors of Oppositional Defiant Disorder are typically of a less severe nature than those of Conduct Disorder and do not include aggression toward people or animals, destruction of property, or a pattern of theft or deceit. Furthermore, Oppositional Defiant Disorder includes problems with emotional dysregulation that are not included in the definition of Conduct Disorder.

Conduct Disorder

Conduct Disorder has three subtypes based on the age of onset of the disorder. These three subtypes are Childhood Onset (312.81), Adolescent Onset (312.82) and Unspecified (312.89). In childhood-onset conduct disorder, individuals are usually male, frequently show physical aggression toward others, have disturbed peer relationships, and may have had Oppositional Defiant Disorder during early childhood. Many children with this subtype also have concurrent ADHD or other neurodevelopmental difficulties. As compared with individuals with childhood-onset type, individuals with adolescent-onset Conduct Disorder are less likely to show aggressive behaviors and tend to have healthier peer relationships.

The essential feature of Conduct Disorder is a repetitive and persistent pattern of behavior in which the basic rights of others and major age-appropriate societal norms or rules are violated. These behaviors fall into four main groupings: aggressive conduct that causes or threatens physical harm to other people or animals; non-aggressive conduct that causes property loss or damage; deceitfulness or theft; and serious violations of rules. Individuals with Conduct Disorder often initiate aggressive behavior and react aggressively to others. They may display bullying, threatening, or intimidating behavior; initiate frequent physical fights; use a weapon that can cause serious physical harm; be physically cruel to people or animals; steal while confronting a victim; or force someone into sexual activity. Physical violence may take the form of rape, assault, or homicide. Intended destruction of other's property may consist of predetermined fire setting with intention of causing serious damage or destroying other people's properties in other ways such as smashing car windows or vandalizing school property. Acts of deceitfulness or theft may incorporate breaking into someone else's house, building, or car; frequently lying or breaking promises to obtain goods or favors or to avoid debts or obligations; or stealing items of nontrivial value without confronting the victim.

Children with Conduct Disorder often have a pattern, beginning before age 13 years, of staying out late at night despite parental prohibitions. Children may also display a pattern of running away from home overnight. Personality features include poor frustration tolerance, irritability, temper outbursts, suspiciousness, insensitivity to punishment, thrill seeking, and recklessness. Substance misuse, suicidal ideation, attempts, and completed suicide occur at a high rate in individuals with Conduct Disorder.

First significant symptoms usually emerge during the period from middle childhood through middle adolescence; the onset is rare after age 16 years. Family-level risk factors include parental rejection and neglect, inconsistent parenting, harsh discipline, physical or sexual abuse, lack of supervision, early institutional living, frequent changes of caregivers, large family size, parental criminality, and certain kinds of familial psychopathology.

Community-level risk factors include peer rejection, affiliation with a delinquent peer group, and neighborhood exposure to violence. Males with a diagnosis of conduct disorder frequently exhibit fighting, stealing, vandalism, and school discipline problems. Females are more likely to exhibit lying, truancy, running away, substance use, and prostitution.

Conduct disorders behaviors may lead to school suspension or expulsion, problems in work adjustment, legal difficulties, sexually transmitted diseases, unplanned pregMichelle, and physical injury from accidents or fights. Conduct Disorder is often associated with an early onset of sexual behavior, alcohol use, tobacco smoking, use of illegal substances, and reckless behavior. Individuals with Conduct Disorder may come into contact with criminal justice system for engaging in illegal behavior.

Intermittent Explosive Disorder (312.34)

Intermittent Explosive Disorder also incorporates high rates of anger. However, individuals with this disorder show serious aggression toward others that is not part of the definition of Oppositional Defiance Disorder. Individuals with personality disorders or disorders with disruptive behaviors such as Oppositional Defiant Disorder, Conduct Disorder, and ADHD, are at a greater risk for developing Intermittent Explosive Disorder. Intermittent Explosive Disorder can be diagnosed when impulsive aggressive outbursts have a rapid onset. Outbursts usually last for less than 30 minutes and typically happen in response to a major provocation by a close intimate or associate. Regardless of the nature of the impulsive aggressive outburst, the core feature of this disorder is a failure to control impulsive aggressive behavior in response to subjectively experienced provocation (i.e., psychosocial stressor) that would not typically result in an angry outburst.

Pyromania (312.33)

An individual is diagnosed with Pyromania when there is a presence of multiple episodes of deliberate and purposeful fire setting. Pyromania happens much more often in males, especially those with poorer social skills and learning difficulties. Pyromania in childhood appears to be rare. Juvenile fire setting is usually associated with Conduct Disorder, ADHD, or Adjustment Disorder.

Kleptomania (312.32)

The essential feature of Kleptomania is the recurrent failure to hold off impulses to steal items even though the items are not needed for personal use or for their monetary value. The individual experiences a rising subjective sense of tension before the theft and feels pleasure, gratification, or relief when committing the theft. The stealing is not committed to express anger or vengeance, is not done in response to a delusion or hallucination, and is not better explained by Conduct Disorder, a Manic episode, or Antisocial Personality Disorder. The stealing is usually done without assistance from others. The individual often feels depressed or guilty about the thefts. Females outnumber males at a ratio of 3:1. The disorder often begins in adolescence. The disorder may continue for years, despite multiple convictions for shoplifting.

Case Description

Jack, age 9, is brought by his mother to a mental health clinic because he has become increasingly disobedient and difficult to manage at school. Several events during the past month convinced his mother that she had to do something about his behavior. Several weeks ago he swore at his teacher and was suspended from school for three days. Last week he was reprimanded by the police for riding his bicycle in the street, something his mother has repeatedly cautioned him about. The next day he failed to use his pedal brakes and rode his bike into a store window, shattering it. He has not been caught in any more serious offences, though once before he broke a window when he was riding his bike with a friend.

Jack has been difficult to manage since nursery school. His problems have slowly escalated. Whenever he is without close supervision, he gets into trouble. He has been reprimanded in school for teasing and kicking other children, tripping them, and calling them names. He is described as bad-tempered and irritable, even though at times he seems to enjoy school. Often he appears to be deliberately trying to annoy other children, though he always claims that others have started the arguments. He does not become involved in serious fights, but does occasionally exchange a few blows with another child.

Jack sometimes refuses to do what his two teachers tell him to do, and this year has been particularly difficult with the one who takes him in the afternoon for arithmetic, art, and science lessons. He gives many reasons why he should not have to do his work and argues when told to do it. Many of the same problems were experienced last year when he had only one teacher. Despite this, his grades are good and have been getting better over the course of the year, particularly in arithmetic and art, which are subjects taught by the teacher with whom he has the most difficulty.

At home Jack's behavior is quite variable. On some days he is defiant and rude to his mother, needing to be told to do everything several times before he will do it, though eventually he usually complies; on other days he is charming and volunteers to help; but his unhelpful days predominate. Jack is described as spiteful and mean with his younger brother Rickie; even when he is in a good mood, he is unkind to Rickie.

Jack's concentration is generally good, and he does not leave his work unfinished. His mother describes him as "on the go all the time", but not restless. His teachers are concerned about his attitude, not about his restlessness. His mother also comments that he tells many minor lies, though when pressed, he is truthful about important things.

What Does Oppositional Defiant Disorder Look Like?

A child with Oppositional Defiant Disorder is the one who displays a set of negative behaviors. He or she is frequently defiant, hostile, and disobedient. Defiant children may display confrontational behavior. They do not like responding to instructions or taking orders from others, and they actively turn down simple requests. Individuals with Oppositional Defiant Disorder are often disobedient at home and at school, rebel against rules, and continuously act out, which compromises their ability to get along with others. Jack is not cooperative when being asked to do things. He appears to blame others for their mistakes, can get annoyed easily, and act in an angry and irritated manner. They get upset often and act in a hostile and spiteful way, which makes them hard to deal with. Children may deliberately argue and annoy people, refuse to do simple tasks, and take the most difficult paths to do things. These behaviors are typically directed towards parents, teachers, and other authority figures.

Adults can get overwhelmed and frustrated when coping with children's consistently disruptive attitude. Defiant children also tend to irritate others with their behavior. It is difficult to be around those children because their destructiveness and disagreeableness are persistent. They produce strong feelings in people by trying to get attention and reaction from them. Other defiant behaviors may include arguing, claiming not to care about losing privileges as a consequence of negative behavior, declining responsibility for actions, ignoring directives, refusing to go to timeout, stubbornness, testing limits, and unwillingness to compromise or negotiate. They can purposefully make people fight with each other by lying and setting things up. Jack tends to annoy other children in school as a way to show his opposition and dislike.

Usually a child will present with co-occurring disorders such as ADHD, anxiety disorder, or depression. Girls may show their oppositional behavior in a different way than boys. They are prone to show their aggressiveness and negativity by verbally expressing it. They may lie and be uncooperative while boys have temper tantrums and argue excessively. Involvement in bullying is usually a sign that a child is engaged in violent and aggressive behaviors.

How Oppositional Defiant Disorder Feel?

Many defiant children may have low self-esteem, are moody, and get easily frustrated. They are rarely truly sorry and believe they are not to be blamed for things they do. They usually feel calm and organized after a huge blow up like nothing happened. Defiant children believe they are identical in authority to adults. Jack is disobedient at home because he feels it is not fair to blame him for everything happening. The biggest fear a child with Oppositional Defiant Disorder has is a fear of lost control. Because they blame others for their behavior they lack responsibility. They question the rules imposed on them, get annoyed by others, and seek revenge. They may see their behaviors as justified and do not see a problem. A child with Oppositional Defiant Disorder believes that unreasonable demands are placed upon him.

Defiant children may experience rejection by classmates because of their poor social skills, aggressive and annoying behavior. They may feel anxious or doubtful due to an unstable situation at home or school. They may also have difficulty maintaining friendships, have low self esteem, and academic problems. Even though Jack likes to study, it is hard for him to make friends and find a way to cope with his mistakes. Children with co-existing ADHD may perform even poorer at school than those with Oppositional Defiant Disorder alone.

A child with Oppositional Defiant Disorder feels like he cannot manage his anger and stress, and has to develop new ways to cope with it. They may feel anxious or uncertain and develop disruptive behaviors as a coping mechanism to deal with stress.

The Client's Dilemma

A child with Oppositional Defiant Disorder usually experiences very difficult years that are problematic for both the child and primary caregivers. Nicholas (10) struggles in school and cannot make friends. He gets easily annoyed with people and their demands. Nicholas feels insecure and stressed out many days of the week. He has anxiety about his life and does not know how to control it. He feels angry at the whole world for making him do things he does not like. Nicholas often loses temper when things do not go his way. Sometimes he celebrates in his room that he did not follow directions and made someone feel bad.

His or her parents feel ineffective, weak, and exhausted. Oftentimes, they feel ashamed of him and their parenting skills. Every time Nicholas wants to be nice to his parents they suspect he is lying. When it happens he feels an edge to argue and disobey even more.

How did he become a child diagnosed with Oppositional Defiant Disorder? Some experts consider that the disorder is so common because of changing definitions of normal childhood behavior, and potential racial, cultural, and gender biases. This behavior typically starts at age 8 but may start in preschool years. Inconsistent parenting, rigid discipline, and maladaptive parent-child interactions may have been causal factors in developing the disorder. Because of possible risk factors and dysfunctional family patterns, a child may develop a tendency to disrupt the environment around him. Overwhelmed parents often get out of control and do not know how to deal with a defiant child.

Theories and Explanations

The exact cause of Oppositional Defiant Disorder is unknown, but it is said to have biological, genetic, and environmental factors, which may add to the condition.

Biological

Some explanations for development of Oppositional Defiant Disorder may be attributed to injuries or defects in certain areas of the brain. Oppositional Defiant Disorder can also be associated with abnormal amounts of some types of neurotransmitters, such as serotonin. According to some propositions, if neurotransmitters are out of balance, brain messages may not be properly transmitted, leading to symptoms of Oppositional Defiant Disorder or other mental disorders. Many children diagnosed with Oppositional Defiant Disorder may have other co-occurring mental disorders such as ADHD, depression, learning disorders, or anxiety disorders.

Problems in emotional regulation may lead to the development of the disorder. Some studies suggest that parents' emotion coaching and emotion regulation may play a protective and preventive role for children with Oppositional Defiant Disorder.

Neurobiological correlates include higher adrenal androgens levels for individuals with Oppositional Defiant Disorder. Their heart rates tend to be higher after aggravation and frustration. Their autonomic nervous system may be more sensitive to the outside triggers.

Furthermore, brain scans propose that there are differences in areas associated with judgment, reasoning, and impulse control in individuals with Oppositional Defiant Disorder. Limitations or developmental disruptions in a child's ability to process thoughts and feelings may be also attributed to the symptoms development. Improper nutrition, smoking, and exposure to other toxins by pregnant mothers may play a part in the symptoms development.

Genetics

Genetic components may be related to the development of Oppositional Defiant Disorder but specific genes are not recognized. However, many children with the disorder have family members with a history of mental disorders such as anxiety disorders, mood disorders, substance use disorders, and personality disorders.

Environmental factors

Environmental risk factors may include a dysfunctional family life, inconsistent discipline at home, harsh or neglectful childrearing practices, and alcohol and drug abuse in the family. Family risk factors also include a poor relationship with one or both parents, a neglectful or absent parent, abuse, neglect, lack of supervision, uninvolved parents, family instability such as divorce or location change.

Some research indicates that children of alcoholic parents, or those in trouble with the law, have a greater chance of developing the symptoms. Social factors incorporate poverty, chaotic environment, and violent neighborhood.

Therapy Techniques

Early detection of symptoms of the disorder is likely to increase chances of behavior change (Bierman, et al, 2011). Moreover, many children diagnosed with Oppositional Defiant Disorder get better and improve over time. Medication alone has not been proven effective in reducing Oppositional Defiant Disorder symptoms. However, it can be helpful with co-existing mental conditions such as ADHD, mood disorders, and anxiety. Antidepressants and antianxiety medications are helpful in reducing symptoms of anxiety and mood disorders. Multimodal treatment may be the best option (Steiner & Remsing, 2007).

There are many treatment options available. Children respond best to treatment that rewards positive behavior and teaches them skills to manage negative behavior. Moreover, treatment works best when parents are involved. Multisystemic Therapy, Parent Management Training, Family

Therapy, Behavioral Family Therapy, Parent-Child Interaction Therapy (PCIT), Cognitive Problem Solving Training, Social Skills Training, and Parent Training are the effective for Oppositional Defiant Disorder treatment.

Multisystemic Therapy

Multisystemic Therapy (MST) is a family-focused treatment program that focuses on multiple systems, targeting disturbance in the behavior of individuals, family, and peers. MST combines strategies from Cognitive Behavioral Therapy, Parent Management Training, and various family therapies (Weiss et al, 2013). The program may concentrate on behavior, family discipline, school performance, and peer pressure. Multisystemic Therapy has been found to be a very effective treatment for individuals with Oppositional Defiant Disorder (Henggeler & Sheidow, 2012). It seeks to integrate individual, school, and family settings. Treatment should also address familial conflict such as marital discord or maternal depression. This treatment addresses many of the possible triggers of defiant problems.

Parent Management Training

Major part of the multisystemic treatment is Parent Management Training (PMT) in which the therapist teaches parents how to encourage desired behaviors, using Cognitive Behavioral Therapy, and also by working on interactions with authority figures at school (Hautmann et al, 2009). Parents are the primary agent of change and are taught how to alter their child's behavior. The focus is on helping parents to manage a child's behavior, enforce stable rules and limits, negotiate compromises, and reward good behavior. PMT enables the family and the child to identify problems, recognize causes, learn about consequences, learn how to talk about feelings, and consider alternative ways of handling difficult situations (Orr, 2008).

The focus of PMT is usually on the child at home. The parents are trained to use points, marks on a chart, or start on a temporary basis to foster behaviors such as completing chores, doing homework, and getting ready on time. Those simple techniques are an excellent way to avoid nagging and punishments. Praise as a reinforcer is found to be very effective. To change, develop, or increase a specific behavior, the reinforcer must be given when that behavior occurs. School has to create a special arrangement for the child such as allowing him to do only the important part of the homework. This way the child can achieve academic success and improve his self-esteem. Parent management training may be used in combination with other therapies.

Behavioral Family Therapy

Behavioral family therapy incorporates family factors that lead to disruptive disorders such as parental stress, cognitions about the child, and child temperament. Families learn stress-reduction techniques and work on developing problem-solving skills. Behavioral Family Therapy focuses on problematic interactions and behavior in a system.

Parent-Child Interaction Therapy (PCIT)

PCIT is an evidenced-based treatment with step-by-step live coached sessions with both parents and a child. In Parent-Child Interaction Therapy, therapists instruct parents while they interact with their children. In this approach, the therapist is located behind a one-way mirror and, using an "ear bug" audio device, and directs parents through strategies that reinforce their children's positive behavior. As a result, parents learn more effective parenting techniques including positive discipline, the quality of the parent-child relationship improves, parental stress reduces, and problem behaviors decrease.

Cognitive Problem Solving Training

Cognitive Problem-Solving Training is focused on children with problematic behavior and poor social skills. This type of training helps a child to learn new skills for approaching situations that previously aggravated negative behavior. Both cognitive and behavioral techniques are used to decrease disruptive behaviors and work on cognitive processing.

The cognitive part of training includes changing faulty views of daily events, working on irrational beliefs, and generating alternative solutions. By changing a child's perceptions and looking at different options, it is possible to identify ways to change disruptive behavior (Matthys et al, 2012).

The behavioral part incorporates modeling positive behaviors, role-playing challenging situations, and rewarding positive behavior. Brainstorming is used as a problem-solving technique to find possible solutions for difficult situations.

Parents are also coached on how to reward positive behavior, and practice new skills with a child (Cunningham & Boyle, 2002). Parents learn to work together with a child to come up with solutions that work for the whole family. Cognitive problem-solving training is more effective when combined with Parent Management Training.

Social Skills Training

Social Skills Training tends to be effective for children with Oppositional Defiant Disorder. It includes training of various emotional, behavioral, and social skills. Specific skills include communication, anger control, and reduction of aggressive behaviors, problem-solving skills, self-monitoring, sharing, and cooperation (Greene et al, 2002). Techniques include verbal instructions, role-playing, coaching, skill reinforcement, and homework. Social Skills Training is helpful for defiant children in teaching more positive and effective interaction with peers.

Parent Training

Parent training is helpful for frustrated and overwhelmed parents whose child is diagnosed with Oppositional Defiant Disorder. Parents are taught to develop skills that allow them a more positive interaction with a child. If a child participates with parents, it lets the whole family develop common goals for how to handle problems (Hautmann, 2009). Parents may learn how to give effective time outs, avoid power struggles, remain calm in the face of opposition, recognize and praise a child's good behaviors and characteristics, offer tolerable choices, establish schedules for family rituals, and chose specific activities to do with children (Bierman et al, 2011). Learning these skills involves consistent patience and time from parents (Kazdin, 2005).

Family Therapy

Family therapy focuses on making changes within the family system. A family therapist reflects on family dynamics and parent-child relationships. There is an established relationship between parenting behavior and a child's defiant behavior (Henggeller, 2012). Family functioning is thus considered the most important factor in causing and maintaining the problem. Lack of interconnectedness among family members and lack of dyadic parental responsiveness seem to complicate the clinical picture. When assessing the family, a therapist relies on parents or other primary caregivers for the core of the information about the symptomatic behavior. Attention is focused on the family's story of problematic behavior with emphasis on the nature of behavior and its impact on the family. A family therapist also looks at the risk factors associated with family such as stressful family environment, family instability, maladaptive parenting techniques, and a troubled marriage. Family dysfunction and family conflict are considered to be causal factors for the disorder development.

Low levels of parental skill and lack of combined effort in children's rearing result in arrested socialization. Lack of appreciation for intimate human relationships is seen in children with Oppositional Defiant Disorder (Frick et al, 1992). A defiant child's identity formation interferes with the development of an adequate self-image. A child's noncompliance is often seen as early precursor to more severe forms of aggressive behavior. When such skills as self-regulation and affective modulation are compromised early in the development, a child may potentially develop disruptive behavior. Inability to label and process emotions may also contribute to oppositional behavior development. Additionally, adult-child interactions may be critical at the point at which oppositional behavior develops.

Marital discord may be a factor for the disorder development. The more severe the marital discord, the more severe the defiant problems (Shalini & Ahalya, 2005). The problem can be aggravated by the child's observation of the parental discord and by internalizing it. Parental conflict can exacerbate the symptoms and the maintenance of the disorder. Family therapists may discuss the parent-child relationship as the primary target and promote couples therapy as a means to helping them meet their goals as parents. There is a need to fully engage parents in the process and reduce parents' defensiveness and skepticism before attempting any interventions. Family therapy target family conflict and promote harmonious parent-child and marital relational processes.

A family therapist can also help parents learn how to modify the child's environment, including changing their own typical responses to non-compliant behavior, and avoid situations in which a child can become overwhelmed. Finally, family treatment should focus on enhancing cooperation between parents and children, and between parents as a couple.

When to Refer

A child psychiatrist or mental health professional is usually the mental health professional who diagnoses the Oppositional Defiant Disorder. Oppositional Defiant Disorder treatment depends on the age of the child, co-existing mental health conditions, and severity of symptoms.

Co-occurring mental disorders would often be a reason to refer a client to a psychiatrist or other mental health professional. When a client displays severe mood disturbance, there may be a possibility of diagnosing with Disruptive Mood Dysregulation Disorder instead of Oppositional Defiant Disorder (APA, 2013). Furthermore, Oppositional Defiant Disorder must be distinguished from Intellectual Developmental Disorder, Language Disorder, and Social Anxiety Disorder.

Often an individualized plan for treatment is required. In many cases, treatments may last for several months and require active parent participation. Marriage and family therapists can provide meaningful support and direction for a child struggling with Oppositional Defiant Disorder. Family therapy can improve emotional connectedness and harmony among family members. Family therapy helps parents to learn techniques to manage a child's behavior, ways to discipline consistently, and teaches about positive reinforcement. Family therapy also looks at the patterns of interaction in a family with a defiant child. Family therapy with clients diagnosed with Oppositional Defiant Disorder is usually helpful.

References

American Association for Marriage and Family Therapy. (n.d.). Retrieved February 20, 2015, from http://www.aamft.org

American Psychiatric Association (2013). *Diagnostic and Statistical Manual of Mental Disorders* (5th ed). Arlington, VA: American Psychiatric Publishing.

Bierman, K., L., Coie, J., D., Dodge, K., A., Greenberg, M., T., Lochman, J., E., McMahon, R., J., & Pinderhughes, E., E. (2011). The Effects of the Fast Track Preventive Intervention on the Development of Conduct Disorder across Childhood. *Child Development*, Vol 82.

Burke, J., D., Loeber, R., & Birmaher, B. (2002). Oppositional defiant disorder and conduct disorder: A review of the past 10 years, part II. *Journal of the American Academy of Child and Adolescent Psychiatry*, 41: 11.

Brown University Child & Adolescent Behavior Letter (2004). Conduct Disorder and Oppositional Defiant Disorder Trends and Treatment, Vol. 20, No. 5.

Child Mind Institute. (n.d.). Retrieved April 1, 2014, from http://www.childmind.org

Cunningham, C., E., Boyle, M., H. (2002). Preschoolers at risk for attention-deficit hyperactivity disorder and oppositional defiant disorder: Family, parenting, and behavioral correlates. *Journal of Abnormal Child Psychology*, Vol 30, 6, 555-569.

Diagnostic and Statistical Manual of Mental Disorders: DSM-V. (5th ed.) (2013). Washington, D. C.: American Psychiatric Association.

Dunsmore, J., C., Booker, J., A. & Ollendick, T., H., (2013). Parental emotion coaching and child emotion regulation as protective factors for children with oppositional defiant disorder. *Social Development*, 22: 444-466.

Frick, P., J., Lahey, B., B., Loeber, R., Stouthamer-Loeber, M., Christ, M., G. & Henson, K (1992). Familial risk factors to oppositional defiant disorder and conduct disorder: Parental Psychopathology and Maternal Parenting. *Journal of Consulting and Clinical Psychology*, *61*(1), 49-55.

Greene, R., W. & Doyle, A., E. (1999). Toward a transactional conceptualization of oppositional defiant disorder: Implications for assessment and treatment. *Clinical Child and Psychology Review*, *2*, 3.

Greene, R., W., Biederman, J., Zerwas, S., Monuteaux, M., C., Goring, J., C., Faraone, S., V., (2002). Psychiatric comorbidity, family dysfunction, and social impairment in referred youth with oppositional defiant disorder. *The American Journal of Psychiatry*, 159: 1214-1224.

Hautmann, C., Stein, P., Hanisch, C., Eichelberger, I., Pluck, J., Walter, D., & Dopfner, M. (2009). Does parent management training for children with externalizing problem behavior in routine care result in clinically significant changes? *Psychotherapy Research*, 19 (2).

Henggeler, S., W., & Sheidow, A., J. (2012). Empirically supported family-based treatments for conduct disorder and delinquency in adolescents. *Journal of Marital and Family Therapy*, *38*, 1.

Kazdin, A., E. (2005). Parent Management Training: Treatment for Oppositional, Aggressive, and Antisocial Behavior in Children and Adolescents. *Oxford University Press*.

Loeber, R., Burke, J., & Pardini, D., A. (2009). Perspectives on oppositional defiant disorder, conduct disorder, and psychopathic features. *The Journal of Child Psychology and Psychiatry* 50:1-2.

Matthys, W., Vanderschuren, L., J., M., J., Schutter, D., J., L., G., & Lochman, J., E. (2012). Impaired neurocognitive functions affect social learning processes in oppositional defiant disorder and conduct disorder: Implications for interventions. *Clinical Child Family Psychology*, Review 15.

(n.d). Retrieved April 1, 2014, from http://www.clinic.psych.ubc.ca

(n.d). Retrieved April 1, 2014, from http://www.cnn.com

(n.d.) Retrieved April 2, 2014, from http://www.disabled-world.com

(n.d). Retrieved April 2, 2014, from http://www.empoweringparents. com

(n.d). Retrieved April 2, 2014, from http://www.kellybear.com

(n.d). Retrieved April 3, 2014, from http://www.kidsmentalhealth.org

(n.d). Retrieved April 3, 2014, from http://www.learningrx.com

(n.d). Retrieved April 3, 2014, from http://www.mayoclinic.com

(n.d). Retrieved April 3, 2014, from http://www.mentalhealth. vermont.gov

(n.d). Retrieved April 4, 2014, from http://www.minddisorders.com

(n.d). Retrieved April 4, 2014, from http://www.monohasen.org

(n.d). Retrieved April 4, 2014, from http://www.msu.edu

(n.d). Retrieved April 4, 2014, from http://www.netdoctor.co.uk

(n.d). Retrieved April 7, 2014, from http://www.nlm.nih.gov

(n.d). Retrieved April 7, 2014, from http://www.rightdiagnosis.com

(n.d). Retrieved April 7, 2014, from http://www.thetotaltransformation. com

(n.d). Retrieved April 8, 2014, from http://www.psychcentral.com

(n.d). Retrieved April 9, 2014, from http://www.psychologytoday.com

(n.d). Retrieved April 11, 2014, from http://www.webmed.com

Orr, M., J., (2008). Clinical Update: Oppositional Defiant Disorder. *Family Therapy Magazine.*

Shalini, A., & Ahalya, R. (2005). Marital conflict among parents: Implications for family therapy with adolescent conduct disorder. *Contemporary Family Therapy*, 27.

Spitzer, R., L., Gibbon, M., Skodol, A., E., Williams, J., B., W., First, M., B., (2002). *DSM-IV-TR Casebook.* A Learning Companion to the Diagnostic and Statistical Manual of Mental Disorders, 4th ed.

Steiner H. & Remsing L. (2007). Practice parameter for the assessment and treatment of children and adolescents with oppositional defiant disorder. *Journal of American Academy of Child and Adolescent Psychiatry*, 46,1.

Weiss, B., Han, S., Harris, V., Catron, T., Ngo, V., K., Caron, A., Gallop, R., & Guth, C. (2013) An independent randomized clinical trial of multisystemic therapy with non-court-referred adolescents with serious conduct problems. *Journal of Consulting and Clinical Psychology.*

Chapter 4

Anxiety Disorders and Related Problems

Liat Rinat, M.A., MFT

What is Anxiety Disorder and How To Recognize It?

Anxiety is a difficult term to define fully and precisely because it actually refers to a complex set of events involving all the dimensions of behavior; particularly the affective, motivational, cognitive, biological, and interpersonal dimensions. Moreover, the pattern of anxiety may vary considerably from person to person and from time to time. What one person experiences as anxiety may be very different from what another experiences, and different yet again from what either of them would experience at another point in time.

This chapter focuses on the most common types of anxiety: Generalized Anxiety Disorder and Panic Disorder.

Generalized Anxiety Disorder

Generalized anxiety disorder (GAD) is characterized by chronic worrying about different events and activities, with recurrence of acute and disabling anxiety episodes. Generalized anxiety disorder is diagnosed when a person worries excessively about a variety of everyday problems for at least six months. The major emotional component of generalized anxiety disorder is an unpleasant sense of apprehensiveness and an approaching disaster. It is called a free-floating anxiety as the anxiety may be vague, diffused, and does not seem to result from any specific threat. These anxiety episodes can occur at any time. The intensity, duration, or frequency of the anxiety and worry is out of proportion to the actual impact of the anticipated event (APA, DSM-V). In most cases the anxiety is so severe it dominates and interferes the person's functioning at work, home, relationships and more.

People with generalized anxiety disorder experience symptoms such as: rapid heart rate, shortness of breath, muscle aches, diarrhea or constipation, loss of appetite, fainting, dizziness, nausea, sweating, sleeplessness, insomnia, nightmares, headaches, frequent urination, and tremors. They tend to be overly sensitive in their relationships, and often feel socially and emotionally inadequate and depressed. They have difficulties concentrating and making decisions as they fear of making mistakes. Not only are they indecisive, but also after they have finally made a decision, they worry excessively over errors and unforeseen consequences that may eventually lead to disaster. They always find something to worry about until most of their friends and relatives lose patience with them.

Even after going to bed, people who suffer from generalized anxiety disorder are not likely to find relief from their worries. They seem to be unable to relax, often spending hours reviewing every mistake, real or imagined, recent or remote. When they are not reviewing and regretting the events of the past, they are anticipating all the potential difficulties they may have to face in the future. After they finally manage to fall asleep, they frequently have anxiety filled dreams. They dream of being choked or shot, their teeth falling out, falling from high places, or of being chased by murderers with the horrible sensation that their legs will move only in slow motion.

Diagnosis criteria 300.02 (F41.1)

A person may be diagnosed with anxiety disorder if they have been anxious more days than not for at least 6 months, the individual finds it difficult to control the worry and the anxiety, worry, or physical symptoms cause clinically significant distress or impairment in social, occupational, or other important areas of functioning. Additional symptoms can involve restlessness or feeling keyed up or on edge, being easily fatigued, difficulty concentrating or mind going blank, irritability, muscle tension, and sleep disturbance.

Panic Disorder

Panic disorder refers to recurrent unexpected panic attacks that is characterized by acute anxiety and extreme autonomic arousal. A panic attack is a sudden surge of intense fear that reaches a peak within minutes. Panic attacks can be perceived as an immediate defensive reaction in response to imminent or perceived danger (Hoyer, 2012). The person experiences intense apprehensiveness and terror, and a sense that something terrible is about to happen. Panic attacks are sudden and last from a few seconds to an hour or more. Symptoms, although vary from one person to another, usually include palpitations, a choking feeling, pounding heartbeat, chest pains, shortness of breath, trembling, profuse sweating, faintness and dizziness, coldness and pallor of the face and extremities, urinary urgency, gastrointestinal sensations, and terrifying feeling of imminent death. The person feels he or she is losing control. The physiological symptoms, together with the sense of impending death or catastrophe, make an anxiety attack a truly terrifying experience. It is crucial that the therapist takes the experience seriously, recognizes the high intensity and irrationality of the feeling.

The panic attack generally subsides within a few minutes, however, it may last longer, even up to a few hours. If it continues, the individual may frantically implore someone to summon a doctor or beg to be taken to a hospital emergency room. After medical treatment has been administered, commonly in the form of verbal reassurance and a minor tranquilizer, the person usually feels better and quiets down. In fact, these individuals often calm down by the time they arrive at the hospital and feel rather ridiculous when the physician or nurse attempts to ascertain the presenting problem. According to Clark (1986) people who experience panic attacks are more likely than people who don't to interpret harmless bodily sensations as precursors to a physical (e.g. heart attack) or psychological (e.g. insanity) catastrophe.

Such attacks vary in frequency of occurrence. They may occur several times a day, once a month or less often. They may occur during the day, or the person may awaken from a sound sleep with a strong feeling of dread or apprehensiveness; which rapidly develops into a full-blown attack. Between attacks the individual may be relatively unperturbed; sometimes though, mild anxiety and tension persist. In some cases, excessive use of tranquilizers, hypnotics, and alcohol complicate the situation. Since these individuals do not know when a panic attack will occur and anticipate disastrous events, they tend to become reluctant to venture far from home, fearing that they might be seized with panic while walking on the streets or while driving. Clinicians often misdiagnose such cases of anxiety disorder as agoraphobia - the fear of open places. However, the real fear here is not of going out of the house; rather, these individuals fear that the panic symptoms will occur if they do go out. In this case, while agoraphobia may be complicating the picture, the primary problem is panic disorder. Once these individuals learn how to control the panic attacks, they typically resume their normal lifestyle.

Cognitive formulations of panic disorder emphasize anticipatory anxiety as a consequence of the apprehension of events as both highly aversive and uncontrollable, leading to attempts to avoid those events or prevent their anticipated negative consequences (Salkovskis, Clark and Gelder, 1996; White, Brown, Somers and Barlow, 2006). According to Barlow (1988) individuals with a panic disorder have a genetically based biological vulnerability. It is a neurobiological overreaction that occurs because such individuals perceive life stressors as if they were truly dangerous or life threatening. In some of these individuals, the initial overreaction becomes associated with the somatic sensations that accompany feelings of anxiety such as dizziness. This conditioning leads to the development of 'learned alarms', where these individuals learn to become fearful of these somatic sensations because they believe they will lead to another attack.

Diagnostic criteria 300.01 (F41.0)

A panic attack is an abrupt surge of intense fear or intense discomfort that reaches a peak within minutes, and during which time any of the following symptoms occur: Palpitations, pounding heart, or accelerated heart rate, sweating, trembling or shaking, sensations of shortness of breath or smothering, feelings of choking, chest pain or discomfort, nausea or abdominal distress, feeling dizzy, unsteady, lightheaded, or faint, chills or heat sensations, paresthesias, derealization or depersonalization, fear of losing control or "going crazy", and/or fear of dying.

Case Description

Peggy B. is a 38-year-old single parent of two boys, ages 7 and 10. She had been divorced for about 5 years, after having been married to a heroin addict for about the same number of years. She was employed as a legal secretary for a large law firm not too far from her home. She first came in for therapy because she was suffering severe anxiety attacks. Whenever she would experience an attack - and she could not predict when they would occur - she would feel as though her legs were going to cave in and as if she could not breathe. She would also become preoccupied with the pounding of her heart, and she believed her throat was closing up. Often she thought that she was going to have a heart attack. She felt terrified, but she did not know what was causing her terror. She initially thought she had some terrible physical disease, and she had consulted many physicians, desperately seeking the source of her problem.

She was especially terrified in the car. Since she could not predict when her "illness" was going to appear, she was constantly on the alert for manifestations of the symptoms. She reported that the attacks most often began when she was in the car, where she always felt on the verge of passing out. She thought that if she did, she would get into a fatal accident. She would drive to work each morning with a thermos of ice water and cold facecloths, which she would place on her neck whenever she started to feel weak. While driving, she would sip the cold water and hold the cold facecloth on her neck and face; this seemed to make her feel somewhat better. One day she forgot the facecloths. When she realized this, she began to panic. She was so desperate to alleviate her terror that she grabbed some old rags from the floor of the car, poured some of the thermos water on them, and laced them on her neck, whereupon she felt better.

She had stopped going out socially. She was afraid that if she went anywhere, the symptoms would surface. In order to avoid the symptoms, then, she would go straight home from work and get into bed, where she felt somewhat safe. Her days consisted of work and bed.

She had developed elaborate systems for ordering things over the phone and on the Internet and having them delivered. This enabled her to keep the family intact while hardly ever having to go out. She had not been in a department store for over a year. When the children needed new school clothes, she called the department store and ordered their clothes over the phone or bought it on the Internet. She would not go into a supermarket, so the family's diet consisted mainly of pizza and various macaroni dishes, all of which could be delivered. A pharmacy nearby also delivered to her. She would pay a teenager who lived next door to take her clothes to the cleaners and pick them up. She paid everything with a check or credit card. She would occasionally force herself to go to the bank, but it always took great preparation and courage. She went only during off hours, and only if she was armed with her thermos and magical facecloths. If there was a line she would go home, drained of energy for the rest of the day.

At the point when Peggy began therapy, she had been to about ten physicians, most of whom had suggested psychological counseling. However, she still believed that she had an undiscovered physical ailment that was responsible for her symptoms. If only her mysterious ailment could be diagnosed, she could take medication to cure it. She was unaware that she was having rather common anxiety attacks. Because of Peggy's refusal to leave the house, her friends were beginning to dwindle, tiring of her inability to take hold of herself and her life. This added to Peggy's depression, and she felt very alone. She had not had a boyfriend in over a year and felt that she would be alone for the rest of her life. She believed that she was a failure as a mother because she could not go on family outings with her children. Her life was bleak and she could see no hope for the future. She wished that she could feel like she did before she got "sick". This was the picture Peggy presented during her first therapy session.

What Does Anxiety Look Like?

The anxious person appears tense, as though in a constant state of agitation. They seem continuously on the alert and energized to meet the impending calamity, whatever it may be. If they are sitting, their knuckles may be white because they are grasping the arm of the chair so tightly. Or they may be twisting their fingers or wringing their hands. If they are standing, they may pace back and forth. Their facial muscles are strained, so that they often appear frozen. Often, they will clench their jaws, biting down hard on their back molars. A person in the middle of a panic attack may pace rapidly. They are terrified and fearful for their lives, believing that they may die at any moment or that they will lose control over themselves and their feelings. Anxiety may cause problems with thinking, sleeping, eating, and functioning. It can be debilitating, hindering people's family, social, educational, and occupational circumstances. Anxiety disorders affect physical health, morbidity, health care costs, and workplace productivity (Ghinassi, 2010).

When Peggy first came in for therapy, her lips were quivering. She was so nervous, she could barely talk. Her whole body was trembling. She was afraid she wouldn't make it up the stairs to the office that her legs would cave in before she got there. Once in the office, she clutched her purse, twisting the handle. She could concentrate only on herself, barley focusing on the therapist's questions. She seemed to be reading from a script of symptoms and feelings that she needed to report to the therapist; she was unable to focus on anything else.

Although Peggy was in a state of high anxiety during that first session, she was not having a panic attack. A panic attack is dramatic, frightening. The individual seems to be losing control of his/her body and his/her life. During a later session, Peggy did in fact have a panic attack and, although it lasted only a few minutes, it seemed to drain her of all energy. In the throes of the attack, she hyperventilated and paced rapidly back and forth in the office. Believing that she was choking to death, she begged the therapist to call an ambulance. When the episode passed, she sat on the couch and for the remainder of the session seemed to be on the verge of falling asleep. Such a relaxed state could not have been predicted from the agitated one that she had been in just a few minutes earlier.

How Does the Anxious Person Feel?

Anxious persons are scared to death. They feel like they have no control over what is happening to them. They feel terrified, and if asked what they are frightened of, they say, "I don't know." This is the most frustrating aspect of the disorder. They feel an impending sense of doom, but they don't know what form the doom will take. They feel that they are "terrified out of their minds," but they cannot isolate the cause. Peggy initially thought that some physical disease was the cause of her distress. Even though many physicians had found nothing physically wrong with her, she insisted that they just had not given her the right diagnostic test. She desperately hoped that they would find an illness to which her symptoms could be attributed, and that a rational explanation for her dreadful condition could be found.

The Client's Dilemma

Peggy was overwhelmed with the many responsibilities in her life. Since her ex-husband was unable to hold a job for more than a few weeks at a time because of his drug problem, Peggy was the sole supporter of her two young sons for many years. When she began treatment, she was barely able to survive; after she paid the bills, there was little money left over to buy food, never mind luxuries.

Peggy constantly compared herself to her two sisters, who had married very wealthy men. They had beautiful homes and were more than able to buy their children anything they wanted. Peggy had a modest home and felt guilty about the quality of care she gave her children. Her sisters had very expensive cars, while Peggy's was barely able to get her back and forth to work.   Whenever Peggy would fall behind on her bills, she would ask her parents for money. They lived in Florida, having retired early in order to travel and enjoy the rest of their lives in a warm climate. Both had been successful professionals and were now financially secure. When Peggy was first contemplating the divorce they had encouraged her, promising to help her financially for as long as she needed it. They had disapproved of Michael, her ex-husband, from the beginning, feeling that he was not good enough for Peggy. This was nothing new for Peggy; they had disapproved of all her boyfriends. Peggy's parents agreed to send her a set amount of money every month in order to help her pay her bills. This arrangement went smoothly for only a few months. Then they began sending the money late, and Peggy worried about when and if she was going to be able to pay the mortgage on her house. Peggy eventually began to having to call them each month and ask them for money in order to survive. They send the money in response to her request, but the price she paid for their financial help was high. Every time she called to "beg" them for the money, they would barrage her with questions: What had she fed the children for supper? What did they wear to school that day? What did she wear to work? Had she lost any weight that month? Had she made any efforts to meet a man?

Their questions undermined her ability as a parent and her functioning as an autonomous person. Peggy had fainted in the middle of one of these barrages, perhaps the only way that she could turn her mother off and shut out her anger, anxiety, and humiliation.

Peggy had never firmly established herself in the first stage of separation/ individuation (Mahler 1975). Her emotional separation from her husband had forced her to be solely responsible for the care of her children before she felt ready and required her to be financially and emotionally dependent on her parents once again. A diagnostic appraisal of her ego functioning indicates that upright locomotion, or "standing on one's two feet," was filling her with anxiety and unconscious conflict. This manifested itself in the trembling in her legs and the fear that she would not be able to seek help or physically complete the tasks necessary to care for herself and her children. Her automobile terror unconsciously pictured for her state of entrapment, morbid helplessness, and dependency that would ensue should she not reach her desired destination.

Peggy's mother was both critical and intrusive, and felt free to question her daughter's ability to adequately take care of herself and to make appropriate decisions. Peggy's mother was unable to help her child clearly differentiate between the child's internal self-representation and that of an internalized adequate mother who protected Peggy from an overwhelming, disastrous world. As an adult, Peggy no longer saw the world as her oyster, and even her ritualistic verbal recitations of her symptoms and feelings for the therapist only elaborated her internal self-representation as that of a deprived, humiliated child who sought the approval of the idealized parent. Her present life events reactivated separation anxiety and fear of engulfment by the internalized aggressive mother who was out of tune with her child's needs for self-gratification at her own psychological level of maturation (Mahler 1976).

On the positive side, Peggy never completely regressed to a point of losing ego functions, and she enlisted help by unconsciously coercing others in her plight to cope. On the one hand, she saw people as a source of help; on the other hand, she felt like a dependent child who needed to coerce them into helping her. She tried to comfort herself by using cold cloths to dampen her anxiety and temporary dizziness. She also had a beginning awareness of her own separateness from her mother.

Not only did Peggy feel financially responsible for the children; she also felt solely responsible for all their needs, which frightened and overwhelmed her. She would often say, "If anything happened to me, what would happen to the boys? There would be no one to take care of them. They have no one but me."

When Peggy began therapy, her parents were running her entire life. She felt that there was little she could do or say to them because they were being kind enough to give her money each month. Any time she did verbalize any discontent, she would quickly negate it by saying, "Yes, but they're so good to me. If it weren't for them, I don't know what I'd do. I would be lost." She psychologically pictured both herself and her sons in the same situation, both dependent upon their parents for survival.

Theories and Explanations For Anxiety

Psychodynamic

Freud believed that the motivation to avoid both awareness and overt expression of unacceptable impulses centered on the concept of anxiety, a powerful and unpleasant emotion that he believed to have primitive beginnings. He distinguished between two kinds of anxiety-provoking situations. In the first kind (which birth may be taken as the prototype) the infant's initial experience is that of being overwhelmed by uncontrollable stimulation. In this case, the anxiety is caused by excessive stimulation that the organism does not possess the capacity to handle.

In the second kind of anxiety-provoking situation (which occurs later in the child's psychosexual development) there is an accumulation of instinctual energy, which is blocked from expression by internalized inhibitions and taboos. A traumatic state ensues, which mobilizes the ego's defenses. In pathological situations, the ego becomes overwhelmed, but the defenses do not help the person to cope and ego functions begin to break down, which can then be accompanied by symptoms of panic and terror. In other words, according to Freud, many common anxiety-provoking situations occur after the ego has matured somewhat. As the child matures, anxiety takes on a new role: It begins to serve as a way of helping it to avoid a panic or traumatic state. The danger that the ego perceives may be *internal*, in the form of some disturbing instinctual impulses that threaten to break into conscious awareness and may be expressed in overt behavior.

In these cases, the anxiety may arise because the individual has learned to recognize it at a preconscious level; or the anxiety may serve the ego as a signal that unconscious derivatives from earlier, once-traumatic situations threaten the ego boundaries.

The perceived danger may also be *external*, such as a threat, loss, withdrawal of love, or a physical injury. This is sometimes referred to in analytic literature as *objective reality anxiety*. The child, as a result, learns various defense mechanisms to prevent these anxiety-arousing impulses from entering awareness or being overtly expressed in ways that might evoke negative consequences from significant others (Freud 1953).

Repression was the defense mechanism in which Freud focused on in his early writing. He believed that repression was the unconscious, but intentional forgetting of memories associated with anxiety-arousing impulses and conflicts. In Freudian theory of neurosis, anxiety played a central role, especially anxiety associated with an unresolved Oedipal conflict. The Oedipal conflict is an assumed inevitable sexual attraction that a young child will have toward the opposite-sex parent and the resulting competition with, and fear of, the same-sex parent. In boys, for example, irrational fantasies involving death wishes toward their father and expected retaliation in the form of castration are thought to be the basis for most neurotic anxieties. The Oedipal conflict becomes most intense when the child is 4 to 6 years of age. In an effort to reduce the associated anxiety, the entire conflict is repressed at that time. Children deal with this anxiety and conflict by identifying with the parent of the same sex and developing an unconscious guilt and superego, which will monitor the actions of the ego at its various levels of functioning. The ego is then supplied with guilt or self-approval to guide it in its reactions to and judgments of others.

As was pointed out earlier, the overt tension and turmoil that appears in anxiety is seen as a failure of ego defenses to control anxiety. Overt anxiety reactions, represent behavior in search of more adaptive ego responses and better-functioning defenses. An anxiety reaction or attack represents an effort by the individual to rid himself of excessive tension by direct discharge, for example, in autonomic dysfunctioning. The person with an anxiety disorder has not developed more adequate methods for dealing with threatening affect and overwhelming tension. While psychodynamic theorists assume that infantile conflicts underlie anxiety reactions in later life, the conflicts themselves usually are not apparent in the person's conscious experiences. Defense mechanisms succeed in repressing conflicts and unacceptable impulses and fantasies. Only the indirect derivatives of this unconscious material (together with indirect derivatives of unconscious defenses and the superego) get through to the preconscious mind. Thus, according to Freud, poorly repressed unconscious forces introduce strange contradictions in adult attitudes and lead to sustained fruitless, self-defeating behavior.

Some of the more modern neo-Freudians and the ego psychologists mention the following as cases of anxiety: perception of oneself as helpless in coping with environmental pressures; separation or the anticipation of separation or abandonment; privation and loss of emotional supports as a result of sudden environmental changes; unacceptable or dangerous impulses that are close to the point of breaking into consciousness; threats or anticipation of disapproval and withdrawal of love (Blanck & Blanck 1974).

Social Learning

Social-learning theorists have a tendency to argue that there is no reason to attribute neurotic disorders to complex and elusive unconscious processes. Many have long insisted that symptoms are merely learned behaviors and, like any other learned response, symptoms can be acquired through simple conditioning and stimulus generalization. A combination of both ego psychology and behavioral theory can lead to a more comprehensive understanding of what is happening at an internal subjective level as well as an external objective behavioral level.

Social-learning theorists believe that (as a response that is susceptible to learning) fear can be treated like any other response and studied in terms of classical conditioning, operant conditioning, and observational learning. From a social-learning point of view, most defense mechanisms are learned behavior patterns by which we try to avoid or escape circumstances that produce fear or anxiety. This kind of learning, known as *avoidance* or *escape learning*, has the following characteristics: if a person is exposed to some intensely unpleasant stimulation, they will usually learn to make some response that will reduce the unpleasant situation or permit them to escape it entirely. When such a response is made, it is reinforced by the cessation of the aversive stimulation. In many instances the person eventually learns to avoid the unpleasant experience altogether by making an avoidance response before the unpleasant stimulation begins.

With regard to panic disorders, behaviorists believe that by classical conditioning, at some point in a person's life, an association is formed between a particular stimulus and anxiety. The two variables involved could have initially been paired randomly. After the initial pairing, this anxiety reaction is elicited in the presence of other similar stimuli in the person's environment. At a later point, the stimuli that once elicited the anxiety response may bear no resemblance to the original traumatic association. Thus, the behavioral explanation for panic disorders centers on the notion of classical conditioning and stimulus generalization.

Cognitive Behavioral

Cognitive behavioral theories believe that any emotion can be influenced by what an individual believes (or does not believe) about a particular situation. These emotions and beliefs can then generalize to a great many other situations. If an individual has learned a particular negative belief about a given situation, more negative emotions and reactions can in turn generalize to many situations. In other words, given the same objective situation, the magnitude of the negative emotion can be greatly influenced by what a person "tells" oneself about the situation. Covert thought processes, such as beliefs, interpretations, and consequent expectations, can have a negative or positive effect, depending on whether one is thinking negatively or positively about the situation. When one makes a covert interpretive response to a situation that reduces negative emotions and anxiety, the response is then positively reinforced and hence is more likely to occur in the future in similar situations. Cognitive therapy attempts to modify the individual's cognitive interpretation of environmental events, rather than to alter the environment or behavior.

Rational emotive therapy typifies the cognitive approach to anxiety. This approach is a broad system of therapy developed by psychologist Albert Ellis (1962, 1970) based on the following assumption: When individuals are faced with stressful situations, they interpret the situation in terms of pairs of declarative sentences. For example, a person who fears rejection and humiliation might react to meeting an attractive woman with the following two sentences: (1) "She may not like me enough to go out on a date." (2) "That would mean that I am hopeless and no good." Ellis suggests that individuals with anxiety disorders are creating their own anxiety and negative evaluations through the second type of sentence. Treatment, therefore, is aimed at teaching the anxious individual to reinterpret stressful situations in more adaptive ways; for example, "If she doesn't like me, that's okay, because someone else will.". "It also does not mean that I am not a good person." Cognitive behavioral therapy can be used alone, or in conjunction with medications. The therapist helps the client identify thought patterns that contribute to the anxiety and panic attacks. Once these harmful thoughts have been identified, the clients can then focus on altering their destructive thoughts and learn to engage in more helpful behaviors.

Strong empirical evidence has proven that a combination of psychotherapeutic medication and cognitive-behavioral therapy (CBT) is the most effective treatment for most anxiety disorders. At the initial assessment the therapist should indicate whether the disorder is severe enough to warrant treatment with medication. Some patients prefer to try CBT first with no medication. However, the therapist still needs to refer the patient for a medication evaluation if the anxiety is too overwhelming to allow full engagement in the therapy (Ghinassi, 2010).

Biological

Is anxiety, as an affective state, the same regardless of the person experiencing it, and is the affect only qualitatively different? Recent psychopharmacological findings indicate that differential diagnoses vary according to the person's ego state. For example, anxiety suffered by neurotics is not the same as anxiety suffered by schizophrenics. Antianxiety drugs such as chlordiazepoxide hydrochloride (Librium) and diazepam (Valium) are very effective when administered to neurotics. However, the antipsychotic phenothiazines are poor agents for neurotic anxiety. The antipsychotic drugs affect different biochemical systems and in psychotics prevent the pervasive kind of primitive anxiety that may break down certain ego functions (Sahakian 1979).

Family Therapy

Family is very important in the recovery of a person with an anxiety disorder. In some cases the source of the disorder is in the family dynamics, the family structure, conflicts between family members, the way a family utilizes coping strategies with stress and more. For example, the quality of the parent–child bond, referred to as attachment, has been theorized to play a role in the development of anxiety disorders (Drake et al. 2012). Moreover, insecurely attached children have greater risk for developing anxiety disorders in general and social anxiety specifically (Bohlin et al. 2000). There is a growing body of literature that suggests parents play an important role in the development and/or maintenance of child anxiety and may also have an impact on treatment outcome (Ginsburg et al. 2004; Wood et al. 2003).

Family therapy can be very efficient for individuals with anxiety disorders as relatives' hostility, relatives' hostile criticism, and patients' perceptions that their relatives are critical of them have prospectively predicted poor treatment outcome with CBT for patients with GAD (Chambless and Steketee, 1999). For example, with the right training, learning about the disorder and with biblio-therapy, the family members can assist the client with homework assignments. This might involve accompanying the client into anxiety-producing situations (in vivo exposure) and providing encouragement to stay in the situation by using anxiety-reduction techniques. Family members can help the client adhere to a behavior, which is developed with the therapist to control anxiety responses in situations when the therapist is not present

A family therapist can help the client and other family members to recognize familial stressors, and work together to reduce its effects. For example, it has been proven that when parents are included and engaged in the therapeutic sessions, children experience improved treatment gains (Kendall and Podell 2011). Family therapy can also help other members of the family to understand what is anxiety, what are the triggers, and increase their support. Ideally, the family should be supportive but not help perpetuate the anxious person' behavior. Family members should not trivialize the disorder, and they need to realize they are a major part of the treatment and the preventative relapse.

Systemic family therapy is an approach to promote family problem-solving skills, communication and positive interactions between family members (Nichols, 2010). It operates from a neutral perspective; looking at the family as a whole and not blaming a specific person. According to this perspective an anxious member affects the entire family, and therefore the whole family needs to help solve the problems and be supportive. The family can help reinforce the suggestions of the therapist, explain situations and explore solutions. This in turn will help members feel that the problem is under control and will reduce the anxiety (Csoti, 2003).

Couples and families come to therapy because their usual ways of managing stress and anxiety are not working. The therapist becomes the third point in the triangle in the dyadic relationship. Therapy is one way to reduce anxiety and stabilize the system. According to Bowen, the therapist himself or herself has to stay calm, not reactive and find answers for the family. It is crucial that the therapist differentiates himself or herself from the system and will not get pulled into the anxiety of the system. As a result, the therapist enables the family to rethink what is happening, and find solutions. A family map or genogram can assist the family to observe information about the relationships, conflicts, and patterns of functioning. This in return can assist them to change their positions and patterns of behavior (Hecker and Wetchler, 2013). Another important role of the family therapist is to look for the family's underlying feelings by being empathic, using clarification and helping all members of the family to express their emotions. The family therapist has to control the sessions and assist all family members to slow down, process their thoughts and share the many feelings that one may be experiencing. This will allow all the members to be heard and will enable him or her to pay attention to any hidden feelings, rage or anxiety the members have (Glick, Berman, Clarkin and Douglas, 2000).

Therapy Techniques

1. *When treating anxious clients, it is crucial to first neutralize some of their intense anxiety.*

Peggy's psychotherapy could not proceed until some of her anxiety was dissipated. She was too focused on her physiological responses to the anxiety to think about anything else. Various methods can be used to help clients relax. First, speak in a soft voice slowing down your own verbal pace. This helps to set the tempo and climate for the client, helping him/her pace himself/herself with tolerable levels of anxiety. Second, universalize the client's experience. Tell him/her about other clients who have had panic disorders. Describe some of their symptoms. Often the client will say, "Yes! That's it! That's what I have." Reassure the client that there are successful techniques for dealing with this disorder. This helps the client selectively identify with the helpful, empathic feelings and attitudes of the therapist and thus neutralizes the anxiety.

If anxious, catastrophic feelings can be infused with care and some confident predictability, they become less overwhelming and the client feels ministered to in a time of dreadful anticipation. Repeated moments of feeling cared about need to be internalized by the client instead of defended against (denied, projected, and displaced). Of course, helping the client own up to these more comfortable moments becomes the continual struggle of the therapeutic process. In the initial therapeutic intervention, Peggy realized that she was not alone in her anxiety - that other people had not only experienced anxiety as severe as hers, but they had also overcome it.

Generally, after these initial techniques are used, the client noticeably relaxes. This relaxation may be short-lived and the client may call in a few days in the same state of terror as s/he was in initially. This is why it is sometimes wise to start off by seeing the client two or three times a week until the anxiety subsides substantially. In the more severe cases, it may be useful to refer the client to a psychiatrist for prescription of an antianxiety agent. Once the anxiety is more manageable, psychotherapy can proceed. The therapist thus establishes, by actual deed as well a verbal example, comforting and caring events for the client to cathect, creating positive memories and hopeful experiences that later will aid the client in coping on his/her own.

2. Teach the client deep muscle relaxation techniques and thus gain mastery over overwhelming effect and an uncontrolled physiological state.

Clients who are experiencing panic attacks feel as though they are losing control over their affect and over their own physiological reactions.

It is very useful to teach them a technique that will enable them to dissipate some of their anxiety and thereby give them some sense of control. The deep muscle relaxation exercise is one such technique. Explain some of the theory behind the procedure - which a person cannot be in a state of anxiety and relaxation at the same time. Demonstrate the exercises and tell the client how often to practice them and when to use them.

Peggy was taught the exercises during the second session, and due to her agitated state, she was very motivated to learn. It was explained to her that the relaxation exercises were a technique that would help her gain control over what her body was doing. She was told that once she mastered them, she would be able to put herself into a state of deep relaxation within seconds. Peggy's therapist explained that her anxiety might disappear initially once she started the exercises, but that it would probably return a few more times before it finally disappeared. Peggy was thus prepared for any further bouts of anxiety, which lessened the potential for feelings of failure and helped prevent her from becoming overwhelmed by future stirrings of anxiety. After Peggy had mastered the exercises, she learned how to proceed quickly from an anxious state to a relaxed one, and to use the exercise whenever she felt a panic attack conning on. At this point, Peggy finally began to believe that she could control her panic attacks; therefore she no longer had to fear becoming overwhelmed by anxiety or by her own helpless self-representation. As a consequence, she experienced fewer and fewer attacks and began to feel better about her deprived internal self. The fear aroused by the panic attack may awaken in clients the earlier infantile ego state in which they possessed no defenses or coping ability.

3. *Help these clients realize that they can effect positive changes in the environment. Help them test their internal subjective experiences and fantasies against objective reality.*

Anxious clients feel as though they have no control over their lives. Outside forces seem to dictate what course their lives take. Peggy felt that everyone had control over her life - and that she had none. This was partly due to her experience of her internal self as a helpless, deprived child who was unable to manage without the idealized parent who could give her constant nurturance and approval. During the course of therapy, she learned that she could tell her parents to stop criticizing her and intruding in her life, and that even if she did this, they could still love her. She learned that it was alright if she did not conduct her life exactly the way her parents dictated. If she did not feel like washing the dinner dishes, she learned that she did not have to - that she was not a bad person or a failure for not being the flawless housekeeper that she thought her mother was.

Once Peggy developed some self-respect, her identity was no longer tied up in an externally defined self, dictated by her mother. She began to master both her internal self-representation and her environment. Once she believed that her house did not always have to be as spotless as her mother's, it became less overwhelming for her to maintain it with some semblance of order. She also learned that her children did not have to be above reproach, and she was therefore able to feel better about her own unique maternal abilities. When she learned that her clothing and hair did not have to be beyond criticism, it became easier for her to take care of herself in a conflict-free way. She began to become her own person and establish her own identity when she ceased to live by her mother's definitions and standards. She became free of the depriving, critical internalized parent and learned that she did not have to fear abandonment by her parents if she did not behave properly. She was on the road to bridging the dichotomy between the good and bad parent, between the critical, depriving one and the benevolent, approving one. Stated another way, the chasm between the internalized angle and the witch mother was no longer as wide.

4. Help the anxious client to establish a support system of peers rather than of relatives.

Clients who are suffering from generalized anxiety or panic disorders tend to gradually isolate themselves from their friends, mainly because they fear suffering an anxiety attack if they go out. After a while, their support systems begin to dwindle, and they are soon left friendless. At this point, the only people who will tolerate their behavior are their relatives - the very people who are generally involved in precipitating their anxiety.

Peggy had isolated herself from her friends, and at the point when she entered therapy, she socialized only with her sisters. Unfortunately, her sisters reminded her of all the things she thought she failed at. They often acted as spokespersons for her mother, reminding her of all the things she needed to do or all the things she hadn't done. When Peggy learned that she could tell her sisters to mind their own business without fearing retaliation, she felt freer. Her declaration of independence and emotional separation somehow made it reality. She then began to seek out old friends and make new ones, encouraged in this pursuit by her therapist, who also encouraged her to begin dating.

When Peggy terminated therapy, she was relatively free of anxiety attacks. She would occasionally begin to feel an attack coming on, but she would do her relaxation exercises and the feelings would disappear. Thus, while the relaxation techniques were not necessarily a cure, they certainly helped Peggy proceed with her life. She eventually developed a support structure that consisted of four or five close girlfriends and a boyfriend whom she had been dating for about six months. She was able to go out at will, and she took her children on more outings. Her family no longer had such a devastating effect on her, and she was able to tell them to "get off her case" if they tried to interfere with her life. Peggy finally felt some sense of mastery over her environment.

When to Refer

When evaluating the anxious client's progress, it is important to ask the following types of questions:

1. Has the client's anxiety subside to a great degree? If not, it might be necessary to reduce his/her discomfort by referring him/her to a psychiatrist for medication.
2. Has the client been able to establish some awareness of his/her patterns of interaction and of the feelings that threaten to overwhelm him/her?
3. Has the client managed to maintain relative control over the anxiety? If the client's anxiety had initially subside, only to return and continue at a high level of intensity, it is possible that the initial change was an artificial one and that more frequent and extensive therapy is needed.

References

Atwood D. J., & Chester, R. (1987). *Treatment techniques for common mental disorders.* Jason Aronson Inc. Northvale, New Jersey, London.

Austin, D.W., & Richards, J.C. (2006). A Test of Core Assumptions of the Catastrophic Misinterpretation Model of Panic Disorder. *Cognitive Therapy & Research. 30(1),* 53-68.

Barlow, D. H. (1988). *Anxiety and its disorders: The nature and treatment of anxiety and panic.* New York: Guilford.

Bohlin, G., Hagekull, B., & Rydell, A. (2000). Attachment and social functioning: A longitudinal study from infancy to middle childhood. *Social Development, 9, 24–39.*

Chambless, D.L. (2012). Adjunctive couple and family intervention for patients with anxiety disorders. *Journal Of Clinical Psychology. 68(5), 548-60.*

Chambless, D. L., & Steketee, G. (1999). Expressed emotion and the prediction of outcome of behavior therapy: A prospective study with agoraphobic and obsessive-compulsive outpatients. *Journal of Consulting and Clinical Psychology, 67, 658–665.*

Clark, D. M. (1986). A cognitive approach to panic. *Behaviour Research and Therapy, 24(4), 461–470.*

Csoti, M. (2003). *School Phobia, Panic Attacks and Anxiety in Children.* Jessica Kingsley Publishers, Ltd.

Drake K.L., & Ginsburg G.S. (2012). Family factors in the development, treatment, and prevention of childhood anxiety disorders. *Clinical Child And Family Psychology Review. 15(2), 144-62.*

Ghinassi, Cheryl Winning (2010). *Anxiety in Biographies of Disease Series.* Santa Barbara, Calif: Greenwood/ABC-CLIO.

Hecker, L.L.,& Wetchler, J.L. (2013). *An Introduction to Marriage and Family Therapy.* Routledge

Ginsburg, G. S., Siqueland, L., Masia-Warner, C., & Hedtke, K. A. (2004). Anxiety disorders in children: Family matters. *Cognitive and Behavioral Practice, 11, 28–43.*

Glick, I.D., Berman, E.M., Clarkin, J.F., & Douglas, R.S. (2000). *Marital and Family Therapy, 4th Edition.* **American Psychiatric Publishing, Inc.**

Kendall, P., & Podell, J. (2011). **Mothers and Fathers in Family Cognitive-Behavioral Therapy for Anxious Youth.** *Journal of Child & Family Studies. 20(2),* **182-195.**

Nichols, M.P. (2010). *Family Therapy: Concepts and Methods, 9th edition.* **Pearson.**

Salkovskis, P. M., Clark, D. M., & Gelder, M. G. (1996). **Cognition-behaviour links in the persistence of panic.** *Behaviour Research and Therapy, 34,* **453–458.**

White, K. S., Brown, T. A., Somers, T. J., & Barlow, D. H. (2006). **Avoidance behavior in panic disorder: the moderating influence of perceived control.** *Behaviour Research and Therapy, 44,* **147–57.**

Wood, J. J., McLeod, B. D., Sigman, M., Hwang, W. C., & Chu, B. C. (2003). **Parenting and childhood anxiety: Theory, empirical findings, and future directions.** *Journal of Child Psychology and Psychiatry, 44, 134–151.*

Chapter 5

Depressive Disorders

Alexandra Laudisio, M.A. MFT

What is Depressive Disorder and How Do You Recognize It?

There are eight categories of depression: (1) major depressive disorder, (2) persistent depressive disorder (dysthymia), (3) premenstrual dysphoric disorder, (4) substance/medication-induced depressive disorder, (5) disruptive mood dysregulation disorder (6) depressive disorder due to another medical condition and (7) other specified depressive disorder and (8) unspecified depressive disorder. In this chapter we focus on disorders 1-4.

Major depressive disorder is a disorder characterized by persistent and pervasive low mood accompanied by feelings of sadness that go beyond the temporary feelings of sad or blue. It is a serious illness that affects one's behavior, feelings, thoughts, physical health, and mood. It usually has physical components and behavioral consequences.

Symptoms of major depressive disorder will include: poor concentration, depressed mood (sadness), fatigue, insomnia, excessive guilt, thoughts of suicide, and appetite disturbances. Clients will actively report feelings of hopelessness, sadness, and feeling of emptiness. There is also a marked diminished interest or pleasure in all or mostly all activities, occurring nearly every day.

A different, more chronic form of the disorder is known as Dysthymia or persistent depressive disorder. This can be diagnosed when the client experiences a mood disturbance for a minimum of two years in adults and a minimum of one year in children.

Premenstrual dysphoric disorder has recently (2013) been moved out of the appendix of the DSM and to Section II. After 20 years of additional research, it has been confirmed that there is a treatment-responsive form of depressive disorder that begins at some point after ovulation and has a definitive mark on functioning.

Substance/medication-induced depressive disorder were brought to light because research suggests that there are a large number of substances that may be abused which may give an individual a sense of being depressed. However, it may be difficult to determine which came first, the substance induced depressive disorder or a major depressive disorder. To find out the best diagnosis for an individual, it is important to go over an individual's history in regards to substance use. According to the research, the best way to identify a diagnosis is "depressive symptoms begin prior to the onset of a substance use disorder or during extended abstinence are typically diagnosed as an independent major depressive disorder episode, whereas depressive symptoms that only occur in the context of substance use and exceed the expected pharmacological effects of the particular substance are typically diagnosed as substance induced depressive disorder" (Magidson, Wang, Lejuez, Iza & Blanco, 2013). Having conversations and asking the client to be truthful and honest about their substance use history may allow for a determination to be made in regards to a specific diagnosis.

Depression is a mood or affect that involves subjective feelings, thoughts, fantasies, or wishes. It usually has physical components and behavioral consequences. One type of depression appears to be precipitated by *external* stress. The individual may become depressed because of stress at work, the loss of a loved one, or a psychosocial crisis such as divorce or unemployment. This type of depression is called *exogenous depression*. It is caused by something outside the individual, arising from the social environment. The stressful event contributes to the individual's feelings of worthlessness and guilt, and thus precipitates a depressive episode (Michael, 2012).

In a second type of depression, the causes are unrelated to external factors; they arise from *within* the individual, as the result of a biochemical or hormonal imbalance. This type is called an *endogenous depression* (Michael, 2012). The bipolar disorders, involutional depression, and postpartum depressive psychosis are believed to be of an endogenous nature. Early developmental difficulties, later inabilities to cope with stress, preexisting ego deficiencies, and cognitive problems may contribute to this major depressive disorder. Psychotherapy is usually the treatment for exogenous depression. For endogenous depression, medical intervention is often essential. For example, lithium carbonate is a drug that is used to stabilize the highs and lows of manic-depression. The tricyclic antidepressants and the monoamine oxidase (MAO) inhibitors are effective for major depressive episodes.

In endogenous depression, the physical dysfunction of biochemical disharmony occur first, and social factors further contribute to the downward trend. Even in the most severe cases, there may be some identifiable environmental factors contributing to, or at least reinforcing, the endogenous problem. An example is the family that needs an ill member in order to divert its attention from problems within the family system.

The distinction between endogenous and exogenous depression, although helpful, tends to create an artificial dichotomy between biological and social stressors. It is only in an artificial sense that biochemical depression or psychological losses and psychosocial stressors cause the depression. It is probably more accurate to see depression as an interaction of factors, with a prominence of one set of causal factors over the other.

Depression can be categorized as *primary* or *secondary*. In *primary* depression, the depressive disorder exists first; there is no history of psychiatric or a physical disorder. Primary depression is characterized by an episode of illness of mood change lasting at least two weeks. Dysphoric mood, anorexia, loss of energy, lack of joy (anhedonia), lower self-esteem, and poor concentration are other important symptoms to look for. There is also secondary depression. Secondary depression results from other psychological or physical disorders. For example, an individual can become depressed if he or she is continuously anxious, is an alcoholic, or has a nervous system disorder. In such cases, the anxiety, the alcoholism, or the nervous disorder is the primary dysfunction, and the depression follows as a consequence.

In order for a person to be diagnosed as having one of the depressive disorders, according to the, they must exhibit certain symptoms over a certain period of time. (For a more detailed listing of the diagnostic criteria, please refer to the DSM-V).

Depression Symptoms

Depression affects 5-8 percent of adults every year. This statistic means approximately 25 million Americans will have an episode of major depression this year. Depression occurs more frequently in women than in men (70 percent) for reasons that are not fully explicit (What is depression? 2013). Depression also frequently occurs among young people. Some 75 percent of a large sample of college students reported experiencing at least mild depression at some time during their freshman year; 41 percent reported moderate to severe depression during the same time period (Bosse et al. 1975).

Diagnostic Criteria

The following are the diagnostic criteria for Major Depressive Disorder. A person experiences a depressed mood most of the day, nearly every day, as indicated by either subjective or observation made by others; there is a markedly diminished interest or pleasure in all, or almost all, activities most of the day, nearly every day; there is a significant weight loss when not dieting or weight gain or decrease or increase in appetite nearly every day. Additional symptoms may include: insomnia or hypersomnia nearly, psychomotor agitation or retardation, fatigue or loss of energy, feelings of worthlessness or excessive or inappropriate guilt, diminished ability to think or concentrate, or indecisiveness, thoughts of death, recurrent suicidal ideation without a specific plan, or a suicide attempt or a specific plan for committing suicide, and the symptoms cause clinically significant distress or impairment in social, occupational, or other important areas of functioning. These symptoms occur nearly every day.

Persistent Depressive Disorder (Dysthymia) 300.4 (F23.1)

Diagnostic Criteria

Here, the person experiences Depressed mood for most of the day, for more days than not, as indicated by either subjective account or observation by others, for at least two years.

Some symptoms are: poor appetite or overeating, insomnia or hypersomnia, low energy or fatigue, low self-esteem, poor concentration or difficulty making decisions, and making decisions.

Premenstrual Dysphoric Disorder 625.4 (N94.3)

Diagnostic Criteria

Persons who fall into this category, experience the majority of the menstrual cycles, symptoms that are present in the final week before the onset of menses, start to *improve* within a few days after the onset of menses, and become *minimal* or absent in the week post menses. There may be a marked affective, irritability or anger or increased interpersonal conflicts, depressed mood, feelings of hopelessness, or self-deprecating thoughts, marked anxiety, tension, and/or feelings of being keyed up or on the edge, decreased interest in usual activities, subjective difficulty in concentration, lethargy, easy fatigability, or marked lack of energy, marked change in appetite, overeating; or specific food cravings, hypersomnia or insomnia, a sense of being overwhelmed or out of control, and physical symptoms such as breast tenderness or swelling, joint or muscle pain, a sensation of "bloating," or weight gain.

Substance/Medication-Induced Depressive Disorder

Diagnostic Criteria

Here the person experiences a prominent and persistent disturbance in mood that predominates in the clinical picture and is characterized by depressed mood or markedly diminished interest or pleasure in all, or almost all, activities. The symptoms developed during or soon after substance intoxication or withdrawal or after exposure to a medication; and the involved substance/medication is capable of producing the symptoms.

Coding note: The ICD-9-CM and ICD-10-CM codes for the [specific substance/medication]-induced depressive disorders are indicated in the table below. Note that the ICD-10-CM code depends on whether or not there is a comorbid substance use disorder present for the same class of substance. If a mild substance use disorder is comorbid with the substance-induced depressive disorder, the 4th position character is "1," and the clinician should record "mild [substance] use disorder" before the substance-induced depressive disorder (e.g., "mild cocaine use disorder with cocaine-induced depressive disorder"). If a moderate or severe substance use disorder is comorbid with the substance-induced depressive disorder, the 4th position character is "2," and clinician should record "moderate [substance] use disorder" or "severe [substance] use disorder," depending on the severity of the comorbid substance use disorder. If there is no comorbid substance use disorder (e.g., after a one-time heavy use of the substance), then the 4th position character is "9," and the clinician should record only the substance-induced depressive disorder.

	ICD-9-CM	With use, disorder, mild	ICD-10-CM With use disorder, moderate or severe	Without use disorder
Alcohol	291.89	F10.14	F10.24	F10-94
Phencyclidine	292.84	F16.14	F16.24	F16.94
Other hallucinogen	292.84	F16.14	F16.24	F16.94
Inhalant	292.84	F18.14	F18.24	F18.94
Opioid	292.84	F11.14	F11.24	F11.94
Sedative, hypnotic, or anxiolytic	292.84	F13.14	F13.24	F13.94
Amphetamine (or other stimulant)	292.84	F15.14	F15.24	F15.94
Cocaine	292.84	F14.14	F14.24	F14.94
Other (or unknown) substance	292.84	F19.14	F19.24	F19.94

Case Description

Leslie S. is a 38-year-old woman, married to James, a 40 –year-old service manager at a department store. When Leslie began therapy, she was about 30 pounds overweight. While she was attractive, her demeanor was not. Her facial expression was sad and pained, her eyes were lifeless, and the corners of her mouth turned down as if she were in constant anguish. There was a joyless expression in her eyes, and her hair was limp and oily.

Her presenting problem was indecisiveness about getting a divorce. Although she was unhappy in her marital situation, she was not sure that she would be able to take care of herself if she were to live alone. She cited as reasons for her unhappiness in her marriage infrequent and unfulfilling sexual intercourse, James' lack of ambition, too little money for their needs, and the fact that they had no children. She believed that she led a miserable existence because her husband did not want to make enough money to support the lifestyle she wanted.

In this case description, Leslie was diagnosed as having a primary depression. Her depression was primarily because it was a consequence of her inability to deal with herself and her external stress. She viewed the world in negative terms and, although she tended to focus on superficial external causes for her depression, such as her inadequate husband, she was merely blaming him for her negative internal state. If he were not there to bear the brunt of her negative internal view of self, she would have found some other person or reason for her unhappiness. In other words, the source of her view of self and the world was generated from within, probably due to a genetic predisposition and to unresolved early developmental problems, possibly resulting in biochemical dysfunction. Her unhappy marriage contributed further to those problems. If one had listened superficially to Leslie, however, one would have believed that correction of the marriage alone would change the depression, without Leslie's ever having to alter her self-view.

What Does Depression Look Like?

Depressed individuals *look* sad. Everything about them seems unhappy. They *speak slowly*, as though every word is a tremendous effort. Their bodies droop and lack tone. Their clothes seem to hang limply on their bodies. Their shoulders seem to sag, as though they carry the worries of the world on their shoulders. In Leslie's case, every facial feature seemed anguished and sad. Her shoulders, her mouth, every facial expression, and every action indicated sadness and loss of tone. She walked slowly, sighing frequently. To her, every aspect of her life seemed sad and listless.

What Does Depression Feel Like?

Depressed persons feel sad. They believe their lives are hopeless and futile. No one cares about them. No one can help them. They sometimes say that they would just like to be left alone to die. They have no energy reserves to draw upon. They often preface sentences with "I can't." Although seemingly preoccupied with themselves and events in their own lives, they actually do very little and often accomplish nothing all day long. Sometimes they are so depressed that they cannot energize themselves to get dressed in the morning or take care of their personal hygiene. Every activity seems insurmountable. Taking a shower drains all of their energy. Leslie would often report that she didn't get dressed all week because it would just have taken too much energy. Why bother? She had no place to go and no one to see. And, even if she did, no one would care anyway.

The Client's Dilemma

Leslie's affective state of well-being was solely dependent upon others' responses to her. If her husband was tired when he came home from work and fell asleep on the couch, Leslie would become depressed. She would think, "Poor me, I'm married to such a boring, useless person. Other women are married to romantic, interesting men." In this way, she devalued the very person on whom she wanted to depend and from whom she needed help. She discounted most, if not all, of his efforts. In doing so, she set up the expectation on his part that he could do nothing to satisfy her, that nothing he could do was right, and that he was generally a useless person.

Because there was a part of Philip that believed Leslie's definition of their situation, he often acted as she expected him to. In this manner, a mutually self-fulfilling prophecy was set up by Leslie with Philip, who cooperated to ensure the accuracy of her definition of both him and their situation. Feeling unable to achieve her goals and unable to get her husband to achieve these goals for her, Leslie felt useless and helpless. She experienced this as a blow to her view of herself as an achieving, accomplishing person. Thus, if Philip was not able to meet some of her needs, or if she had difficulty gratifying herself, he was perceived by her as similar to her emotionally depriving parent.

From James' point of view, he could never satisfy Leslie anyway, so after a while, he stopped trying. In doing so, he reinforced her negative perception and feelings. And so the dysfunctional cycle persisted, each reenacting the emotional psychodrama of childhood, redoing in adulthood an early childhood script that seemed fixed in its outcome.

According to Leslie, her husband did not earn enough money to buy her the house she desired. They would never be able to afford the material possessions that would make her feel happy and fulfilled. She believed that if she had a more dynamic husband who could give her more in terms of romantic attention and material possessions, she would then be happy and fulfilled.

For Leslie, life weighed her down. By comparison, her friends and acquaintances had life situation that were far happier than hers. She was not as charming, not as smart, did not have as fine a house, and was not as pretty as the women around her. Leslie believed she had many physical flaws. She was overweight, she thought her nose was too large, and she had a slight imperfection in her left eye which she was convinced spoiled her appearance because she believed everyone noticed it.

She felt incapacitated by people in her life. She had always wanted to go to college, but her mother never gave her the support she needed in order to complete her degree. She felt burdened and trapped by people around her who failed to fulfill her expectations. The self-fulfilling prophecy was realized. Philip failed to provide her with the lifestyle she felt she deserved. She saw no way out of her situation except to leave her marriage in the hope of finding another man who would fulfill her needs and wishes.

She saw Philip as the cause of her problems, blind to the part *she* played. For example, Philip did not want children. They had discussed (and supposedly settled) this issue before they married. Leslie had agreed to go through with the marriage anyway. She never hesitated to remind him, though, that it was his fault that she was deprived of children. She ignored the fact that she had agreed to remain childless. Leslie continually complained about the frequency and quality of their sex life. They managed to have sex once a year; after they did, she would bitterly deride him for his inadequacy as a lover and blame him for depriving her of an active sex life. Leslie's critical attacks made Philip hesitate to approach her again. They thus, colluded in maintaining a sexless, joyless marriage. The fact was that Philip had strong desires for sex, but he kept them from Leslie.

Theories and Explanations for Depression

Depression is related to many factors. To assume that it is uni-causal is an oversimplification. Thus, the theories presented in this section are not necessarily mutually exclusive. Psychoanalytic, social-learning, and biological theories of depression are briefly considered and are viewed as interacting causal factors contributing to what seems to constitute and uninterruptable chain of events.

Psychodynamic

Freud (1917) drew a parallel between bereavement and depression. He believed that the depressed individual was communicating a sense of grief similar to the feelings associated with bereavement. Depression, according to Freud, represents the unconscious and symbolic loss of a love relationship. Depressives feel just as unloved and bereft as they would if someone close to them had died or abandoned them. They experience feelings of dependence and vulnerability.

According to Freud, children ambivalently both love and hate their parents. This same unresolved ambivalence is present in depression. The individual feels abandoned and at the same time feels enormously angry and frustrated about the abandonment. Yet for some unconscious reason, depressives cannot express this hostility openly. They preserve their dependent attachment to the powerful parent and fear losing control over their own murderous rage. The rage is then directed inward and turned against the self. It becomes the source for their own terrible self-accusations. Since they have been unable to verbally acknowledge and attack the person who has disappointed them, they attack themselves.

It is believed that unresolved feelings of loss and deprivation lead to increased feelings of unconscious hostility and guilt, which, in turn, increase the dependency on the depriving or abandoning love object. The depriving object is primitively incapacitated and unconsciously fused to such an extent that the cruel and sadistic feelings of the love object become part of the ego and result in feelings of self-derogation and worthlessness.

Bibring (1953) pays less attention to object loss and its impact on the ego. For him, depression is a product of the ego state itself and its inability to self-gratify, which is not necessarily connected to the aggressive drive. Helplessness in obtaining what the person desires and finds valuable is the key issue. The ego is aware of certain goals and may also be unconsciously aware of the unattainability of these goals. It therefore suffers narcissistic injury and collapse of self-esteem. The individual cannot live up to such unconscious, unrealistic, and unattainable ideals, so conscious depression and self-blame occur.

Hostility is not the primary cause of depression, according to Bibring. He believes that feelings of inability to achieve desired goals are a more important factor. Depressed individuals, because they cannot obtain the valuable things they desire, often feel like small children, completely vulnerable and defenseless in a world they cannot control, and in an inner world on which they cannot depend for supplies of self-esteem.

Social Learning

Liberman and Raskin (1971) assert that people become, and remain, depressed because of the social rewards they obtain when they appear to be dejected. They elicit sympathy and concern from others. However, the well-meaning people surrounding the depressive only sustain the client's symptoms. Although focusing on the present interacting world of the adult person, this model somewhat resembles the previous analytic model, which also emphasizes the helplessness and depletion of the childish ego.

Lewinsohn and colleagues (1979) argue that people are depressed because of the reinforcement contingencies they experience, but these theorists focus instead of the *lack* of reinforcement in the client's environment. Many depressives may never have acquired the social skills they need to ensure themselves of a high possibility of positive reinforcement. This deprivation helps account for their depressive behaviors.

Seligman (1972) states that individuals become depressed when they are confronted by an uncontrollable and painful series of events that leads them to believe that they will continue to suffer regardless of what they do. Thus, he believes that depression occurs, not so much because of early loss and its traumatic early influence, but rather through the reinforcement of "learned helplessness." Depressed individuals are not assertive. They have not learned to cope. Learned helplessness is a way of life. Seligman argues that when we are children, we are indeed helpless; consequently, we feel overwhelmed. As adults, we return to those feelings. Depressives have a pervasive negative self-view. Life becomes overwhelming and traumatic due to their inability to change that negative self-view.

Beck (1972, 1976) focuses instead on the "faulty logic" and "selective abstractions" of depressives. They easily misinterpret events so that they fit into their negatively distorted belief pattern that they are worthless, unlovable, and incompetent. Their impressions are largely negative and selectively distorted. They define their future as bleak and grim. Beck's theory proposes negative thoughts are triggered by dysfunctional beliefs that cause depressive symptoms (Nemade, Staats-Reiss & Dombeck, n.d.). One model that Beck used to explain depression is the cognitive triad. The cognitive triad describes three negative views in which an individual thinks; the self, the world and the future (Possel & Black, 2014). Within an individual's thinking, according to this model, an individual's negative view of the self would in turn carry over to negative views of their world and eventually their future. The individual would have a constant cycle of having these negative feelings that would allow for the depressive symptoms to be maintained.

Another theory in looking at depression in individuals is the hopelessness theory of depression. Along the same lines as Beck's model, this too discusses how an individual has a negative view of the self and the world and that by having these hopeless negative thoughts/feelings, depression will eventually follow (Auerbach, Webb, Gardiner and Pechtel, 2013). For an individual who may be at risk or vulnerable to a depressive disorder diagnosis, it is said "the theory asserts that the interaction of the negative cognitive styles and stress leads to the development of hopelessness" (Auerbach et al, 2013). This suggests as well the significance that stress may place on an individual in any given circumstance. It is vital to look at all aspects of an individual's environment to look for what may be playing a role in these negative cognitions.

Biological

In order for the brain to function properly, neurotransmitters, must be released at certain rates. It is believed that if too much or too little of the chemical serotonin is [et al. 1977), Schildkraut 1977). Other theorists (Post et al. 1977, Sweeney et al 1979, Weiss et al. 1979) believe that the chemical involved is noradrenaline or norepinephrine.

Women are twice as likely as men to experience depression (see Weissman and Klerman 1977). These theorists report that the changes in hormone levels which occur in women as a result of the menstrual cycle is a possible cause of depression in at least some cases. However, to assume that depression is unicausal even on a biological level is an oversimplification. There are several precursors involved in depression, including genetic, developmental, physiological, and psychological factors. It would appear that the potentially reversible state of neurophysiological hyperarousal may be based on disordered biogenic amine or electrolyte disturbance, which coexists with environmental stressors that signal impending decompensation, hopelessness, and negative self-perception.

According to the National Institute of Mental Health, women are 70% more likely to experience depression in their lifetime. Comparing statistics to adults over the age of 60, people ranging from 18-29 years old are 70% more likely to experience depression during their lifetime, ages 30-44 are 120% more likely, and 45-59 year olds are 100% more likely to experience depression (2008).

According to Richard H. Hall (1998), there are two additional biological theories of depression. The first includes *Monoamine Hypothesis* and the second, *the autoreceptor subsensitivity theory*. Monoamine Hypothesis is the assumption that depression is caused by the result of an underactivity of monoamines, specifically 5-HT. Antidepression drugs have **reserpine**, a "monoamine agonists" which are now rarely used to treat high blood pressure due to the high side effects of depression. Statistics prove monoamine agonists such a reserpine induce depression. Another part of the theory includes evidence supporting that high levels of 5-HT are also correlated with depression. Statistics show that patients with low levels of 5-HT metabolite were more likely to commit suicide (Hall, 1998).

The second theory still relies on the concept of subsensitivity and neural compensation. The difference relates to the **autoreceptor subsensitivity theory**, which in one theory is seen as the post synaptic receptors that become sensitive; but in this theory, the 5-HT autoreceptors become subsensitive. The initial effect is for the monoamine agonists to stimulate the autoreceptors in a way that can prevent the increased levels of monoamines from releasing from the drugs. However, after two or three weeks, the autoreceptors become extremely subsensitive because of constant stimulation. This process stops the autoreceptors from sending their inhibitory signals, leading the client to have feelings of depression (Hall, 1998).

Cultural Theories

Ethnicity and culture are very important aspects of illness and health. The study of sociology of depression engulfs cultural contexts such as social stressors as well as the cultural contexts in which people live. Ethnomedicine, a new branch of medicine, focuses on perception, roles, and context of culture and how it shapes individuals lives. Ethnomedical research suggests that focusing on oneself with cultural differences and the social hierarchy of individuals is linked to the prevalence of depression. Often times, happiness is sacrificed for the stability of cultures and groups. There is not much thought given to individuals and their roles in society and their larger cultural communities (Nemade, Reiss, & Dombeck).

Our culture shapes our daily norms, obligations, and responsibilities. An example of this would be an individual that comes from a culture with demanding family obligations that are non-negotiable which can lead to feelings of restrictedness, feelings of being limited, and even powerless. Another example would be in an Asian culture where it is common for one person to work very hard and share a paycheck with their entire immediate family as well as extended family. As a result, lack of focus on oneself and constant pleasing of others can lead to an increase in depressive disorders. We can also take into thought a family where the cultural norms are for a woman to stay home and not work, while their spouse is out a majority of the day making money for their family. If there is a social stressor which forces a change to the norm of the household such as the death of the spouse, the stress can cause the person to become severely depressed (Nemade, Reiss, & Dombeck).

It is important to note that cultural identity influences the degree to which an individual may show somatic or physical symptoms of depression. To word it differently, some cultures are comfortable in reporting feelings and symptoms that are more physical in nature than mental. Some cultures may think depression is a normal response for people emotionally to specific life events. There are cultures where it is not socially accepted to express physical or emotional discomfort and depression would not be as widely accepted. Some cultures do not believe that depression exists at all. There are cultures that may find the depressive symptoms to be problematic. For example, an individual from China that came to the United States may reject the idea that a biochemical imbalance is causing them to have depressive symptoms to explain the low energy flows and sad thoughts because these are not concepts that are accepted in Chinese medicine (Nemade, Reiss, & Dombeck).

There are many cultures in the world that do not accept the term of "depressed" as it is seen as morally unacceptable, experientially meaningless, and shameful. Treatment for a person from a culture such as the one explained may not be successful due to the resistance of the client. A person's cultural background is a very influential part of a person's biological make up. Such differences can influence whether people are receptive to diagnoses and treatment when stressed and their backgrounds can also influence their response to medications (Nemade, Reiss, & Dombeck).

Looking at Depression Systemically From a Family Therapy Framework

More than half of individuals today with major depression report they have experienced problematic and distressing family functioning (Coyne et al., 2002). It is not a secret to state that families with individuals who have chronic forms of depression experience similar feelings of dysfunction as the individual with the diagnosis. The most frequently reported events brought up prior to the onset of depression are marital difficulties, focusing specifically on arguments in a household (Paykel et al., 1969). It has been noted that lack of support from a spouse or family member or inability to confide in family members or spouses can increase the risk for depression (Parry & Shapiro, 1986). However, because family functioning is directly related to relapsing or maintaining wellness; depression has been shown to last for shorter periods with families that are able and willing to improve their family or relational functioning (Keitner et al., 1997, 1995).

When families come to therapy there is often something therapists call an "identified patient." This person is a symptom bearer for all the complaints in the family as well as the dysfunction. Again, just because one family member may attend to this name of the "symptom bearer," the whole family is generally in distress. The interventions used for family therapy are aimed toward the family unit itself with the perspective that each symptom individually are products of relational struggles within the family unit. The symptoms arise from being complicated by the family system. A family therapist utilizes the connection that exists between the patient and family with the goal of assisting to improve the family functioning overall (Broderick & Weston, 2009).

Helping to Create the Connection with Families

An important principle to consider when meeting with families and/ or spouses of clients with depression is to meet with all family members that are available in the household. The therapist will be able to see the family dynamic and function as a whole in order to help the family function differently, the therapist will have the opportunity to see the family dynamic. It is important for the therapist to assist the family to be supportive and non-judgemental in the process. Many family members benefit from the group setting as well after being blamed for the reason behind their loved ones depression (Keitner, 2005).

Case History

Danielle is a 13 year old girl who first encountered mental health treatment after she was found in the bathroom of her middle school with ten cigarettes in her hand and threatening suicide. Danielle stated she was cutting herself every day and she just wanted to die. Danielle admitted to have feelings of depression for several months after her father left when her parents decided to get separated. She no longer wanted to attend school and her grades were declining significantly.

She admitted to having trouble fitting in because the kids that did not go to school were often into drugs and pills and Danielle was not into that. The students that did well in school did not want to associate with her because of her multiple attempts to act out in school by standing on chairs and leaving class without permission.

Danielle's family consisted of her mother, father, brother and sister. Her parents were going through a separation for the second time and had both contacted lawyers for a divorce settlement proceeding. Her mother reported she was abused by her father growing up and at one point her father tried to hit her while she was holding Danielle as an infant. Her mother had little contact with her father after that day. Danielle's mother reported symptoms of posttraumatic stress disorder (PTSD) from the abuse she suffered from her father growing up and as an adult. She also experienced constant fatigue and headaches that limited her involvement with her children. She felt her family of origin was unstructured and she had "too much freedom" which she felt contributed to her constantly getting in trouble and hit. She became involved with drugs and alcohol at a young age because no one was around to watch her. She felt Danielle had a similar temperament and feared that without more supervision she would end up like herself but in more dangerous situations.

Danielle had a distant relationship from her father. He was a police officer and highly valued order and discipline. He viewed psychiatric symptoms as a sign of weakness or as an excuse. This caused more fighting in the divorce proceedings with Danielle's mother and a strained relationship for her because she wasn't sure if she should listen to her mother and get help or listen to her father and stop being weak. Danielle became aggressive and made constant threats toward her father since the first time he left the home when her parents decided to separate

Although Danielle presented to therapy as the identified patient we can see there is a lot happening within the family dynamic that may be affecting her feelings of depression and suicide. The types of therapies that will be focused on are; psychodynamic family therapy, Structural family therapy, and cognitive behavioral therapy.

Psychodynamic Family Therapy

According to Broderick & Weston (2009), there are many schools of therapy that have had a positive outcome for people with depression. The psychodynamic approach to family therapy comes from the basis of psychoanalytic theory. This viewpoint is based on intrapsychic processes of each individual member of the family system. The processes of all members collectively, merge into something called the "family neurosis."

These intrapsychic processes take place in the unconscious and include projective identification, repression, transference, and some grief. "Psychic determinism refers to the idea that mental events do not occur at random and that every behavior has a cause or source embedded in the individual's history (Broderick & Weston, 2009, p. 34)." Transference is a process that occurs frequently within many relationships. This process occurs when an individual's thoughts or feelings are projected onto another person.

Psychodynamic family therapy will involve bringing the unconscious conflicts between family members into the conscious. This can be done using a technique such as interpretation. "Change is facilitated by 'working through' the unconscious transference distortions of each family member. Through this process, parents become aware of how conflicts in the present family system are related to their unconscious attempts to master old conflicts arising from their family of origin (Broderick & Weston, 2009, p. 34)"

Treatment Using Psychodynamic Family Therapy

When the therapist see's the family through the psychodynamic lens, the conflict between Danielle and her father was rooted in past relationships. Her father was extremely resistant to engaging in treatment because of his thoughts that psychiatric symptoms were a sign of weakness, however, with non-judgmental acceptance and time that was offered by the therapist, all members of the family attended therapy in a safe environment.

During therapy it was brought up that Danielle's father came from a household where there was harsh discipline and his father was an extremely masculine figure. Danielle had a lot of built up hatred toward her father because of his relentless attempts to keep her on "lock down" and for running such a strict, disciplined household. Danielle's father was able to look inside about his projection of his own fears and childhood memories that he appeared to be punishing his daughter for.

The mother's conflict with her daughter was also embedded in her past. Her identification with Danielle came from her projective identification with herself as an out of control child. She was trying to enforce rules and a strict, disciplined household due to her own unresolved conflict with her mother and father for not being successful in providing her with that household as an adolescent. Her mother's unconscious anger toward both her parents (her father for beating her and her mother for never defending her) was most likely being internalized into her somatic symptoms that included her constant fatigue and headaches. These symptoms also kept her mother out of direct confrontation with Danielle's husband and leaving the difficult decisions to him.

Danielle's symptoms of depression also had an unconscious purpose. Danielle spent a lot of her time growing up with her mother and her siblings. Danielle also perceived her parents relationship as a relationship that took attention away from her. She felt her mother spent more time caring about fixing the relationship with her father and that time was taken away from loving her. This created conflict in which Danielle began having feelings of aggression toward her father and this unresolved conflict in the home wanting attention from her mother manifested itself through her current symptoms.

The psychodynamic family therapist used the technique of interpretation to help increase the family's insight into how each individual's past was affecting their current relationships. The therapist assisted in expanding the family's repertoire of emotional expression which would help the family solve its present conflicts without bringing the past into play (Broderick & Weston, 2009).

Structural Family Therapy

"The structural family therapist views symptoms that occur in a particular family member, often the identified patient, to be directly linked to the organizational context of the family (Broderick & Weston, 2009, p. 35)." A family unit that dictates and participates in how other family members relate along with how family functions are carried out is known as *family structure*. This structure is often invisible to the members of the family and it is the therapist's goal to decipher the structure as well as facilitate transformation by means of problem solving.

Structural family therapy includes important elements such as alliances, hierarchies, coalitions, and boundaries. The formation and use of boundaries in a system is vitally important for the family to function and the family will have ranges from enmeshed to disengaged. If a family member is disengaged with someone, it means they have little to no contact with that person. If a person is enmeshed, the relationship is too close with too much contact with one another. The boundary formation is extremely important in 'subsystems' within each family. For a family to function appropriately and effectively, children should have contact with their parents but not interfere with one another (Broderick & Weston, 2009).

The first task of a structural family therapist is to determine the family structure. The therapist will carefully observe how each family member interacts with one another inside the therapy room. This therapy involves shifting the family structure and how this occurs is through enactment or the re-creation of family dialogues in addition to manipulating seating arrangements. The therapist will direct a family member to speak directly to the person they are speaking about instead of telling the therapist how they are feeling. This forces the families to enact their transitional patterns instead of describing them. The other technique that includes changing seating arrangements, helps to challenge the existing family structures that include their hierarchies and alliances. While out of session, the therapist gives assignments that will aim to either strengthen or weaken family boundaries that already exist. These assignments will aide in changing the existing boundaries into more appropriate ones (Broderick & Weston, 2009.

Treatment Using Structural Family Therapy

Through careful observation of a structural family therapist, the therapist would uncover the dysfunctional structure of the family and help to transform it into a more functional one. The boundaries in this family are clear examples of both enmeshment and disengagement. Danielle and her mother were enmeshed while Danielle and her father were clearly disengaged. Danielle's mother was also enmeshed with Danielle's other siblings.

The hierarchy of the family was skewed as well with the father at the top and a large gap between him and Danielle's mother. This position placed the mother closer to the children. Danielle also had an alliance with her mother against her father, although Danielle was not able to see her enmeshment with her mother.

To shift this structure, the therapist recreated a dialogue with Danielle and her father about one time when he caught Danielle smoking in her room at home. The therapist ensured each individual spoke more to each other than to her directly.

SFT (Structural Family Therapist): **Danielle, can you tell me what you remember about that time you were caught smoking in your room?**

Danielle: **I was in my room one day and I thought both my parents were out and next thing I knew but Dad burst open the door and started screaming at me. I was so afraid and thought he was going to hit me!**

SFT: **Danielle, can you look at your father and tell him the event again?**

Danielle: **I guess…. Dad, I felt really scared when you came into my room and were screaming. I know I was wrong but….**

Father: **(looking at the therapist) I really did not intend to scare her.**

SFT: **Dad, are you able to tell Danielle that?**

Dad: **Dani, I didn't mean to scare you. I just know deep down you are a really good kid and it really hurts me to see you making bad decisions.**

At this point, the seating arrangements were structured in accordance with the desired changes in the alliances and hierarchies of the family. The therapist had placed the mother and father sitting next to one another with equal footing between their three children. To resolve the boundary problems in the family, behavioral assignments were assigned to bring Dad and Danielle closer together which in turn would create more space between Danielle and her mother. The therapist assigned for Danielle and Dad to

take a hobby together one time per week while Mom was assigned to find an interest or an activity outside the home, allowing time for the siblings to have some time together and space of their own (Broderick & Weston, 2009).

Cognitive Behavioral Family Therapy

Although Cognitive Behavioral Therapy (CBT) is not seen to be a systemic therapy, many of the basic principles can be applied to each individual during a family therapy session. This form of therapy relies heavily on psychoeducation. Opposite to psychodynamic therapy (which emphasizes intrapsychic forces) CBT emphasizes external social forces and their importance. The basic principle is that all behavior is learning-based and with use of behavior modification, all behavior can be "unlearned." The therapist in CBT plays the role as the coach or teacher and assists with change by using positive and negative reinforcements after understanding how each family member influences one another (Broderick & Weston, 2009).

Techniques that are used with CBT therapy include thought diaries, psychoeducation, communication training, operant conditioning strategies, and contingency contracting. Thought diaries assist the client to write down and track thought patterns with a goal of, "uncovering and then correcting common cognitive distortions like catastrophic thinking or overgeneralization" (Broderick & Weston, 2009, p. 37). Contingency contracts assist family members with replacing destructive patterns in relation to the presenting problem. This behavioral plan is a contract between the client and the therapist. Operant conditioning attempts to use positive and negative reinforcements in order to shape behavior. Time out procedures may be employed with younger family members. The therapist also works as a coach to help employ communication techniques such as how to show empathy, how to listen, and how convey negative emotions in a more respectful way. Psychoeducation is also a large part of CBT and is tailored to the needs of each client (Broderick & Weston, 2009).

Treatment Using Cognitive Behavioral Therapy

Using one of the most fundamental techniques, operant conditioning, and behavior can be shaped in a positive way. Positive reinforcements such as playing a video game, getting a piece of candy, or gaining an allowance are three good rewards to use for Danielle. This reward would be earned if she improves her grades in school. Negative reinforcements can also be employed such as not increasing the allowance amount each week if Danielle is caught smoking. Operant conditioning was also used for Danielle's brother and sister who also often complained about somatic symptoms such as stomach aches. If either brother or sister wanted to stay home from school, their father would stay home with them which would not be the reward the children wanted which was to spend more time with their mother. Each child received a pizza party, prize, or a movie out if they did not miss any school for one month.

Communication skills were employed for all family members. The therapist coached Mom and Dad with listening skills and sharing their ideas and thoughts in a respectful safe place and manner. Mom and Dad, after the 5th session in therapy, decided to work on their relationship instead of proceeding with divorce. Psychoeducation was employed with assisting Danielle's father to see that psychiatric symptoms, such as depression, was not a sign of weakness. The therapist was also able to assist Danielle's father with some anger management skills and training (Broderick & Weston, 2009).

Seeing a family system as opposed to treating an individual alone helps the focus of therapy to be shifted away from the "identified patient" and for the symptom to be spread around the family. Although there are many forms of Family Therapy that exist, each family will need to work with a therapist that matches their needs and the therapist's style (Broderick & Weston, 2009).

Therapy Techniques

It is important to remember that these techniques are not mutually exclusive. They should be thought of as interacting techniques, geared toward creating change and alternatives for the person in order to replace previously existing, interlocking dysfunctional behaviors and attitudes. In looking at the following practice techniques, the initial case description about Leslie will be the main focus.

1. In treating depressed persons, it is important to help them begin to clarify the boundaries between themselves and the people they need.

Leslie, for example, was unable to understand that her husband's needs were different from hers. She was at the time appalled by the fact that he had his own thoughts. She failed to see that he was a separate person. When he did act independently of her, she considered him wrong, bad, or unreasonable and tried to convince him of the error in his ways. She set up rules of conduct for him, and if he deviated, she punished him by withdrawing her affection and pouting. She wanted him to desire the same things she wanted.

With therapeutic intervention, Leslie was able to recognize that other people have rights and needs of their own and that Philip had a separate existence that was not necessarily a reflection of hers. In other words, Leslie learned that people are not machines that automatically see and satisfy her needs. She thus began to develop a self-separated from her husband. She was no longer symbiotically tied to him out of ambivalent caring, nor was she solely dependent on his nurturance and positive responses. She could plan, think, and wish on her own. She was no longer tied to controlling him or punishing him should he not respond as she wished. She also did not feel compelled to set up a prearranged dependent hostile relationship as the only outcome of their marriage.

2. Help depressed persons to see their active part in their own gratification.

At one point during her therapy, Leslie decided that she could not live another day without having the bathroom redecorated. This, according to Leslie, was James' responsibility because it was the type of thing that "men were supposed to do." According to her, he was responsible for financing the plan and for doing the actual work. Leslie's part in this project was to choose colors, curtains, and wallpaper. Philip wanted to delay beginning the project until there was a slow period at work so he could give it more time. He also wanted to wait until he had more money.

While Philip was willing to redecorate the bathroom, he felt some resentment because he was compelled to live up to Leslie's role expectations and to be responsible for the major part of the project. Although Leslie was earning money at the time, she could not accept responsibility for any household financial matters. She thereby avoided taking responsibility for meeting her own needs. When this was brought to her attention, she complained that she *did* assert herself with Philip (which she defined as evidence of her psychological growth). It never occurred to her that *she* did not have to depend on Philip to begin a project, or that she could fulfill some of her own needs. A part of the therapeutic intervention was important to help Leslie see that she had a part in her own destiny and that she could in fact positively affect her environment. The therapist helped her understand that some of her anger and unresolved ambivalence was a need to see herself as a victim of James' deprivation rather than of her own self-deprivation and guilt. In this negative way, she had believed that she was controlling her own life. This only led to feelings of helplessness and self-deprivation.

3. Help depressed persons to see that there are alternatives to their negative view of self and the world.

Leslie focused on the negative side of most situations. She was unable to see the positive aspects of her house or positive traits in her husband and generally considered most people in her world to be lacking in some way. The therapy often focused on teaching her to see that there were alternatives to her negative self-definitions. If Leslie verbalized that Philip was totally useless, the therapist would ask, "*Totally*, Leslie?" Leslie then started to consider some of James' positive traits. The therapist then asked her to consider some of James' positive traits. The therapist then asked her to elaborate on some of James' more positive aspects. In other words, she was encouraged to generate some positive attributes of her husband and not to see him or other aspects of her world in dreary, dismal terms.

Leslie also saw *herself* in negative and unfulfilling ways. She felt that she excelled at nothing and would never be able to be a professional person, a goal that was very important to her. Because of this self-definition, she felt guilty and became increasingly dependent on Philip to fulfill her every self-desire. In therapy, Leslie learned that she did in fact have office skills, which were then utilized to help her find a job. She learned also that she had academic skills, which she later used to acquire a bachelor's degree. Her new definitions of her situations were thus broadened to include alternatives to her negative and distorted view of self and the world. In so doing, Leslie was able to bring some personal and social rewards and satisfactions into her life, which in turn helped her to recast her depression and hopelessness. She discovered that she was in charge of those rewards and gratifications and that she could even initiate some ideas and rewards of her own.

4. Help depressed persons to partialize their needs and wishes.

When Leslie began therapy, she was overwhelmed with depression. *Everything* in her life felt hopeless. She defined herself and her life situation in persistent, global terms. *Nothing* in her life was going right. There was *no* part of her that was at all useful. She was *completely* stupid and *totally* unhappy. Her husband was a *complete* jerk- unable to be successful in even the most minor endeavor. As long as she continued to see the world in these bleak, global terms, Leslie would, of course, remain depressed.

In therapy, Leslie learned to partialize her problems. Was she *completely* stupid? Or were there times when she was minimally intelligent? Was Philip *always* boring? Or were there times when she felt that he was somewhat interesting? Was there *never* a time when she felt happy? Or did she sometimes enjoy being alive? Leslie would actually answer affirmatively to a few of the second questions in each pair. The therapist would then ask her to elaborate on the tiny bit of positive potential in her life. Leslie was then taught to *create* positive situations on her own. In therapy, Leslie learned to enhance, always in small increments, any positive moments in her life; she thereby decreased her overwhelming feeling of depression and her internalized negative view of herself and the world.

When to Refer

When evaluating the depressed client's progress, it is important to ask the following questions:

1. Has the treatment progressed?
2. Has the client reached some of his/her self-defined goals?
3. Does the client feel better?
4. Does the client feel as though s/he has achieved more control over the environment, and has s/he taken on some of the responsibility for his/her own well-being?
5. Does the client have control over internal reinforcers and satisfactions? Is s/he able to provide some positive experiences for himself/herself?
6. Is the client sabotaging treatment in any way? For example, is s/he blaming the therapist for lack of progress in treatment or for ongoing unhappiness?
7. Is the client becoming increasingly depressed? Does s/he have suicidal thoughts?

If after answering these questions, you decide that client either is not progressing or sinking into a more serious depression, it would be wise to refer the client for further psychiatric evaluation, hospitalization, medication, or any appropriate combination. If you feel the client is expressing suicidal ideation, it is crucial that s/he be referred for psychiatric evaluation. At this time also involuntary hospitalization should be considered.

References

Auerbach, R. P., Webb, C. A., Gardiner, C. K., & Pechtal, P. (2013). Behavioral and neural mechanisms underlying cognitive vulnerability models of depression. *Journal of Psychotherapy Integration*, *23*(3), 222-235.

Broderick, P., & Weston, C. (2009). *Family therapy with a depressed adolescent*. Retrieved from (Broderick & Weston, 2009).

Coyne JC, Thompson R, Palmer SC (2002), Marital quality, coping with conflict, marital complaints, and affection in couples with a depressed wife. J Fam Psychol 16(1):26-37.

Hall, R. H. (1998). *Theories of depression.* Retrieved from http://web. mst.edu/~rhall/neuroscience/07 disorders/depression theory.pdf

Keitner, G. (2005). Family therapy in the treatment of depression. *Depression, Major Depressive Disorder, Addiction, 22*(11).

Keitner GI, Ryan CE, Miller IW et al. (1995), Role of the family in recovery and major depression. Am J Psychiatry *152*(7):1002-1008.

Keitner GI, Ryan CE, Miller IW, Zlotnick C (1997), Psychosocial factors and the long-term course of major depression. J Affect Disord *44*(1):57-67.

Magidson, J. F., Wang, S., Lejuez, C. W., Iza, M., & Blanco, C. (2013). Prospective study of substance-induced and independent major depressive disorder among individuals with substance use disorders in a nationally representative sample. *Depression and Anxiety, 30,* 538-545.

Major depressive disorder among adults. (2008). Retrieved from http://www.nimh.nih.gov/statistics/1mdd adult.shtml

Michael, K. (2012, 03 9). *Endogenous depression.* Retrieved from http://www.healthline.com/health/depression/endogenous-depression

Nemade, R., Staats-Reiss, N., & Dombeck, M. (n.d.).*Cognitive theories of major depression: Aaron beck.* Retrieved from http://info.epmhmr.org/poc/view_doc.php?type=doc&id=13006&cn=5

Nemade, R., Reiss, N., & Dombeck, M. (n.d.). *Sociology of depression-effects of culture.*

Retrieved from http://info.emergencehealthnetwork.org/poc/view_doc.php?type=doc&id=13009&cn=5 Paykel ES, Myers JK, Dienelt MN et al. (1969), Life events and depression. A controlled study. *Arch Gen Psychiatry 21*(6):753-760.

Possel, P., & Black, S. W. (2014). Testing three different sequential meditational interpretations of Beck's cognitive model of the development of depression. *Journal of Clinical Psychology, 70*(1), 72-94.

What is depression? (2013). Retrieved from http://www.nami.org/Template.cfm?Section=depression

Chapter 6

Obsessive Compulsive Disorder

Alexandra Laudisio. M.A., MFT

What is Obsessive Compulsive Disorder and How Do You Recognize It?

An *obsession* is persistent, recurring preoccupation with an idea or thought. A *compulsion* is an impulse that is experienced as irresistible. Obsessive-compulsive individuals feel compelled to think thoughts that they say they do not want to think or to carry out actions that they say are against their will. These individuals usually realize that their behavior is irrational, but they cannot control it. In the case that will be presented in this chapter, the client's obsession was the fear that she was going to poison her children. The compulsion was the urge to ritualistically wash her hands in order to prevent this from happening.

Most people resort to minor obsessive-compulsive patterns under severe pressure or when trying to achieve goals that they consider critically important. An example is the student who feels that she cannot pass an exam unless she brings her lucky charm with her. People with compulsive disorders however, feel *compelled* to perform some act that seems absurd to them and that they say they do not want to perform. Such compulsive acts vary from relatively mild ritual-like behavior, such as skipping over every third crack in the sidewalk, to more extreme forms of behavior, like washing one's hands fifty times a day. They can involve actual physical acts or can be essentially cognitive in nature, involving feelings and thoughts. The performance of the compulsive act usually results in reduced anxiety and a feeling of relief. If the person tries to avoid the compulsion, however, tension, anxiety, guilt, and fear usually increase.

An individual who has an obsession or compulsion can be almost as impaired as an agoraphobic; in this case, however, the anxiety is not quite as overt. People who suffer from obsessions and compulsions find their lives extensively governed by strange ideas or rituals. The obsession may take the form of an alarming, disruptive thought that creeps into the client's mind, seemingly of its own accord and not of the person's own volition. Client's claim that they cannot account for the idea and that even though is seems crazy or alien, it continually recurs. A typical example of such a thought is the belief that some harm may befall the client or a relative. An obsessive-compulsive disorder is considered maladaptive both because it is characterized by irrational, exaggerated behavior in the face of stressors that are not upsetting to most people and because such behavior reduces the client's flexibility and capacity for self-direction.

Compulsions complicate obsessions. Here, a persistent fantasy is accompanied by an irrational but irresistible need to perform the same act over and over again. Part of the phenomenon is *obsessive doubting*, which involves the person's inability to tolerate uncertainty about himself and his life situation. While the phobic individual feels compelled to *avoid* certain ideas and activities, the obsessive-compulsive person *must* entertain a particular idea or perform a particular activity. But the underlying concern in both cases is quite similar. People with both types of disorders fear losing control over their own behavior and being humiliated or experiencing inadequacy or helplessness. As Salzman (1968) aptly pointed out, phobias often develop when persons utilizing an obsessive-compulsive defense system face a situation (often set up to be avoidable) in which they can no longer maintain control. Obsessive compulsive disorder causes sufferers to fixate on one anxiety-ridden thought which later develops into a phobia or fear of the thought (Fritscher, 2009).

Neurotic obsessive thoughts center around a wide variety of topics, such as bodily function's committing suicide, immoral acts, or even finding the solution to some seemingly unsolvable world problem. Particularly common are obsessive thoughts about committing some immoral or humiliating act- shouting out obscene remarks in a crowded church, for example. Even though obsessive thoughts are not generally acted upon, they can remain a source of torment. Examples of thoughts or actions designed to counteract these forbidden, distressing thoughts include almost any kind of thought ritual, such as counting to oneself or memorizing license plate numbers; cleanliness rituals; excessive orderliness or neatness; and inordinate attempts to conform one's activities to a precise timetable.

Most people engage in some compulsive behaviors (stepping over cracks in sidewalks, not walking under ladders, throwing salt over their shoulders if they break a mirror), but they are generally not compelled to the extent that the neurotic obsessive-compulsive person is. Most of us have experienced minor obsessional thoughts, an upcoming trip, or a favorite old song that we cannot seem to get out of our minds. In the case of obsessive-compulsive reactions, however, the thoughts are more persistent, tend to appear irrational, even to the individuals involved, and tend to interfere considerably with everyday life.

The precise incidence of obsessive-compulsive reactions is difficult to determine. Scattered anecdotal evidence suggests that this disorder has occurred throughout history. Obsessive-compulsive individuals are often secretive about their neurotic behavior and are frequently able to work effectively in spite of it. Consequently, the problem is probably underestimated. A relatively high proportion of obsessive-compulsive people remain unmarried; some surveys report that up to 50 percent are married. Obsessive-compulsive reactions are more commonly found among upper-income, highly intelligent groups (Nemiah 1967). The incidence of obsessive-compulsive disorder has been estimated to comprise 12 to 20 percent of the anxiety disorders. Age and sex have not been systematically studied. According to NAMI (National Alliance on Mental Illness), this disorder is two to three times more common than bipolar and schizophrenia disorder. This disorder will strike all walks of life including people of all ethnic and social backgrounds. Symptoms often begin during childhood, teenage years, or young adulthood (Duckworth & Freedman, 2012).

Obsession Compulsive Symptoms

Obsessions are recurrent and persistent thoughts, urges, or images that are experienced, at some time during the disturbance, as intrusive and unwanted, and that in most individuals cause marked anxiety or distress. The individual attempts to ignore or suppress such thoughts, urges, or images to neutralize them with some other thought or action (i.e., by performing a compulsion).

Compulsions are repetitive behaviors (e.g., hand washing, ordering, checking) or mental acts (e.g., praying, counting, repeating words silently) that the individual feels driven to perform in response to an obsession or according to rules that must be applied rigidly.

The behaviors or mental acts are aimed at preventing or reducing anxiety or distress, or preventing some dreaded event or situation; however, these behaviors or mental acts are not connected in a realistic way with what they are designed to neutralize or prevent, or are clearly excessive. The obsessions or compulsions are time-consuming (e.g., taking more than 1 hour per day) or cause clinically significant distress or impairment in social, occupational, or other important areas of functioning. The obsessive-compulsive symptoms are not attributable to the physiological effects of a substance (e.g., a drug of abuse, a medication) or another medical condition. The obsessions or compulsions are a significant source of distress to the individual or interfere with social or role functioning. They are not due to another mental or neurological disorder, such as Tourette's disorder, schizophrenia, major depression, or organic mental disorder.

Case Description

Gail R. is a 29-year-old woman married to Tom, a 34-year-old certified public accountant. This is her second marriage. She was first married when she was 18 to Craig, a repairman for the telephone company. This marriage lasted three years, after which they divorced. Craig, by Gail's definition and description, was an alcoholic. He would go out with his friends after work and drink until about 11:00PM. He was often abusive and loud when he returned home. Gail reported that she had tried on many occasions to leave him but "just couldn't". Whenever she would tell him that she wanted a separation, he would beg her to stay, promising he would change. One night he knocked her against a wall, and she decided to leave him "once and for all."

Two years later she married Tom. She had become pregnant while they were dating and she had an abortion. She became pregnant again about a year later, but this time they decided to get married. Tom's parents were very upset about her pregMichelle and the fact that she was "forcing" their son to marry her. She gave birth to a boy and three years later, to a girl. When she entered therapy, the children's ages were 4 and 1. Between the births of her two children, she had a miscarriage.

Her presenting problem was that she was extremely fearful that she was going to poison her family, especially one of the children. She feared that poisonous chemicals would get on her hands and that she would then unwittingly contaminate her family's food. In order to prevent this from occurring, she felt that she had to wash her hand at least twice an hour.

Gail related a history of events in support of her obsessive fear. She stated that the week before her miscarriage, her cesspool had backed up into the house, and chemicals had to be poured into it to clear it out. She believed that she had somehow ingested these chemicals, causing her to have a miscarriage.

Later there was another episode, this time involving Gail's daughter. Dishwashing liquid had accidentally contaminated their drinking water and the daughter had begun choking on it. Tom corroborated this. Gail thought that she might have had the chemical on her hands and somehow poisoned her daughter. At her mother-in-law's hysterical insistence, she called a poison control center and asked if it was possible for her to have poisoned her child. They, unfortunately, said yes, which only served to reinforce her worst fears.

Prior to this episode, her son drank some of her perfume, necessitating a trip to the hospital, where his stomach was pumped. These events served as "proof" for Gail's' belief that she could very easily poison her children. Confirmed for her was the underlying thought that she was a dreadful, dangerous person who had magical powers and could eliminate others just by thinking about it.

What Does Obsessive Compulsive Behavior Look Like?

In general, the person who suffers from obsessive-compulsive disorder feels insecure and inadequate, and has a rigidly developed conscience. There is a tendency toward feelings of guilt and remorse and a high vulnerability to feelings of fallibility. Gail was brought up in a strict Catholic home where thinking about an evil deed was just as morally wrong as doing the deed. Her early background and development did not help her discriminate between the trivial, inconsequential thought and the horrendous deed. Religion had been very important in her life during her childhood. Because of her strict religious upbringing, whenever she felt stressed, she would pray to God or other omnipotent beings to relieve her of her evil thoughts so that she could again be the perfect child. She thought that this would please her frustrating, unpleasable parents.

Unlike most obsessive-compulsive individuals, Gail was much disorganized with her daily activities, often complaining that she accomplished nothing all day. She had trouble getting out of the house, and at times, when her husband returned from work, he would find her in her nightgown playing with the children. He would become angry and helplessly frustrated, shouting that she seemed unable to adequately run the household. She seemed unable to provide them with a predictable, stable life. Procrastinating for most of the day, she often would not find the time to go food shopping, complaining that the children took up too much of her time. If she was scheduled to meet her husband, she would invariably be late. In fact, she was chronically late for every appointment she made, including her therapy sessions.

Gail's presentation was usually pleasant and affable. Although she was quite upset during the first session, she was later able to compose herself and articulately present her problems. She was an attractive woman, neatly dressed. She did not appear to be excessively anxious, and it was in this manner that she approached the remainder of the sessions.

What Does Obsessive Compulsive Behavior Feel Like?

Obsessive individuals are preoccupied with ruminations, doubts, and thoughts that maintain for them a low level of well-being (Sullivan 1956). Gail felt that she had to monitor whatever she touched to make sure that she did not come in contact with anything poisonous. Obsessive-compulsive individuals feel as though they are driven by forces they can sometimes (but not always) name but cannot change or ignore. They also find themselves pushing to attain goals that never seem satisfying once they have been achieved. To be mediocre, to make an error or make mistakes are human foibles to be avoided. To avoid being wrong or mistaken, one must never take a firm stand or advocate only one side of an issue. They cannot allow themselves unbridled participation in life or its projects, other than as a disinterested spectator or uncommitted bystander. Obsessive individuals cannot relax, enjoy, or savor life; instead, they struggle and worry. Gail constantly worried about poisoning her children. She could not enjoy being their mother.

At times, obsessive people are able to recognize the absurdity of their actions. They are sometimes even able to laugh about their preoccupations. There were times, when Gail would laugh at her behavior. Unfortunately though, after a while, obsessive people generally begin to worry again, this time worrying about why they cannot stop worrying. These individuals are constantly evaluating themselves, examining whether they are "doing it right." The obsessive person sets up firm expectations of specific reactions and responses from significant others. The obsessive individual may relate more to the expected response than to the person from whom the response is expected. This expected agenda now provides a vehicle for social interaction. The obsessive individual is too preoccupied with his/her own agenda that he/she often misses the chance for social intimacy and close communication. Anger, hostility, and unfriendliness are more easily recognized and acknowledged because they encourage distance.

The obsessive person often becomes completely preoccupied with details and documentation of experiences with the uncaring and uncommunicative world. This often makes genuine communication and focused clear thinking quite difficult. For this reason, obsessive individuals often have problems with interpersonal relationships.

Despite the rigid defenses attributed to them, obsessive neurotics often feel very anxious. Beginning in early childhood, Gail had a difficult time coping with the problems of everyday life. She mentioned one experience that typified her parents' overprotection and misguided concern for her.

As a child, Gail had had a very close relationship with her paternal grandfather. They lived in the same house, and he would often take Gail to the park and play with her. She remembered these as the only moments of genuine tenderness and concern she had ever experienced. When her grandfather died, her parents did not inform her of his death for many months. She could not imagine what had happened to him, and she later doubted whether he really cared about her. Many years later, as an adult, she still becomes anxious and tearful whenever she thinks about that time in her life, doubting whether she will ever again experience caring and happiness. It is not surprising that the two men Gail later married were also initially overprotective of her and enabled her to avoid coping with everyday reality.

The degree of anxiety manifested in obsessive individuals depends on how successfully they use their defensive systems to maintain feelings of self-worth and effective operation of their ego systems. Doubt and rumination beset obsessive-compulsives because of continuous uncertainty and concern about what they have or have not done, or about the efficacy of their ritualistic behavior. In psychoanalytic terms, their id-ego boundaries are too permeable and their ego-outer world boundaries are too rigid. Insight-oriented psychotherapy is often directed at realigning those boundaries. Investigation of the origin and history of their anxiety and self-doubts may prove fruitless if the day-to-day doubts, ruminations, and overwhelming lack of self-worth is not understood and dealt with in terms of their present day functioning. As is true of most forms of maladaptive behavior, the longer the history of obsessions and compulsions, the more resistant they are to modification. The behaviors of roughly three-quarters of hospitalized obsessive-compulsives remain unchanged ten to twenty years after admission (Kringlen 1968).

The Client's Dilemma

Significantly, a large proportion of obsessive-compulsive individuals are found to have been unusually preoccupied with issues of control long before their symptoms appeared. These individuals often have a history suggesting marked discomfort in any situation in which they did not have a large measure of control. Obsessive-compulsive individuals need to be in control of all phases of their lives and are typically driven by anxiety about being controlled by other people or events that undermine their security. If the obsessive person's ritualistically ordered existence fails to protect him/her from exploitation by another, he/she might have to submit to the fearful impulse.

This kind of anxiety is typified by Gail's behavior when she first started having sex. Because she felt that her sexual wishes were dirty and contaminating, she would take three or more showers a day in order to cleanse herself. She felt that she was doing something bad by giving in to her sexual desires, and that God would punish her. Each time Gail would wash herself, there would be a temporary feeling of relief, but this short term feeling of satisfaction would not last long (obsessive-compulsive disorder, 2013). This became her preoccupation. Interestingly, when Gail was a child, her father had threatened to wash her with a scrub brush if she did not take a bath. Thus, the importance of cleanliness was coupled with the childish sexual wish for her father's loving care and concern.

The compulsion represents the once feared parental command to "go and wash yourself," now internalized as a superego command to prevent dirty thoughts or wishes. It could also have represented a threat to Gail that unless she washed (or omitted a certain act), she might lose parental care and concern (Fenichel 1945).

The extraordinary concern with self-imposed regularity and control in the pre-obsessive-compulsive individual can take the form of exaggerated perfectionism or concern that one's actions might lead to terrible consequences. Two other characteristics common in obsessive-compulsive disorders are indecisiveness and highly controlled emotions. Indecisiveness results from strong conflicting tendencies. Some individuals become almost incapacitated by endless compulsive rituals and immobilize their will and actions with obsessive indecision and doubt. The excessive inhibition of emotion is reflected in the cold, detached, and unemotional fashion in which persons experience their obsessive ideas and compulsive acts. It is also reflected in the lack of spontaneity associated with rigid patterns of orderliness and timetable living, and in highly formalized interpersonal relationships.

Theories and Explanations for Obsessive Compulsive Behavior

Psychological theories tend to focus on conditions that would produce the observed conflicts. Since the obsessions and the counteracting responses almost always involve the expression of unacceptable aggressive or sexual impulses, it is natural to look for environmental learning experiences that promote strong conflicts in this area.

Psychoanalytic

The Freudian contention is that three defense mechanisms are especially significant in the development of obsessive-compulsive neurosis: isolation, undoing, and reaction formation. The contention is that *isolation* separates the affect from a thought or act, which then becomes obsessive or compulsive in nature. The affect is usually experienced as an impulse not completely barred from consciousness and constantly threatening to break through the ego controls and defenses that have been imposed on it.

Obsessive people use the defense mechanism of isolation to separate feelings from intellectual content so that their obsessive thoughts become detached from their emotional roots; an over-intellectualized pattern of life is the result. In their desire to be overly cautious or protective of their loved ones, they often rob them of their affectionate loving care.

Undoing refers to many features of compulsive rituals in which the person attempts to undo the harm (real or imagined), that could result from the unacceptable impulse. Engaging in a certain ritualistic behavior "cancels out" the dangerous impulse. Undoing is illustrated by the individual who, whenever he turns off a light thinks, "My father will die," which is the unconscious wish. This thought compels him to turn around, touch the switch, turn on the light, and say, "I take back that thought." The compulsive act thus undoes that which he feared would result from the initial thought. The initial thought might have had its roots in an unresolved underlying aggressive or death-wish impulse toward the father.

Reaction formations are also quite common. Obsessive concern with cleanliness may be a defense against sexual wishes or underlying urges to be dirty. Compulsive orderliness may protect the person from the fear of unleashed aggression, from the wish to smash everything in sight. Excessive politeness and formality may protect the person from urges to be cruel and sadistic. Reaction formation is illustrated by the mother who is overly solicitous of her children because of her underlying aggressive feelings toward them. Thus, she compulsively checks their room dozens of times a night to make sure they are safe. She thereby undertakes an attitude contradictory to the original thoughts.

Reaction formations are often used with undoing defenses, except that they are expressed in broad personality styles rather than in highly specific rituals. To protect their loved ones from hostile wishes, compulsive neurotics so rigorously and devoutly guard them from danger that they often torment them with their doubts. They will then inadvertently express the unconscious hostility despite their need to prevent it.

From a developmental point of view, the obsessive person has regressed, in the face of an intense oedipal conflict, to the anal stage. Compulsive concerns with cleanliness and orderliness represent reaction formations against anal impulses to be dirty and messy. Compulsive tendencies to inhibit emotion or to be formal or excessively good, on the other hand, reflect reaction formations against anal-sadistic impulses, originating in the child's defiance of parental efforts to force compliance with toilet training.

It is interesting to note that at one point during Gail's therapy, the therapist requested that she question her mother about her toilet training. Gail's mother informed her that she was trained when she was 1 year old because her mother was pregnant with her second child and wanted Gail trained before the baby was born. Her wish for Gail's mastery and control was based on her own needs, not the child's developmental readiness. Unfortunately, her mother had a miscarriage. Her mother was 27 years old at the time, exactly the same age as Gail was when she had her miscarriage, leading the therapist to wonder whether Gail felt incapable of caring for the child, just as she had felt that her mother was incapable of loving and caring for her. In this way she may have unconsciously contributed to aborting her own child.

Interpersonal

In Sullivan's interpersonal and social view, the obsessive social self-system is a crude but stable attempt to deal with the interpersonal world, which never really achieves for them a true sense of a well-defined, competent self. Neither do they have a clear sense of how poorly they have interacted with others. This helps them to avoid a great deal of anxiety and self-doubt. Their internal, unconscious self-representation reflects a great need for grandiosity and perfection to exclude or minimize any feelings of inferiority or badness.

In spite of their arrogance and grandiose contempt for others, they feel inferior to others. They invariably make inordinate demands on friends, spouses, and coworkers, not so much out of the need for unconscious hostility, as the Freudians maintain, but due to their need to have others maintain their shaky self-esteem and their grandiose self-expectations. They are often not above a certain amount of cruelty to others if it helps to maintain their own tenuous self-operations. The underlying fear is that despite their rituals and compulsions and expansive self-idea, they will never quite be capable of being rescued or regenerated from their feelings of badness and evil. Their rather desolate early life experiences do not inoculate them from misunderstanding and future exploitiveness in their relationships with others (Sullivan 1956).

Social Learning

The social-learning explanation holds that most of the stratagems of an individual with obsessive-compulsive disorder are responses learned and maintained because they reduce or avoid anxiety and negative emotions. Parents of obsessive-compulsive individuals not only fail to model humor, spontaneity, or fun, but may also actively punish the child's expression of these traits. They seem to have carried to an extreme the conditions thought to promote the internalization of parental admonitions. There is generally a history of clearly repeated rules of expected thought and conduct. These parents typically have themselves modeled conscientious behavior of a compulsive quality. They have also conditioned the child to experience positive emotion upon behaving (or thinking about behaving) in a desirable way and to experience negative emotions such as anxiety, shame, or guilt upon behaving (or thinking of behaving) in an undesirable way. Obsessive children have internalized their parents' rule to such an extreme degree that their whole world is dominated by striving for imagined parental approval by thinking good thoughts and by avoiding imagined parental disapproval by engaging in all manner of magical and ritualistic thoughts and behaviors.

The treatment of obsessions and compulsions has taken somewhat different directions from the treatment of other anxiety disorders. The goal in treating individuals who engage in compulsive behaviors is to stop the behavior long enough for them to discover that the vague dreaded consequence does not happen (Marks 1973). Mills and colleagues (1973) used the *response-prevention method* to treat five individuals with serious compulsive behaviors. In the case of a woman hospitalized for excessive hand-washing (over fifty times a day), they removed the handles on the sink so that the woman could not turn on the water. Her hand-washing behavior fell to zero; after this period, when the handles were replaced, the frequency of hand washing remained much lower than it had been before intervention. Correspondingly, the client's compulsive urges gradually approached zero. Implementation of this procedure generally involves finding some effective way of temporarily blocking a compulsive behavior, although some clients are able to voluntarily stop the behavior when urged to do so by a therapist.

Turner and co-workers (1979) confirmed the effectiveness of response prevention in the treatment of compulsive disorders; however, they found that this approach did little to reduce the problems that are often associated with obsessive-compulsive behavior, such as depression and interpersonal difficulties. Obsessive thoughts and compulsions also can often be eliminated by mild aversion conditioning (Bandura 1969, Bandura and Bareb 1973, Stern et al. 1973). Here, the conditioning works best when combined with reinforcement of more adaptive alternative behaviors.

Therapy Techniques

1. Be supportive yet firm in your initial approach.

Where there exists better ego functioning and less preoccupation with obsessive thoughts and rituals, the therapist can engage the conflict-free ego in making its own decisions and taking action, that is, to use judgment. Initially, Gail contacted the therapist three or four times a week. Her reason for calling typically was that she was facing ambivalent feelings, confusion, and doubt and could not decide what to do next. For example, an entire day would go by and she would not have accomplished anything because she could not get out of the bathroom. Washing her hands in the bathroom often took up a good portion of her day. The magical ritual substituted for decision making and leading her own life. Now it was evening and her husband would see be home. Gail knew that he would be angry when he saw that she had accomplished nothing all day.

At this point, perhaps a half hour before her husband returned home, she would call the therapist, overreacting, upset, and in crisis. Should she just remain in her undressed state and prepare for his screams, or should she make some attempts at organizing herself? The husband in this case became a displacement and projection of the originally loved and yet feared, punitive, frustrating parent (superego figure), complete with commands and cautions. At the same time, he also represented the desired protector against feared impulses, who would guide Gail toward desirable actions. For some reason, Gail never resolved her conflicted and dichotomous feelings about the punitive or loving parent; perhaps because she had never felt enough genuine caring and concern as a child to counteract the punitive, commanding parent with the loving one.

When Gail telephoned with this question, the therapist, always in a supportive manner, would ask Gail what needed to be done in order to avoid the yelling and the feared humiliation. Then the therapist would tell Gail what to do next. The therapist thus became the protective parent who was lacking in Gail's internal ego system. Gail would make a list and follow the therapist's instructions, thereby minimizing her chances of being lectured by her "punitive husband." After a while, Gail was able to compose her own list and deal with her husband more realistically and less as a commanding, punitive protector. This can only be accomplished though, if the therapist is felt to offer options and beliefs that add to the client's self-esteem, which in turn helps to negate some of the evil thoughts.

2. Help the client to gain some control over the obsessive thoughts.

Obsessive thoughts have been successfully treated using a technique known as *thought stopping* (Wolpe 1958). This is a form of thought "suppression" that is a self-help technique that is recommended to clients that have a desire to gain control over their obsessive thoughts (Druckman & Bjork, 1994). This procedure involves telling the client to focus on the obsessive thought for a moment, after which the therapist shouts, "Stop!" This will usually distract the client and momentarily stop the obsessive thought. The procedure is repeated several times until the client can silently give the command to him/herself and thereby terminate the obsessive thought. Another method of thought stopping could be the use of the "rubber-band." Every time the client has a negative thought, they 'snap' the rubber band on their wrist which will stop the unwanted thought for a moment. Once this is done, the client will want to add a positive thought or image in their head such as lying on the beach, which will help the client feel calmer. The thought or image should not have anything to do with the unwanted thought. The idea is to "replace" the negative thought with positive thought or image (Romito & Barton, 2010).

Rimm, Saunders, and Westell (1975) used a modified version of this method, in which the client also reduced anxiety by repeating positive thoughts to take the place of the obsessional thoughts- "I will keep control of my mind and never hurt anyone!" This study indicated that thought stopping was generally effective, confirming other reports by Hays and Waddel (1976), Marks (1973), and Rimm (1973). The therapist presents the client with the reasonable limits to his/her painful suffering and a rational, loving approach to protect him/her from losing control over his/her life and his/her "evil, disordered impulses." This technique is used for negative thought replacement and is used within a cognitive-behavioral context or therapy. Practicing this technique everyday will help to foster healthy thinking that comes naturally. Once the client begins to replace their negative thoughts with positive thoughts, the client will be able to relax more, lower their stress, and be calmer (Romito & Barton, 2010).

Gail was told during the initial sessions that it would be helpful if she talked to herself. In other words, whenever she started to think of the possibility of her hands being contaminated with chemicals, she was told to tell herself that she was being ridiculous, that she was not going to poison anyone, that there were no poisons on her hands, and that she did not have to wash her hands.

Another aspect of this technique was to help Gail to see the inaccuracy of her thoughts. The therapist would encourage Gail to indulge in her secret fantasies, "What would happen if you *did* get bleach on your hands?" The purpose of this technique was to lead her through the fantasy from beginning to end in order to help her see whether she was going to hurt anyone. By answering questions about what she would do next, Gail was able to rationally explore and "know" that she was not going to hurt anyone.

3. *Encourage the expression of anger, frustration, and a host of other feelings that become possible when the client is not preoccupied with loss of control and evil thoughts.*

As was stated earlier, Gail was chronically late for appointments. At first, the therapist was supportive, saying it was all right. In doing so, the therapist was colluding with the negativistic child in Gail. However, as time went on, the therapist became less and less understanding. When Gail arrived late with her many excuses, the therapist would say nothing. At one point, the therapist told Gail that when she arrived on time for her appointment, they could indeed have a celebration. Interestingly, this statement led to an important insight for Gail. Shortly thereafter, the therapist was about five minutes late for a session. It happened to be the first time that Gail was there on time! The therapist, after apologizing, asked Gail how she felt about her being late. Gail said that it was all right, that she understood; she was submissive, compliant, and understanding, as was usual for her.

Three weeks later Gail reported during a session that on the day when the therapist had been late, she had been waiting outside, pacing back and forth, and feeling frustrated and disappointed. She had dropped her glove in the snow and later became terrified that the glove had gotten contaminated with dog urine and that she would poison her children. The therapist asked how Gail felt about the disappointment and frustration she experienced when the therapist arrived late. Gail expressed her annoyance, disappointment, and anger. She admitted that she actually had been annoyed with the therapist for being late, especially since it was the first time that she was on time and she had wanted to show the therapist that she really could be on time. It was shortly thereafter that Gail realized that whenever she had a negative feeling about something or someone, that she had the urge to wash her hands. Gail had spent most of her life being an obedient, good child who ritualistically obeyed her mother regardless of her own secret wishes. However, she was also the naughty child who would put on a pleasant face to hide her desire to rebel against her mother's strong, domineering will. If she only secretly rebelled against the frustrating, bad mother, perhaps she did not have to risk losing the loving, protective one. Her passive, disobedient behavior with her husband enabled her to go along with his demands and controls so that she did not have to deal with being a competent, loving mother.

4. Teach the client to use assertiveness techniques to express their needs and help them to express these needs no matter what the feared consequences.

After Gail had the initial insight into why she was washing her hands, the hand-washing ritual began to occupy a secondary place in her life.

At this point in the therapy, whenever the client began to feel annoyed at her parents or her husband, she talked about it. If she did not want to do something, she was better able to express herself and define her own desires. She could also discriminate between appropriate and inappropriate behavior. The inappropriate behavior was a false front, needed to convince her mother and husband that she was not a terrible, unlovable person-that she was not a bad person that nobody could love, not even Gail herself.

Soon after Gail started expressing herself, her husband began having trouble at work and wanted Gail to get a job to add to the family finances. The therapist was somewhat concerned about the responsibilities involved and questioned Gail as to whether she felt ready and willing to work. Gail believed that she was ready, and she found a job working as a receptionist in an office. Gail functioned very well at this job and found the role gratifying. After a few months she terminated the therapy.

The therapist needs to allow the client to make the decision to terminate treatment in order to enable him/her to deal with his/her own self-doubts. This helps the client to establish an inner self-representation that is competent to make decisions and to deal with the punitive superego, which may try to undermine constructive actions.

It is now two years since Gail terminated therapy. The therapist received a Christmas card from Gail each year. On both occasions, Gail included a short note describing how happy she is with her life.

In reviewing this case, one would have to wonder whether Gail had unresolved feelings of guilt and whether she feared punishment for having an abortion. She must have unconsciously believed that she had indeed killed the child. When she became pregnant again, she felt compelled to marry the father. This excused her from having to make the decision as a mature adult to marry him and give birth to their child. After all, hadn't her parents led her to believe that she was incapable of leading her own life? Even her future in-laws felt that the marriage was "wrong in the first place." These circumstances and events combined to contribute to Gail's doubt, and her guilt and ambivalence about her children confirmed for her that she did not deserve to be a mother. The message was conveyed that it was better for her to symbolically displace these thoughts and unconsciously eliminate the children altogether. In that way she could be protected from both her evil thoughts and her punitive and guilt-inducing superego. The compliant, helpless child could then feel protected from the powerful, frustrating, depriving parents, and perhaps even gain from them the love and protection that she was so unable to give to herself.

Family Therapy Treatment

Often when thinking about a disorder, we believe the disorder lies within one individual; but as new research develops and systemic therapy becomes more popular, we reach out to friends, family and significant others to see where the disorder is being fostered. Exposure and response prevention (ERP) has considerable evidence in the effectiveness in treatment of individuals with obsessive-compulsive disorder (OCD), but not all patients respond well. Some patients will relapse and continue in their obsessive thought cycles. It is important to note that often times family and significant others often become involved in a patient's symptoms (e.g., by providing reassurance, refraining or checking to make sure there is no contact with contaminants), and possibly creating a relationship dynamic that contrasts with the treatment of the individual diagnosed. The systemic focus on treatment for many individuals serves as a risk factor and long term problems for people with OCD. Preliminary studies and outcome treatment suggests that involving spouses, partners, and family in the treatment process to act as "coaches" for the OCD loved ones improves efficacy of ERP.

For the individual with OCD, there is an internally consistent "logic" that ties compulsions and obsessions. "For example, someone with obsessional images of harming a loved one might repeatedly seek assurances- such as from a partner or spouse- that he is unlikely to act on such thoughts. In a similar way, someone with obsessional doubts that she will be responsible for starting a house fire might spend hours checking and rechecking that appliances are unplugged and lights are turned off" (Abramowitz, Baucom, Wheaton, Boeding, Fabricant, Paprocki & Fischer, 2012). Research indicates anxiety that is reduced for a short period of time, usually follows performance of rituals, "which negatively reinforces these behaviors leading to their proliferation" (Abramowitz, et al 2012).

Frequently, OCD has a negative impact on the sufferer's relationships such as a relationship with a spouse or a romantic partner. Dysfunctional relationship patterns may promote and maintain the OCD symptoms leading to the development of a vicious cycle.

The following will describe the primary ways this process may be manifested.

1. A partner, spouse, or family member maintains the symptoms by "helping" and "assisting" with the compulsive rituals out of the love for the sufferer. This is also known as *symptom accommodation*.
2. The anxiety symptoms can create conflict and distress in a relationship therefore, exacerbating the anxiety.
3. "The couple might struggle with general relationship distress that does not result from the OCD; in this instance, the chronic stress of a discordant relationship can exacerbate OCD symptoms for an individual who is vulnerable to the disorder" (Abramowitz, et al 2012, p. 192).

Accommodation in a relationship can be subtle or overt and can be helpful as well as detrimental to the individual suffering from obsessive compulsive disorder. "Accommodation occurs when a partner or spouse of someone with OCD participates in their loved one's rituals, facilitates avoidance strategies, assumes daily responsibilities for the sufferer, or helps to resolve problems that have resulted from the patient's obsessional fears and compulsive urges" (Abramowitz, et al 2012, p. 192). For example, Patrick is a 66-year-old grandfather with obsessive thoughts about molesting his own grandchildren. Finding himself disgusted with these thoughts he avoided his grandchildren. Patrick's wife Norma also refrained from discussing their grandchildren, putting pictures of the grandchildren in the home, and agreed to only watch "wholesome" TV channels to avoid triggering Patrick's obsessions. Norma followed these directions in order to keep her husband from becoming irritable and anxious. Norma reported that by accommodating her husband's symptoms, it was her way to show him how much she loved and cared about him. This fostered the OCD symptom, never leading to exposure or treatment for Patrick.

Avoidance and compulsive rituals prevent the "natural extinction of obsessional fear and ritualistic urges (Abramowitz, et al 2012, p. 193). The partner perpetuates OCD symptoms by accommodating to these symptoms. For example think of a woman who has fears of acting on impulses to molest her newborn child. Her husband accommodated his wife by being the sole person to change their newborn daughter. By doing this, the husband prevents his wife from learning "her intense anxiety over the senseless obsessions is temporary and will subside and that she is unlikely to act on her unwanted obsessional thoughts" (Abramowitz, et al 2012, p. 193).

Accommodating the symptoms may also lead to a negative effect on the individual because it may decrease their motivation to participate in treatment. For instance, John is afraid to leave his house because believes he will inhale pesticides and become contaminated. His wife goes out and does all the grocery shopping and errands, and changes her clothes every time she arrives home at her husband's request. His wife's accommodations lead John to think he had control over his compulsions and obsessions, leading him to never confront his fear of going outside.

Abramowitz et al. (2012) created a list of questions for assessing System-Symptom Fit within a couple with OCD. Some questions during an assessment may include:

> When and how did the partner become aware of the patient's problem with OCD?
>
> What effects have OCD symptoms (obsessional fear, avoidance, rituals) had on the relationship in terms of daily life?
>
> If there are any patterns that seem to have developed because of the patient's OCD symptoms, what are they?
>
> How does each partner think their relationship might be different if the patient did not have difficulties with OCD?
>
> Is there anyone else (e.g., children) who is affected in any way by the patient having problems with OCD? (If so, explore who and how.)
>
> What types of strategies has the couple used to try to cope with the patient's OCD?
>
> When the patient is experiencing obsessional fear or performing rituals, does it ever lead to anger or arguments?

What happens in these situations? Does the unaffected partner ever have a tendency to help the patient escape from the anxiety, avoid situations that cause obsessions, or assist with the compulsive rituals to lower the anxiety?

How well has this worked?

Describe how the two of you communicate about the OCD problem (p. 197).

Once a partner or family member is educated and understands the principles of the underlying exposure therapy, he/she/they can assist as a coach for the individual. Studies have indicated that close relatives that have assisted in treatment have helped to improve the effectiveness for OCD as well as the interpersonal relationship with the individual (Abramowitz, et al 2012). However, partner-assisted exposure is more successful when there is minimal conflict and accommodations in the relationship. By learning to be a "coach" for a loved one, the family member or partner begins to offer emotional support as the individual is working on their exposure practices. The coach is taught to provide gentle reminders to not engage in safety behaviors or avoidance behaviors, and to help implement exposures without provoking anxiety or rituals. The goal is to not have the partner or family member alleviate the anxiety, but to emphasize to help the client "get through" the obsessional moment of anxiety until it dissipates on its own (Abramowitz, et al, 2012).

Systemic Therapy

There are two important reasons for bringing a couples system or a family system into therapy for the treatment of OCD. First reason being, the relationship distress, such as chronic stressors, can exacerbate the OCD symptoms as well as psychiatric symptoms. Second, the interventions discussed above are most successfully implemented when the two partners or family can work together as a team working toward a common goal (Abramowitz, et al 2012)

When to Refer?

The therapist must ascertain whether the client is able to render objective judgments and to envision the possibility of engaging in more constructive behavior. With the therapist's help, the client can differentiate between the evil thoughts and the compulsion to act on them. It is difficult to determine whether to refer this type of client because it is sometimes difficult to ascertain when the ritual will take on a secondary, delusional meaning in the client's life. If there is no decrease in the ritualistic behavior after three months of regular (at least once a week) therapy, the patient should probably have a psychiatric evaluation completed. A more severe underlying disorder may be operating, and a second opinion might help the therapist to make this determination. Differential diagnosis is necessary because obsessional thoughts and rituals sometimes operate as a defense against a more serious mental disorder, such as schizophrenia.

References

Fritscher, L. (2009, 06). *Obsessive-compulsive disorder*. Retrieved from http://phobias.about.com/od/glossary/g/ocddefinition.htm

Duckworth, K., & Freedman, J. (2012, 04). *Obsessive-compulsive disorder*. Retrieved from http://www.nami.org/Template. cfm?Section=By_Illness&Template=/ContentManagement/ ContentDisplay.cfm&ContentID=142546 *Obsessive-compulsive disorder*. (2013). Retrieved from http://medical-dictionary. thefreedictionary.com/obsessive-compulsive disorder

Druckman, D., & Bjork, R. (1994). *Learning, remembering, believing: Enhancing human performance*. Washington D.C.: National Academic Press.

Romito, K., & Barton, S. (2010, 08 26). *Positive thinking- stopping unwanted thoughts*. Retrieved from http://www.webmd.com/ mental-health/positive-thinking-stopping-unwanted-thoughts

Abramowitz, J. S., Baucom, D. H., Wheaton, M. G., Boeding, S., Fabricant, L. E., Paprocki, C., & Fischer, M. S. (2012). Enhancing exposure and response prevention for ocd: A couple-based approach.

Chapter 7

Phobias

Nirveeta Charles, M.A., MFT

What is a Phobia and How Do You Recognize It?

A *phobia* is an intense, irrational fear that greatly interferes with a person's life. As a result, phobic individuals tend to bring structure to most, if not all, of their daily activities around the feared object, situation, or event. It is sometimes difficult to distinguish a phobic person from one who is experiencing panic disorder, but there are several distinguishing characteristics. A panic attack seems to appear suddenly, with no obvious precipitating factor; a phobia, by contrast, appears to be much more directed and specific. Phobic people are overcome with anxiety *only* in the presence of what they fear. A woman with a dog phobia may feel quite content until she actually meets up with a dog; only then will she be seized with terror. A man who cannot bear riding in elevators may remain free of anxiety as long as he avoids these conveyances and make all his journeys between floors by using the stairs. People who turn pale at the very thought of looking down from the top of the Empire State Building may feel safe as long as they stay on the ground.

Phobias sometimes begin with an anxiety attack, but the anxiety becomes crystallized around a particular object or situation. As long as these individuals can avoid the feared object or situation, their anxiety level does not reach disturbing proportions. A phobia then, is an intense, irrational fear of some object, event, activity, or situation. It is irrational in the sense that the fear greatly exceeds any danger that might be inherent in the feared stimulus. People who suffer from phobias know this on a rational level and will often state that they have nothing to be afraid of; yet when in the presence of a feared object, they exhibit severe anxiety symptoms. Phobias involve levels of fear which are not only intense but also interfere with normal living patterns. People who experience such intense specific fears strive to organize their lives in such a way as to minimize their exposure to the fear-arousing stimuli. The most prominent maladaptive features of phobic disorders are the amount of fear experienced, the accompanying autonomic arousal, and the behaviors engaged in to avoid the feared stimulus. The term *phobic disorder* is used only when the fear and avoidance behavior are sufficiently intense to seriously disrupt the individual's life. Although phobias are common among children, they are generally relatively transient before adulthood.

Simple phobias involve maladaptive fear and avoidance of discrete objects or situations. Some of the most common simple phobias are fear of animals and insects; fear of heart attacks, cancer, and other diseases; fear of heights; and fear of closed spaces. These phobias rarely cause a serious problem for the phobic person, unless the feared stimulus happens to be something that is commonly or necessarily encountered, as in the case of person who fears riding in elevators but works in a high-rise office building. Unlike other phobias, simple phobias usually are not associated with generalized anxiety or other problems. Except for animal phobias, which afflict women 95 percent of the time (Marks 1969), the incidence of simple phobias is approximately equal in males and females.

The individual with a *social phobia* is fearful of and avoids social situations, especially those in which there is potential for public scrutiny and evaluation, such as meeting new people, speaking in public, or going on a date with a new acquaintance. Intense fears of this sort are generally quite maladaptive since they interfere with important areas of normal social functioning. Individuals with social phobias often experience diffuse anxiety, depression, and other phobias, but they generally do not have other serious behavior problems. This diagnosis is usually first assigned in late childhood adolescence, or early adulthood. Slightly more women than men receive this diagnosis (Marks 1969).

Agoraphobia is defined by intense fear of leaving a familiar setting, and accompanying restriction of activities. *Agoraphobia* literally means fear of open spaces. The agoraphobic individual becomes anxious at the thought of leaving home or when outside, particularly when alone. Many phobic persons rarely, if ever, go out in public, but they can often function fairly well within the home. The great majority of agoraphobic individuals also suffer from panic attacks, either preceding the development of the agoraphobic pattern or concurrent with it. Fear of having a panic attack outside the home is often cited as the reason for staying home. The agoraphobic pattern is more closely related to panic attacks than are other phobias. As with panic disorders, its onset is generally in late adolescence or early adulthood, and it usually follows a course of repeated episodes of anxiety interspersed with periods of mild, diffuse anxiety. Agoraphobia is three times more common in women than in men (Marks 1969). in addition, its onset in most cases is clearly precipitated by stress, particularly marital and interpersonal stress (Goldstein and Chambless 1978).

More than any other phobia, agoraphobia is frequently accompanied by a variety of other behavior problems. The most common of these are social difficulties, depression, the abuse of alcohol and other anxiety-reducing drugs, and other phobias.

Phobias are common at all levels of society, at all ages, and in both sexes. Phobias are generally more common in females than males but this varies according to the type of phobia. It is difficult to determine the incidence of phobias because people often can deal with phobias simply by avoiding what they fear. It is generally only when the phobia results in a great deal of inconvenience that the person decides to seek therapy. For example, if a person works on the 21st floor of an office building and has an intense fear of elevators, he or she may decide to seek therapy to eliminate the fear because of the degree to which it interferes with his/her life. Based on a survey of a Vermont community, Agras and colleagues (1969) estimated that the overall presence of phobic individuals in the general population was 7.7 percent, though less than 1 percent of the population were bothered by severely disabling phobias.

There are different subtypes of phobias that exist. These different subtypes are as follows; animal type, natural environment type, blood-injection-injury (BII) type, situational type and other type (Reuther, Davis III, Grills-Taqueehel, & Zlomke, 2011). The phobias that have been discussed earlier are some of the more common types, but there are many more. Here is a list of just a few phobias that may not commonly be known or discussed. "Alliumphobia- Fear of garlic, Chionophobia- Fear of snow, Emetophobia- Fear of vomiting, Necrophobia- Fear of death or dead things, Rupophobia- Fear of dirt, and Xyrophobia-Fear of razors" (Culbertson, 1995). These are just a few of a long list.

Phobias Symptoms

"Specific Phobia" are listed under the general category of Anxiety Disorders. A key feature of this disorder is that the fear of anxiety is circumscribed to the presence of a particular situation or object. Furthermore, "the 12-month community prevalence estimate for specific phobia is approximately 7%-9%" (American Psychiatric Association, 2013, p. 199). Some symptoms include: a marked fear or anxiety about a specific object or situation; the phobic object or situation almost always provokes immediate fear or anxiety; the phobic object or situation is actively avoided or endured with intense fear or anxiety; the fear or anxiety is out of proportion to the actual danger posed by the specific object or situation and to the sociocultural context; the fear is usually present at least six months and the fear, anxiety, and/or avoidance causes clinically significant distress or impairment in social, occupational, or other important areas of functioning. (For a more detailed description, and additional specifications, please refer to DSM-V, American Psychiatric Association, 2013).

Case Description

Pat H. was a 53-year-old woman married to John, a 59-year-old town clerk. She was also mother to Bill, a 33-year-old bachelor who worked in Manhattan as a keypunch operator. Bill lived in his parents' home and traveled to his job every day. Pat had married John when she was 20 years old, and she had been a homemaker and mother all these years. Prior to her marriage, she had been a bookkeeper.

Approximately ten years earlier, Pat had begun feeling anxious; diazepam (Valium) was prescribed for her by her family physician. Since the prescription was refillable, she continued to take it for the next ten years. When she first entered therapy, she was basically addicted to the drug.

Pat was an intelligent, attractive woman who over the years had withdrawn from the outside world. She gradually stopped attending social functions with her husband, who was active in various clubs. Going to the supermarket became more and more difficult for her. About five years before entering therapy, she began to have trouble leaving the house. She simultaneously stopped driving the car, giving the excuse that it made her too anxious because of all the terrible drivers on the road.

As the years went by, she gradually became more and more dependent upon her husband; when she entered therapy, she was basically dependent upon him for her daily survival. She reported that whenever she left the house, she felt as though she were going to faint. She could barely go a block when she went out for a walk, and would only do so if John were there to hold her up. The two appeared as though they were many years older as they walked slowly down the street, holding each other up. Pat could manage to travel only to her therapist's office and to the office of her family physician. She felt it imperative to visit her family physician at least once a week in order to make sure that there was nothing physically wrong with her. She believed that she had some sort of gastrointestinal disorder and spent a good deal of the day monitoring her internal gas levels and physical examples of her evacuation process. She also monitored her food intake because she believed that that food she ate might be responsible for her discomfort. According to all the medical tests, she was in good physical health. Clearly, then, she suffered from hypochondriacal concerns, anxiety about her appearance, and fear of losing control over certain physiological processes.

While Pat's husband was at work during the day, she would roam about the house, refusing to clean or to do much of anything. She would eat the breakfast her husband prepared for her and then pace back and forth waiting for John to come home. When John was at work, he was required to call her every hour to make sure that she was all right. Her greatest fear was that she would lose consciousness as a result of her gastrointestinal disorder and that no one would find her. She begged John to rush home from work, but when he did, he would find her crying and upset, despairing over her supposed physical deterioration. Since her gall operation two years before, she had lost quite a bit of weight, which only served to reinforce her belief that she had a serious disorder. She insisted that this weakness rendered her totally dependent on John.

Their typical interaction proceeded as follows: John would rush home from work and begin cooking supper while he listened to Pat's description of her symptoms and fears of the day. If he asked her to accompany him to one of his club's social functions, she would burst into tears, insisting that he knew she could not endure the pressure of going outside the house. "And besides," she would shout, "nothing fits me anymore. All my clothes are too big." Pat had stopped going shopping for clothing because she could not bear to be in a large building. As a result, she wore old clothes that were much too large for her. This only served to emphasize her pitiful appearance.

Whenever Pat would meet someone she knew, she would describe her ailments in great detail, repeatedly listing her symptoms, until the person found an excuse to leave. Needless to say, her friends and relatives were dwindling, becoming annoyed with Pat's self-preoccupations

What Does a Phobia Look Like?

Phobic persons look much like the anxious persons, so much so that they appear tense and exhibit "nervous" symptoms. If they attempt to approach, rather than avoid, the phobic situation, they will become overwhelmed with anxiety, which can vary from mild feelings of uneasiness to distress to a full-fledged anxiety attack. These individuals also experience a wide range of symptoms in addition to their phobias, including tension headaches, back pains, stomach upsets, dizzy spells, and fear of going mad. During times of more acute panic, these individuals often complain of feelings of unreality, of strangeness, and of not being themselves. Feelings of depressions often accompany phobias, and many patients report serious interpersonal difficulties. Some also have serious difficulty making decisions.

At the start of therapy, Pat was unable to leave her home for more than fifteen minutes, unless she was going to visit one of her doctors, in which case she could stay out for extended periods of time. She was constantly anxious, dreading the time when she would have to go outside for a walk down the block. Like Peggy in Chapter 2 who suffered from panic disorder, Pat also was somewhat comforted by drinking cold water, and she carried a thermos with her wherever she went. When in the presence of another person, she spoke of either her fear of going outside or the wide array of physical symptoms she experienced. During her therapy sessions, she was often unable to sit still and would pace back and forth. She lived in a state of constant fear. Most of her day was spent waiting for John to come home so that she could feel somewhat safe, although she never really did. Her speech was rapid and she spoke constantly, describing either her symptoms or her plight in life. Her body movements were fast and jerky rather than gradual and harmonious.

What Does a Phobia Feel Like?

Like the person who experiences panic disorder, the phobic individual is petrified whenever the feared object or situation is close by. Unlike the person with a panic disorder, however, the phobic person can reasonably predict when the anxiety will begin. Severely phobic individuals experience anxiety even when thinking about the feared object. In other words, the phobic anxiety generalizes so that objects, person, events or other stimulus patterns that even slightly resemble the feared object elicit the fear response to varying degrees. When Pat even thought about going outside, she began to feel anxious. Phobias can become so severe that the client is forced to lead an exceedingly constricted, inhibited life. As a consequence, they become housebound.

Pat often reported that she felt as though she was out of control - which her physiological processes were taking hold of her and she did not have any control over them. The feeling of loss of control results when certain feelings and reactions are removed from consciousness and defended against. In another sense, however, Pat had a great deal of control in the household. The entire family structured their lives around her, the "sick one." It is important to examine this family from a family-systems perspective because the incapacitated person is often getting needs fulfilled as a "victim" that are not obvious at first glance. In Pat's case, her phobic behavior relieved her of many adult responsibilities, won her a great deal of attention and concern from her husband, and allowed her to control the lives of other family members. It created the necessity for them to structure their lives around her "sickness," to help take care of her, and to see her former responsibilities and tasks. Thus, Pat received many secondary gains from remaining phobic.

The Client's Dilemma

Regardless of how Pat's phobia initially began, it is crucial to recognize how her phobic behavior was reinforced. By avoiding the feared object (the outside world), she felt somewhat safer (anxiety reduction). In addition, her phobia was at least partially maintained by secondary gains. In other words, Pat received many rewards by remaining "sick." Some of those gains were increased attention and concern from John, together with some general concern on part of her relatives and family. By remaining a dependent, helpless victim, she was also able to give up many of the responsibilities involved in housekeeping and cooking. She relinquished numerous adult responsibilities and remained in the role of the child, totally helpless and dependent on others.

Pat's agoraphobia was the overriding concern in her life. She has little enthusiasm or energy for anything else. Her entire illness was tied up in her self-involved, dependent, helpless role. When Pat's sister-in-law was dying of cancer, for example, Pat could not bring herself to visit her in the hospital because she was too afraid to leave her home. She was completely self-absorbed and had little time for anyone else. By the time she entered therapy, she was unable to concern herself with any of the needs of others, including those of her immediate family. The paradox of her behavior was that while the immediate effect of remaining at home seemed initially to reduce Pat's anxiety, she was ultimately doomed to a life of misery and entrapment.

No long-range solution was possible for her, and she was becoming more and more absorbed by her phobic processes. At one point in the beginning of therapy, Pat was considering wearing adult diapers in order to prevent an accident because of her "intestinal problems." She had thus regressed to almost total dependency, and in many ways her life was out of control. She experienced a notable submissiveness and clinging dependency to John, which created in her another dilemma. While she desperately needed his nurturance and support, she tremendously resented her dependency on him. It was not unusual for her to lash out at him, "Why are you so good to me? Why don't you get a divorce and get away from me?"

In some way, this was Pat's secret wish. When they were first married, John would occasionally disappear with his friends for days at a time. There would be no warning, no phone call, nothing. One day, he would simply fail to come home from work, only to return four days later, having left his young bride and infant son to fend for themselves. Pat said she learned to adapt to these situations, but later on in therapy she revealed her fury at his irresponsibility. As John got older, he gradually stopped this behavior.

After she had been married for about four years, Pat began an affair with the husband of a couple with whom she and John had been very friendly. The relationship lasted until the man died about seven years prior to Pat's entering therapy. Throughout the years, the foursome remained good friends, socializing on a regular basis. Pat believed that John knew nothing of this affair. Pat said that on a few occasions she wished that she could leave John for this man but, at the last minute, always decided to stay. As was typical of women who were Pat's age, she said she did "what was expected of her" and stayed with John. Her phobic symptoms worsened after the death of her friend, and it was around this time that she also increased her drug usage. In this way, she unconsciously thought she could contain her anxiety and guilt. Her own sense of autonomy was submerged, as was her sexuality, although she must have feared exposure of these painful feelings that she felt made her a bad person.

Theories and Explanations for Phobias

Psychoanalytic

Psychodynamic interpretations of phobias center around the notion that phobias develop when people find themselves in situations that cause them a great deal of internal conflict. In the past, these people had successfully used ego defense mechanisms to deal with this sort of conflict, but at this point the stress is so intense that their defenses start to give way. As a consequence, they start to regress and display various neurotic symptoms. As with the patient's original ego defenses, they represent a way of binding and symbolizing the patient's internal conflict. The symptoms express indirectly what the patient cannot express directly and finds too painful to experience.

According to Freud, the phobic individual not only readily uses the defense of displacement, but they also make use of projection. These defenses displace an internal danger (eruption of previously unconscious material into preconscious awareness) onto an external danger and a concrete situation. The result is an irrational, but avoidable, fear. The person now gives control of his life to a fear- evoking, overwhelming external situation and forces that to guide his life while simultaneously enabling him to suspend judgment and guilt about the situation.

Phobic symptoms also represent a concretization of thought processes. According to Arieti (1955), this concretization is an active, unconscious process that not only simplifies emotional issues for the client but also makes concrete, focused, and specific that which is often vague and not clearly demonstrable. It undermines conceptual, abstract notions and thought processes, thus making the ego more fragile and childish psychic structure. This, in turn, undermined the client's ability to perceive and test her internal feelings and resources against what she perceives as an overwhelming, fearful world. This hinders the process of separation/ individuation and the establishment of an active, aggressive, autonomous self.

Many phobic people are characterized by a strong desire to be nurtured. In Pat's case, it could be said that she had a need for a dependent relationship that was similar to an emotional symbiosis. It is not unusual for a phobic person to have a companion or spouse who serves as protection from acting out forbidden impulses and comforts them from anxiety and pain. It is perhaps true that as children, phobic individuals were not adequately protected from excessive internal or external stress, and their present fears are regressions under stress to a more infantile level of psychosexual adjustment. The protector and symbiotic partner appears to be in charge of the victim's life, accountable for all the decisions and responsibilities.

Pat had always envied her friends who worked, and she often spoke of wanting to do "something meaningful." She was a very bright woman who quickly became bored with household chores. John refused to agree to her working. He felt that he could adequately support his family, and that Pat's working would only serve to show the world that he was inept as a breadwinner. In a sense, this represented her dilemma; by becoming fearful of leaving home, she was expressing her own conflict - her desire to hold a job coupled with the unspoken knowledge of her husband's insecurities. Thus, her symptoms were protecting her from having to make a choice that could at some point jeopardize her marriage.

Pat's fear communicated a wish - a wish not to have to examine her marriage, which might prove to be ultimately very painful and for which she felt unprepared; thus, the symptoms carried secondary gains. By holding on to the symptoms, Pat did not have to face the painful unconscious conflict underneath. The symptoms themselves represented an outlet - a way of expressing the conflict in disguised fashion. Her helplessness and demanding behavior enabled Pat to partially express her anger and blame John for her life situation. She was the good girl who saved him and marriage from her sexual feelings, her accusations of his wrongdoings, and her wish to leave this uncaring man.

Social Learning

Wolpe (1952, 1953) noted that if an animal was fed in the presence of an object that it had come to fear, the fear would gradually diminish. He decided to put this technique to use with humans in a procedure that came to be called *systematic desensitization*. As a first step he asked his clients to describe a "graded hierarchy" of fears, moving from objects or situations that terrified them to those that evoked only mild anxiety. Then, starting with the least feared item on the list, Wolpe encouraged his patients to relax by using several techniques, the best being known as Jacobson's method (1938). One example of using relaxation techniques would be to educate the client on mindfulness meditation. The idea with this as expressed in the research would be that a person would bring their attention to the present moment as opposed to looking in the past or even the future ("Focusing on the good things", 2013). In doing this practice, it should be during a time when the individual has something that they do every day (i.e.; traveling for work, having lunch…) but now instead of just eating their lunch they will set a purpose or intention for that half hour. It should also be told to the client's that "your mind will wander off" and that is perfectly normal, however, when that does occur bring your thoughts back to the proposed intention. Remind the client that to acknowledge all feelings they may experience during this time and then let it go so that they may become more relaxed ("Focusing on the good things", 2013). By practicing this relaxation daily, they may improve their overall health, boost the immune system, improve psychological conditions and increase activity in a number of brain regions ("Focusing on the good things", 2013).

Wolpe believed that phobias can be explained, not be complexes and unconscious conflicts, but by concepts like conditioning, generalization, and drive reduction. People acquire irrational fears merely because they have undergone a traumatic experience. Once they have suffered this sort of overwhelming anxiety, they will try to avoid similar situations - including perfectly harmless objects that happened to have been present at the time of the trauma.

Another behaviorist explanation is put forth by Skinner (see Sidman 1960). The key concepts for Skinnerians are reinforcement and punishment. Pat's phobia, as was stated earlier, enabled her in many ways to be a privileged person. She received a great deal of attention and love for remaining the sick, helpless victim. These "fringe benefits" of her phobia are called *secondary gains*. Unlike the psychoanalysts, who feel that unresolved unconscious conflict is the cause of phobias specifically and neurotic behavior in general, the behaviorists look at the here-and-now environment for the reinforcers. They also look for the secondary gains the person receives as a result of maintaining the dysfunctional behavior. As we saw in Pat's case, however, certain unspoken words and feelings that have been removed from awareness sometimes need to be discovered and verbalized.

Cognitive-Behavioral

Although Beck's cognitive behavioral therapy was developed initially for the treatment of depression (Beck et al. 1979, Hollon and Beck 1978), it can also be used to explain phobic behavior. The main thesis is that problems arise from people's illogical thinking about themselves, the world they live in, and the future. These illogical ideas are maintained even in the face of contradictory evidence, because these individuals typically engage in self-defeating and self-fulfilling behaviors in which they selectively perceive the world as harmful while ignoring evidence to the contrary. They overgeneralize on the basis of limited examples, seeing themselves as totally worthless and magnifying the significance of undesirable events ("This is the end of the world") and engaging in absolute, "all-or-none" thinking - "I am always successful or else a failure."

Beck believes that there is a connection between patients' thoughts and the symptom. He believes that such ideas are the primary source of all neurotic symptoms. He would state that Pat had "morbid fantasies" about the catastrophes that might befall her if she went outside. Pat exhibited symptoms because of what she told herself. She lacked a sense of self-efficacy and was convinced that she could not master a particular situation. She engaged in negative self-talk and was anxiously preoccupied with herself and her impending catastrophe. Thus, her images of the world were entirely negative and her own self-perceptions were faulty.

Biological

More recently, biological theories have put forth the notion of "preparedness" to explain neurotic behavior. A number of behaviorists have noted that symptoms do not appear at random (Seligman and Hager 1972, Marks 1976, Lader 1976). While a good many people are afraid of snakes, heights, driving, and going out alone, very few people are fearful of kitten or foods. They believe that some objects seem to elicit fears more readily than other. Mark (1976) suggests that there may be a link between "neurotic" behavior and man's "phylogenetic inheritance." Because of our biological constitution, and as an evolutionary adaptive response, we may be more "prepared" to avoid certain situations or objects. Thus, certain phobias may be indicative of some sort of biological predispositions to avoid certain dangers.

Family Therapy View

Family therapy views individuals suffering from phobias as a part of a family system that helps maintain the ongoing appearance of symptoms of the individual through the interaction of the members. The family systems approach according to Cerio (1997) places less focus on the individual who presents problematic symptoms and instead pays more attention to the patterns of interaction that happen in the family. Madanes explained that "the dysfunctional behavior of the child is seen as a symptom of a larger problem within the family or as the child's inappropriate way of helping the family" (as cited in Cerio, 1997). Furthermore, family systems theory also includes members of the family beyond the nuclear family as well as other social institutions that have an effect on the family (Cerio, 1997).

Some strategic approaches to treating phobias are based on models of family therapy by Haley, Madanes and some structural approaches include models by Minuchin and Fishman in particular (Cerio, 1997). In general, these approaches are "problem driven" as opposed to proposed methods that are to be followed. This means that these approaches can be tailored to fit each family's situation as necessary.

The first basic concept in looking at an individual who has presented as having a phobia in terms of a systemic approach is that that the individual, or identified patient is just the person who carries the symptom of the dysfunctional family as a whole (Cerio, 1997). Next, this systemic approach recognizes the hierarchy that the family has set up themselves. This structure either helps the family function ideal, or hinders them from doing so. An ideal structure would include parents at the top, next to one another, followed by their offspring in the order in which they were born (Cerio, 1997). In situations in which individuals are phobic, there may be some disruption in their family structure that throws them off balance which results in the symptoms of phobia appearing among one or a few of the members of the family system.

Therapists who are more strategic also recognize patterns among the family that resemble triangles. Problems arise because amid two conflicting individuals, a third gets pulled into the dynamic (Cerio, 1997). This "triangulation" is problematic as it drags more people into the conflict and it also helps maintain distance between the original conflicting parties which does not help solve the problem.

Cerio (1997) lists important interventions that start with getting as many members of the identified patient's family in session. This can include those in both the nuclear and extended family system. Next, both the identified patient and the other family members should be asked to define the problem and describe when the phobic symptoms started and events that may have caused it at the time. Then, a reframe can be used to introduce the family to a new way of viewing the problem. As in the example given by Cerio (1997) in which systemic interventions are used on a family with a child is experiencing school phobia, a possible reframe for such a family could be "that doesn't sound much like a phobia to me as it does a child who is allowed to worry too much". Here, the responsibility is spread around to not only the symptom bearer who worries too much, but to the parents or other family member who allow it, thereby contributing to it. This introduces control over the symptom beyond just the individual (Cerio, 1997).

Once the members who are under involved and those who are over involved are identified, the therapist can then help them switch places in relation to the identified patient (Cerio, 1997). So an under involved parent for example, could be asked to perform tasks or relate to the phobic individual more often and the over involved parent would be distanced.

Barrett (2000) points out that "It seems reasonable to hypothesize that addressing parental psychopathology and family functioning in treatment could lead to greater child treatment response rates. Theorists have argued that because children are incredibly reliant on their family environment, an improved model of treatment would be one that is premised on an interpersonal conceptualization of youth anxiety and that aims to employ interventions at the social (e.g., familial) rather than individual levels" (as cited by Podell & Kendall, 2011). Hughes et al (2008) also explain that a child's distress may be maintained by behavior that their parents are engaging in (as cited by Podell & Kendall, 2011). Though these are instances that speak to situations in which the phobic individual is a child, the circumstances could present in different ways. The phobic individual may not be a child, and the individuals that could be helping the phobic individual maintain his or her symptom could just as well be a spouse.

In terms of Pat's case history, although Pat could most certainly attempt to work through her phobic behaviors individually, combining the following therapy techniques along with having sessions that include at least both Pat and her husband could be useful. Upon examining Pat's symptoms and when they started, it is easy to see how both her son and husband have learned to accommodate to her "sickness" over the years. By continuously helping her, they have contributed to her helplessness. They have also slowly given her the power to control them to a certain extent as well. Looking at the family system as a whole, it can be said that Pat slowly gave up her responsibilities as a mother and wife and traded them in for a much easier deal of being "handicapped". She was perfectly capable for doing many things for herself prior to experiencing phobic feelings but both her son and husband enabled her actions of helplessness as time passed and have been helping to maintain her symptoms for quite a while now.

By reframing the family situation to one in which Pat is seen to be as helpless as a child who has two parents, rather than a son and husband, the family may begin to see the role they play in keeping Pat "sick". In addition, the therapist could frame their family structure as one in which Pat has everyone wrapped around her pinky in that she gets help whenever she wants for whatever she needs and does not have to contribute toward much of the household duties. Once they see how they have been contributing to her phobic experience, they can begin to figure out new ways of interacting with her that would help her become more independent.

Therapeutic Techniques

1. Train clients to use relaxation techniques.

The first step is to train the client to relax. Try to accomplish this in the first four sessions. The relaxation techniques require the client to first contract and gradually relax specific muscle group until a state of complete relaxation is achieved. Instruct the client to start with the right foot, then the left, and gradually work his or her way up the body to the facial muscles. Direct the client to flex the particular muscle until a certain level of tension is achieved and to focus on the tension, and then relax the muscle and focus on the tension flowing out of the system. Emphasize the shoulder, face and neck area where tension typically accumulates. (An example of this relaxation procedure is provided in the Appendix.)

It took Pat quite a while to learn to use these exercises; when she first practiced them, she would focus on how much tension was built up in her system and was then unable to focus on the tension *leaving* her system. Initially, she was *increasing* her tension level instead of decreasing it. With practice, however, she was soon able to relax and thereby experience a sense of control over her physiological responses. Her autonomic arousal had precipitated loss of control over these responses. Perhaps she has unconsciously given up control over her body so that she would require constant care.

2. Create a hierarchy of concerns and responses ranging from the least feared activity to the most feared activity.

The least feared activity on Pat's list was walking to the front door. The most feared activity was being in a large department store. Pat was first told to put herself in a deep state of muscle relaxation and then to picture herself at home, all by herself. She was then told to imagine herself walking out of her bedroom to the front door. If at any point during the session she experienced anxiety, she was told to signal the therapist by raising her finger, at which point she would be instructed to resume the exercises in order to maintain the relaxed state.

After one item of the hierarchy has been successfully accomplished, Pat would progress to another, more fear-evoking item. Pat was taught, at each step of the way, to imagine herself in the fearful situation, with the result that she was imagining herself in the situation while still in a relaxed state. The goal, then, was to break the association between the feared situations and the anxiety. Pat progressed slowly up the hierarchy until she was able to go outside for short periods of time and drive the car for a few blocks. She then gradually increased the time she spent outside until she was able to go quite comfortably to the places she had been able to go to in the past.

It should be noted that the therapist and Pat were working together to master the feared external situation. The therapist helped Pat to gain control over her fearful fantasies and responses to them. The client's participation at first is minimal: She has only to raise her finger. The therapist responds by giving the client permission to discontinue, to go back to a more comfortable state. In so doing, the therapist begins by allowing the client to be dependent and ends by encouraging more independence and mastery as the client becomes ready.

3. Help client's put themselves in some "win" situations.

It was crucial for Pat to accomplish something on her own. For all of her adult life, she had been largely incapacitated and dependent on her husband. She had to start to develop a life apart from his. In order to help her accomplish this, she was given homework assignments - very small ones at first because that was all she could handle. She was sent to the store once a day to purchase the newspaper. She was then asked to read one article in the newspaper and report on it to her therapist, under the guise that the therapist was so busy that she did not have time to read the newspaper and in this way they both would benefit. Later on Pat would then be sent to the library to take out a variety of sources (i.e.; books, magazines, journals…) and report back to the therapist.

At one point, during a setback when she was feeling particularly fearful again, Pat decided that she wanted to enter a psychiatric hospital. The therapist agreed that this might be restful for her, but that before she entered the hospital she would have to research the various hospitals on Long Island. So Pat went back to the library. By the time she finished researching psychiatric hospitals, she was feeling better about her abilities. Thus the therapist never challenged her decision to have control over her life, even if it meant being sick and returning to a more dependent and helpless state. Her helpless state would thus be decided by her own actions and decisions, and she made a conscious choice that undermined her own helplessness. She had unconsciously reached a healthier position in her life even if she ultimately chose to be hospitalized.

4. *Help clients to express anger about their life situation, and help them take responsibility for their own guilt.*

Pat carried a great deal of unexpressed anger at her husband. She was furious because he used to leave her without warning when they were first married. She was angry because she felt forced into an extramarital affair. She believed that if John had been more attentive to her and fulfilled her sexual needs, she would not have had to engage in extramarital sex. Thus, she never took responsibility for her own sexual feelings; instead, she projected blame onto John, and felt herself to be a victim of his lack of caring. Helping the client become aware of *herself* as a sexually active participant, rather than a sexually disinterested bystander, is the long-range goal toward which the therapist guided the client.

Pat was angry about John's relationship with their son. Bill resented his father because John could have helped him obtain a good position in the town clerk's office. Instead he refused, and Bill had to work for less money at a job which he defined as uninteresting. Pat was also furious at

John for this decision, and for his general disinterest in their son. Further, Pat was angry with John for catering to her every whim, for taking her to psychiatrists, dieticians, and every other medical specialist she decided to consult. She was angry with him for having forced her to sell her mother's house and moving them into a much smaller, less expensive house. On many levels Pat was aware that John was enabling her to continue her phobia. She understood that he was helping her to be incompetent. It was crucial for her to express and dissipate some of her anger. During the course of therapy, she learned first how to express her anger to the therapist and then how to express some of her sexual and autonomous needs to her husband in a way that could be constructive.

After the client has faced what initially appeared to be an overwhelming situational fear, with an accompanying threat of loss of ego control, the client is then ready to face other fearful emotions. After the therapist has helped the client build trust and take risks with their environment, the next step of taking risks with feelings does not seem so dreadful. As before, the client can continue at his own pace, temporarily retreating (if necessary) from overwhelming fear and anxiety without "loss of face" or fear of humiliation or inadequacy. The therapist, then, helps the client deal with safe dosages of feeling, working toward the goal of enabling the client to manage his approach-avoidance behavior in the phobic situation.

5. Help the client's family to adjust to the client's "wellness".

When pat started to take charge of her life, John began feeling insecure. His role of caretaker was disappearing; his role as the only competent one was disintegrating. As Pat became increasingly healthy, John became more unstable. In order to counteract these feelings in John, couple counseling was needed. John had to learn that he could be competent in other areas, and that it was unnecessary for him to cater to Pat's every whim and need. Pat had to learn that she could receive constructive attention and concern from John. They could discuss some of the painful negative feelings that had previously not been verbalized without the threat of marital dissolution. It is often necessary for the therapist to help the couple see the disruptive and "negative" feelings can be dealt with if they have a commitment to a stable marriage. Differences in feelings and values can be negotiated and resolved If the couple can make compromises within their marital relationship.

When to Refer

It was crucial for Pat to have psychiatric evaluation upon entering therapy because of her dependence on tranquilizers. After her psychiatric evaluation, it was decided by the psychiatrist and the therapist that Pat should be gradually weaned from the drug. She remained in therapy on a weekly basis and had once-a-month sessions with the psychiatrist to determine the appropriate level of tranquilizer.

Clients must be referred to a psychiatrist for an evaluation whenever drugs are involved. A phobia should initially be dealt with from a behavioral perspective using systematic desensitization techniques and setting up a hierarchy of fears. Once the phobia has successfully been eliminated, it becomes important to examine the client's psychodynamics on a comprehensive level that long-lasting cure and a stable adjustment to a more rewarding life can be achieved. If, during any point in the process, the phobic behavior remains or returns and becomes entrenched, consultation of referral for a more extensive treatment may be necessary.

Phobias also play a part in other mental disorders, such as borderline personality disorders and schizophrenia. In these cases, they serve to stabilize a fragile ego structure, preventing further overwhelming anxiety and decompensation. The phobia thus serves a different purpose for these individuals than it does for the "true" phobic, and treatment therefore involves recognition of the more serious underlying disorder.

References

Atwood, J. D. (1987). Treatment techniques for common mental disorders / Joan D. Atwood, Robert Chester. Northvale, NJ: Aronson, c1987.

Cerio, J. (1997). School phobia: A family systems approach. Elementary School Guidance & Counseling, 31(3), 180.

Culbertson, F. (1995, July 17). *The phobia list*. Retrieved from http://www.phobialist.com

Dange, J. K., & J., M. (2012). Adolescent Fears and Their Family Relationship. Golden Research Thoughts, 2(3), 1-9.

Drake, K., & Ginsburg, G. (2012). Family Factors in the Development, Treatment, and Prevention of Childhood Anxiety Disorders. Clinical Child & Family Psychology Review, 15(2), 144-162. doi:10.1007/s10567-011-0109-0

Focusing on the good things. (2013). *Occupational Health, 403.*

Podell, J., & Kendall, P. (2011). Mothers and Fathers in Family Cognitive-Behavioral Therapy for Anxious Youth. Journal Of Child & Family Studies, 20(2), 182-195.

Priest, J. B., & Denton, W. (2012). Anxiety Disorders and Latinos: The Role of Family Cohesion and Family Discord. Hispanic Journal of Behavioral Sciences, 34(4), 557.

Reuther, E. T., Davis III, T. E., Grills-Taqueehel, A. E., & Zlomke, K. R. (2011). Fear of anxiety in fearful adults: an analysis of heterogeneity among phobia types. *Current Psychology, 30.3*, 268.

Chapter 8

Post-Traumatic Stress Disorder

Nirveeta Charles, M.A., MFT

What is Post Traumatic Stress Disorder and How Do You Recognize It?

Coconut Grove nightclub fire in Boston took the lives of 492 people. More than 50 percent of the survivors required treatment for severe psychological shock (Adler 1943). In 1972, two commuter trains collided in Chicago. The collision left 44 person dead and over 300 injured. The tragedy also left scores of persons with feelings of fear, anxiety, and guilt. Psychological evaluation of 8 of the 64 survivors after the collision of two jet planes on Santa Cruz de Tenerife Island in 1977, in which 580 people died, indicated that all the survivors studied suffered from serious emotional problems which stemmed directly from the accident (Perlberg 1979).

With few exceptions, people who are exposed to plane crashes, automobile accidents, explosions, fires, earthquakes, tornadoes, sexual assault, or other terrifying situations experience severe psychological shock. The symptoms vary widely, and depend on the nature and severity of the terrifying experience, the degree of surprise, and the personality of the individual.

Stressful events may be characterized as *acute* or *chronic*. Acute stress results from sudden, intense events, such as natural disasters, rape and other violent crimes, and loss of a spouse. Chronic stressors, on the other hand, are the relatively constant demand of living in social systems, attending school, working, and maintaining personal relationships. These events may impart meaning and purpose to life, but they are also inevitable sources of stress. This chapter focuses on acute stress.

A "disaster syndrome" has been delineated which appears to characterize the reactions of many victims of such catastrophes. This syndrome may be described in terms of the reactions during the traumatic experience, the reactions initially following it the acute post-traumatic stress - and the complications that may arise later or be long lasting- the chronic or delayed post-traumatic stress.

Initial Disaster Syndrome and Acute Post-Traumatic Stress

The initial responses to a disaster typically involve three stages: 1) shock, 2) suggestible, and 3) recovery stage. It is in the third stage that acute post-traumatic stress disorder may develop.

During the shock stage, the victim is stunned, dazed, and apathetic. Frequently unaware of the extent of personal injuries, the victim tends to wander about aimlessly until guided or directed. The victim is generally unable to make more than minimal efforts to help either themselves or others. In extreme cases, the victim may be stuporous, disoriented, and amnesic about the traumatic event.

During the suggestible stage, the victim tends to be passive, suggestible, and willing to take direction from rescue workers or others less affected by the disaster. The individual often expresses extreme concern over the welfare of other victims and attempts to be of assistance, however, performance of even routine tasks tends to be inefficient.

In the recovery stage, individuals may be tense, apprehensive, and generally anxious, but they gradually begin to regain psychological equilibrium. The person may feel a need to repeatedly describe the catastrophic event. The clinical picture may be complicated in some cases by intense feelings of grief and depression. If victims feel that their own personal inadequacy or incompetency contributed to the loss of loved ones in the disaster, they may experience strong feelings of guilt. In this case, the post-traumatic stress may continue for months. Many victims experience *survivor guilt* which seems to center around the feeling that they did not deserve to survive.

Chronic or Delayed Post-Traumatic Stress

Some individuals who undergo terrifying experiences exhibit a reaction pattern that may endure for weeks, months, or even years. As has been noted, the post-traumatic stress reaction would be clinically diagnosed as *chronic* if it continued for longer than six months. If it did not begin until six months after the catastrophe, it would be diagnosed as *delayed*.

In either case, post-traumatic stress includes the following symptoms:

1. *Anxiety*, varying from mild apprehensiveness to episodes of acute anxiety, commonly associated with situations that recall the traumatic experience.
2. *Chronic tensions and irritability*, often accompanied by feelings of fatigue, insomnia, inability to tolerate noise, and the complaint of "I just can't seem to relax"
3. *Repetitive nightmares*, reproducing the traumatic incident either directly or symbolically
4. *Impaired concentration and memory.*
5. *Depression*

Some individuals withdraw from social contact and avoid experiences that may cause excitement. This is commonly manifested in the avoidance of interpersonal involvement, loss of sexual interest, and a need for peace and quiet at any price.

Post-traumatic stress disorder may be complicated by a physical mutilation that necessitates changes in the victim's way of life; it may be complicated by the psychological effects of receiving disability of legal compensation or damage suits, which all tends to prolong post-traumatic symptoms (Okura 1975).

Post Traumatic Stress Symptoms

PTSD is generally found more in females than in males and that females tend to experience the symptoms for longer time periods compared to males. Individuals with PTSD are 80% more likely than those without PTSD to also experience at least one other mental disorder (e.g., depressive, bipolar, anxiety, or substance abuse disorders) (p. 280).

In terms of prevalence among U.S. adults, it is estimated that PTSD affects 3.5% of the population (American Psychiatric Association, 2013).

A person can be diagnosed with PTSD if they have directly experienced a traumatic event, witnessed, in person, the event as it occurred to others, learned that the traumatic event occurred to a close family member or close friend, the event must have been violent or accidental, experienced repeated or extreme exposure to aversive details of the traumatic event (e.g., first responders collecting human remains; police officers repeatedly exposed the details of child abuse). Additional symptoms are: recurrent, involuntary, and intrusive distressing memories of the traumatic event, recurrent distressing dreams in which the content and/or affect of the dream are related to the traumatic event, dissociative reactions (e.g., flashback) in which the individual feels or acts as if the traumatic event were recurring, intense or prolonged psychological distress at exposure to internal or external cues that symbolize or resemble an aspect of the traumatic event, marked physiological reactions to internal or external cues that symbolize or resemble an aspect of the traumatic event, and a persistent avoidance of stimuli associated with traumatic event. There may be avoidance of or efforts to avoid distressing memories, thoughts, or feelings about or closely associated with the traumatic event, avoidance of or efforts to avoid external reminders (people, places, conversations, activities, object, situations) that rouse distressing memories, thoughts, or feelings about or closely associated with traumatic event. Additional symptoms may include: irritable behavior and angry outbursts typically expressed as verbal or physical aggression toward people or objects, reckless or self-destructive behavior, hypervigilance, exaggerated startle response, problems with concentration, disturbance difficulty falling or staying asleep or restless sleep, the disturbance causes clinically significant distress or impairment in social, occupational, or other important areas of functioning.

Case Description

Michelle R. is an unmarried 52-year-old woman. While on vacation in the Poconos, she was abruptly awakened in the night by an unidentified male, beaten, and raped. She entered the center of Service to Rape Victims Program in crisis three months later. Michelle's presenting problem included extreme feelings of anger and periods of panic during the night. She was experiencing eating and sleeping disturbances and periodic flashbacks of the attack, all common to rape trauma syndrome. The symptom that led Michelle to seek treatment was an uncontrollable flashback during which she reported she could actually feel the weight of the rapist's body on top of her and still smell him.

Michelle was masculine in appearance. She wore no makeup, her hair was cropped short, and her fingernails were cut straight across, causing even her hands to appear mannish. Michelle sat with her legs apart, leaned forward, rested her hands on her knees, and spat anger with every word during the first sessions. Her anger was directed at everyone. Her venom had alienated many of her friends and her job was in jeopardy because of displacement of her angry feelings onto her coworkers.

Michelle had never seen her assailant. He woke her as he clubbed her on the head, causing bleeding, while he was threatening to kill her. Michelle believed him and her eyes avoided his face at all times in order to survive. It was as though as a survivor, she was unable to fix the feelings of anger and hate on a particular face. To complicate matters, the police had arrested a black male several months later for a similar crime and were trying to tie the two cases together. Michelle was even unsure of the men's race.

The initial focus of the crisis intervention was to enable Michelle to focus her anger on an appropriate object or person. For Michelle, this became the motel in which the assault occurred. The lack of appropriate locks and the absence of a telephone became the basis for a lawsuit.

Several sessions later, Michelle began to feel that she was making progress. Her anger with the world had subsided considerably, and she appeared to be functioning at a level comparable to that prior to her assault. It was at this point in treatment that someone knocked at her door at 1:00 A.M., and her world fell apart. She reported that she grabbed an 8-inch knife, and in a panic, waited near the door. It was not until her landlord called at the door that she was able to move. She screamed at him for frightening her. She then reported that she sat on her bed, knife in hand, clutching her knees, for over an hour before the taste of fear in her mouth left and she was able to put the knife down.

Michelle feared her world would never be safe again. She discussed her deceased mother frequently and expressed a longing for the comfort and safety of the past. The focus of sessions in this short-term type of counseling revolved around exploring how safe her world was before the attack and the manner in which she negotiated her surroundings at that time as opposed to after the attack. Achieving insight into the fact that the world is not less safe now, nor was it entirely safe before, Michelle was able to call on her inner strength, She drove to New York to meet a friend and gradually became more confident in both familiar and unfamiliar situations.

What Does Post Traumatic Stress Syndrome Look Like?

Individual reactions to stress vary considerably, but when stress is prolonged or intense, it often brings about some pattern of reaction that includes one or more of the following characteristics (Davidson 1978, Dubos 1965, Horowitz 1976, Selye 1976).

Affective reactions

The most common reaction to severe, sudden stress is *anxiety*. This may occur during the period of stress or some time afterward. In addition to anxiety, specific fears of things or events related to the stress (for example, fear of driving automobiles after an accident) may also result. After a stressful event, the individual may become and remain depressed for a considerable period of time. Depending on the individual and the situation, this depression may be intense or mild and may be accompanied by disturbing thoughts, physical complaints, and guilt. Stress may also leave the person more vulnerable to other minor stressors and irritations. Perhaps the most serious damage done by stress-induced irritability is that people often think that minor irritations are the cause of their anger rather than recognizing them as the precipitating factor. The minor irritants are so much the focus of attention that the real cause, stress, often goes unnoticed.

Cognitive reactions

Under intense stress, individuals sometimes find it difficult to concentrate or think clearly. This effect of stress on concentration often leads to accident proneness. After the stress has receded, unpleasant recollections of the event may intrude in thoughts, sometimes repeatedly (Becker et al. 1973).

Biological reactions

Stress sets off an automatic physiological reaction through the sympathetic nervous system that prepares the body for a "fight or flight" response. Blood is diverted from the skin and digestive system to the crucial skeletal muscles; heart rate, blood pressure, and respiratory rates increase in order to better supply the body with oxygen; adrenaline is released; muscles are tensed; and so on. These reactions, while perhaps adaptive hundreds of years ago, are not adaptive in today's society. People are generally not able to fight or run from stressors facing them today. As a result, physiological arousal is often useless and may even be harmful.

When stress is intense, especially when it is prolonged, over arousal can result in a variety of problems, including migraine headaches, urinary and bowel dysfunction, muscle aches, sleeplessness, trembling, and increased menstrual discomfort. Excessive arousal also commonly produces high blood pressure and releases blood fats that may contribute to heart disease (Ursin et al. 1978). Whether these physiological symptoms will occur, and their seriousness if they do occur, depend on the severity and duration of the stress and on the individual psychological constitution of the person involved.

In addition, people often react to stress through changes in what they eat and drink They may eat more or less than usual and often will consume more alcohol, caffeine, tranquilizers, tobacco, or other drugs. It is clear that the drugs counteract the effects of stress to some extent. Overeating may accomplish the same thing by distracting the eater or even by lowering arousal by diverting blood from the brain (Selye 1976). At other times, stress can produce a loss of appetite.

Other reactions

Stress reactions may affect other behavioral dimensions. Severely stressful events can bring about a brief period of "irrational" or "bizarre" behavior. However, such reactions are infrequent and are usually transient.

Not all reactions to stress are maladaptive. Stress can call forth bravery, corporation, and our best coping strategies. In floods and fires, some men and women risk their lives to save others rather than flee in panic.

Disasters, enemies, and other stressors often bring people together and a common cause that allows them to forget minor animosities. Many factors influence reactions to stress.

Intensity and duration of stress

In general, the more intense or prolonged the stressful event, the more serious the stress reaction will be. The intensity of the traumatic reaction also seems to be dependent on the suddenness of the event and the degree to which the situation is life threatening. Events such as the death of a spouse or loss of a job are more likely to produce serious stress reactions than a cancelled vacation (Rabkin and Stuening 1976).

Presence of other stress

Each source of stress is assumed not only to produce its own reactions in the individual but also to make the individual more vulnerable to other stresses. The studies of Homes and Rahe (1967), show a link between serious illness and the number of stress events in an individual's life which provides some evidence for this belief.

Prior experience and forewarning of stress

Stress reactions are generally more severe and intense when an individual has had no prior experience with the particular stress or with similar events, and when the individual has had no warning of the stress (Cassel 1970). Michelle never had a concern or worry that the world was not safe. She felt the motel she was staying at was safe and never gave it a second thought. The farthest thing on her mind was that someone may break in.

Characteristics of the individual

Some individual characteristics and circumstances have been identified that appear to typify the people most likely to react strongly to stress. A survey conducted at the University of Chicago and the National Institute for Mental Health (Uhlenhuth et al. 1974) suggests that individuals who are young, female, white, Protestant, of lower socioeconomic status, and living alone tend to experience more severe reactions to stress than others. However, there appears to be individual differences with regard to how people react to stress. Psychologists also often speak of the differences among individuals in their abilities to cope with stress and in their tolerance for stress (Dohrenwend and Dohrenwend 1969). Because these terms are often not operationally defined there is little research to help specify what the components of coping and tolerance are and to determine if they differ in some meaningful way. Research has demonstrated, however, that some individuals chronically react more intensely to stress than others (Glass and Singer 1972, Golin 1974, Horowitz et al. 1973). It is difficult to determine whether this reaction stems from genetic or other causes, or some unknown combination.

Social support

A clear relationship is apparent between the magnitude of the stress reaction and the presence of social support, which can be defined as satisfying relationships with friends and/or family (Habif and Lahey 1979). Individuals who live alone are much more likely than those who live with families to react to intense stress with serious illness or behavior disorders (Webb and Collette 1975).

Personal control

An additional factor influencing the severity of stress reactions is the degree to which the individual can predict what controls the stress events. Symptoms of stress may persist because the person's customary sense of self-confidence and mastery has been badly undermined. The world, which previously seemed at least reasonably safe and predictable, has now become an untrustworthy place. Now that the stressful event has occurred, the victim is continually on the alert for new threats (Krupnick and Horowitz 1981). In Michelle's case, a knock on her door in the middle of the night frightened her so much that she grabbed a knife and could not go back to sleep for over an hour. At the same time, however, the person feels somewhat "shaky," no longer sure of being able to cope with any situation that might arise.

Stress takes a toll on the body. It causes the pituitary and adrenal glands to over secrete their hormones and throws the nervous system out of balance. It disrupts the individual's efforts to preserve a sense of homeostasis (Cannon 1929, 1932). When the mind is stressed, so too is the body, and the effects are presumably all the more powerful when the stress is unusually intense.

Once all these vital functions have become altered, the body may not return to its former, comparatively tranquil, well-balanced state. The nervous system may continue to overreact for considerable period after the traumatic event.

How Does Post Traumatic Stress Syndrome Feel?

Like phobias, post-traumatic stress disorder is precipitated by specific events. The object or events that set off the phobia are quite commonplace; for example, crowds, embarrassment, cats, illness, and so on. The precipitant of post-traumatic stress disorder, in contrast, is a catastrophic event *beyond* the normal range of human suffering - for example, an earthquake, a rape, combat or imprisonment in a concentration camp, etc. Three symptoms that result from the catastrophe are: (1) numbness in experiencing the world, (2) reliving the trauma in memory and in dreams, and (3) symptoms of anxiety. Anxiety symptoms include: excessive arousal, hyper alertness, poor concentration, memory impairment, and phobic avoidance of situations that are reminders of the trauma. In addition, the individual may be wracked with guilt about surviving the catastrophe when others did not. For Michelle, she experienced many symptoms. Michelle would have flashbacks and be awoken in the middle of the night with panic. She became consumed with so much anger that she began to alienate her friends and put her job in jeopardy.

The Client's Dilemma

The catastrophe that brings about post-traumatic stress disorder need not be experienced en masse, as is the case in flood, war, and concentration camp confinement; it can be solitary. Rape is perhaps one of the most common such catastrophes in modern American society. The rape situation itself involves severe psychological and physiological reactions on the part of the victim - reactions that reveal the shock and trauma of the event. Psychologically, the victim experiences feelings of anger, terror, exhaustion, racing thoughts, worry, shame, humiliation, helplessness, and fear. Physiologically, victims experience common fear reactions: racing heartbeat, rapid breathing, shaking and trembling, as well as pain (Veronen et al. 79). A person's reaction to rape looks very much like post-traumatic stress syndrome and has been called *rape trauma syndrome* (Burgess and Holmstrom 1979).

Most power-oriented and anger rapes result in extreme trauma for the victims. The reactions can be divided into two phases: the *acute* (disorganization) and the *long-term* (reorganization). The acute phase begins immediately following the raping and may continue for hours, days and often several weeks. The acute phase is characterized by severe disorganization of one's life, accompanied by strong psychological and physiological reactions. In the hours immediately after the attack, the victim experiences a variety of emotions, including shock, disbelief, fear, anger, and extreme anxiety. Although these reactions tend to be the same for almost all victims, the outward behavior may be *expressive* (releasing feelings through crying, smiling, restlessness, or tenseness). In the *controlled* reaction, the victim will generally appear subdued and matter of fact. Her feelings are constricted and inhibited.

Physiological reactions in the acute phase include the physical trauma of being beaten, general soreness from the attack, and muscle tension including headaches, fatigue, and severe sleep disturbances. Gastrointestinal problems are common in the form of stomach pains, loss of appetite, and nausea from anti-pregMichelle medication and from the attack itself. Genitourinary problems are also frequent, including vaginal discharge, itching, burning upon urination, and general vaginal pain. Some physical symptoms may be due to the assault itself and not to the emotional trauma. Injury such as bruises, abrasions, and vaginal or rectal tears require a period of healing.

After the initial shock or disbelief begins to fade, rape victims typically experience deep feelings of fear, anger, and anxiety. Some victims appear hysterical, others try to mask their horror with a calm façade. Many are in terror that the rapist will return. Some extend their fear to all strangers or situations. At this time, the victims need to talk about the experience to try to make sense of their horror, to be reassured that they are not alone and are not still prey to the assailant, and to make them feel that they are still valued and cared for by their friends and loved ones.

The acute phase continues for several weeks after the attack, and feelings of humiliation, fear, embarrassment, anger, revenge, self-blame, and concern about future physical violence are common. The fear experienced by victims is a central part of the rape trauma. Even though these reactions diminish greatly after about 3 months, there still remains a core of fear and anxiety concerning many previously routine aspects of social life. Some victims never lose their fear in any situation in which there is the potential that they might be treated aggressively or in which they might lose control.

Next, the victim experiences symptoms that strongly resemble reactions to other scenarios, for example; floods, combat, and concentration camp confinement; particularly anxiety and reliving the rape. Physical symptoms also appear - inability to fall asleep or sudden awakening, stomach pains, genitourinary disturbances, and tension headaches. Persons/victims who had suddenly been awakened by the rapist found that they would awake each night, at about the same time the attack had occurred, screaming from rape nightmares. Dreams and nightmares of the rape continue for a long time, with one third of the victims reporting terrifying rape dreams.

Like flood victims, rape victims startle easily in response to even minor episodes, such as being alone. In addition, fear, depression, humiliation, embarrassment, anger, and self-blame became dominant emotions, particularly fear of violence and death. Like the victims of flood and concentration camp confinement, these victims sometime develop phobias. People who had been attacked indoors develop phobias of the indoors, and those who had been attacked outdoors develop phobias of the outdoors.

Even though the extreme fear and anxiety reactions of the acute phase diminish three to six months after the attack, they are still very much present. Nightmares are common and fear of places and situations suggestive of the rape are frequent (Kilpatrick et al. 1979, Veronen et al. 1979). The reason for these fears is that a very crucial learning process takes place during the rape. Through classical conditioning, characteristics of the rape situation (activities, body parts, and the person) become associated with the fear and violence experienced. After the rape, similar places, situations, noises, people, and other reminders evoke the same fear and anxiety responses the victim experienced during the rape. One of the very real problems in dealing with rape in the counseling situation is that these situations must be unlearned and removed from the victim's life.

During the *reorganization phase* of rape trauma, severe reactions seem to diminish, but the problems of restoring one's life to normal remain. How quickly and completely the victims reorganize their lives depends on several factors including psychological characteristics, their social support networks (including friends, relatives, spouses, and rape counselors), and the manner in which they were treated as a victim (Burgess and Holmstrom 1978, Atkeson et al. 1982).

In the long term process of reorganization, most victims take action to ensure safety. Feelings of fear and nervousness often continue during the second, long-term reorganization phase. Victims may fear retaliation by the rapist. Women often change their place of residence during this time. Many people who are raped change their telephone numbers, and approximately half of them make trips home to seek support from family members. Half of the victims move. Many of the victims begin to read about rape and write about their experiences. Some become active in rape crisis centers and assist other victims; of these, 70 percent recover in a few months. When contacted four to six years after the rape, three quarters of the victims in this study felt that they had recovered, half of these within a few months and the other half within several years. One quarter of the victims felt that they still have not recovered (Burgess and Holmstrom 1979).

Clinicians have reported two of the long-term consequences that occur more frequently than others; they are difficulty trusting members of the opposite sex and avoidance of interpersonal involvement. Metzger (1976) suggests that in the case of women victims, they see men as protectors and providers and are therefore profoundly affected by the sense of betrayal the rape produces. Survivors of acquaintance rape are especially fearful of men and distrust their ability to judge who is safe. Young women and recently divorced women have the highest incidence of acquaintance rape. In addition to their relationship problems, these women, whose egos may be fragile or immature either developmentally or as a result of their circumstances, are often left with severe, self-concept and self-esteem problems.

Most women are terrified when they are raped, for they are afraid they are going to be killed. Even the minority who do not consider the possibility of death; experience rape as extremely frightening, degrading, and stressful.

Burgess and Holmstrom (1976) found that rape victims tried a variety of coping mechanisms. Before the attack, many got the vague sense that something was wrong - noticed that a man was hanging around and wondered uneasily what he was up to. Reactions to this awareness of impending danger included: trying to escape, memorizing what the man looked like in order to identify him afterward, talking to calm him down, dissuade him, or at least stall for time, bargaining, asserting their rights, threatening, joking; screaming, trying to fight the attacker off, and blowing a rape whistle to attract attention. However, one third of the victims were too frightened to do anything. They were paralyzed by fear, totally overpowered physically, or too shocked by an acquaintance's unexpected behavior to do anything to prevent it.

Women, who have been raped report that they are depressed and afraid, plagued by nightmares and mood swings. The immediate impact of rape brings about a wide variety of reactions. After the extreme fear of a life-threatening situation, the woman may be glad simply to be alive. But they may also feel humiliated, angry, vengeful, embarrassed, or guilty. Their moods may change unpredictably. Thoughts of the attack may haunt them night and day. Many find it hard to eat and sleep and their bodies may be sore all over. According to Resnick et al. and Ellis (1981), depressive symptoms seem to disappear in most rape victims within about four months. Rape continues to disrupt victims' lives for weeks and months afterward. Many women find it difficult to work but feel vulnerable at home. They may change their locks, telephone numbers, and apartments, however, the fear of being attacked again persists. Disturbing dreams, terror at being alone, and paranoid reactions to strangers and even acquaintances make it difficult for victims to feel free and safe anywhere.

Sexual fears are fairly common after rape, and some women are unable to resume normal sexual activity. Rape can precipitate sexual difficulties for the woman. She may have fearful or negative feelings about sexual relations in general, particularly about intercourse. Becker (1984) theorizes that sexual problems are a result of a "two factor" social-learning theory. They explain that the fear and anxiety or negative reaction experienced by the assault survivor at the time of the incident is generalized to other sexual situations, resulting in a conditioned response to avoid or withdraw from sexual activity or inhibit sexual feelings entirely.

Given the sexual focus of the violence and fear in rape, most victims find themselves conditioned by the rape to have certain responses to sexual activity. This figure included 38 percent of people who refrained from sex entirely for at least three months following the rape. Only a small amount of rape victims studied by Burgess and Holmstrom (19 percent) reported no change in sexual activity. Among these women, however, 50 percent reported changes in their responses to sex, including flashbacks, worrying about their partner's reaction, aversion to certain sexual activities, discomfort and pain, difficulty with sexual feelings in general, and lack of orgasmic response. A small number (9 percent) of the victims in this study increased their sexual activity following the rape. Sometimes this increase was an attempt to counter the negative rape experience with positive sexual interaction. In other cases however, the increase reflected a change in sexual self-concept along the lines of abandoning previous sexual values. Burgess and Holmstrom (1979) reported that some women engaged in sexual intercourse with almost any available male, and some began prostitution. The incidence of these reactions is not clear, but they can be assumed to be relatively rare.

Sexual relationships are thus no comfort for these women, for they are usually marred by associations with the rape. Sensitive partners may wait patiently until the woman's fear is gradually replaced by a willing interest in sex, but some insist on asserting their own "sexual rights" immediately, much to the rape victim's distress. Some double-standard husbands have subtlety blamed their wives for what happened and have even divorced them, saying, "I don't know how I could forgive her, although I know it's not her fault" (Renshaw 198, p. 717).

The rape experience affects not only sexual activity, but sexual satisfaction as well. Feldman-Summers and Linder (1979) measured the self-reported sexual satisfaction of rape victims one week before the attack (retrospectively), one week after the rape, and two months after the rape.

They found that for several dimensions of sexuality, sexual satisfaction dropped significantly one week after the attack and then increased slightly in the following two month period. The level of sexual satisfaction two months after the rape was still significantly less than it has been before the rape.

These findings have important implications for helping rape victims recover and regain their previous sexuality. Reentry into sexual interaction is best accomplished gradually, by means of those activities that are not fear-conditioned by rape. This approach allows for positive feelings to be associated with sexual interaction and opens the way for communication with one's partner about fears and anxieties, about life in general and particularly about sex.

Re-entry into sexuality can be a complex and difficult process. In addition to making the decision to resume sexual activity and dealing with her own emotional and physiological responses to sex, the victim is often concerned about her partner's reactions (Burgess and Holmstrom 1979). Common concerns include how her partner feels about the rape itself: Does he think it was her fault? Does he believe her? Does he think she enjoyed it? Does he think she wanted to be raped? She is also anxious about how her partner feels about her. Does he see her as spoiled and undesirable? Does he see her as different? How does he feel about her being sexual with another man? These are all concerns which are frequently difficult for the victim to discuss with her partner, but which may be confronted in the counseling situation in the context of understanding and communication.

The time it takes rape victims to learn to cope with their experience depends on their ego strength, how close and supportive their friends and relatives are able to be, and how health and law enforcement officials treat them as victims. The support, or lack of it, from people around her makes a significant difference in a woman's ability to cope with the trauma of rape. If she decides to report the rape and suffer the additional stress of police, hospital, and court-room procedures, she should be accompanied by an advocate to help her handle the difficulties she most assuredly will encounter.

Short-term rape counseling usually has two major goals. One is to help the victim gain control over the stressful memories of the rape. Confronting the victim directly by talking about what happened tends to dilute the pain and fear they experience. The second goal is to help the victim feel accepting about herself again. Some rape victims may feel that others will reject them. They need supportive people around who will reassure them that they are worthwhile, loved and appreciated. Other women need help with feelings that they have lost control over their emotions. They may feel that it is wrong to express anger and want very much to be emotionally stable again. Others need help with feelings of weakness, helplessness, and insecurity. Women who believe that they were not powerful enough to fight off their assailants may need to feel that they are strong in all situations. Courses in self-defense may restore their sense of physical competence. Also, opportunities to counsel other rape victims may give them a sense of usefulness and accomplishment (Burgess and Holmstrom (1974).

In a later study, Burgess and Holmstrom (1979) found their rape victims differed in their recovery rates and the types of strategies they used. These researchers found that the victims who recovered most rapidly used more adaptive strategies, including positive self-assessment, defense mechanisms of explanation, minimization, suppression, and dramatization. Victims who had not yet recovered used less-adaptive mechanisms, such as negative self-assessments, inaction, substance abuse, and acting on suicidal thoughts.

"Teenage rape trauma syndrome" refers to a pattern of behavior common to some victims after being raped. The syndrome typically has three phases: a phobic phase, followed by a denial phase, followed by a psychosomatic phase. In the phobic phase, the young women demonstrate many fears: fear of leaving the house, fear of strangers, resistance to relationships with the opposite sex, and frequent nightmares that reenact the rape scene. The girls may request tranquilizers or sleeping pills. It is more important, though, for the young woman to be encouraged to talk about her fears and nightmares to her counselor.

In the denial phase, about two months after the rape, these girls begin to socialize again generally denying that the rape continues to trouble them, in spite of evidence to the contrary. This includes persistent nightmares, insomnia, sleeping with a nightlight, and completely avoiding the location of the rape. They may begin to dress sloppily and wear loose fitting clothing. At this point in the therapeutic relationship, these victims may discontinue follow-up care, claiming that they have no need for it.

Later, six to eight months after the rape, these girls enter the psychosomatic phases, complaining of headaches, abdominal pain, or dizzy spells. The time of onset is often vague, and the victim may not inform a new physician that she has been raped.

A rape victim should immediately call a crisis center and a sympathetic friend. Her first priority is to get medical care for injuries and instructions on dealing with possible disease or pregMichelle. The presence of a close friend and a knowledgeable rape crisis counselor will help ensure that the victim receives proper comforting treatment. A rape victim also needs sound advice, without pressure, to make a decision about whether to report the crime to the police and whether to pursue prosecution if the rapist is apprehended. The crime should be reported promptly, and the victim should save all physical evidence, make note of her assailant's characteristics, and obtain a written report of her injuries and laboratory results. A number of counseling modalities have been described that seem to be effective with rape trauma survivors during the first three months following the incident.

The following are general suggestions for counseling teenage rape victims. (1) Offer all adolescent rape victims the opportunity for counseling immediately after the rape or in the near future; (2) Avoid unnecessary repeated descriptions of the details surrounding the rape; (3) Look for signs of suicidal ideation; (4) Be alert to signs of the "teenage rape victim syndrome"; and (5) Offer support in dealing with family community, and police.

For an example of a step-by-step early intervention program for counseling rape survivors, refer to Kilpatrick and colleagues (1979). For further information, write to the National Center for Prevention and Control of Rape, U.S. Department of Health and Human Services, 5600 Fishers Lane, Rockville, Maryland, 20857.

Theories and Explanations for Post Traumatic Stress Syndrome

Ego Psychological

The ego-psychological view is that coping ability and adaptability require a degree of order and predictability (Erikson 1950, 1968, Hartmann 1939, Kardiner and Spiegel 1947). The challenges that one faces must remain within reasonable limits and not overtax existing resources - which, as Erikson describes it, is one's ability to make sense of experience. If these challenges prove too overwhelming or become more than one can bear, then, almost inevitably, one will cease to function normally and begin to become disorganized.

Cognitive Behavioral

Seligman (1975), a cognitive behaviorist, offer a similar explanation. Excessive stress causes individuals to become disturbed because it is uncontrollable and unpredictable. Previous learning is suddenly upset. The connection between what people do and what happens to them has been disrupted.

A great deal of attention has recently been devoted to the topic of preventing maladaptive reactions to stress through *stress inoculations*. The idea involves using cognitive techniques to inoculate persons to stress so that they are better able to deal with difficult life situations. Meichenbaum (1974) has proposed a more elaborate program of cognitive stress inoculation for use with adults under stress. This procedure involves (1) explaining the relationship between stress and anxiety and stress reactions, (2) teaching clients that they can consciously control reactions to stress, (3) teaching progressive muscle relaxation, and (4) giving clients controlled laboratory practice in reacting calmly to stressful films, imagine stressful events, and even unpredictable electric shocks.

Social Learning

More recently, social-learning therapy has been adapted for the treatment of serious acute stress reactions (Sank 1979). In the case of chronic stress, perhaps changing occupations, for example, or seeking marital counseling can help reduce stress (Bourne 1969), Fraser 1973). Learning theorists believe that stress is a reaction to situations in which reinforcement has abruptly become noncontingent. Thus stripped of their usual ability to anticipate and control life events, people give way to feelings of helplessness and fail to cope with normal, everyday stressors.

Systemic View

Systemic treatment has been shown to be effective in treating posttraumatic stress disorder as well as many other issues that are normally viewed as originating and having to do with solely the individual. Posttraumatic stress disorder symptoms may be found in an individual if they have been the only one to endure a traumatic experience, yet the people that closely surround the individual, such as family members, also deal with the effects of the traumatic experience (Allen & Bloom, 1994). Part of the aim in taking the family into consideration in treating individuals diagnosed with PTSD is based on the idea that the individual's trauma "disrupts attachment bonds and severs important internal and external connections" (Allen & Bloom, 1994, p. 430). Furthermore, "The family becomes unable to provide adequately the safety, affect modulation, and training that its members require. Psychological trauma produces not only biological and psychological, but also social wounds, and social wounds require social healing" (Allen & Bloom, p. 430). There are four ways in which families can be affected by trauma which are as follows: "(1) simultaneous effects as when natural disaster hits an entire community; (2) vicarious effects as when a family member is the victim of the trauma, and the response of the other family members results in the experience of trauma, as in hostage situations; (3) chiasmal effects as when the traumatic stress actually "infects" other members of the family; (4) intrafamilial trauma as when the family itself is the source of trauma" (Allen & Bloom, 1994, p. 431).

In order to treat the posttraumatic stress disorder in a systemic context, some considerations must be made. Extensive psychoeducation must be done in the family of choice. This will help with developing a "cognitive framework" that is "trauma based" in order to help reframe the problem within the family's history. In this way, the trauma can be viewed as "a family challenge and survival mission" (Allen & Bloom, 1994, p. 432). If there is any trauma that has been caused by the family system itself, exploring enactments can help the therapist show the family members the roles they are actively playing that contribute to maintaining the posttraumatic stress. In doing so, more productive "scripts" can be created to help guide the family in the respective direction. In addition, therapists can help clients learn how to "self-protect" in session in order for the client to be able to translate this behavior in other instances in his or her life (Allen & Bloom, 1994). Confrontation in instances where traumatic situations have occurred within the family, must be done toward the later stages of therapy when the client is able to tolerate perhaps the loss of attachment that may come along with the confrontation (Allen & Bloom, 1994).

Figley & Figely (2009) state, "Trauma is by nature interpersonal and is, therefore, a systemic entity." According to them, "meaning-making" actually comes from "intimate, relational" contexts (Figley & Figely, 2009). What becomes important in dealing with trauma, is a family that holds the belief that they have the means to be able to have some level of control over whatever traumatic experience occurred. With family members that hold this belief, they are more readily able identify strengths that have come from traumatic incidents and by extension, are better able to move toward recovery (Figley & Figely, 2009).

Amstadter, McCart, & Ruggiero (2007) pointed out that the main areas of intervention with adult PTSD clients are exposure, cognitive therapy, anxiety management, and psychoeducation. So along with cognitive restructuring approaches with the individual for PTSD symptoms, psychoeducation with family members may be helpful in creating more of a safe support network.

In Michelle's case, in addition to cognitive restructuring, Michelle could be seen with some of her more close family members, so if she was unmarried, that might mean her family of origin which could include parents or siblings and perhaps if she was married, she could be seen with her spouse. Reassurance would be a central theme in the process and the family could function as reinforcement. Helping the family to understand Michelle's cognitive processes as well is important so that they may begin to think about ways in which they can assist her rather than struggle with not knowing how to deal with her symptoms as they may appear, even if they decrease.

Therapy Techniques

Until recently, there was a lack of awareness of all the therapeutic alternatives available for those suffering from post-traumatic stress disorder. Due mainly to the mental health movement, clinicians are now more familiar with the problem. Although many victims may not be aware that therapy is available (Katz and Mazur 1979), they can benefit from providers such as walk-in clinics that practice crisis intervention, "rape groups" for Vietnam veterans and rape counseling centers.

Post-traumatic stress disorders develop in people whose sense of control and mastery has been powerfully undermined. The world that once seemed orderly and benign now appears unpredictable and menacing. An extraordinarily threatening experience - or series of incidents - has completely shaken their very identity and sense of self, and their trust in themselves and their ability to cope has been shattered. Whether or not they are explicit about it, most therapists seem to assume that they are helping their traumatized clients regain what they have lost - their self-confidence and ability to cope.

1. Help clients to express their feelings about the terrifying event.

It is most important to bring clients face to face with the traumatizing experience. It is necessary that they express their emotions to achieve some sort of catharsis. Even therapists who are not psychodynamically oriented may unwittingly be providing their clients with some type of emotional release. Discharging tension and anxiety to a comforting and reassuring expert reduces the feelings of terror associated with the traumatizing events.

2. Help clients establish social support systems.

If social support can help prevent post-traumatic stress disorders, it can also help victims recover (Butcher and Maudal 1976). In some situations, the best person to offer such support may be another victim. Clients often report that they originally thought that their symptoms were unusual and that no one else has felt as distressed as they did after ordeal. They are often relieved to discover that others have felt the same way.

3. Help clients to control their symptoms.

After victims have brought their experiences and feelings into the open, their symptoms can be worked through and brought under control. The client's feelings should be explored to a point at which both therapist and client feel comfortable with them. Using triggering situations to enable the client to experience some of the symptoms without losing control and feeling humiliated is helpful. The ability to control both internal and external events at their own discretion can rebuild the client's sense of environmental mastery. Progressive muscle relaxation and systematic desensitization can be employed to relieve anxiety. For a detailed description of these techniques, see Benson 1975, Goldfried and Trier 1974, Jacobson 1938, Mathews and Gelder 1969. A number of studies have also demonstrated that meditation, modified to remove its metaphysical-religious aspects, may be as effective as more formal relaxation techniques (Clopton and Risbrough 1973).

4. Help clients to increase their assertiveness and sense of environmental mastery.

Clients can be trained in assertiveness and other skills that will help them feel less vulnerable. In Michelle's case, resuming her friendships, exploring her social encounters, and moving progressively back into the world all helped her to feel like an active, competent person again. By the end of the twelve sessions offered by the rape counseling program, Michelle had begun to wear makeup and nail polish. Her hairdo was less severe and she wore the color pink to a session for the first time. Although Michelle believed that she was over the worst and that her crisis had passed, one of the coping mechanisms upon which she relied heavily was blocking the memory of her assault.

The knowledge that she would have to relieve the entire event in detail for her lawsuit was sometimes anxiety provoking. She planned to rely on her feelings of hate, anger, and revenge to carry her through her ordeal. Michelle perceived the lawsuit as necessary to her mental health, and she believed that she would be able to utilize the support of her friends to sustain her.

When to Refer

Rape counseling typically does not involve long-term psychotherapy. Most victims need to feel as though they have gained control over the effects of the memories of the rape. They also need to learn to feel comfortable with themselves again. They may fear that others will reject them. Helping them to mobilize a support group is an effective way of enabling them to cope with these feelings.

For other women, however, the impact of the rape is long lasting. These women carry the emotional scars of the rape for years and seem unable to come to terms with the emotional aftermath of the traumatic event. Years later, they may be afraid to venture out of the house or may feel extremely vulnerable when left alone. Others may be very reluctant to enter into an intimate relationship with a member of the opposite sex. For these women, long-term psychotherapy would be more appropriate.

Post-traumatic stress disorder in general often involves short term therapy. Adjustment times typically do not exceed 24 months. Prior levels of functioning should be taken into consideration. Prior to the traumatic event, clients who were high functioning and had adequate coping skills tend to return to their normal level of functioning more readily than those who were not. If, after 6 months of psychotherapy, the client has made little progress, psychiatric evaluation is warranted.

References

Agazarian, Y., & Gantt, S. (2011). Systems-centered Therapy: In Clinical Practice with Individuals, Families and Groups. London: Karnac Books.

Allen, S. N., & Bloom, S. L. (1994). Group and family treatment of post-traumatic stress disorder. *Psychiatric Clinics of North America*, *17*(2), 425-437.

Amstadter, A. B., McCart, M. R., & Ruggiero, K. J. (2007). Psychosocial interventions for adults with crime-related PTSD. *Professional Psychology: Research and Practice*, **38**(6), 640-651.

Atwood, J. D. (1987). *Treatment techniques for common mental disorders* / Joan D. Atwood, Robert Chester. Northvale, NJ: Aronson, c.1987.

American Psychiatric Publishing (2013). Posttraumatic stress disorder. Retrieved from http://www.dsm5.org/Documents/PTSD%20 Fact%20Sheet.pdf

American Psychiatric Association. (2013). Diagnostic and statistical manual of mental disorders (5th ed.). Arlington, VA: American Psychiatric Publishing.

Bernardon, S., & Pernice-Duca, F. (2010). A family systems perspective to recovery from posttraumatic stress in children. *Family Journal*, *18*(4), 349.

Figley, C. R., & Figley, K. (2009). Stemming the Tide of Trauma Systemically: The Role of Family Therapy. *Australian & New Zealand Journal of Family Therapy*, 30(3), 173-183.

Milenković, T., Simonović, M., Stanković, M., & Samardžić, L. (2013). Disturbed family functioning in patients suffering from posttraumatic stress disorder. *Medicinski Glasnik*, *10*(1), 120-125.

Monson, C. M., Macdonald, A., & Brown-Bowers, A. (2012). Couple/ family therapy for posttraumatic stress disorder: Review to facilitate interpretation of VA/DOD Clinical Practice Guideline. *Journal of Rehabilitation Research & Development*, 49(6), 717-728.

Saxe, G. N., Heidi Ellis, B. B., Fogler, J., & Navalta, C. P. (2012). Innovations in Practice: Preliminary evidence for effective family engagement in treatment for child traumatic stress-trauma systems therapy approach to preventing dropout. *Child & Adolescent Mental Health*, *17*(1), 58-61.

Stanković, M., Grbeša, G., Kostić, J., Simonović, M., Milenković, T., & Višnji, A. (2013). A preview of the efficiency of systemic family therapy in treatment of children with posttraumatic stress disorder developed after car accident. *Vojnosanitetski Pregled: Military Medical & Pharmaceutical Journal Of Serbia & Montenegro*, 70(2), 149-154.

Saxe, G. N., Heidi Ellis, B. B., Fogler, J., & Navalta, C. P. (2012). Innovations in practice: Preliminary evidence for effective family engagement in treatment for child traumatic stress-trauma systems therapy approach to preventing dropout. *Child & Adolescent Mental Health*, *17*(1), 58-61.

Chapter 9

Eating Disorders

Michelle Wiley M.A., MFT

What is Anorexia Nervosa and Bulimia and How Do You Recognize These Clients?

The client with *Anorexia Nervosa* loses so much weight by refusing food or by vomiting shortly after eating, that she risks dying of starvation. Sufferers of this disorder typically envision themselves as "fat," no matter how emaciated they really are. Some theorists consider anorexia nervosa to be related to hysterical conversion disorders, however, because of its widespread and often very serious effects on various organ systems, it seems fitting to include it within the psychophysiological category.

According to a number of experts (Bruch 1973, 1978; Rosman et al. 1975; Van Buskirk 1977), anorexia nervosa appears to follow a characteristic course. The typical client grows up in a fairly affluent home where food is plentiful and takes on a magical role. The future client has distinguished herself as a "model" child; obedient, cooperative, bright, and very industrious. She is a child who always obeys her parents' commands. She often empties her plate, to her parents delight. Such children play this role so well that the parents are indulgently content with their ritualistic conformity. These children rarely dare to shed this role, possibly for fear that if they were to do so, their parents will be unable to recognize them.

The parents of these children seem to count on them to maintain the system's stability. It is as though if these children were not obedient, conforming, and well fed, the narcissistic security system of the family would be seriously threatened and the parents would become ridden with anxiety. "Aren't you eating today?" "Don't you feel well?" "Is there anything wrong with you?" The parents of the future anorectic appear to be blind to their child's emotional and physical needs for self-validation. The "pre anorectic" is too good to be true. There appears to be something ominously "driven" about her desire to please. She cannot be satisfied with being good; she must be perfect. She also seems somewhat anxious and phobic, remaining close to home and giving the impression of being strongly attached to her mother.

In addition, the future anorectic often has a history of problems with food. She may always have been a "picky" eater, or (a much more likely possibility) she may always have had trouble controlling her weight and may tend to be slightly overweight. In any event, at some point during adolescence (usually between the ages of 12 and 18), she decides she is too fat and proceeds to go on a diet. Any extra pounds disappear quickly. People compliment her on her altered appearance, telling her how nice and thin she looks. Despite her success, however, the anorectic is convinced that she still is not thin enough and continues to try to lose weight. Gradually and insidiously, her dieting gets completely out of hand and out of control. No matter how gaunt and emaciated she becomes, even if she tips the scale at a meager 70 pounds, the anorectic insists that she is too fat.

At this point her concern with food is an all-consuming obsession. Often she measures out her daily rations in advance. If she happens to take in more than her allowance, she may resort to laxatives or force herself to vomit. She may begin to engage in excessive physical exercise in order to ensure her continued slim state. Strangely enough, until her weight drops dangerously low, the anorectic tends to have enormous energy and adheres to a very active schedule. Even after she has become significantly underweight, she still may be able to maintain a strenuous exercise program.

The typical client is an adolescent female who becomes obsessed with fear of becoming overweight and who then places herself on a rigidly controlled diet, often accompanied by rigorous exercise routines. She proceeds to lose a substantial amount of weight. As she loses weight. She becomes even more frightened of becoming overweight, so she restricts her diet even more. The client is now obsessed with food and its preparation. She may collect recipes and cookbooks, and may even contemplate a career in nutrition. Bizarre habits of hoarding food, cutting food into small pieces, playing with food, and concocting weird food combinations are quite typical behavior of the anorectic female. Although many clients with anorexia also have depressive symptoms and eventually become socially isolated, their thinking, outside of their distorted body perception, is usually not grossly disturbed. They are not suffering from a psychotic disorder.

Bruch (1973) describes three basic symptoms of disordered psychological functioning in primary anorectics. First, there is a disturbance, of delusional proportions, in the individual's body image and self-concept. Even when reduced to a grotesque, pitiful, skeleton like appearance, the anorectic may deny that she is too thin and indeed continue to worry about being too fat. As Arieti (1974a) and Bruch (1978) observe, the adolescent who suffers from this disturbance appears to be somewhat delusional about her body image and the reality associated with it. She may look like a refugee from a concentration camp. She may have grown so weak that she can barely walk from room to room. Yet she continues to insist that the image she sees reflected in the mirror is obese. If asked to show the examiner where she is fat, she will point to some excess fold of skin. Her alarmed family, friends, and physician may plead with her to eat-to no avail. She will eat for no one. The diet she is following utterly dominates her existence, often to the point of threatening her life. It appears as though the diet regimen becomes the instrument through which she can subdue her body and exert some control over her helpless, impotent existence.

Second, there appears to be a disturbance in the accuracy of the perception, or cognitive interpretation, of stimuli arising in the body. Rather than a mere loss of appetite, there is a failure to recognize cues of hunger, a failure similar to that occurring in many obese individuals. The anorectic may also fail to recognize bodily cues indicating fatigue. Despite severe malnutrition, the client may exhibit hyperactivity.

Finally, there is usually a paralyzing sense of ineffectiveness-a feeling of acting only in response to the demands of others, rather than to one's own needs and wishes. This feeling of lack of control is typically masked by a surface negativity and stubborn defiance, which unfortunately, makes treatment difficult. These clients reject their bodies, reject the notion of life through a positive somatic existence, and, reject the notion of death as an inevitable consequence of disregarding their corporal needs.

In anorexia nervosa, eating is reduced to a point at which severe weight loss occurs. Although it was once apparently quite rare, the incidence of this disorder has alarmingly increased in recent years for reasons that remain obscure. It is estimated that approximately 1 percent of women between the ages of 12 and 25- approximately 260,000 women-suffer from anorexia nervosa. Anorexia nervosa is typically a disease of young women. It occurs in women nine times as frequently as in men, and although it may appear at any age, its onset is typically in adolescence or early adulthood.

Anorexia nervosa can be fatal. In a survey of studies, estimates of the death rate ranged up to 19 percent, with about half of the studies reporting a death rate below 5 percent. Since it can be fatal, anorexia nervosa should always be regarded as a clinical emergency, requiring prompt therapeutic intervention.

A study released in November 2013, published in *JAMA Pediatrics*, surveyed 5,527 teenage males nationwide from 1999 to 2011. The results indicated that 17.9% of teenage males were extremely concerned about their physique — and more likely to engage in dangerous behaviors such as alcohol and drug abuse. Though women with eating disorders tend to be concerned with thinness, men become concerned about their muscularity and athletic build. The survey said 2.4% of men experienced anxiety about muscularity and used supplements, growth hormone derivatives and/or steroids to control their body shape. Most estimates indicate that 1 out of 10 people with an eating disorder is male. It is possible that the ratio is smaller given that the diagnostic criteria for eating disorders are designed about women. So although uncommon, it is possible that a therapist will see a male in therapy for an eating disorder (Newlon, November 2013).

Bulimia, the second eating disorder discussed in this chapter, is characterized by recurrent episodes of binge-eating. These episodes appear uncontrollable. The bulimic individual consumes large amounts of food in a short period of time, which leads to feelings of shame and revulsion. Following binge eating, most clients attempt to rid themselves of calories by inducing vomiting or abusing laxatives. The use of purgatives is not deemed mandatory in diagnosing bulimia in the DSM-III criteria. Johnson and Larson (1982) found that 74 percent of respondents to their magazine survey met the criteria for the psychiatric diagnosis of bulimia. Of the bulimics, 6 percent were also classifiable as anorectic. The respondents tended to have never married (70 percent), were white (97 percent), had some college education (84 percent) and had a median age of 22 years. Although 62 percent were of normal weight when they responded, 43 percent reported weights during adolescence (at 15 years of age) that were classified as overweight. Binge eating usually began at around 18 years of age.

Of those who binged, almost half reported doing so at least once a day. The average number of calories consumed during a typical binge was estimated at approximately 4800, usually in the form of sweets (94 percent). Of those who reported purging (71 percent), 69 percent vomited, 39 percent used laxatives, and 26 percent used both. These bulimic women reported normal sexual interest and experience but unusually low frequencies of alcohol, drug, and cigarette use. What was surprising about this study was the apparent widespread incidence of bulimia among ostensibly normal young women.

Most individuals with bulimia or binge eating who present themselves for therapy are of normal weight. This pattern of binge eating may also occur in clients who are anorectic and in clients who are substantially overweight. While dietary habits of the two groups are dissimilar, there is substantial overlap between the two syndromes. About half of the clients currently hospitalized for anorexia nervosa are also bulimic. A significant number of normal-weight bulimics have histories of anorexia nervosa. Thus, the disorders of excessive food deprivation and consumption appear linked in some way.

Bulimics are usually people who are frightened, lonely, and emotionally unfulfilled. Characteristically, the binge-purge cycle is a substitute method of dealing with poor self-esteem, depression, and a deep sense of inadequacy that they are unable to cope with more directly. It is important to note that in some cases, the purge part of the cycle is the real end sought. The binge eating, in these cases, is associated with shame, guilt, and panic. Purging is associated with the release of these emotions.

Although individuals with anorexia, bulimia and binge eating disorder frequently report feelings of failure and isolation, it is basically their preoccupation with food and their association with it that often leads to the isolation and loneliness. Their low self-esteem puzzles their friends, family, and teachers since, in other areas, they are often successful in their accomplishments. They harbor overwhelming fears that they will fail or be rejected.

Binge eating disorder (BED) is characterized by insatiable cravings that can occur any time of the day or night, usually secretive, and filled with shame. Bingeing is often rooted in poor body image, use of food to deal with stress, low self-esteem and tied to dysfunctional thoughts.

More common than anorexia nervosa or bulimia, binge eating disorder occurs in 1 out of 35 adults in the U.S. This translates to 3-5% of women (about 5 million) and 2 % of men (3 million). Although eating disorders are typically twice as common in women, BED seems to be an "equal opportunity" disorder, with 40% occurrence in men. Data also indicates the BED does not discriminate against race. BED is as common in African American women as it in Caucasian and Hispanic women (www.anad.org).

BED does not exist in the presence of anorexia nervosa or bulimia. Although there are similar characteristics between those with bulimia and BED, those with BED do not purge. There are no compensatory mechanisms associated with the binge to get rid of the calories, so individuals with BED are more likely to be overweight or obese, while patients with bulimia may be underweight, normal weight or overweight.

Symptoms: Anorexia Nervosa

Diagnostic Criteria 307.1

Anorexics suffer from a lack of of energy intake relative to requirements, leading to a significantly low body weight in the context of age, sex, developmental trajectory, and physical health; there is an intense fear of gaining weight or of becoming fat, or persistent behavior that interferes with weight gain, even though at a significantly low weight; there is a persistent lack of recognition of the seriousness of the current low body weight.

Bulimia Nervosa

Diagnostic Criteria 307.51 (F50.2)

With this disorder, there are episodes of binge eating. An episode of binge eating is characterized by both of the following: eating, in a discrete period of time (e.g. within any 2 hour period), an amount of food that is definitely larger than what most individuals would eat in a similar period of time under similar circumstances; a sense of lack of control over eating during the episode (e.g. a feeling that one cannot stop eating or control what or how much one is eating); inappropriate compensatory behavior in order to prevent weight gain, such as self-induced vomiting; misuse of laxatives, diuretics, or other medications; fasting; or excessive exercise.

Binge-Eating Disorder Diagnostic Criteria 307.51 (F50.8)

In this case, there are recurrent episodes of binge eating. An episode of binge eating is characterized by both of the following: eating, in a discrete period of time (e.g. within any 2 hour period), an amount of food that is definitely larger that what most people would eat in a similar period of time under similar circumstances; a sense of lack of control over eating during the episode (e.g. a feeling that one cannot stop eating or control what or how much one is eating); eating much more rapidly than normal; eating until feeling uncomfortably full, eating large amounts of food when not feeling physically hungry, eating alone because of feeling embarrassed by how much one is eating, feeling disgusted with oneself, depressed, or very guilty afterward, including marked distress regarding binge eating is present.

Case Description For Anorexia Nervosa

Janine W. is an 18 year old girl, who upon entering therapy, weighed 62 pounds. Originally approximately 20 pounds overweight, she decided to diet. After losing the initial 20 pounds, she decided that she was still too fat and continued to lose weight. Upon entering therapy, the only food she would eat was ice cream, which she would eat only when no one was watching. Her appearance was pitiful. She was a small girl to begin with, only about 5 feet tall. Her small frame combined with her thinness created a look of total fragility, as though even the slightest touch would be dangerous to her.

She was a good student, always getting A's. Her career goal was to be a graphic designer. Throughout the period of her weight loss, she never missed a day of school, insisting that there was nothing wrong with her. If the therapist pressed her about her weight - or the lack of it - she would point to a place on her thigh or buttock where she would find a fold of skin, proof of her "battle of the bulge." Janine had a lot of friends with whom she seemed to interact appropriately. When asked how they felt about her loss of weight, she said they accepted it or did not even notice it because she always wore very loose clothing.

Janine's family situation was poor. Her father was a carpet installer who worked long hours. Her mother, who ran his business from home, spent most of the day answering telephones and keeping the books. For the major portion of Janine's early life, she was responsible for taking care of her brother while her mother answered telephones. The two children were told to go play in the basement, where they would be out of earshot of the phones. They then had to amuse themselves all day, lest they anger their mother. At lunch time, their mother would quickly run downstairs to feed them and then return upstairs to continue answering the phones. Janine had full responsibility for caring for her younger brother. At the time Janine was only 4 years old and her brother was 2- an unusually young age for so much responsibility. This pattern continued for many years, until the children were old enough to fend for themselves. So for most of Janine's childhood years, she was responsible for her younger brother, forced to focus on his needs rather than on her own.

When Janine was about 16 years old, she was about 20 pounds overweight and decided to go on a diet. She still felt fat after she lost the initial 20 pounds, so she continued to diet. Early on, she learned to make herself vomit. If she ate more than she felt she should have, she would excuse herself from the table, go into the bathroom, and stick her finger down her throat and vomit. It was difficult the first time, but after that it was quite easy. She used this technique any time she happened to "eat by accident."

It soon became obvious that there was a problem. Janine's parents encouraged her to eat, but she refused. Every time she refused their requests that she eat, she felt a sense of victory-like she had won a major battle. She felt that she had finally gotten even with her mother; on a conscious level, however, she was not aware of the meaning of the battle and its overwhelming intensity. Her parents at one point took her to see a psychiatrist. The psychiatrist asked her many questions, but once again Janine refused to answer. The psychiatrist told her parents that if she would not speak, he could not help her. Once again Janine felt victorious. She had won, and they had lost! She walked through life existing only for these secret little victories, losing more and more weight until finally her life was in danger. However, these small victories seemed to add only temporarily to her feelings of power, resulting eventually in her distorted self-worth.

Case Description for Bulimia Nervosa

Elaine K. is a 29 year old overweight, drably dressed young woman who came in for therapy accompanied by her mother. She had been binge eating for the last 3 months and had done so episodically for the last 10 years. Elaine had been in and out of treatment with numerous prestigious therapists, without success, for the preceding 5 years. During that time, she had lost three jobs in her career as a registered nurse, usually due to an uncontrollable need to binge.

Elaine's binge eating was followed by induced vomiting. After vomiting, Elaine felt humiliated, shamed, out of control of her life, and "disgustingly fat." Her weight varied from within normal range to being 50 to 60 pounds in excess. She was using large quantities of syrup of ipecac to induce vomiting in order to rid herself of the calories from the ingested food. She had developed a high tolerance for this emetic drug.

A pattern of behavior typically associated with Elaine's binge-purge pattern was to call her mother and demand help in controlling her need to binge. The help she requested was that her mother place her in a motel room without money or clothing in order to prevent her from compulsively seeking food. In spite of these precautions, however, she would find ways to escape from these external restrictions and would proceed to steal food from nearby stores; her objective was to obtain high calorie "junk food." Unconsciously, she needed to lose the inner tension from her primitive, rage-filled impulses, which threatened her ego stability. After her secret eating orgies, she would vomit, and then feel guilty, depressed, worthless and hopeless.

Elaine was brought up in a middle class Catholic family, the middle child of three girls. She viewed herself as the "ugly duckling" in the family constellation, when compared with a bright, very pretty older sister. She blamed many of her difficulties on her mother, who forced her to transfer from a public school to the parochial school where she worked as a school nurse. She believed that her family and others always drew attention to her unattractiveness and lack of success, and unfavorably compared her with her older sister.

Despite her academic achievement- she had graduated with a B average from a respected university school of nursing- Elaine felt inferior in her ability to perform professional tasks when she compared herself with her colleagues. She had obtained employment at several teaching hospitals but had left each without notice. Sometimes she was terminated, usually due to problematic interpersonal relationships with coworkers or roommates in the nursing quarters. She would then feel rejected, unaccepted, and angry, and would seek solace in her binge eating. She would subsequently withdraw from her social milieu.

Elaine attributed her difficulties to her belief that she was not the "star" that her sister was. In fact, during the course of her treatment, her mother had allowed her sister to return home because she was in the process of a difficult divorce and was feeling very depressed. Elaine reacted with intense rage and envy. How could her mother do this to her when she was desperately trying to gain control over herself and her life? She had very little empathy for her sister, nor any real understanding of why her mother might be sympathetic to her sister's plight. Once again, Elaine felt second best to her sister.

Case Description for Binge Eating Disorder

(Journal of Addiction Medicine, March 2010)

A 48-year old African American woman presented for treatment for binge eating and weight loss. She presented for treatment following a recent routine physical examination during which her primary care physician noted concerns about her increasing weight. The physician recommended that she try to lose weight but did not provide any specific or further guidance. In light of her previous "failed" experiences with commercial weight loss programs, she decided to seek treatment at a university-based program. At initial evaluation, she was 64 inches tall and weighed 230 pounds yielding a body mass index (BMI) of 39.5, which reflects obesity. She had moderately elevated blood pressure and high cholesterol but was otherwise in good health. The patient completed college and a master's degree in education and had been employed as a special education teacher in the same job for 11 years. She lived with her husband of 24 years, and one of her two adult children. She reported that her relationships with her husband and family were good, that her job was enjoyable and rewarding, and that she had a good circle of close relationships.

The patient reported an onset of overweight during adulthood. She reported having been involved in sports throughout childhood, and although she viewed herself as 'big-boned', she did not have body image concerns nor did she recall feeling dissatisfied with her weight or shape when younger. She denied any significant dieting behaviors until age 29. She reported maintaining a weight of approximately 150 pounds (BMI = 25.7) until age 28, at which age she became pregnant with her second child. She reported that she never fully lost the 'baby weight' and subsequently began to gradually gain weight throughout her 30s despite numerous dieting efforts. She reported a rapid weight gain of approximately 25 pounds in the past 6 months.

The patient reported an onset of "eating binges" at approximately age 16. The binge eating began soon after she began babysitting for neighborhood children. She estimated that she would engage in binge eating approximately 1-2 times per month which occurred during times that she babysat at night and had access to assorted snack foods. During those times she would 'load up on junk food' that the family had provided. She recalled that she would eat chips, cookies, and brownies "non-stop," and that these eating episodes often lasted throughout the evening. She recalled feeling a loss of control during these episodes and stated that she would continue to eat despite not feeling physically hungry and that she would not stop until feeling physically ill. She reported that she was very embarrassed and secretive about these eating behaviors. She also recalled feeling embarrassed when worried that it was likely that the missing food was apparent to the family for whom she was babysitting. She denied any history of extreme inappropriate weight control or purging behaviors such as self-inducing vomiting or misusing laxatives.

The patient reported infrequent and sporadic binge eating throughout her late teens and early 20s, estimating a frequency of once per month which tended to correspond with social functions. During her 30s, however, the frequency of her binge eating increased considerably and became more regular except during periods of dieting efforts. The patient reported that she had enrolled in commercial weight loss programs approximately five different times, and had, in addition, tried to follow multiple self-help diets. She reported that when she was following a weight loss plan, she could successfully lose approximately 10 pounds, but that she would 'hit a wall' and discontinue after about one month of dieting. She reported that in-between diets, her binge eating would resume at a frequency of 2 to 3 times per week, and persist at that level until the next dieting attempt. The patient reported that she had not engaged any formal dieting in the past 18 months, although she frequently skipped meals in an effort to reduce her weight.

The patient noted an increase in binge eating frequency approximately six months ago, corresponding with her mother's hospitalization and rapid physical decline. The patient was the primary caregiver for her mother, and noted that the months preceding her mother's death were extremely stressful. She reported that her binge eating increased in frequency to 3 to 4 times per week during her mother's illness, and increased to 6 to 7 times per week following her mother's death.

The patient described her typical binge episode as starting with an evening meal and extending for several hours. Her daily pattern of eating was to skip breakfast, and to consume a standard school cafeteria lunch at 11:30 a.m. She would then not eat again until preparing the evening meal, at which point she would 'graze' while cooking. The patient reported that most nights she would eat a 'normal' meal with her family, consisting of 5-6 ounces of meat, 2 or 3 types of vegetables, and bread. However, she would then eat the 'leftovers' while cleaning up after the meal, such that overall she would have consumed the equivalent of two full meals. She would then eat various foods throughout the rest of the evening until bedtime. During these episodes, she would alternate between salty and sweet snacks. One example binge episode, occurring approximately 30 minutes after the evening meal and spanning the two hours before bedtime, included: a roll of Ritz crackers with 6 ounces of cheese, 2 doughnuts, 4 handfuls of Chex mix, and ½ of a large (12 oz.) Cadbury candy bar.

The patient reported that she had recently quit smoking 'cold turkey' and had successfully maintained abstinence for four months. She reported quitting smoking following the death of her mother because she died of cancer. She quit smoking without any professional help and without the use of any nicotine replacements or medications to assist with the smoking cessation.

In terms of her smoking history, the patient reported that she began smoking at age 18, that she had successfully quit smoking upon becoming pregnant at age 24, but resumed when she returned to work 11 years ago. She reported a daily smoking frequency of 15 to 20 cigarettes per day. She reported no serious efforts to stop smoking during the past 11 years prior to this recent period of complete abstinence. The patient reported that since quitting smoking, she has experienced more frequent and intense urges to binge eat, and that in the few weeks prior to intake the urges to smoke had increased in frequency and intensity. She reported urges to smoke primarily in the evenings.

What Does An Eating Disorder Look Like?

Several psychological characteristics have been noted among anorectic clients. They are usually from upper socioeconomic levels. Onset of the disorder is confined largely to the adolescent or young adult years. A history of unusual or bizarre eating habits is quite common. A distorted body image, particularly in overestimation of their physical dimensions, is almost universal. These patients are usually described as sensitive, dependent, introverted, anxious, perfectionistic, selfish, and unusually stubborn. They almost invariably report little or no interest in sex. They have typically been extremely conscientious in regard to conventional duties, such as school work. They sometimes feel that eating blunts their intellectual acuity.

Janine presented the typical case of anorexia nervosa. Her physical sense of herself was so distorted that it was almost delusional. Even when she weighed less than 65 pounds, she truly believed that she was overweight. Her defiance of her mother was remarkable. It was perhaps true that the only way Janine could become a person separate from her mother was to direct all her energy toward not eating - the exact thing that her mother was demanding. By doing the opposite, Janine made a statement: "I can't be you, because you want me to eat. I am not eating; therefore I am separate." Eating meant giving in to passivity and receptivity, the qualities from which Janine needed to dissociate herself in order to free herself from feeling impotent. She had to resort to these drastic measures in order to free herself from her mother's consuming control. In this sense, Janine's anorexia represented a healthy symptom-a drastic attempt to individuate herself from her intrusive mother.

It is not unusual for anorectic girls to describe their mothers in very unflattering terms. During childhood and latency, the parent's insensitivity, criticism, and interference in all aspects of the child's life prevents her from developing vital feelings of her own that accrue to a self-affirming experience. The girl is therefore not able to differentiate and identify with a loving, appropriate, caring parent.

Janine saw her mother as excessively dominant, intrusive, overbearing, and ambivalent. While it is possible that Janine's mother responded in these ways because of her concern over her daughter's failing health, it is much more likely that her domineering traits contributed to the etiology of anorexia. For the major portion of Janine's life, her behavior was controlled by her mother. All of Janine's life decisions were made by her mother. At age 16, it was time for Janine to begin preparing to go to Art College, a dream she had since she was a little girl. Psychologically, though, Janine could not have handled a life that involved independent decision making. She had not achieved a separate identity. Her mother had always told her what to do; how could she know what to do by herself? Unfortunately, Janine had not achieved an autonomous identity and had no confidence in her own ability to function as a separate being.

As it occurred in Janine's situation, anorexia often begins when life changes are requiring new or unfamiliar skills about which the person feels inadequate; such changes include going off to college, getting married, or even reaching puberty. The characteristic conflict activated by such events seems to be, on the one hand, a desire to achieve autonomy, and on the other, a pronounced fear of obtaining the status of an independent adult. Food then becomes the phobic and obsessional context in which this drama is played out.

Not infrequently, the disorder begins as an extension of the ritual of normal dieting, which is very common in young women. What distinguishes the normal dieter from one who converts dieting into a dangerous flirtation with disaster still remains a mystery. In any event, there seems to be increasing acknowledgement that the syndrome of anorexia may be the extreme end of a continuum. Thus it is somewhat reasonable to speak of a pre anorectic state, in which individuals have extreme, but not yet self-injurious, aversions to food.

Anorexia in young women is thought by some psychoanalytic theorists to represent sexual conflicts, possibly involving fear of impregnation, and to function as a stratagem for avoiding the adult sexual role. Whether or not this theory holds true, anorexia does indeed severely modify the female sexual characteristics; breasts and hips shrink dramatically, and amenorrhea is common. In Janine's case, her feelings about losing her breasts and menstrual cycle were negligible, possibly indicating that other factors were operating. It was the therapist's sense that Janine's overriding wish was too unconsciously "get even" with her mother, and that defiance of her mother's wishes was a most important factor.

What Does An Eating Disorder Feel Like?

Typical of the anorectic syndrome is, in the face of dwindling energy sources, an unfailing denial of the growing seriousness of the condition. The anorectic individual feels out of control. As was stated earlier, when the backgrounds of anorectic adolescents have been examined by researchers, the initial impression is usually one, not of pathological disturbance, but rather an unusual freedom from developmental difficulties. As children, these patients generally appeared to have been outstandingly good and quiet. If one were to superficially examine Janine's scholastic record and interactions with peers, the picture would have been one of normalcy.

Upon closer investigation, however, these presumably positive personality characteristics, and the parental reactions to them, turn out to have a distinctly negative aspect. Foremost is a history of a lack of individual initiative and autonomy, a lack of sense of oneself as a distinct individual, capable of determining and accomplishing one's goals. Instead, consciously and unconsciously, anorectics are likely to have feelings of being enslaved, exploited, and not being permitted to live lives of their own. Janine felt enslaved to her brother. She was not allowed to have a life of her own beyond that of a babysitter. She lacked a clear sense of her emerging self, despite prolonged struggles to be perfect in the eyes of others. She eventually had an obsessional need to be in control of every aspect of life, with particular concern about losing control over her body.

Janine was preoccupied with thoughts of food and engaged excessively in food- and weight-related behavior.

Janine's mother exerted such firm control and regulation during childhood that Janine found it difficult to establish a sense of identity and confidence in her decision-making ability. Her parents manifested intrusive concern and overprotection; not encouraging Janine's separation and autonomy. Parental discomfort with the child's autonomy leads the parent (usually the mother) to reinforce reliance on her, which in turn, stifles the child's development of self. These parents are likely to have encouraged their children to become perfectionistic overachievers. Furthermore, such a regulated child may become so focused on external cues and controls as determinants of behavior that, like the obese child, they have not learned to respond appropriately to differential cues originating within herself, both physiologically and psychologically.

Many bulimics have extremely low self-esteem, particularly regarding their bodies; self-loathing is not uncommon when they fail to meet their own expectations. Self-denial and need for approval are also features of their struggles with themselves. The act of purging seems to be an attempt to regain the power and control that they lost as a result of their binge eating. They seem to harbor an all-consuming rage, which is often expressed through eating. Boskland-Lodahl (1976) seem to feel that the rage stems from the guilt bulimics feel at not living up to parental standards of "adorableness." They also report that the women observed in their study both feared and hated men. They saw them as defaming their self-worth and as being capable of destroying their self-respect.

Anorexia and bulimia appear to revolve around certain family dynamics. The mothers of bulimics tend to doubt their own ability to be tender and are unresponsive to their daughters' needs, which results in the daughters' doubting their own self-worth. Self-sufficiency is seen as a desired trait because dependency is seen as "bad." Although bulimics appear to be dependent, their needs are actually meshed with pseudoindependence because they feel that others do not want to respond to their dependency. Fathers are seen as maintaining distant relationships but having high expectations, especially concerning their daughters' personal appearance and performance. It appears the integration of associated ideals of independence and ambition with the traditional concepts of femininity may be particularly difficult for these women.

In Elaine's case, as soon as she was able to achieve some separation from her family and was succeeding in her first year at a small college, she abruptly left. She then went on to a larger university, where she felt just like one of a number of competing students. Her first year of tranquility and stability was still disrupted, however, this time by intense striving for achievement with the other students. This rivalry and competition for the position of her parents' best child was first noted in her rivalry with her older sister. It repeated itself many times, even in treatment, when she attended a support group for compulsive eaters and began to insist that the other members were more attractive and successful than she. At this point, her tenuous control over her eating was quickly broken, and she again returned to binging and purging, which always resulted in self-loathing. She would also often project onto the therapist a feeling of not getting anywhere, not accomplishing anything in treatment or in her life. This seemed to underlie an accusation that the therapist-mother would never be able to give her anything worthwhile.

The Client's Dilemma

The anorectic woman is viewed by some theorists as fearing an unconsciously hated domineering mother. The intrusion of this mother into the anorectic's psyche and body image then forces her to reject eating, which would ultimately render her similar to her mother. The anorectic therefore rejects the feminine qualities of receptivity and passivity, which both oral and sexual needs would only accentuate.

On the other hand, some theorists believe that bulimic women seem to fear sexual contact, not because of fear or pregMichelle or sexuality, but because of a fear of rejection. Performance anxiety and resultant rejection were critical childhood issues for them. The conflict with mother and the resultant hatred was more of a conscious phenomenon. Moreover, rather than rejecting the female role and its socially accepted aspects, the bulimic appears to identify *too* intensely with what she perceives as the "proper female role." In contrast to the anorectic's defense against anxiety and depression by ritualism and perfectionism, the bulimic tries to become a caricature of a perfect little woman. This notion is partly supported by Boskland-Lodahl (1976), who found that bulimic women were particularly sensitive to rejection by men. This fear of rejection often resulted in avoidance of men to the extent that it prevented the possibility of their gaining any nurturance and pleasure at all from male companions.

Conflicted and assailed by self-doubts, the "pre anorectic" girl becomes distressed as she experiences all the physical changes of adolescence; undeniable proof that she is turning into an adult. She is dismayed as her menstrual cycle begins and her body starts to assume a more womanly shape. The menses is a sudden and mysterious change over which the pre anorectic feels no control. Consciously, she may be obsessed with the thought that she is "too fat", but at a deeper level she is very depressed. The prospect of having to leave the safety and security of childhood with all its comforting rules and regulations is more than she can bear.

What is far more traumatic to the pre anorectic adolescent, however, is that she experiences sexuality in a passive and receptive way. This realization of the passive-receptive aspect of feminine life makes puberty an unbearable transition which the potential anorectic dreads and is determined to fight with her divided ego. Thus, she experiences the body as an object outside of the self on which to spy, destroying its needs, fighting its demands, and creating a sense of false euphoria from which she foresees a final state of emancipation.

The hunger strike thus serves a multitude of purposes. As the anorectic diets, her feminine curves disappear, and she becomes as flat-chested and angular as any prepubertal girl. Once she drops below a certain weight, her pituitary gland shuts down, and she stops menstruating-almost as if she has managed to turn back the biological clock. Her unwillingness to eat understandably arouses all sorts of parental concerns because she is seen as sick, and has reverted to a more childish role. Her half-starved condition requires her family to take care of her. At the same time, her refusal of food and her emaciated appearance seem to constitute an unconscious accusation. It is as if she is saying to her parents-in particular to her overprotective mother "See what you've done to me? I'm afraid to grow up." There may also be an element of defiance: "I've had to be such a good child all these years, and now I'm not going to listen to you. I won't even eat. This is a part of my life that I, and only I, can control, no matter what you want me to do."

Anorexia nervosa, then, is a very puzzling and paradoxical disorder. Its victims, seemingly without intention, engage in a protracted program of self-destruction, refusing others' desperate efforts to rescue them. The young girl, often in response to maternal encouragement to lose weight, embarks on a physical program which reaches obsessional levels, in an all-out defiant stance against an intrusive and domineering mother.

Elaine never perceived herself as a competent, worthwhile person who had a unique place in her family. She felt pushed to the side, rejected, and unfavorably compared with others by her family. Underneath her constant need to succeed, to compete with her sister and later on her peers and colleagues, was an unconscious fear that she would amount to nothing. She was at times convinced that others did not notice her and that her sister could obtain and easily consume all the praise, loving care, and nurturance to which she did not feel entitled. She hated her sister and envied her attractiveness, success, and the respect she could so easily obtain from others. If she, Elaine, could not obtain it, then perhaps she could destroy everyone else's happiness and gratification. These were, after all, only momentary and transitory kinds of feelings.

The client's compulsive need to feed herself was meant to satisfy ambivalently held needs. It reassured her that she could love and feed herself without having to depend on the attention of others, with whom she could not establish trust. It humiliated and disgusted her that she needed to "stuff down" the mounting tension and anger that threatened to overwhelm her control and her life. Her increasing use of "junk food" for quick gratification and a feeling of self-control, comfort, and pleasure could never really satiate her. In fact, she doubted whether anybody could satisfy her and whether life itself could ever be a rewarding or satisfying experience. The tireless efforts of others to reassure and rescue her provided only momentary reassurance that she was not an unattractive, unlovable, unworthy person who could quickly negate their efforts into nothingness. If her rage could destroy both their efforts and herself, then her life had no meaning or feelings, except through the magic of food and the people it enabled her to control.

Often, the <u>signs and symptoms of eating disorders</u> happen during the teen year's right after puberty hits. According to the <u>National Institute of Mental Health</u> (NIMH), a new study published in the *Journal of Abnormal Psychology* has looked at the biology behind the development of <u>binge eating in teens</u>. The theory was that changes during puberty may affect the development of binge eating and other eating disorders – a theory tested on rats. The outcome? The study suggests that puberty indeed contributes to the development of eating behaviors, a result that solidifies the role of biology in eating disorder issues.

Theories and Explanations of Eating Disorders

Psychodynamic

Psychodynamic theorists conceptualize the etiology and treatment of the various psychophysiological disorders in essentially the same way they conceptualize neuroses. Thus explaining the causes of anorexia, psychodynamic theorists are still concerned with anxiety, defense mechanisms, and trauma at various psychosexual stages. Janine had remained at an early stage of development; she had failed to individuate from her mother. The supportive, nurturing environment and the encouragement she needed in order to develop a separate identity were missing.

These theorists have proposed that anorectic individuals, when faced with anxiety-arousing prospect of genital sexuality at adolescence, regress to an already existing oral fixation. Denial of eating is thought to reflect denial of sexuality over the unconscious, defended-against wish to be impregnated through the mouth. Some of Crisp's et al. (1980) findings place particular emphasis on the biological regression of the anorectic client to a sub pubertal weight, which he views as avoidance or as a defensive posture of the anorectic character. He also suggests that both the anorectic and her family emphasize oral, dependent aspects of development rather than aggressive, sexual, and independent strivings. The result is a narrow range of coping mechanisms and restricted ego growth.

Traditional psychoanalytic theorists place the core of a problem within the individual and his or her unique personal history. Infancy and early experience are considered particularly important in predisposing the person to symptoms that some psychoanalytic theorists see as serving powerful unmet needs and unfulfilled wishes. Treatment is directed at looking for the symbolic meaning of the symptoms to understand what is motivating the behavior. Contemporary psychoanalysis deals with eating disorders in the context of personal relationships as well as the organization of the self. It still emphasizes the patient's unique history and finding a safe haven in which to process that history to claim a more thorough understanding of the antecedents of the eating disorder symptoms (Fishman 2004).

Ego Psychology and Object Relations

Bruch (1978) focused on the early feeding relationship between mother and child as the prototype of learning experiences for later relationships. If the maternal response is disjunctive, and if she superimposes her own needs on the child so that she cannot distinguish fatigue, helplessness, and frustration from nutritional needs, then the ego center of the child's cognitive structure become fixated in Piaget's preconceptual stage. Due to this confused conceptualization of body stimuli and the parent's rigid attitude toward verbalizations, the child's language usage is determined not by conceptual notions, but by literal mindedness.

The child's present subjective experience is not distinguished from the concept of the object and object reality. The anorectic equates her own maturing body with her experience of the maternal object. She attributes unacceptable experiences of herself to a concrete expression of her bodily processes. The liberal incorporation of the bad object (mother) becomes equated with her own body. The anorectic ego's aggressive, hateful feelings need to be defended against in order for her not to become depressed. Thus, the anorectic retains just enough loving feelings of symbolic oneness with mother to prevent a schizophrenic catastrophe. She also defends herself against a hateful, frustrating mother in order to forestall a permanent state of depression.

Palazzoli (1978) believes that anorexia nervosa is a special defense structure between schizo-paranoia and depression. The incorporated bad object can never be split, but remains whole, just like the body with which it is identified. The anorectic hovers between schizophrenia and depression, and her body experience is equally ambiguous, lying halfway between the non-I and the bad-I, both alien and her own, a destructive non-self-invading the self. Using the defense mechanism of projection, the client protects herself from experiencing personal delusions and preserves the ability to socialize and relate.

Family Systems

Minuchin (1978) asserts that operant conditioning is necessary to initiate weight gain. Subsequent, family therapy plays a central role. It is his view that although lifesaving is the most important goal in the initial stage of treatment, long-term success without relapse depends on reorganization of maladaptive patterns of family interaction. Those who emphasize family factors tend to rely on data that suggest that families of anorectics engage in disturbed patterns of interaction.

Family systems theorists have emphasized conflicts around issues of independence and the transition from childhood to adulthood. They feel that anorectic children are likely to appear in families that are excessively enmeshed. They assert that anorectics tend to have overprotective parents and lack effective ways of directly resolving conflicts. Thus the anorectic girl may be seen as asserting her independence in the only way she can- by refusing to eat. Although Janine's parents may not have been overprotective, they certainly were over-controlling and intrusive, refusing to allow her the freedom of expression she needed in order to grow psychologically. This intrusive concern with the child's psychological needs results in a hyper-vigilance on the part of the child, who becomes a "parent watcher."

In a study of 15 females, Crisp and colleagues (1974) provide some evidence that is consistent with a family systems point of view. They found that parents of daughters who showed the least improvement with therapy had significantly higher levels of psychopathology, as measured by a questionnaire. Even more relevant is their finding that successful treatment of the daughters was associated with an *increase* in parental disturbance. This increase in parental disturbance was especially marked when the marital relationship was poor; mothers tended to show an increase in anxiety and fathers an increase in depression. The authors concluded that the daughter's illness sometimes served as a protective function for one or both parents when they were threatened by the prospect of the daughter's independence.

Minuchin and colleagues (1978) report a success rate for family therapy of 86 percent after follow up periods ranging from three months to four years. This impressive result is probably reflective of the substantial degree of effectiveness of Minuchin's family therapy approach to the disorder.

The family is an integral system in the healthy development of a child and can play an important role in the recovery process. Unfortunately, in the past, parents were often blamed as the sole cause of their child's eating disorder. As more research is done on the diverse contributing factors, it becomes more and more clear that this is not the case. While stressful or chaotic family situations may intersect with other triggers to exacerbate or maintain the illness, they do not cause eating disorders. It's also important to note that some family dynamics, which were once assumed to be precursors to an eating disorder, may develop as a response to a family member's struggle with an eating disorder. The Academy of Eating Disorders (AED) recently released a position paper that clarifies the role of the family in the acquisition of eating disorders. The paper points out that there is no data to support the idea that anorexia or bulimia are caused by a certain type of family dynamic or parenting style. Alternatively, there is strong evidence that family-based treatment for younger patients, implemented early on in their illness, leads to positive results and improvements in conjunction with professionally guided family intervention. While parents and families are not to blame for eating disorders, they can play a role in helping kids establish a positive body image, one of the most important protective factors against eating disorders (www.eatingdisorder.org).

Social Learning

Some psychologists view family factors and social learning as causes of anorexia nervosa. From this viewpoint, the adolescent is likely to get considerable attention and reinforcement for early attempts at weight loss. Later, when the condition becomes serious, the child gains even more attention and may in fact become the center of family concern as the parents seek various treatments. Modeling of parents who are very slender or are highly concerned with weight and diets is suggested as an additional cause (Bemis 1978) by these theorists.

Janine's family seemed to be over concerned with weight. Her mother tended to be weight-conscious, as were the other women in the family. Thus, thin women were set up as positive role models. Certainly, once Janine became anorectic, she received additional attention from relatives, who expressed concern over her failing health. In this sense, Janine received a great deal of secondary gain by remaining "sick."

Biological

It seems likely that anorexia nervosa involves a substantial psychological component, although its features and modes of operation remain largely a matter of speculation. There is some suggestion of biological cause, since there are some known physical conditions, such as pituitary gland disorders, that can result in massive weight loss. It is speculated that at some point in the process of withdrawal from eating, biological factors seem to develop their own demands, taking the behavior beyond conscious control and making it exceedingly difficult to reverse.

The best guess is that the biological component that is responsible is located in the region of the hypothalamus, a richly interconnected structure in the brain involved in the regulation of motives and emotions. Although biological factors may play a part in the etiology of primary anorexia, perhaps an impairment of the release of gonadotropin from the anterior pituitary gland or a defect in the feedback control mechanisms for certain neurotransmitters (for example, dopamine) psychological influences appear to be dominant. Most individuals who are diagnosed with primary anorexia have had all known physical etiologies ruled out. Therefore, the belief that all these individuals suffering from a biological disorder is highly speculative. The motivating effects of the associated psychological factors and the use of the body as a receptive vehicle for the management and discharge of distraught emotional feelings are, without doubt, significant factors in illness.

Therapy Techniques

The approach used by the therapist in treatment of anorectics needs to be one of careful timing in order to avoid prematurely interpreting their unconscious motives. Such premature interpretations will only add to the anorectic's denial and reinforce her sense of alienation from the world. An approach of first gathering the facts of their lives, and a focus on understanding what they have to say and how they feel, reinforces their sense of self and reality. These clients, as previously stated, do not have a firmly established use of language and concepts appropriate to their age and background. They sometimes use language oddly or differently. Therefore, premature cognitive clarification of reality or premature use of interpretation of their mysterious behavior is discouraged, for it would be dangerous to their fragile egos and might overwhelm them. In any case, a close scrutiny of the client's ego capacity for facing her primitive emotions and an assessment of the state of her ego defenses are necessary prior to beginning work towards helping the client realize her underlying self-destructive motivation.

Bruch's (1978) position that clients need to feel, act and learn about themselves and their lives, sharpened by their coming to grips with reality expectations, makes sense that it helps eliminate the deep-seated cognitive and perceptual blocks that have dissociated from consciousness and from an anorectics early primitive body cues. With these precautions in mind, the following multidimensional approach is suggested when treating those with eating disorders.

1. *Induce the client to begin to eat again.*

The most effective therapy for anorexia nervosa is probably one that involves a combination of techniques. First, the patient must be induced to begin eating again, and here some form of behavior modification seems useful. This involves shaping the client's eating behavior with a behavior modification approach. The behavioral method is based on operant reinforcement procedures. The client is given social rewards, for example, time spent with peers for the appropriate consumption of food. Since the primary initial concern is the weight gain, clients can be reinforced with special privileges whenever they show improvements in their eating or when they gain weight. If the client is not hospitalized, the client and therapist can create a contract to increase rewards as the client begins to gain weight. In Janine's case, since she was not hospitalized, she and the therapist agreed upon a food regimen, which involved Janine monitoring her own behavior and presenting the therapist with a summary during each session. Maintaining a weight sufficient for survival is the goal. This reduces the client's suspicions of the therapist's motivation. Janine's intake was steadily increased until it reached a normal level. Before progressing to a higher increment, however, the client should show signs of clear judgment and they should initiate, rather than responding just to please the therapist.

The fact that most patients are initially treated in a hospital makes it somewhat easier to arrange for reinforcement. The patient can eat meals with the therapist and improvement can be reinforced. In a hospital setting, other reinforcers, such as access to television, could also be provided when the client eats a certain amount of food. Some hospitals use modified bed rest, high calorie intake, and supportive nursing care. The use of bed rest, the gradual increase in levels of activity, and the increase in privileges are all dependent on weight gain, thus producing a positive schedule of increased reinforcement. It may be more than that, however; putting the client to bed helps break through the denial and restricts her activity under medical supervision, thus providing needed external structure which does not easily enable loss of control.

2. Help the client deal with feelings of hopelessness and despair.

Try to help the client overcome her underlying sense of conflict and despair. Younger clients often dread growing up. Both their attempts to starve themselves and their bodily preoccupations represent a desperate attempt to exert control over events that are threatening to overwhelm them-namely, adult responsibilities.

Underneath Janine's good, conscientious, cooperative facade was a paper-thin kind of person, pathetically unsure of herself. She had never experienced pleasure in most of her accomplishments and had never felt a sense of control over her life and relationships with others. She was never allowed to think for herself, so whenever self-determination was called for, she became terribly insecure. Therapy helped Janine to understand that she could be less than perfect and still succeed in life. Her primary psychotherapeutic goal was personal and self-reorientation to enable her to see herself as having a separate identity from her parents, and therefore deserving of self-respect. It was crucial to build her self-confidence and to assist her in acquiring a greater sense of autonomy so that she could direct her own life and choose self-satisfying goals.

3. Help the client deal with cognitive deficits and distortions.

Another treatment goal is to enable the client to avoid the retreat in the solace of the perfect body as a solution to her existential problems in living. One client had a magical, concrete goal of 95 pounds, to which she felt she must return if she was to ever feel in control and happy again. She almost completely avoided and denied having to come to grips with her problems of not having an adequate job (despite college graduation with honors), not having dated in college, and feeling trapped in her home, which is where she felt forced to live with a deprecating, blaming mother. Her episodic hysterical crying, yelling and sobbing while living with her parents can be viewed as a need to be dead psychologically in order to be immune from the pain and disgrace she felt living in her mother's home.

Anorectics' need for concretization of their interpersonal shortcomings and of daily problems, all of which are focused on their bodies, is like a macabre drama in the theatre of the absurd of which they seem quite unaware. A therapeutic dialogue must be directed at helping the client realize (later on in the treatment) the secrets locked into their needing to express their deprecatory attitude toward their body and living through body language and primitive regressive symbolism.

4. Enlist the support of the client's family.

Once the anorectic is out of immediate danger, she and her family can benefit from a more dynamic form of treatment. After Janine had started eating again and was out of immediate danger, it was important to work with her family in an effort to alter the family dynamics that might have encouraged Janine's anorectic behavior. How had the family sustained and inadvertently nurtured the anorectic behavior? How had the family transmitted the mental attitudes of anorexia as the only solution to the complex issues of individuation and separation?

In family therapy, one must proceed cautiously with the mothers of anorectics, who feel that their sacrifices for the families have already been overwhelming. The therapeutic goal does not stop with the immediate need to gain weight. In fact, focusing solely on the weight within the family sessions serves merely to reinforce the client's fear that the family wants to "stuff" her with food while ignoring her anxiety. It also serves to reinforce the notion that the problem lies within the anorectic individual (the identified patient) and that her problem is separate and apart from the family situation.

The family's role in the ongoing maintenance of the anorexia must be examined. What gains did Janine's mother receive in keeping Janine dependent upon her? If it served the purpose of helping her to feel needed and adequate as a mother, then what other roles could she develop in the family that would serve to nurture her child's psychological growth? The families of these clients are often rigidly defensive about maintaining the status quo, present loyalties and secret coalitions, so that the family stability is preserved at the cost of individual growth. How did the family benefit from Janine's "sickness" and her accompanying constricted emotional role within the family? If Janine were not "sick" would the family focus then shift-perhaps to marital dysfunction? If that were to happen, would the parents be prepared to confront their marital issues so that their needs would not intrude on Janine's fragile autonomy?

It was crucial to examine these questions in order to alter any dysfunctional patterns so that long-term symptom-free behavior would be maintained. Thus, opening up some poorly resolved issues on which harmony was tenuously achieved shakes the basis of family stability. Perhaps that is necessary for a while, but with therapeutic support and empathy, a new harmony can be achieved. The family need not fear disintegration; powerful forces kept it together in the past, and so it will remain together in the future- but for different reasons.

5. *Utilize long-term group treatment*

Once Janine had gained a sufficient amount of weight and had worked through separation and individuation issues with her parents, and once the family's dysfunctional patterns had been explored, it was the therapist's opinion that Janine could benefit from participating in supportive group psychotherapy. These sessions allowed her to express her concerns, thoughts, fears and enabled her to develop psychological autonomy and growth.

In group therapy, participants are encouraged to share their feelings and experiences about food, weight, and body shape and to see the relationships between eating, body image and interpersonal relationships. The goals of each group therapy can vary, however, most are based on enhancing self-esteem and assertiveness and providing the participants with coping skills and social and emotional support (Fishman, 2004).

Family Therapy Treatment

Family therapy, in treating clients with eating disorders, encourages parents to play a pivotal role in restoring their child's weight while trying to avoid hospitalizations. The most widely documented research on the efficacy of family therapy for treating eating disorders is a series of studies carried out by a group at the Maudsley Hospital in London, England. The study compared family therapy in Anorexia Nervosa patients, where the family was encouraged to take charge of the patient's eating, with individual therapy. Outcomes at 1 year follow up showed family therapy to be superior for younger patients (those under 19 years of age) with a short history of the disorder (less than 3 years), while individual therapy was more effective with older patients (Fishman 2004).

Called the Maudsley method, the treatment is a demanding program in that for the first 2 weeks, at least one parent must be available around the clock to supervise meals and snacks, and monitor children between meals to make sure they do not burn off the <u>calories</u> with excessive exercise. At one of the first sessions of the Maudsley method, the therapist sits in on a family meal to observe the dynamics. Everyone in the family has a role: siblings are instructed to clear out once they are finished eating, not jump up and yell at their sister for not eating or yell at the parent. This method shows that parents are not to blame for the problem. It shows that they are part of the solution. Their job is to be calm, supportive and consistent. The parents have to be on the same page when it comes to therapy. One parent cannot be telling the child to eat while the other is saying just give her a break tonight.

Another treatment that can be used is the Intensive Structural Therapy Model (IST). It is based on four theoretical tenets: 1) the problem is being maintained by the patient's contemporary social context, 2) certain isomorphic (structurally equal) patterns pervade the context, 3) it is essential to search for the homeostatic maintainer (homeostasis of the system is maintained by the emergence of the system), and 4) therapeutic crisis induction can be invaluable in transforming systems (Fishman 2004). IST is a 5 step model of therapy. Step 1: gathering the members of the system. For individuals with eating disorders this would be the family i.e. parents, siblings and possibly grandparents. It is important for family members to come to sessions, especially the first one, so the therapist can see the familial interactions, dysfunctional patterns and who or what is maintaining the homeostasis in the family system. Step 2: generating goals and planning treatment. This step exposes the homeostatic maintainer. Once this person has been identified, he or she is the one that the therapist can use to help reach therapeutic goals. Step 3: addressing the dysfunctional patterns. When dysfunctional patterns are realized, along with the homeostatic maintainer, transforming the system can begin. The therapist challenges the family to change by destabilizing the system. He or she does not allow the system to return to its former homeostasis. This creates a crisis that makes the family look at its old patterns of interaction. Step 4: establishing and maintaining a new organization. Because the system cannot rely on its old patterns of interaction, new ones have to be created. The family learns to directly address their conflicts. For individuals with eating disorders, the changes in the family are usually enough to replace the dysfunctional patterns. The new patterns are "often established in the behavioral paradigm that is set up to take the place of the parental stratagems that have not worked to get their child to eat" (Fishman, 2004). Step 5: ending therapy. The system has been reorganized with new interactional patterns so therapy can safely be ended. If the family feels that further treatment is needed, they may always come back. They do have regular follow ups so the family is reassured that help is still available to them if necessary. For some families, therapy will not be successful and should be ended. This will sometimes trigger a crisis within the system and therapy will continue to see if change can happen. Other times, it is best for therapy to end, "leaving the door open" for further work, should the family request it, or referring them to an alternate therapist.

When to Refer

If the client is not adhering to the behavioral routine suggested by the therapist (e.g., not eating to gain weight in a consistent, scheduled way), then hospitalization and medical supervision is required. Although this may interfere with the transference and may induce feelings of being controlled or exploited by the therapist, the issue of failing health or of life and death is the more important issue that must take priority in the treatment. The need for medical supervision is explained to the client, and when her health is restored, treatment can resume. The therapeutic problem becomes one in which neither the therapist nor the client is any longer in control.

Medical emergencies do exist for anorectics, and the services of an internist may also be necessary to monitor the client's disturbed electrolytic balance and general health. In bulimic, the excessive use of laxatives or purgatives may have caused a chemical imbalance in the body, so that the psychological issues cannot be addressed at this time.

Severe under eating and the consequential malnutrition and serious weight loss may accompany a variety of psychological disorders ranging from schizophrenia to depression. However, the clinical picture in primary anorexia nervosa is remarkably similar from one client to another.

The eating disorders generally respond best to long-term psychotherapy. It is believed that a multimodal treatment approach is most appropriate. As stated earlier, referral for medical evaluation is always necessary, and a team approach is usually the most effective.

References

American Psychiatric Association. (2013). *Diagnostic and statistical manual of mental disorders* (5th ed.). Arlington, VA: American Psychiatric Publishing.

ANAD. (n.d.). Retrieved June 5, 2014, from http://www.anad.org.

Arieti, S. (1974a). An overview of schizophrenia from a predominantly psychological approach. *The American Journal of Psychiatry, 131*(3), 241-249.

Asen, E. (2002). Outcome research in family therapy. *Advances in Psychiatric Treatment, 8*, 230-238.

Atwood, J. & Chester, R. (1987). *Treatment Techniques for Common Mental Disorders.* New Jersey: Jason Aronson.

Bemis, K. M. (1978). Current approaches to the etiology and treatment of anorexia nervosa. *Psychological Bulletin, 85*, 593-617.

Boskland-Lodahl, M. (1976). Cinderella's stepsisters: A feminist perspective on anorexia nervosa and bulimia. *Signs, 2*(2), 342-356.

Bruch, H. (1973). *Eating Disorders: Obesity, Anorexia Nervosa, and the Person Within.* New York: Basic Books.

Bruch, H. (1978). *The Golden Cage: The Enigma of Anorexia Nervosa.* New York: Vintage.

Crisp, A. H., Harding, B., & McGuinness, B. (1974). Anorexia nervosa: Psychoneurotic characteristics of parents: Relationship to progress. *Journal of Psychosomatic Research, 18*, 167-173.

Crisp, A. H., Hsu, L. K., Harding, B. & Hartshorn, J. (1980). Clinical features of anorexia nervosa: A study of a consecutive series of 102 female patients. *Journal of Psychosomatic Research, 24*(3-4), 179-191.

Fishman, H. C. (2004). *Enduring Change in Eating Disorders.* New York: Brunner-Routledge.

Johnson, C., & Larson, R. (1982). Bulimia: an analysis of mood and behavior. *Psychosomatic Medicine, 44*(4), 341-351.

Minuchin, S., Rosman, B.L., & Baker, L. (1978). *Psychosomatic Families: Anorexia Nervosa in Context.* Cambridge: Harvard University Press.

National Eating Disorders Association. (n.d.). Retrieved June 6, 2014, from http://www.nationaleatingdisorders.org.

Newlon, C. (2013, November 12). A Guy Thing: Eating Disorders Increase in Men. Retrieved June 5, 2014, from http://www.usatoday.com.

NIMH · Home. (n.d.). Retrieved June 7, 2014, from http://www.nimh.nih.gov/index.shtml.

Palazzoli, M. S. (1978). *Self-starvation: From Individual to Family Therapy in the Treatment of Anorexia Nervosa.* New York: Jason Aronson.

Rosman, B. L., Minuchin, S., & Liebman, R. (1975). Family lunch session: An introduction to family therapy in anorexia nervosa. *American Journal of Orthopsychiatry 45*:846-854.

Van Buskirk, S. S. (1977). A two-phase perspective on the treatment of anorexia nervosa. *Psychological Bulletin,* 84, 529-547.

White, M. A., Grilo, C. M., O'Malley, S. S. & Potenza, M. N. (2010). Clinical case discussion: Binge eating disorder, obesity and tobacco smoking. *Journal of Addiction Medicine.* 4(1), 11-19.

Chapter 10

Sexual Dysfunctions

Michelle Parisano M.A., MFT

What Are The Sexual Dysfunctions and How Do You Recognize Them?

Maintaining a sexual relationship involves all levels of human behavior. On the biological level, a delicate series of hormonal, physiological, and muscular functions work together to produce an integrated response during the act of sexual intercourse. However, things are more complicate on the psychological level. This is where the pleasure associated with sexual activity is frequently accompanied by anxieties, inhibitions, questions, and doubts about social definitions and expectations, emotional reactions to one's partner, and the interpersonal patterns of sexual and social relationships. On the sociocultural level, one's sexuality is affected by cultural prescriptions and proscriptions, social patterns, expectations, and norms that help to determine where, how, with whom, and under what circumstances sexual behavior will take place (Atwood & Klucinec, 2008).

It is only in recent times, thanks in large part to the pioneering work of Kinsey and associates (1948, 1953) that we have come to understand how widespread and severe individual problems are with sexuality in our own culture. Because of the very nature of the sexual dysfunctions, the format of this chapter differs slightly from previous formats. In this chapter, instead of one case history presentation, several shorter case histories will be described. One reason for this is that there are many sexual dysfunctions. The second, more complicated reason is that the practice of counseling and sex therapy requires specialized training. To present counseling techniques for sexual problems in the space of one chapter would be oversimplifying the issues and perhaps misleading readers. Most training programs for counselors and therapists provide one or, at best, two courses in sexuality, which does not prepare the student to practice sexual counseling or sexual therapy. We will focus here, therefore, on providing the reader with a description of the various disorder and we will take the professional stance that individuals with sexual dysfunctions should be referred to professionals trained in the field of sex therapy.

The term *sexual dysfunction* refers to impairment either in the desire for or in the ability to achieve sexual pleasure or gratification or both. With few exceptions, such impairments generally occur, not as a result of anatomical or physiological pathology, but rather because of faulty psychosexual adjustment and learning. The dysfunctions vary markedly in degree and, regardless of which partner is alleged to be dysfunctional, the enjoyment of sex by both parties in the relationship will probably be adversely affected. Whatever the dysfunction may be, it is reasonable to assume that it can create much misery and unhappiness in the lives of both the individuals affected by the disorder and their partners.

Several dimensions of maladaptive behavior can occur in sexual dysfunctions. As stated before, the *biological reaction* is clearly influenced since sexual arousal and behavior can be easily disrupted by a malfunction in this area. Major problems are also likely to occur in other dimensions of behavior. For example, common *psychological reactions* to sexual behavior are intense anxiety prior to or during sexual activities, guilt over certain sexual behaviors, or depression because of the difficulties caused by the sexual dysfunction. Another dimension involved is the *cognitive reaction*. In cases of sexual dysfunction, there is typically some negative evaluation of sexual behavior in general. These negative beliefs are often based on cultural or religious proscriptions against sexual activity. These proscriptions against sexual behavior also affect individuals at a psychological level. Both men and women with sexual dysfunctions tend to develop diminished self-esteem and self-confidence. Like people with any type of problem, those with sexual dysfunctions often tend to worry excessively about the disorder. These affective and cognitive effects usually lead to decreased interest in sex, which usually then interferes with current or potential sociosexual relationships.

The individual with a sexual dysfunction generally does not have any other major forms of maladaptive behavior and may be well adjusted to other aspects of life, such as work settings or nonsexual social relationships. Munjack and Stapes (1976) found that, based on psychological tests, women with sexual dysfunction were virtually identical to "normal" controls. The only difference was that the controls were slightly less depressed.

Thus, difficulty achieving satisfactory sexual relations has significant physiological, emotional, interpersonal, and cultural effects. Psychotherapists tend to emphasize the psychological factors, however, and most professionals agree that psychological factors seem to account for nearly three fourths of all sexual difficulties.

Sexual dysfunction is probably one of the most common of all human problems. Practically every man has had trouble at one point or another achieving or maintaining an erection and almost every woman has had difficulty reaching orgasm from time to time. For some people such sexual dysfunction may be chronic. Some men are impotent; that is, they can rarely, if ever, sustain an erection long enough to enjoy sexual intercourse. There are also women who are completely anorgasmic; some experts prefer the term *preorgasmic* (Ersner-Hershfield and Kopel, 1979). Such women are never able to have an orgasm. The variety of sexual behaviors is vast, and in our increasingly permissive contemporary culture, it is basically up to couples to decide for themselves what kind of sexual relationship they wish to have. This makes the definition of sexual dysfunction largely subjective and experiential.

Male Sexual Dysfunctions

Male Hypoactive Sexual Desire Disorder (302.71)

Male Hypoactive Sexual Desire Disorder is defined as persistently or recurrently deficient (or absent) sexual/erotic thoughts or fantasies and desire for sexual activity, where the judgment of deficiency is made by the clinician, taking into account factors that affect sexual functioning, such as age and general and sociocultural contexts of the individual's life (American Psychiatric Association, 2013, p. 440). In the case of males, no erection occurs and no urges to engage in sexual behavior are felt.

The causes of male hypoactive sexual desire may include organic as well as psychogenic factors. Approximately 10-20% of men with low sexual interest have pituitary tumors that cause too much of the hormone prolactin to be produced. Prolactin reduces the amount of testosterone and can lead to low sexual desire or erectile disorder (Buvat, 2003; Schwartz, Bauman, & Masters, 1983). Sexual unresponsiveness can also be caused by psychogenic factors such as shame, poor self-esteem, a bad relationship, guilt, or embarrassment about sexual activity or one's body, or a history of sexual abuse. Before any treatment can begin, the etiological factors must be identified.

The goal here is to create a non-demanding, relaxed, and sensuous environment in which mutually gratifying sexual activity can take place.

Erectile Disorder (302.72)

The two most widely recognized experts in the field of sexual dysfunction are Masters and Johnson (1970). According to them, the most common male sexual dysfunction, *erectile disorder*, refers to the repeated failure to obtain or maintain erections during partnered sexual activities. In many cases, a male, for some reason or other, begins to worry about whether or not he will be able to achieve erection. This fear can become so anxiety-eliciting that it can eventually lead to erectile disorder. Other psychological factors involved in erectile disorder are performance anxiety, spectatoring (mentally observing and evaluating one's sexual performance while it is occurring), and guilt (see also Atwood, 2001).

Masters and Johnson (1970) differentiate between lifelong and acquired erectile disorder. In *lifelong* erectile disorder, the most difficult to cure of all the forms of inadequacy, the male has never been able to sustain an erection sufficient for the successful completion of intercourse, usually defined as including intravaginal ejaculation. This is a chronic type of disorder. The individual with *acquired* erectile disorder usually has a history of having been able to have sexual intercourse at least once but currently cannot maintain an erection. This male has had at least one episode, usually many episodes, of successful intercourse. Lifelong erectile disorder is a relatively rare disorder, but it has been estimated that at least half of the male population has experienced the acquired variety at least temporarily, especially in the early years of sexual exploration. It should be noted that the man who occasionally cannot perform sexually because of extreme fatigue, excessive alcohol consumption, or the like would not meet the criteria for erectile disorder. Under some situations, however, these "normal" failures can result in acquired erectile disorder if the individual is overly anxious and allows the temporary condition to distress him to the extent that it interferes with subsequent functioning.

Chronic or permanent erectile disorder before the age of 60 is relatively rare and is usually due to psychological factors. In fact, according to the findings of Kinsey and colleagues (1948, 1953), only about one fourth of males experience erectile dysfunction by the age of 70, and even then many cases are a result of psychological factors. More recent studies have indicated that men and women in their 80s and 90s are quite capable of enjoying sex (Kaplan 1974a; Masters and Johnson, 1976). To the degree that men do experience some difficulties in their older years, it appears that in some cases they may simply be assimilating and complying with the societal expectation and definition of declining sexual performance with age (Tollison et al., 1977).

Some cases of erectile disorder -- estimates are approximately 15 percent (Kaplan, 1974a) -- are caused by a variety of different organic conditions, including certain types of vascular disease, diabetes, neurological disorders, kidney failure, hormonal irregularities, and excess blood levels of certain drugs, including alcohol (Wagner and Metz, 1980). Masters and Johnson (1970) have also listed some psychological and social causes of acquired erectile dysfunction: frequent premature ejaculation, intemperate alcoholic consumption, excessive maternal or paternal domination in childhood, inhibitory religious orthodoxy, homosexual conflict, and inadequate sexual counseling.

The primary therapeutic goals in treating erectile dysfunction are to remove the individual's fear of failure, to eliminate the spectator role by reorienting the client's emotions toward active participation in sexuality, and to remove his parent's fear of his erectile dysfunction. Masters and Johnson's program for erectile dysfunction typically progresses in the following manner: (1) pleasuring without direct attempt to produce an erection, (2) penile erection through gential pleasuring, (3) extravaginal orgasm, (4) penetration without orgasm, and (5) full coitus with orgasm. According to Masters and Johnson (1975), the woman's role in the treatment of erectile dysfunction cannot be overemphasized. They believe that unless she shows compassion over his erectile failure, his feelings of anxiety and guilt will only increase. Masters and Johnson report a success rate of 59.4 percent in treating cases of lifelong erectile disorder and 73.8 percent in cases of acquired erectile disorder.

Premature (Early) Ejaculation (302.75)

Some men have no difficulty achieving erection but ejaculate so quickly during intercourse that both partners are left feeling frustrated. This problem is called *premature (early) ejaculation*. The erection is easily achieved, but the male is unable to postpone his ejaculation long enough to satisfy the female. Ejaculation takes place immediately before, immediately upon, or shortly after insertion, resulting in unsuccessful intercourse.

Exact definition of premature (early) ejaculation is not possible because of pronounced variations in both the likelihood and the latency of female orgasm in sexual intercourse. Premature (early) ejaculation is defined in many different ways by many different therapists. Masters and Johnson (1970), for example, believe that the individual involved has not learned to control his sexual response. Before Masters and Johnson (1976) the definition between premature (early) ejaculations was based on the amount of time insertion could be maintained before ejaculation (Kinsey et al., 1948) or how many thrusts could occur after penetration but before orgasm. Ejaculations occurring less than a minute after penetration were considered to be premature. This emphasis on time, though, was avoided by Masters and Johnson (1970), who defined the problem, as reaching ejaculation before the female reached orgasm on 50 percent of the sexual encounters. However, this definition is not without problems either. For example, if the female partner has difficulty achieving an orgasm even when there is sufficient stimulation over an extended period of time, should this be considered premature (early) ejaculation by the male? LoPiccolo and Heiman (1977) suggest that the inability to tolerate as much as four minutes of stimulation without ejaculation is a reasonable indicator that a male may be in need of sex therapy. Although the exact definition is a difficult problem for the researcher and the clinician, it is usually the man or his partner who decides that it is a problem and who then seeks help.

Generally, the treatment for premature ejaculation involves teaching the individual to recognize the signs of impending and imminent orgasm. Using the *squeeze technique*, which will be discussed later, the woman stimulates the man until the point of inevitability of orgasm. At that moment he signals her, and she then stops stimulation. This start-stop procedure was first discussed by James Semans (1956), who suggests that the couple repeat this procedure several times, after which the man is allowed to ejaculate. Four trials are recommended. The couple then proceed to sexual intercourse, during which the same start-stop pattern is repeated.

Delayed Ejaculation (302.74)

Somewhat the opposite problem is *delayed ejaculation*. Delayed ejaculation is a rare condition in which the male is able to achieve erection and insertion but experiences a marked delay in or inability to achieve ejaculation. He may be able to ejaculate by masturbating or, in the case of the married man, he may be able to ejaculate with a woman to whom he is not married; in other cases, he may be unable to ejaculate at all. Occasionally, a man with a predominantly homosexual orientation will experience delayed ejaculation with women (see Kaplan, 1974a, 333). Relatively few cases of delayed ejaculation are seen by sex therapists, but Kaplan (1974b) believes that the problem is widespread. It is possible that many men are too embarrassed by it even to contemplate therapy for it.

Treatment of delayed ejaculation involves the woman initially stimulating the man to orgasm extravaginally. Once he does ejaculate, even if it is outside of the vagina, Masters and Johnson believe that the couple has overcome a major hurdle. This orgasm means that the man can allow himself to be pleasured by the woman, and it enables her to express to him her positive feelings about having pleasure him. After this has been accomplished on several more occasions, a technique called *bridging* is used. This involves the woman stimulating man to the point of orgasm. Right before he ejaculates, he signals her and she stops. At this point, she places his penis inside her vagina and he continues to thrust, producing orgasm through this means alone. Once orgasm occurs intravaginally, Masters and Johnson believe much of the anxiety and conflict seem to disappear. They report a success rate of 82.4 percent using this technique.

Female Sexual Dysfunctions

Female Sexual Interest/Desire Disorder (302.72)

For females, hypoactive sexual desire disorder and female sexual arousal disorder have been combined into one disorder: Female Sexual Interest/Arousal Disorder (American Psychiatric Association, 2013). Lief (1977) and Kaplan (1979) are responsible for the labeling of low sexual desire as a sexual disorder. This was based on their observations that the lack of motivation to have sex was a crucial factor in unsuccessful sex therapy cases. Females experience a lack of sexual arousal. Physically, she does not lubricate vaginally and no change in the vaginal size occurs to accommodate the penis. The causes of low sexual interest may include organic as well as psychogenic factors. As with males, sexual unresponsiveness can also be caused by psychogenic factors such as shame, poor self-esteem, a bad relationship, guilt, or embarrassment about sexual activity or one's body, or a history of sexual abuse. Before any treatment can begin, the etiological factors must be identified.

The goal here is to create a non-demanding, relaxed, and sensuous environment in which mutually gratifying sexual activity can take place. The sensate focus exercise is critical in assisting women to relax and in some cases to help them learn about their own sexuality. The female superior position is often helpful because it increases female sensitivity. However, a review of the current treatment programs for sexual desire disorders reveals that current approaches are more eclectic than the original behavioral techniques (see Leiblum & Rosen, 1988).

Female Orgasmic Disorder (302.73)

Many women are readily sexually excitable and otherwise enjoy sexual activity, yet they experience difficulty in achieving orgasm. Formerly, *any* failure to gain sexual gratification on the part of the female was listed under the all-inclusive misleading heading of "frigidity." Masters and Johnson (1970), however, have distinguished various forms of sexual dysfunction. The major sexual impairment for women is *orgasmic dysfunction*, which refers to a delay in, infrequency of, or absence of orgasm or reduced intensity of orgasmic sensations. According to these researchers, there are two basic types of this problem. In *generalized* orgasmic disorder, the woman has never achieved orgasm through coitus, masturbation, or any other means. In *situational* orgasmic disorder, the woman is orgasmic only in certain situations and not in others. For example, the woman could have experienced orgasms in the past but is no longer able to do so or can only have an orgasm under specific circumstance. For example, she may experience orgasm only by means of manual stimulation, or only when coitus takes place in the bathroom. The diagnosis of orgasmic disorder is complicated by the fact that the subjective quality of orgasm varies widely among females and within the same female from time to time, making precise evaluations of occurrence and quality difficult (Singer and Singer, 1972). As stated earlier, orgasmic disorder is in some ways the female counterpart of erectile disorder. In recent years, many women have been as concerned about being nonorgasmic as men are concerned about being impotent.

Because of social pressure, personal expectations, and/or the sheer desire to be orgasmic, some women will fake orgasms, presumably to please their partners. Some women seen in therapy report they had faked orgasms for years prior to being able to communicate honestly with their partners about their nonorgasmic condition. Recently, there has been some research indicating that faking orgasms also occurs among men. Many nonorgasmic women report some traumatic sexual experience in the past and/or parents who held extremely rigid and negative views about sex. In some cases, orgasm may have taken on some other meaning to them, such as submission to the male or loss of self-control. In other cases, the intensity of orgasm may be frightening, and the woman may be afraid to "let go."

Treatment of orgasmic disorder involves freeing the woman from the now seemingly involuntary control of the orgasmic reflex. In therapy she is taught to focus on the sensations produced by mounting sexual tension. She is made aware through psychotherapy of her sexual functions and attitudes. She is also told what an orgasm is, what it feels like. She is encouraged to fantasize during foreplay and masturbation. She learns the progression of sexual responsiveness and the sexual events that generally terminate in orgasm.

The woman is usually first taught to experience an orgasm through masturbation. This may involve working through feelings of shame and guilt about the activity. Once she is able to have orgasm alone, she then learns, by bridging, to have one with her partner. Next she learns to experience orgasm through clitoral stimulation by her partner and, finally, she experiences orgasm through sexual intercourse, usually, again, through the use of bridging. Masters and Johnson report an 83.4 percent success rate for generalized orgasmic disorder and a 77.2 percent in cases of situational orgasmic disorder.

Genito-Pelvic Pain/Penetration Disorder (302.76)

Genito-Pelvic Pain/Penetration Disorder represents the merging of Vaginismus and Dyspareunia, less common sexual dysfunctions which were highly comorbid and difficult to distinguish (American Psychiatric Association, 2013). In Vaginismus, the outer third of the vagina spasmodically contracts when penile insertion is attempted, rendering intercourse either impossible or very painful. For some women, the anticipation or even thoughts of vaginal penetration could induce the contraction, resulting in a tight feeling causing discomfort, making vaginal penetration impossible. Dyspareunia was described as recurrent or persistent painful sexual intercourse.

Binik (2010) reported that the majority of the women diagnosed with Vaginismus also experienced pain and therefore suggested that Vaginismus and Dyspareunia should be combined into a single diagnosis: Genito-Pelvic Pain/Penetration Disorder. Genito-Pelvic Pain/Penetration Disorder refers to persistent or recurrent difficulties with for commonly comorbid symptom dimensions: (1) difficulty having intercourse, (2) genito-pelvic pain, (3) fear of pain or vaginal penetration, (4) tension of the pelvic floor muscles (p. 437).

Masters, Johnson, and Kolodny (1985) estimate that 2 to 3 percent of all post-adolescent women experience difficulty having intercourse and/or tension of the pelvic floor muscles (formerly Vaginismus), but usually do not have a problem with sexual arousal. The causes are generally psychogenic and related to shame, fear, and embarrassment. Masters and Johnson (1970), found that Genito-Pelvic Pain/Penetration Disorder (formerly

Vaginismus) is associated with erectile disorder in a woman's partner, strong religious teachings against sexuality, homosexual feelings, a history of sexual assault, and negative or hostile feelings toward one's partner.

Another aspect of Genito-Pelvic Pain/Penetration Disorder is painful intercourse (formerly Dyspareunia). This pain may be a result of pelvic inflammatory disease, endometriosis, tumors, rigid hymen, yeast infections, creams, or many other factors. Although many women experience pain at some point during sexual intercourse, it is estimated that between 12-20% of women experience ongoing genital pain (Brotto, 2013). The pain can manifest as a cramping or burning sensation, and can occur externally in the vaginal area, or internally in the pelvic area. As a result of the pain women may avoid sexual activity.

The successful treatment of Genito-Pelvic Pain/Penetration Disorder most often utilizes behavioral techniques focused on modifying a conditioned response. Vaginal dilators of progressive size are used, combined with Kegel exercises to teach control of the vaginal muscles, cognitive restructuring to alleviate guilt about sexuality or resolve past sexual trauma, and attention to intrapsychic problems or systemic couple issues. The vaginal dilators are usually used in the doctor's office with or without the partner's presence, learning to allow for the presence of the dilator without the conditioned fear response. The goal here is to decrease the woman's fear and anxiety so that penetration can occur. Support and encouragement from the partner is crucial (Lazarus, 1989; Leiblum, Pervin, and Campbell. 1989).

Symptoms

The sexual dysfunctions appear to be very common (Kaplan 1974b; Khatchadourian and Lunde, 1972; McCary, 1973). They are much more prevalent than one might think. Every sexually active person has probably experienced some dysfunction at one time or another. Masters and Johnson (1970) estimate that fully half the marriages in the United States suffer from some form of sexual inadequacy. The actual number of clients with sexual problems is undoubtedly much higher than the surveys indicate. And the vast majority of cases, particularly those involving female sexual dysfunction, often go untreated. This estimate is supported by Frank and colleagues (1978). They found that, of 100 couples, 80 percent reported having happy and satisfying sexual relationships. However, 40 percent of the men reported problems with erection and ejaculation, and 63 percent of women reported having trouble becoming sexually aroused or reaching orgasm.

Sexual dysfunctions are a heterogenous group of disorders that are typically characterized by a clinically significant disturbance in a person's ability to respond sexually or to experience sexual pleasure. The categories listed include the following: delayed ejaculation, erectile disorder, female orgasmic disorder, female sexual interest/arousal disorder, genito-pelvic pain/penetration disorder, male hypoactive sexual desire disorder, premature (early) ejaculation, substance/medication induced sexual dysfunction, other specified sexual dysfunction, and unspecified sexual dysfunction (see also Atwood, 2004). (For a detailed description of each of these disorders, please refer to DSM-V, American Psychiatric Associate, 2013).

Theories and Explanations for the Sexual Dysfunctions

Psychodynamic

Freudian theory holds that sexual difficulties result from childhood sexual trauma, which led to excessive fear, guilt, or anxiety about sex. Only through a thorough psychoanalysis of these deep-seated feelings could healthy and full sexual pleasure, which Freud believed was one of the most important aspects of life, be achieved. Freud asserted that the healthy person was the one who is able to love, play, and work.

According to Freud (1905), sexual disorders represent a continuation into adulthood of the diffuse sexual preoccupation of the child. Children normally enjoy "showing off" their sexual equipment and peeking at that of others. Furthermore, according to Freudian theory, they are capable of resorting to any number of defensive maneuvers in attempting to deal with the castration anxiety and penis envy supposedly endemic to the oedipal period. In accordance with this line of thinking, psychodynamic theorists generally conceptualize sexual disorders as the result of fixation at a pregenital stage; in general, with sexual disorders as with the sexual dysfunctions, it is the oedipal stage, with its concomitant castration anxiety, that is considered the major source of mischief. Treatment then involves the therapist's interpreting symbolic remarks, behaviors, and dreams in an attempt to bring to the conscious level the unconscious sexual conflict so that it can be confronted and "worked through."

Behavioral

Behaviorists suggest that sexual difficulties may essentially be bad habits that come from the association of sexual feelings with negative outcomes. The behaviorists feel that erectile disorder, for example, might result not from a neurotic childhood conflict, as the Freudians believe, but from a recurrent fear of sexual rejection that interferes with the ability to participate in sexual feelings. Most theorists would agree that behaviorists have had a profound impact upon the treatment of sexual dysfunctions, especially in recent years.

The most notable example of such treatment, unquestionably, is the Masters and Johnson (1970) program, which made headlines in the late 1960s and early 1970s. Theirs is a brief form of therapy, and ideally taking two weeks. Clinicians who favor this approach try to determine how well a given pair of sexual partners communicate. They are more interested in helping couples overcome their symptoms than in probing any deep-seated emotional conflicts. Indeed, candidates for the Masters and Johnson program are carefully screened to be sure that they are free of overwhelming psychological problems. They generally insist on treating couples who are committed to each other or are involved in a long-standing relationship.

The most common behavioral interpretation of sexual inadequacies is that they result from faulty learning, inasmuch as the child learned to associate either guilt or anxiety with sexuality or had several "bad" early sexual experiences. Behaviorists believe that many cultural patterns contribute to sexual performance difficulties. For example, the myth that women do not enjoy sex and should think solely of satisfying their male partners has probably caused many women to neglect or negate their sexual feelings and pleasure. Lack of information about sexual functioning has kept many people from learning how to stimulate themselves effectively to obtain maximum pleasure. In sum, the behaviorists believe that just as sexual dysfunctions are learned, they can be unlearned.

Masters and Johnson's treatment of married couples rests on two basic assumptions. The first is that sexual inadequacy is not an individual problem -- "her" problem is "his" problem -- but a problem of the marital unit, in which sexual communication has broken down. They work only with couples because they feel that there is no such thing as an uninvolved partner in a committed relationship in which there is sexual distress. This strategy shifts the therapeutic focus from the individual to the relationship. The second assumption is that in order to reactivate the individual's natural ability to respond to sexual stimuli, the couple must be relieved of all performance pressures; essentially, they must return to a goalless, nondemand petting stage in order to rediscover their ability to be "pleasured" by touching and caressing. Masters and Johnson's program uses the dual-sex therapy team because they believe that only a woman can fully understand the female sexual response and only a man can fully understand the male sexual response. This team approach increases therapeutic objectivity and balance by adequately representing male and female viewpoints and gives each partner a same-sex therapist to whom he or she can relate more easily.

Techniques used by Masters and Johnson include the following:

Hand riding

Because most sexual dysfunction occurs when the individuals involved are embarrassed to teach each other what is sexually pleasing to them, Masters and Johnson employ a technique called "hand riding." It involves the placing of one's hand upon the partner's hand and gently and slowly guiding the partner's hand over the body, indicating what is sexually pleasing. The situation is then reversed, with the opposite partner doing the guiding over his or her own body. Partners thereby learn to communicate to each other what sexually pleases them.

Squeeze technique

This technique, which is primarily used to treat premature (early) ejaculation, involves the female's squeezing the glans of the penis between her thumb and forefinger after the male communicates to her feeling his feeling of impending orgasm. The female places her thumb below the frenulum and two fingers and two fingers above, one forward of the coronal ridge and one behind, on the shaft of the penis. Pressure is then applied for several seconds until the erection has practically subsided. By squeezing the penis in this fashion, the sensation of impending orgasm disappears and sexual intercourse is continued. In this manner, ejaculation is postponed and sexual intercourse is lengthened. This pattern should be repeated approximately four times, each trial lasting 15 to 20 minutes. The man then ejaculates during the last trial.

This technique will not work if the man himself attempts to use it. It is important also for the couple not to use the technique as a game. Eventually, through overuse of the technique, it is possible that the man will become less and less sensitive to sexual stimulation.

Kegeling

This technique is named after the physician who developed these exercises. Kegeling is designed to strengthen the pubococcygeal muscle in women. The woman is taught to stop and start her urinary flow so that she can learn which muscle is involved. She then practices this exercise regularly in order to strengthen the muscle. Since this muscle is directly involved in the physiology of orgasm in the female, Kegeling has the indirect effect of helping the female learn about her own sexual apparatus and physiological response.

Sensate focus

Sensate focus is an important technique in sexual pleasuring. Masters and Johnson (1966) define sensate focus as the use of touch to provide sensory experiences in reconstituting natural responsivity to sexual stimuli. In this manner, clients are taught to go back in time to when they experienced the uninhibited sensual responses of early childhood. Further clients are removed from the spectator role and placed in a position in which they learn to communicate effectively with the sexual partner. Sensate focus is kept at a nonverbal level and involves the partners' touching each for sexual pleasure. It progresses from nongenital to genital touching in three phase.

In phase 1, purposeful erotic arousal, genital stimulation is carefully avoided. Tender, gentle touching is used instead. The purpose of this phase is to increase intimacy and mutual involvement. The responsibilities of the man to have an erection and the pressure on the woman to create one are removed.

Phase 2 of sensate focus, which typically, but not always, follows phase 1, involves progression to touching the genital areas. The intent of this phase is to produce sexual stimulation and arousal, but not orgasm. The couples are explicitly and implicitly encouraged to engage in progressive sexual behavior not involving orgasm.

The couple progresses to phase 3 only after they consider their response to phase 2 to be positive. Phase 3 involves orgasm by noncoital or coital means. In sum, the purpose of sensate focus is to reinstitute sexual responsiveness to touching. It is a crucial component to most, if not all, of the treatments of sexual dysfunctions, especially for genito-pelvic pain/ penetration disorder and female sexual desire/interest disorder. Helen Singer Kaplan (1974), a psychoanalyst who combined behavioral methods with more traditional psychotherapy, believes that sexual difficulties have immediate specific underlying causes. In her view, human sexual response is best seen as *triphasic*, or consisting of three separate but interlocking phases: desire, arousal, and orgasm. She believes that desire-phase disorders are the most difficult to treat, because they tend to be associated with deep-seated psychological difficulties. She also states that "the standard sex therapy methods seem to be effective primarily for those sexual problems which have their roots in mild and easily diminished anxieties and conflicts" (Kaplan, 1974b, xviii). To deal with the more complex cases, she uses a longer version of sex therapy which seeks a deeper level of insight and addresses unconscious conflicts. One of her underlying theories is that sexual disorder usually results from multiple causes, some more immediate and accessible, and others that are more remote and hidden.

The immediate causes include physiological and medical problems, which she feels account for approximately 20 percent of the cases, and the kinds of negative learning and association that encompass bad habits and negative cultural and social conditioning. Kaplan's method of therapy, like that of Masters and Johnson, focuses first on these immediate causes. In nearly 80 percent of the cases, such therapy is successful in alleviating sexual difficulty. Only then, if couples wish it, or therapy is not successful, are the deep personality conflicts explored.

According to Kaplan, most sexual dysfunctions involve a number of psychological components. The clinician who is trying to evaluate a given client's problem should be aware of four distinct but interrelated factors: (1) the immediate situation, (2) possible intrapsychic conflicts, (3) possible interpersonal conflicts, and (4) prior learning. With some clients, Kaplan suggests, one component may be more prominent than the rest. With others, all components may seem to play an equal part.

The details of Kaplan's treatment method differ considerably in some ways from the Masters and Johnson approach. In the treatment of premature (early) ejaculation, for example, she advocates the use of the "stop-start" technique instead of the squeeze.

Biological

Psychogenic erectile dysfunction is by far the type of erectile dysfunction most frequently encountered by therapists, accounting for more than 85 percent of the cases. There are organic reasons for this sexual dysfunction, however, some of which include such diseases as diabetes, pelvic traumas, arteriosclerosis, multiple sclerosis, cancer, spinal cord injury, and the aftermath of surgery of the prostate, colon, or bladder. Certain drugs, including alcohol, narcotics, antihypertensives, and antidepressants, can also affect sexual potency. Nevertheless, in the great majority of cases, erectile dysfunction has a psychological basis. Some organic causes of orgasmic dysfunction in women are hormonal imbalance, disorders of the nervous system, genital lesions, excessive use of drugs or alcohol, and deficient sexual apparatus (lack of a clitoris or ejaculator ducts).

Genito-pelvic pain/penetration disorder can be the result of disorders of the entrance to the vagina, such as an intact hymen, scar tissue, or infection; vaginal disorders, such as infections, or allergic reactions; thinning of the vaginal walls; scarring of the roof of the vagina; pelvic disorders, such as endometriosis; tumors; cysts; or tears in the ligaments which support the uterus. In general though, genito-pelvic pain/penetration disorder is usually due to the psychological factors of fear and guilt. The pain can involve the vagina, cervix, uterus, or bladder. The vaginal muscles become taut, and intercourse is painful, especially if the male partner is insensitive or clumsy. Genito-pelvic pain/penetration disorder can also occur when the woman has learned to associate gear and pain with sexual intercourse. Postmenopausal women frequently experience genito-pelvic pain/penetration disorder occurs because the mucous membrane of the vagina has become fragile and thin due to the decreased estrogen production. The vagina no longer secretes sufficient lubrication for easy penile insertion.

Organic factors involved in male hypoactive sexual desire disorder and female sexual interest/desire disorder include anemia, hypothyroidism, alcoholism, and Addison's disease. Certain drugs, such as antihypertensives, antihistamines (which dry up the vaginal membrane), heroin, cancer chemotherapeutic agents, and marijuana, can also diminish sexual desire.

Social Systems

Social work clinicians, whose major concern is the person-situation constellation, would agree with Masters and Johnson (1970) that it is frequently advisable to focus therapy on the interaction of the marital pair. However, clinical experiences have led many to believe that the most chronic marital complaints are unconscious wishes. The man who complains that his wife is frigid and cold unconsciously wants his spouse to be that way. Her warmth, intimacy, and sexual impulsivity would only serve to frighten him. Similarly, the wife who complains that her husband is weak and fragiles needs this kind of husband to protect her. His sexual potency would frighten her (Einstein, 1956; Strean, 1976). Moreover, the wife in the first example and the husband in the second are unconsciously conforming to each other's labels of them. If therapists do not take sides in a marital conflict, they eventually will be experienced by the client in the same way that the spouse is experienced (Strean, 1976).

Mental health professionals who adhere to social systems theory, role theory, ego psychology, and psychoanalysis often support their clinical observations with a recognition of the ever-present unconscious collusion between spouses in a sexually conflicted marriage (Strean, 1976). These theorists believe that Masters and Johnson (1970) and other behavioral therapists fail to understand that a sexual conflict is always a manifestation of a psychosocial conflict that had its roots in a client's life story. People with sexual conflicts react like frightened, angry, or inhibited children, and it is their unresolved childhood conflicts that must be addressed in sex therapy. Clients need to be assisted to see the parallels between the therapeutic relationship and their sexual relationship. They need to be helped to realize they are writing their own self-destructive scripts for sexual unhappiness.

Therapeutic Techniques

The treatment of sexual dysfunctions has undergone nothing less than a revolution over the years. Once regarded as very difficult and often intractable therapeutic challenges, most instances of sexual dysfunction now yield quite readily to programs of treatment involving new techniques that are still being developed and improved (Anderson, 1983; Leiblum & Rosen, 1979; Nowinski & LoPiccolo, 1979; Tollison et al., 1977). As a result, success rates approaching 90 percent or more for many of the dysfunctions have become quite routine.

The turning point is uniformly considered to be the publication in 1970 of Masters and Johnson's *Human Sexual Inadequacy*. The success rates claimed by this team of dedicated clinical researchers astonished the professional community and rapidly led to the widespread adoption of their general approach, which combines elements of traditional behavioral therapy in a framework emphasizing direct intervention aimed at the dysfunction itself.

While the early confidence inspired by Masters and Johnson's reported results has waned somewhat in the interim (Leiblum & Rosen, 1979; Vandereycken, 1982; Zildeberg, 1980), their work has unquestionably stimulated a host of new therapeutic techniques. Despite varying emphases and methods among treatment programs, there seems to be a general agreement on the importance of removing crippling misconceptions, inhibitions and fears, and fostering attitudes toward participation in sexual behavior as a pleasurable, natural, and meaningful experience.

Malatesta (1978) has named the following five components of sex therapy: (1) education, (2) relationship enhancement, (3) structured behavioral activities, (4) environmental rearrangement, and (5) anxiety management and other concerns. They feel that, without exception, the effective sex therapy plan should ascertain that the presenting couple or individual has an adequate *understanding of human sexuality*. The therapist should convey to the couple that (1) sexual problems do not necessarily indicate deep-seated emotional problems but probably reflect inadequate or maladaptive learning and experience, and (2) that neither partner is entirely responsible for a sexual dysfunction, and that positive change is entirely dependent on a mutually shared and mutually executed plan of therapeutic activity.

The strength of the couple's relationship is ultimately tied to the couple's motivation and the partner's involvement in the treatment process. Thus a typical therapeutic focus could be on the division of home labor, sex-role differentiation, life-style patterns, and conflict-resolution skills.

The prescription of a systematic plan of structured sexual activities remains an integral part of sex therapy. Another aspect of behavioral prescriptions involves the extent to which couples can disengage from extraneous stimuli such as work or children, promote interesting and creative atmosphere for sexual expression, and focus on self and partner sexuality. Last, when anxiety is a central feature of the sexual dysfunction, it may be important to employ more traditional methods of intervention, such as progressive muscle relaxation training, systematic desensitization, or hypnosis, before or during a sex therapy program (Kroger, 1977, 1981; Wincze, 1982; Wolpe, 1958).

The following are some more concrete therapy techniques:

1. Take an extensive history at the outset of therapy.

Before beginning treatment, the therapist should obtain an extensive history. This basically serves as a psychological examination and will aid the therapist in assessing the extent of the client's problem. It is crucial for the therapist to question the client about sexual fantasies, desires, and wishes. The information obtained will be invaluable to the diagnostic and assessment process. The therapist needs to determine explicit details of the couple's sexual relationship and information about the quality of their relationship in general.

2. *Refer the client for a complete physical examination.*

More so than in any of the other psychological disorders, it is crucial to rule out any organic cause of the sexual problem. For example, Masters and Johnson tell the story of three men who were referred to them with the presenting problem of impotence. These men had all been in therapy prior to coming to the institute; they had a combined fifteen years of therapy with five different therapists. Still the problem persisted. Upon entering the treatment facility, a complete sexual history was taken for these men. As it turned out, none of the men had ever had an orgasm by any means, not even through nocturnal emissions as adolescents. The therapy team referred them to a urinary specialist, a physician who not only specializes in urinary problems but also thoroughly understands the sexual apparatus of men and women.

As it turned out, these men did not have ejaculatory ducts; they would never ejaculate. These men could have gone for therapy for the rest of their lives and the problem would have remained because it was not psychological. Of course, after they were told that they did not not have ejaculatory ducts, they were offered psychological counseling to deal with this finding; however, no amount of psychological counseling could ever "cure" their problem. It is therefore crucial to utilize the expertise of professionals who are specifically trained in therapy, for they know which questions to ask.

3. *When treating a client who has a sexual problem, work closely with a sex therapist who can be utilized for supervisory/consultation purposes.*

Sexual dysfunctions often have different psychological roots than do the other, more psychologically based problems. There are times when clients simply need to be provided with accurate information about their bodies or are ignorant about sexual techniques or the sexual response. In cases such as these, a therapist who is specifically trained in this area should be consulted. These situations can usually be readily treated with sex therapy. Other problems may be more complex, arising, for example, out of either fear or failure, or a need to be in control during sexual activity, or fear of rejection if performance is inadequate. These situations can usually be ameliorated by short-term therapy. The focus here is teaching these clients to communicate their fears and anxieties. Again, a clinician specifically trained in sex therapy should be consulted.

For example, there was a case of a woman who had been in therapy for many years because of dyspareunia. She had explored in great detail with her original therapist her guilt and anxiety about sexuality in general, her feelings toward her husband, and her feelings toward her parents. Still the problem persisted. Frustrated after about five years with the other therapist, the woman decided to consult a certified sex therapist. After a detailed sex history was obtained, it became obvious that some other factor was at work. As it turned out, the woman was taking excessive doses of an over-the-counter antihistamine to relieve symptoms of her sinus congestion. Most antihistamines work by drying up mucous membranes, of which the vagina is one. The antihistamine was drying up this client's vagina, thereby making intercourse painful. The therapist suggested that the woman stop taking the antihistamine for a while. The client later reported that the problem had been eliminated. A therapist untrained in the effects of certain drugs on sexual anatomy and physiology would probably have led the therapy in another direction. It is important, therefore, once it has been ascertained that the client is presenting a primarily sexual dysfunction, to consult with a colleague who is specially trained in sex therapy.

Another case example points to the need for the therapist to be aware of the effect of drugs on sexual behavior. Bob B., a 42-year-old engineer, sought therapy for erectile dysfunction. Divorced, he had functioned adequately while married and initially following the break-up. The problem had first occurred about two months before he began therapy. During the initial sessions, he discussed his anger at his former wife and his fears about reentering the dating world. It was during one of these initial sessions that the therapist asked if he was taking any medication. He quickly answered,

"No, nothing that would cause this problem." The therapist persisted, asking him if he was taking any medication at all. He replied that all the took was blood pressure medication, which he was certain had nothing to do with his sexual problem. In fact, however, it had everything to do with his sexual problem. He was encouraged to discuss the problem with his family physician and to request an alternate medication, one that did not carry the side effect of erectile dysfunction.

Another group of clients who suffer from performance anxiety and fear of rejection are more difficult than the other two groups to treat. Others who fall into this group are those who fear romantic intimacy or sexual success (see Kaplan, 1974b). The sexual problems of these individuals stem from negative attitudes toward themselves, feelings of conflict, and severe insecurity. Sex therapy in these cases is aimed at alleviating basic problems of a fragile self-esteem and guilt following the pleasures associated with sex. Here the therapist must be able to deal with unconscious motivation and conflict. It is necessary in these cases for the therapist to shift from psychotherapy to sex therapy and back again, and to recognize the crucial points at which to do so. Brief psychotherapy is generally inappropriate for these clients; their problems are associated with severe psychopathology, such as pervasive paranoia and marked hostility in relationships.

In recognition of the need for specialized training and certification in the area of sex counseling and therapy, the American Association of Sex Educators, Counselors, and Therapists (AASECT) in 1973 appointed highly qualified professionals to establish training guidelines. AASECT reviews the experience and academic training of clinicians who wish to specialize in sex counseling and therapy. A list of qualified professionals can be obtained at www. AASECT.org.

4. *It is especially important when treating a client with a sexual dysfunction to be aware of one's own values and beliefs so that they are not projected onto the client.*

The case of Sally and Tom L. typifies one of the cautions necessary in the practice of sex therapy. They were an upper-middle-class couple who first came for counseling because of sexual problems. Sally was not interested in sex with Tom and they had not had sex in over three months.

Tom was very upset, not understanding what the problem was. They were observant Catholics, and the therapist assumed because of Sally's strict Catholic upbringing that she felt guilty about sex. The therapist then proceeded with treatment with this assumption in mind, working to help the couple accept and alleviate this anxiety with the ultimate goal of more open sexual communication. These attempts failed, and the couple left therapy shortly thereafter, with the problem unchanged.

When Sally called the same therapist for a session a year later, she informed the therapist that she and Tom had divorced. The major reason for the divorce was that Sally was involved in an affair with her girlfriend. Although it is probably true that the divorce would have occurred anyway, it was an important lesson for the therapist inasmuch as the therapist's assumptions had caused her to lead the therapy in a particular direction. If the assumptions had been examined and perhaps explored in the therapy, it is possible that the underlying fact of Sally's homosexuality would have surfaced, in which case other, more productive, issues could have been examined.

5. Help the clients to learn to communicate openly about sexuality.

Crucial to the process of sex therapy is to teach clients to communicate honestly and openly about sex. Atwood (1985) presents the following communication suggestions for clients who are having sexual problems:

1. Don't collect "trading stamps"; deal with issues immediately.
2. Attempt to reinterpret negative perceptions into more positive ones.
3. Avoid patterns of communication in which someone is a loser; aim instead for two winners.
4. Free yourself from preprogrammed responses.
5. Beware of transforming anxieties and insecurities about self into critical attacks on others.
6. Avoid patterns of denial/discounting. Responsibility shared is more rewarding than responsibility denied.
7. Listen and look. Tune into your partner.
8. Examine and evaluate feelings of guilt and anxiety.

Systemic Therapy

Clinicians should carefully evaluate the couple's general relationship at the beginning of therapy (Zimmer, 1987). Couples in conflict often exhibit some type of sexual disorder. These sexual disorders, however, can play various important roles in the maintenance of the couple system. For example, the sexual disorder may serve to divert the couple from other family interaction, help the couple maintain emotional distance, provide outlets for power positions or hostility, or sustain role-specific behavior. In cases like these, treating the sexual disorder in a sex therapeutic modality alone is likely to meet with failure, as the sexual disorder must be sustained by the couple in order to maintain stability.

This type of conceptualization enables the therapist to accomplish the following: (1) Assess and understand the influences within the couple in the etiology and maintenance of the sexual disorder; (2) Assess the relative strength of the relationship-enhancing forces that could potentially facilitate and support the process of sex therapy; and (3) Assess the relative strength of the relationship-diminishing forces that could potentially inhibit and even undermine the process of sex therapy. Therefore, a comprehensive and multidimensional approach to the treatment of sexual disorders must include a thorough evaluation of the couple relationship. Focusing on couple issues helps to facilitate rapid changes in both couple and sexual functioning.

A major problem in the field of sexy therapy is that for the most part it has not been grounded in or related to systems theory, meaning that sexual disorder continue to be treated as a special area both theoretically and clinically within the field of couple therapy. In other words, there has been little effort to develop a connection between the couple theories and theories of sexual behavior. Systems theorists, on the other hand, generally see sexuality as a symptom or a metaphor of the relationship, so that the couple might avoid dealing with the more essential couple issues. Similarly, there are a variety of ways in which systems theorists, depending on the context of the relationship, may view sexual disorders. In this viewpoint, sexual disorders do not exist in a vacuum, but are often related to problems in the couple's emotional relationship, such as poor communication, hostility and competitiveness, or sex role problems.

Even when the sexual disorder is not related to problems in the couple relationship, the couple's emotional relationship is often damaged by the sexual issue and feelings of guilt, inadequacy, and frustration that usually accompany the sexual disorder.

From this viewpoint, sexual problems hold a cyclical position in the couple's interaction. One partner's demands may be the result of his/her own sexual frustration and feelings of rejection. The other partner's anxiety might be a combination of sexual conflict, self-doubt about sexuality, and fear of failure to please their partner. Therefore, the important features of therapy include interrupting the cycle of interaction that has developed, separating the sexual issue from the relationship as a while, exploring the roots of the sexual disorder, and then integrating it with feelings of love. Therapy from this point of view tends to focus on the couple's interactions and the system dynamics that are maintaining the problematic sexual patterns.

In essence, the major approaches to sex therapy can be divided into two camps. On one hand, with the Masters and Johnson and the newer sex therapy models, sexual disorder is treated seriously and the sexual issue presented is the problem to be worked on. On the other hand, using the psychoanalytic and more systemically based sex therapies, sexual disorder is seen as a manifestation of an underlying conflict, metaphor, or symptom of a problem in the couple relationship. The two major camps represent the division between the fields of couple therapy and sex therapy. Atwood and Weinstein (1989) suggest that it is time for the fields of couple therapy and sex therapy to be brought together. It can be argued that it does not make sense to train people to practice couple and family therapy without adequately training them in human sexuality, nor is it fruitful to train people to practice sex therapy without giving them the context in which to apply it. Rather than referring clients to a "sex therapist," Sager (1976) believed that couple and family therapists need to be versed in sex therapy and able to shift focus when necessary. Lief (1977) also believes that it is impossible to undertake sex therapy without exploring the quality of the couple's relationship.

Recently, postmodern approaches to couple therapy have begun to be used. For a description of one such postmodern approach, see Atwood (1993). Current research (Althof, 2010; Binik & Meana, 2009; McCarthy

& Thestrup, 2008; Metz & McCarthy, 2004) overwhelmingly supports an integrative approach, in addition to the belief that clinicians do not need to specialize in sex therapy to effectively work with the many variations of sexual issues presented by couples and individuals. The assessment techniques remain constant, regardless of one's sexual orientation, preferences, sexual identity, race, ethnicity and culture. A thorough analysis of the sexual history, current sexual practices, relationship history and quality, emotional well-being and satisfaction, and contextual factors combine with all relevant biological and medical components necessary to understand the creation and maintenance of the current relational conditions (Althof, 2010).

When to Refer

1. Refer the client to a medical physician or a urologist if you suspect that the problem has a biological rather than psychological etiology.
2. The clients should be re-diagnosed or referred it is suspected that the sexual problem is secondary to some more disturbing psychological problem, such as schizophrenia or depression. Depression very often leads to a lack of desire for sex. If the therapist focuses only on the sexual problem and not on the person in the context of the environment, the problem may persist.

References

American Psychiatric Association. (2000). *Diagnostic and Statistical Manual of Mental Disorders* (4th ed., Text Revision). Washington, DC: American Psychiatric Association.

American Psychiatric Association. (2013). *Diagnostic and Statistical Manual of Mental Disorders* (5th ed.). Washington, DC: American Psychiatric Association.

Anderson, B. L. (1983). Primary orgasmic dysfunction: Diagnostic considerations and review of treatment. *Psychological Bulletin, 93*(1), 105-36.

Atwood, J. (1985). Techniques to open sexual communication. In *Marriage and Family Living.* St. Meinard, IN: Abbey Press.

Atwood, Joan D. (2001) Invited Chapter. Sexual Dysfunctions and Sex Therapy. In Joseph Wecksler, An Introduction to Marriage and Family Therapy. New York: The Haworth Press.

Atwood, Joan D. (2004) Invited Chapter. Sexual Issues in Family Therapy. In Family Therapy Review.by Robert Coombs, Houghton Mifflin/Lawrence Erlbaum Associates.

Atwood, Joan D. (2002). Invited Chapter. Sexual Issues and Therapy. In Estelle Weinstein and Efrem Rosen's Critical Issues in Sexuality: Implications for Psychotherapy. Boston, Mass.: American Press.

Atwood, Joan D. and Klucinec, E. (2008). Current State of Sexuality Theory and Therapy. Invited Chapter. Handbook of Clinical Issues in Couple Therapy. Routledge.

Binik, Y. M. (2010). The DSM diagnostic criteria for vaginismus. *Archives of Sexual Behavior, 39*, 278-291.

Brotto, L. (2013). Sexual Pain Disorders. Retrieved from http:// http://www.obgyn.ubc.ca/SexualHealth/sexual_dysfunctions/ pain_disorders.php

Buvat, J. (2003). Hyperprolactinemia and sexual function in men: a short review. *International Journal of Impotence Research, 15*, 373-77.

Eisenstein, V. W. (1956). *Neurotic Interaction in Marriage.* New York: Basic Books.

Ersner-Hershfield, R., & Kopel, S. (1979). Group treatment of preorgasmic women: Evalutation of partner involvement and spacing of sessions. *Journal of Consulting and Clinical Psychology, 47*, 750-59.

Frank, E., Anderson, C., & Rubenstein, D. N. (1978). Frequency of sexual dysfunction in normal couples. *New England Journal of Medicine, 299*(3), 111-15.

Kaplan, H. S. (1974a). The classification of female sexual dysfunction. *Journal of Sex and Marital Therapy, 1*(2), 124-38.

Kaplan, H. S. (1974b). *The new sex therapy.* New York: Brunner-Mazel.

Khatchadourian, H. A., & Lunde, D. T. (1972). *Fundamentals of human sexuality.* New York: Holt, Rhinehart and Winston.

Kinsey, A. C., Pomeroy, W. B., & Martin, C. E. (1948). *Sexual behavior in the human male.* Philadelphia: W. B. Saunders.

Kinsey, A. C., Pomeroy, W. B., Wardell, B., Martin, C. E., and Gebhard, P. H. (1953). *Sexual behavior in the human female.* Philadelphia: Saunders.

Kroger, W. S. (1977). *Clinical and experimental hypnosis in medicine, dentistry, and psychology* (2nd ed.). Philadelphia: JB Lippincott.

Leiblum, S. R., & Rosen, R. C. (1979). The weekend workshop for dysfunctional couples: Assets and limitations. *Journal of Sex and Marital Therapy, 5*(1), 57-69.

LoPiccolo, J., & Heiman, J. (1977). Cultural values and the therapeutic definition of sexual function and dysfunction. *Journal of Social Issues, 33*(2), 166-83.

Malatesta, V. J. (1978). The affects of alcohol on ejaculation latency in human males. Unpublished doctoral dissertation, University of Georgia.

Masters, W. H., & Johnson, V. E. (1966). *Human Sexual Response.* Boston: Little, Brown.

Masters, W. H., & Johnson, V. E. (1970). *Human Sexual Inadequacy.* Boston: Little, Brown.

Masters, W. H., & Johnson, V. E. (1976). Principles of the new sex therapy. *American Journal of Psychiatry, 133*(5), 548-54.

McCary, J. L. (1973). *Human Sexuality: Physiological, Psychological, and Sociological Factors* (2nd ed.). New York: Van Nostrand.

Munjack, D. J., and Staples, F. R. (1976). Psychological characteristics of women with sexual inhibition (frigidity) in sex clinics. *Journal of Nervous and Mental Disease, 163,* 117-29.

Nowinski, J. K., & LoPiccolo, J. (1979). Assessing sexual behavior in couples. *Journal of Sex and Marital Therapy, 5*(3), 225-43.

Singer, J., & Singer, I. (1972). Types of female orgasms. *Journal of Sex Research, 8,* 255-67.

Strean, H. S. (1976). A psychosocial view of social deviancy. *Clinical Social Work Journal, 4*(3), 187-203.

Tollison, C. D., Nasbilt, J. G., & Frey, J. D. (1977). Comparison of attitudes towards sexual intimacy in prostitutes and college coeds. *Journal of Social Psychology, 101*(2), 319-20.

Vandereycken, W. (1982). Paradoxical strategies in a blocked sex therapy. *American Journal of Psychotherapy, 36*(1), 103-108.

Wagner, G., & Metz, P. (1980). Impotence (erectile dysfunction) due to vascular disorders: An overview. *Journal of Sex and Marital Therapy, 6*(4), 223-33.

Wincze, J. P. (1982). Assessment of sexual disorders. *Behavioral Assessment, 4*(3), 257-71.

Wolpe, J. (1958). *Psychotherapy by Reciprocal Inhibition.* Stanford, CA: Stanford University Press.

Zilbergeld, B. (1980). Alternatives to couple counseling for sex problems: Group and individual therapy. *Journal of Sex and Marital Therapy, 6*(1), 3-18.

Chapter 11

Substance Abuse

Michelle Wiley M.A., MFT

What Is Alcohol Abuse and How Do You Recognize It?

Drug abuse problems span the globe and have been with us for centuries (Austin 1978). In the early 1600's, the use of tobacco became very controversial in England. Similar historical reactions to opium were observed in China from 1700 through the mid-1980. History provides evidence that various cultures have found it difficult to control drugs. If a sufficient portion of the population provides a demand for a drug, it appears that the laws are never completely effective in stopping its use or abuse. In the United States, the failure of a national prohibition against alcohol, which was instituted in 1920 and repealed in 1933, provides one of the clearest examples of this failure. It is apparent that something other than legal sanctions and controls is necessary to stop the use of many of the substances that have been abused over the past 400 years. One of contemporary society's major concerns is preventing the use of any drug from developing into a maladaptive pattern of abuse.

The use of drugs, including alcohol, provides one of the clearest examples of how a behavior pattern can range from a totally acceptable and adaptive behavior to a serious, maladaptive pattern. Using alcohol is an acceptable social custom in many cultures, and it is kept under control by most individuals who drink. However, there are approximately 9 to 10 million alcoholics in the United States. Of the estimated 90 million people in the United States who do drink, 81 million are social drinkers. The other 9 million are alcoholics, and of these, at least 3 million are female.

Although the incidence of alcoholism is thought to be increasing in women, estimates still indicate that there are about four times as many male as female alcoholics. In some respects, alcoholism in women differs from alcoholism in men. Although many of the basic symptoms are the same, women alcoholics are more likely than men to drink alone, to hide their drinking and to feel guilty and ashamed by it. Because the alcoholic woman is strongly stigmatized in our society, she may make unusual efforts to conceal her drinking. Her best friends may never have seen her drunk. The alcoholic woman bears a double burden- she not only suffers from the stigma of drinking, but she is also looked upon as more of a moral transgressor than the alcoholic man. Alcoholic women more often suffer from associated depression and seek medical help for nervousness and insomnia. Because their drinking is not often recognized as the cause of these complaints, many of the women (more often than alcoholic men) also develop a secondary dependence on prescribed sedatives and tranquilizers. There is also a notable difference in the age of onset and progression. In general, alcoholism starts considerably later in women than it does in men and progresses much more rapidly once it starts.

There does appear to be some clear ethnic differences in the incidence of alcoholism (McCord et al. 1960). Rates of alcoholism in ethnic groups that emphasize the use of alcohol for religious or dining purposes, such as Jews and Italians, are generally lower than in ethnic groups that use alcohol for recreational use, such as the Irish. Alcoholism is also more common in urban areas. The vast majority of alcoholics (70 percent) live at home with their families. The skid row alcoholic who lives from one bottle to the next on the streets or in the woods accounts for less than 5 percent of the alcoholics in America. Although alcoholism is generally a middle-age disorder, there has been an alarming increase in alcoholism among young people, including adolescents and college students. Recent government estimates suggest that 20 percent of 14-to 19-year olds drink alcohol on a regular basis. Estimates for college students indicate that as many as 70 to 95 percent drink, and that up to 25 percent will at some point in their lives have problems with their drinking (Ingalls 1978).

Recent analyses of survey data by Calahan (1978) indicate that a great percentage of alcohol-related problems tend to occur in younger persons. When a number of specific problems, such as excessive drinking; problems at work due to drinking; and problems with spouse, friends, or neighbors, were included, the youngest group studied (21- to 24-year-olds) had by far the highest prevalence of problems. Thus, although we often think of the typical alcoholic as the 40- to 55-year-old, this may be a very misleading impression.

In contrast to approaches that examine only the incidence of alcoholism, Calahan (1978) took a more comprehensive approach by looking at various personal, family, social, health, and behavioral problems associated with drinking. His data suggested that alcohol-related problems are more common than would be expected. Based on summary scores of alcohol-related problems, 15 percent of the men and 4 percent of the women had relatively severe problems associated with alcohol, while another 28 percent of the men and 17 percent of the women had moderate difficulty. These findings suggest that the impact of alcohol abuse and dependency may be more pervasive than might have been anticipated, since 43 percent of the men and 21 percent of the women had at least moderate problems linked to alcohol.

The cost of alcoholism is enormous; to individuals, their families, and society at large. The male alcoholic who has maintained a chronic drinking habit for several years usually creates and experiences the highest cost to himself and to society. He often has lost his family, his health, his employment opportunities, his financial resources, and his self-respect.

A substantial proportion of homicides and suicides are related to alcohol abuse. The majority of highway deaths and accidents involve drivers who were drinking and who would have been considered to have serious problems with alcohol. Problem drinkers usually have poor work performance and high rates of absenteeism. Furthermore, there are the high costs to the local, state, and federal health agencies who provide medical and other treatment services to alcoholics. The total expenditure for dealing with alcoholism is many billions of dollars. Estimates indicate annual costs to industry of more than $9 billion, cost for automobile accidents of more than $6 billion, and a health care bill of over $8 billion (National Institute of Alcohol Abuse and Alcoholism 1974). These personal and economic costs are likely to increase dramatically in the next decade. This is primarily due to increasing rates of drinking problems among adolescents and women. It also appears that a growing number of individuals who formerly abused other drugs are now turning to alcohol.

Although alcohol is America's most abused drug, and although much time and money has been invested in studying it, its action on the brain remains unclear. Many things *are* known, however: (1) It is primarily a depressant drug; (2) tolerance develops to the effects of alcohol; (3) after prolonged use of moderate to high levels of alcohol, addiction occurs; (4) a sudden decrease in alcohol intake in an alcoholic will result in a dangerous withdrawal syndrome called delirium tremens (DTs).

To some degree, the definition of addiction and the identification of addicts is arbitrary. Addiction does not simply imply negative personality traits or criminal behavior. Rather, it is a description of how the body adapts to foreign substances. To be addicted, a person must use drugs to the extent that four conditions are present:

1. *Cellular tolerance.* After a period of time, it becomes clear that more and more of the drug is required to produce the same effects or the level of intoxication experienced initially. Tolerance may develop slowly, over a number of years, as it does in alcoholism, or it may develop rapidly, within a month, as it does with heroin.

2. *Loss of control.* The addicted person eventually cannot control the timing and/or the dosage of the drug he/she uses. Often the individual will crave the drug if they have not used it recently, and taking even one dose will produce the urge to take another and another, until physical or financial disability prevent further use. Another form of loss of control is seen in alcohol users who can control the amount of alcohol they use at any one time, but cannot stop using the drug, even for brief periods of time.

3. *Withdrawal.* Once an individual's body has adapted to the presence of the drug, its absence will initially upset the equilibrium of the cellular environment. Severe discomfort may occur, including pain, tremors, profuse sweating, nausea, and irritability when the drug cannot be obtained. Withdrawal symptoms usually appear within a few hours of the last dose of the drug and may persist for several days.

4. *Disruption of lifestyle.* Often added to the list is a fourth criterion of addiction, which reflects psychological or social changes, rather than physiological ones, attributed to the use of the drug. People addicted to drugs often find themselves unable to meet others' expectations with regard to family maintenance, job performance, and social responsibility. At times even the smallest demand exceeds the addict's capacity. Their coping mechanisms and social responsibilities are hindered.

Although alcohol in moderate quantities generally produces pleasurable changes in mood, its effects are often unpredictable. In some cases alcohol will produce a "glow" or a "high"; at other times it will have no effect at all; sometimes it will intensify a depressed mood. Much depends on the individual's physical and emotional state.

Prior to the 1950's, alcoholism was viewed as a moral problem, and since it was seen as a moral issue, the subject was not discussed in scientific circles. The alcoholic was simply a weak individual who suffered from a lack of moral fiber. Just as Kinsey and Masters and Johnson made sex an acceptable topic for discussion, E. Jellinek developed a disease concept of alcoholism, thereby freeing the alcoholic from moral guilt. Jellinek (1952) provided the classic description of alcohol addiction as a four-stage process.

Stages of Alcohol Dependence

Although the distinction between alcohol independence and alcohol abuse may prove to be an important diagnostic consideration in the future, most research at this time has not attempted to make this differentiation. Thus, most of what is described in this section applies to those who have been classified simply as "alcoholics" in the past.

Although every alcoholic will not show the same pattern, Jellinek (1971) described the typical developmental course in alcoholic dependence. In spite of Jellinek's heavy reliance on a disease model, his discussion of the development of alcoholism is important to non-disease approaches because his view emphasizes the gradual development of alcoholic behavior patterns. In other words, a person does not become an alcoholic overnight. Instead the complex behavior patterns associated with excessive reliance on alcohol develop gradually, over a period of years.

In the earliest stage, the *prealcoholic phase*, normal social drinking provides the individual with considerable relief of tension and anxiety. As drinking increases to achieve tension relief, tolerance to the effects of alcohol develop. The individual, who had previously been drinking only socially, often finds him/herself tense and unable to handle problems. After experiencing relief from these tensions while drinking, the person discovers that it is not the situations or the people that relax them, but the drug. After heavy social drinking for a period of six months to two years, the future addict may enter the second, or prodromal, phase.

In the *prodromal phase*, the complications of excessive drinking begin to accumulate. The individual may begin to experience some subjective discomfort associated with the use of the drug. The individual may notice a "need" for the drug and feel tense and apprehensive when not using it. *Blackouts* loss of memory for certain periods of time- may occur. For example, the person may not remember where he was the previous night or how he returned home. The person may think about drinking throughout the day and engage in it while alone. The actual drinking behavior may change; the individual often begins to drink very rapidly, gulping drinks rather than sipping them. Unpleasant emotional reactions, such as depression, guilt, or extreme anxiety, may also develop during this phase. The person becomes reluctant to discuss their drinking behavior.

During the *crucial phase*, alcoholics lose control over their drinking, and further deterioration in psychological, social, and physical functioning occurs. The transition from the second to the third stage occurs quietly, almost imperceptibly. The alcoholic feels that he cannot abstain from drinking; or, if he can, the first drink leads to continuous use, until unconsciousness or depletion of funds stops the spree or binge. Because the body is now adapted to the presence of alcohol, cessation of drinking may lead to withdrawal symptoms.

Severe psychological and physical disturbances may also occur. Self-esteem and self-confidence decline, and social obligations which were previously met are now ignored. With continued excessive drinking, appetite is lost, and eating is avoided for long periods of time. As nutritional status declines, various physical complications, including brain damage, can occur if this pattern is maintained.

If the person is unable to obtain alcohol for any length of time and blood alcohol levels drop too rapidly, delirium tremens (DTs) may occur. The person's heart may race, their body may shake uncontrollably, and perspiration may be profuse. Visual or tactile hallucinations may occur. The person may be restless, unable to sleep, apprehensive, and fearful. Increased defensiveness, in the form of denial and projection, eventually leads to a lifestyle of social isolation and sudden hostility and aggression towards others.

Physical and psychological deterioration set in during the *chronic phase*, when the more extreme consequences of alcoholism are experienced as the person "hits bottom". During this stage, the alcoholic usually suffers from malnutrition, loss of feeling in the hands and legs, tremors, chronic nausea. Gastritis, and eventually, irreversible brain damage. Unable to work or stay with the family, and possessing little money, the alcoholic typically gravitates to the poorest of neighborhoods, often drinking with those in a lower socioeconomic class. Personal grooming and hygiene may be neglected in favor of obsessions with obtaining the drug.

Jellinek believes that it is only at this stage that the person will give up the struggle with alcohol and seek treatment for the addiction. Drinking is almost continuous during this stage, and the person may drink *any* alcoholic substance- including hair tonic, mouthwash, shoe polish, toxic wood alcohol, and even sterno- when regular alcoholic beverages are not available. Social contacts center around interactions with other alcoholics, as contacts with former friends, family, and employers are usually lost. The alcoholic person may now be living on the streets.

As stated earlier, other psychological symptoms, such as hallucinations and paranoid fear, develop in some individuals. The alcoholic who stops drinking at this time may experience DTs. When these individuals reach the final phase, it becomes increasingly difficult for them to accept their behavior. Some will admit to their addiction and seek help; others will live out this destructive pattern until an earlier-than-necessary death. Again, it must be remembered that these are only general phases of alcoholism. Many alcoholics seek treatment prior to progressing to the advanced stages of alcoholism.

The following list summarizes the four stages of alcohol dependence:

1. Prealcoholic Phase

    In this stage, alcohol produces marked release from anxiety or other discomfort; the frequency of drinking increase; the tolerance for alcohol increases

2. Prodromal Phase

    In this stage, the person has his or her first memory blackouts; there is a preoccupation with alcohol; there is hidden drinking, drinking alone, avoidance of discussion of drinking; the gulping of drinks; there is guilt about drinking and behavior

3. Crucial Phase

   Here, there is a loss of control over drinking (starting to drink usually leads to full drunkenness, but can still sometimes avoid taking first drink; frequent morning drinking); the person rationalizes drinking as acceptable; there is a lowering of self-esteem; there is a loss of friends and family, and impairment of job functioning; the person begins to neglect nutrition

4. Chronic Stage

   In this stage, there is frequent, often constant, drinking, with no control, impairments of thinking, a lack of concern with social standards, shift of friendships to other heavy drinkers, the person will drink any source of alcohol, fears, hallucinations, and tremors often develop, the person often admits defeat

Jellinek's four-stage descent into alcoholism used to be cited almost routinely in textbooks, but as vivid as it appears to be, it is no longer considered entirely accurate. Critics (Marlatt et al. 1973, Pihl and Spiers 1978, Polich et al. 1980) claim that although it appears to capture some features of alcoholism, it is too rigid to apply to every case. In Fact, Knupfer (1972) claims that alcoholics do not conform to any single pattern, perhaps because alcohol abuse is so widespread. She interviewed a sample of adult males drawn at random from the San Francisco area. She discovered that a rather high percentage of the group- about 30 percent- admitted having a serious drinking problem. Approximately half of these men described their consumption as "excessive". Yet relatively few fit Jellinek's four-stage model, and even more intriguing, a third of the very heavy drinkers had already "reformed". Most had quit on their own, and practically none of them could articulate a clear reason for breaking their dependence.

Knupfer's assessment has been bolstered by another very intensive research project. Polich and colleagues (Polich et al. 1980) conducted a four year study of alcoholics, all men who had contacted one of the Alcoholism

Treatment Centers funded by the National Institute on Alcohol Abuse and Alcoholism. These subjects underwent extensive interviews and a variety of tests, both psychological and medical. In order to ensure that the information they were furnishing was accurate, their friends and relatives were also interviewed. Most important of all, the researchers made a strenuous attempt to keep track of their subjects over the four-year period and succeeded in determining what had happened to 85 percent of them (an exceedingly high proportion for any follow-up effort thus far). Some alcoholics were still drinking heavily, some had quit and then resumed, and others had stopped and were remaining abstinent. A small percentage (8 percent) had been able to return to controlled drinking. And finally, quite a few (almost 15 percent) had died-at a rate "two and one half times the rate that would be expected in a population of a comparable age and racial distribution" (p. 175). Thus, while it appears that Jellinek's model may be useful in some cases, it is not relevant in all cases. Recent research also indicates that there is no one alcoholic pattern; rather, people appear to respond to alcohol, at least initially, according to their own unique personality constitutions.

Another significant point to be made is that most of the studies on alcoholism have been limited to males. Experts traditionally believed that alcoholism was far more common among men than among women. They now believe, however, that female alcoholics are quite numerous and that their ranks may be increasing (Gomberg 1974). Some theorists have suggested, in fact, that alcohol abuse has been fairly common among women all along; it has simply been less visible, they claim, because women are generally quieter about their drinking behavior. They are more likely to drink in secret and less likely to become violent when intoxicated (Pihl and Spiers 1978, Wilsnack 1973).

In addition to intoxication, alcohol abuse can lead to other alcohol-induced states that often bring clients to emergency rooms. Alcohol-induced hallucinations and DTs are examples. Alcohol-induced hallucinations are not diagnosed easily. In acute *alcoholic hallucinosis,* the individual generally will experience hallucinations of some type (usually auditory) and will usually have appropriate reactions to the hallucinations (for example, fear if the hallucinations are fear provoking). They will also have no delirium or confusion, and will have no easily identifiable signs of heavy alcohol use.

An example of this process is as follows: First the individual may hear a voice speaking simple statements. With time, however, the hallucinations usually extend to the voices of several people, all of them critical and reproachful. The individual's innermost weakness, particularly sexual ones, may be itemized, and various horrible punishments then proposed. The person may hear the clanking of chains, the sharpening of knives, the sound of pistol shots, or footsteps approaching in a threatening manner. Terror stricken, the individual may scream for help or attempt suicide.

In some cases, the individual may be misdiagnosed as schizophrenic; especially if alcohol abuse is denied, and there is no friend or family member to give accurate information. Alcoholic hallucinations may occur in some long term, heavily drinking alcoholics who have stopped drinking or have reduced considerably their alcohol intake in the previous 48 hours. There are no significant differences in the type of hallucinations or other symptoms experienced by the alcoholic with hallucinosis. The only clear distinguishing characteristic is the individual's history. This condition may continue for several days or even weeks, during which time the person is depressed but fairly well oriented and coherent, apart from the hallucinations. After recovery, the client usually shows considerable remorse and guilt, as well as some insight into what has happened.

Investigators are now less inclined than they had previously been to attribute this type of psychotic reaction solely to the effects of alcohol. Rather, it seems to be related to a broader pattern of maladaptive behavior. In other words, while the psychotic symptoms can be triggered by the alcohol, it is probable that they could have been similarly brought about by other drugs, illness, exhaustion, or other types of stress.

The other alcohol-induced state, *delirium tremens*, is relatively easy to identify. Delirium tremens is probably the best known of the various alcoholic psychotic reactions. A fairly common occurrence among those who drink excessively for a long time, this reaction may occur during a prolonged drinking spree or upon the withdrawal of alcohol after prolonged drinking. The DTs are a sequence of symptoms resulting from a continuing decrease in alcohol levels in an alcoholic. There are usually four stages of symptoms. The first stage begins with the psychomotor agitation and hyperactivity of the autonomic nervous system that continues throughout all four stages. The shakes and anxiety may begin within two or three hours of no alcohol intake. The shakes (most noticeably hand tremors) become progressively more intense and disruptive, until the individual might not even be able to feed himself. This initial stage is also characterized by a very rapid heart rate, profuse perspiration, hypertension, insomnia, and loss of appetite. In the absence of treatment or further alcohol intake, these symptoms progress.

It may be four, six, or eight hours after the last drink, but the appearance of hallucinations will mark the beginning of the second stage. These hallucinations may affect any sensory system-visual, auditory, or tactile-and are similar to those that occur in alcohol hallucinosis. The differential diagnosis is easily rendered, however, none of the first-stage symptoms are present in alcoholic hallucinosis.

In the third stage, delirium develops and delusions begin, intermittently at first and then for increasing durations followed by amnesia for the entire episode. Disorientation to time and place is common. All of the earlier stages may develop in the first 24 hours after the last drink, or it may take 96 hours for the stage to appear. The time course of DTs depends on the rate at which alcohol levels decrease.

Finally, the fourth stage is marked by severe grand mal seizures that may occur frequently, and sometimes cause death. The four stages overlap, merge, and are sometimes missed as discrete stages. The clinical situation is never quite like the typification described here. Thus, the delirium is usually preceded by a period of restlessness and insomnia, often accompanied by general uneasiness and apprehensiveness. Slight noises and objects that appear to be suddenly moving may produce considerable excitement and agitation.

Once the symptoms fully appear, they may include the following: (1) disorientation to time and place (for example, mistake the hospital for a church or a jail, no longer recognize friends, or identify hospital attendants as old acquaintances); (2) vivid hallucinations (particularly of small, fast-moving animals like snakes, rats, and roaches) which are clearly localized in space; (3) acute fear, often provoked by the hallucinated animals' changing form, size, or color in terrifying ways; (4) extreme suggestibility, in which a person can be made to see almost any form of animal if its presence is merely suggested; (5) marked tremor of the hands, tongue, and lips; and (6) any other symptoms which may include perspiration, fever, rapid and weak heartbeat, coated tongue, and foul breath.

The delirium typically lasts from three to six days and is generally followed by a deep sleep. When the person awakens, few symptoms remain, aside from possible remorse, but most clients will have been badly scarred and may not resume drinking for several weeks or months. However, without therapy drinking eventually begins again, only to be followed by a return to the hospital with another attack. The death rate from delirium tremens as a result of seizures, heart failure, and other complications used to be approximated at 10 percent (Tavel 1962). With drugs such as chlordiazepoxide (Librium), the death rate during delirium tremens and acute alcohol withdrawal has been markedly reduced.

In actual practice, a client clearly "going into" DTs would be hospitalized-usually on a medical unit since the medical problems are more critical at that point than the psychiatric problems-and treated with a long-lasting benzodiazepine, usually chlordiazepoxide (Librium). The benzodiazepine has cross tolerance with alcohol and will substitute for the alcohol, thus inhibiting withdrawal (DTs). The amount of benzodiazepine is gradually reduced until discontinuation in four to seven days, at which point the individual has been detoxified to alcohol.

Korsakoff's psychosis, another of the psychoses associated with alcoholism, was first described by the Russian psychiatrist Korsakoff in 1887. The outstanding symptom is a memory defect (particularly with regard to recent events) which is concealed by falsification. Individuals may not recognize pictures, faces, rooms, and other objects that they have just seen; although they may sense that these people or objects are familiar. These people increasingly tend to fill gaps with reminiscences and fanciful tales that lead to unconnected and distorted associations. These individuals may appear to be delirious, hallucinating, and disoriented to time and place, but ordinarily their confusion and disordered conduct are closely related to their attempts to fill in the memory gaps. The memory disturbance itself seems related to an inability to form new associations in a manner that renders them readily retrievable. Such a reaction usually occurs in older alcoholics, and only after many years of excessive drinking.

The symptoms of this disorder are now thought to be due to Vitamin B deficiency and other dietary inadequacies. A diet rich in vitamins and minerals generally restores the patient to more normal physical and mental health. However, some personality deterioration usually remains, in the form of memory impairment, blunted intellectual capacity, and diminished moral and ethical standards.

Another alcohol related disorder is *pathological intoxication*. This is an acute reaction that occurs in individuals whose tolerance to alcohol is chronically low (such as epileptics or those of an unstable personality makeup) or in normal individuals whose tolerance to alcohol is temporarily lessened by exhaustion, emotional stress, or other conditions. Following the intake of even moderate amounts of alcohol, these individuals may suddenly become disoriented and may even commit violent crimes. This confused, disoriented state is usually followed by a period of deep sleep, with complete amnesia afterward.

While 80 percent of alcoholics can be expected to experience some withdrawal symptomatology (Mello and Mendelson 1979), only 5 to 15 percent develop the more serious withdrawal symptoms; convulsions, confusion, disorientation, and hallucinations (Schuckit-Rorpes 1979, Sellers and Kalant 1976). Although most alcoholics experience at least some of the less severe symptoms of withdrawal, DTs occur in only 5 percent of alcoholics hospitalized for major withdrawal (Victor and Adams 1953), with an estimated incidence among alcoholics of between 1 and 15 percent (Gross et al. 1973).

Criteria Grouping for the Substance Use Disorders

In this category, the person experiences, social impairment, risky use, and pharmacological criteria. A problematic pattern of substance use leading to clinically significant impairment or distress occurs. Substance is often taken in larger amounts or over a longer period than was intended; there is a persistent desire or unsuccessful efforts to cut down or control substance use; a great deal of time is spent in activities necessary to obtain, use, or recover from its effects; craving or strong desire or urge to use the substance; recurrent substance use resulting in a failure to fulfill at major role obligations at work, school or home; continued substance use despite having persistent or recurrent social or interpersonal problems caused or exacerbated by the effects of substance use; important social, occupational or recreational activities are given up or reduced because of substance use; recurrent substance use in situations in which it is physically hazardous;

substance use is continued despite knowledge of having a persistent or recurrent physical or psychological problem that is likely to have been caused or exacerbated by the substance.

Substance Induced Symptoms

To give the reader an idea of the experiences of the symptoms in these categories, the following are brief summaries of the disorder.

Alcohol Intoxication Criteria 303.00

In this category, there is recent ingestion of alcohol; clinically significant problematic behavioral or psychological changes (e.g. inappropriate sexual or aggressive behavior, mood labiality, impaired judgment) that developed during or shortly after, alcohol ingestion, slurred speech, incoordination, unsteady gait, nystagmus (involuntary rapid eye movement in one or both eyes), impairment in attention or memory, stupor or coma.

Alcohol Withdrawal 291.81

With the cessation of alcohol where the use has been heavy or prolonged, the person experiences: autonomic hyperactivity (e.g, sweating or pulse rate greater than 100 bpm), increased hand tremor; insomnia, nausea or vomiting, transient visual, tactile, or auditory hallucinations or illusions, psychomotor agitation, anxiety, generalized tonic-clonic seizures.

These symptoms signs or symptoms cause clinically significant distress or impairment in social, occupational, or other important areas of functioning.

Caffeine Intoxication Criteria 305.90 (F15.929)

There has been a recent consumption of caffeine, restlessness, nervousness, excitement, insomnia, flushed face, diuresis (urine production), gastrointestinal disturbance, muscle twitching, rambling flow of thought or speech, tachycardia, or arrhythmia, periods of inexhaustibility, and psychomotor agitation. These signs or symptoms cause clinically significant stress or impairment in social, occupational, or other important areas of functioning.

Caffeine Withdrawal Criteria 292.0 (F15.93)

After a prolonged daily use of caffeine, there is an abrupt cessation or reduction in caffeine use. The person experiences headache, marked fatique or drowsiness, dysphoric mood, depressed mood, or irritability, difficulty concentrating, flu like symptoms, and the signs or symptoms cause clinically significant stress or impairment in social, occupational, or other important areas of functioning.

Cannabis Intoxication Criteria 292.89

This category includes a recent use of cannabis, clinically significant problematic behavior or psychological changes (e.g., impaired motor coordination, euphoria, anxiety, sensation of slowed time, impaired judgment, social withdrawal) that developed during, or shortly after, cannabis use, conjunctival injection, increased appetite, dry mouth, and tachycardia

Cannabis Withdrawal 292.0 (F12.288)

Once cannabis use that has been heavy and prolonged stops, symptoms develop in about 1-3 weeks. These symptoms include: irritability, anger, or aggression, nervousness or anxiety, sleep difficulty (e.g., insomnia, disturbing dreams), decreased appetite or weight loss, restlessness, and depressed mood. These physical symptoms can cause significant discomfort: abdominal pain, shakiness/tremors, sweating, fever, chills, or headache and the symptoms in cause clinically significant distress or impairment in social, occupational, or other important areas of functioning.

Phencyclidine Intoxication Criteria 292.89

There is a use of phencyclidine (or a pharmacologically similar substance) that manifests in significant problematic behavioral changes (e.g., belligerence, assaultiveness, impulsiveness, unpredictability, psychomotor agitation, impaired judgement) that developed during, or shortly after, phencyclidine use and may include the following signs or symptoms: vertical or horizontal nystagmus, hypertension or tachycardia, numbness or diminished responsiveness to pain, ataxia, dysarthria, muscle rigidity, seizures or coma, and hyperacusis.

Other Hallucinogen Intoxication 292.89

Here there can be significant problematic behavioral and psychological changes (e.g., marked anxiety or depression, ideas of reference, fear of "losing one's mind," paranoid ideation, impaired judgment) that developed during, or shortly after, hallucinogen use, along with perceptual changes occurring in a state of full wakefulness and alertness (e.g., subjective intensification of perceptions, depersonalization, derealization, illusions, hallucinations, synesthesias) that developed during, or shortly after, hallucinogen use. Additional symptoms include: pupillary dilation, tachycardia, sweating, palpitations, blurring of vision, tremors and uncoordination.

Hallucinogen Persisting Perception Disorder 292.89 (F16.983)

Once hallucinogen use is stopped, the person can reexperiencing of one or more of the perceptual symptoms that were experienced while intoxicated with the hallucinogen (e.g., geometric hallucinations, false perceptions of movement in the peripheral visual fields, flashes of color, intensified colors, trails of images of moving objects, positive afterimages, halos around objects, macropsia and macropsia. These symptoms cause clinically significant distress or impairment in social, occupational, or other important areas of functioning.

Inhalant Intoxication 292.89

When a person has recently, intended or unintended, short-term, high dose exposure to inhalant substances, including volatile hydrocarbons such as toluene of gasoline, there can be clinically significant problematic behavioral changes or psychological changes (e.g., belligerence, assaultiveness, apathy, impaired judgment) that developed during, or shortly after, exposure to inhalants. In addition, they may experience: Dizziness, nystagmus, incoordination, slurred speech, unsteady gait, lethargy, depressed reflexes, psychomotor retardation, tremor, generalized muscle weakness, blurred vision or diplopia, stupor or coma, and euphoria.

Opioid Intoxication Criteria 292.89

In this situation there is a recent use of an opioid. There are clinically significant problematic behavioral or psychological changes (e.g., initial euphoria followed by apathy, dysphoria, psychomotor agitation or retardation, impaired judgment) that developed during, or shortly after, opioid use, pupillary constriction (or pupillary dilation due to anoxia from severe overdose) and one (or more) of the following signs or symptoms developing during, or shortly after, opioid use: Drowsiness or coma, slurred speech and impairment in attention or memory.

Opioid Withdrawal Criteria 292.0 (F11.23)

When the opioid use that has been heavy and prolonged and then stopped, the following symptoms may occur: Dysphoric mood, nausea or vomiting, muscle aches, lacrimation or rhinorrhea, pupillary dilation, piloerection, or sweating, diarrhea, yawning, fever and insomnia. These symptoms cause clinically significant distress or impairment in social, occupational or other areas of functioning.

Sedative, Hypnotic, or Anxiolytic Intoxication

In this category, there has been recent use of a sedative, hypnotic, or anxiolytic and there has been significant maladaptive behavioral or psychological changes (e.g., inappropriate sexual or aggressive behavior, mood lability, impaired judgment) that developed during, or shortly after, sedative, hypnotic, or anxiolytic use.

Sedative, Hypnotic, or Anxiolytic Withdrawal 292.0

When the sedative, hypnotic, or anxiolytic use has been prolonged and then stopped, the person may experience the following symptoms: Autonomic hyperactivity (e.g. sweating or pulse rate greater than 100 bpm), hand tremor., insomnia, nausea or vomiting, transient visual, tactile, or auditory hallucinations or illusions, psychomotor agitation, anxiety, and grand mal seizures. These symptoms cause clinically significant distress or impairment in social, occupational or other areas of functioning.

Stimulant Intoxication Criteria 292.89

Here there has been recent use of an amphetamine-type substance, cocaine, or other stimulant and clinically significant problematic behavioral or psychological changes (e.g., euphoria or affective blunting; changes in sociability; hypervigilance; interpersonal sensitivity; anxiety, tension, or anger; stereotyped behaviors; impaired judgment) that developed during, or shortly after, use of a stimulant. In addition, there may be tachycardia, pupillary dilation, elevated or lowered blood pressure, perspiration or chills, nausea or vomiting, evidence of weight loss, psychomotor agitation or retardation, muscular weakness, respiratory depression, chest pain, or cardiac arrhythmias, confusion, seizures, dyskinesias, dystonias, or coma

Stimulant Withdrawal Criteria 292.0

When the prolonged amphetamine-type substance, cocaine, or other stimulant use is abruptly stopped, dysphoric mood, fatigue, vivid, unpleasant dreams, insomnia or hypersomnia, increased appetite, psychomotor retardation or agitation, and these symptoms cause clinically significant distress or impairment in social, occupational or other areas of functioning.

Tobacco Withdrawal Criteria 292.0 (F17.203)

Abrupt cessation of tobacco use, or reduction in the amount of tobacco used, can create the following symptoms: irritability, anxiety, difficulty concentrating, increased appetite, restlessness, depressed mood, insomnia, and the signs or symptoms cause clinically significant distress or impairment in social, occupational or other areas of functioning.

Case Description

Richard L. presented himself in a counseling session as a shy, awkward 29 year old man. He complained of anxiety attacks which he could not control. He blamed these attacks on his probation officer, who he felt had intruded excessively into his life. He thereby displaced his problem and disowned his drinking behavior, and he seemed somewhat frightened of certain aspects of his life. He also appeared to have poor interpersonal skills. He gave a life history that indicated enmeshment with his family, who expected him to fail (despite their stated belief that he could accomplish great things). His family had often come to his rescue, but they resented his acting-out behavior and drinking. They felt he had chosen a life of failure and deviance, primarily as a way of punishing them and rebelling against the family mandates.

It was apparent early in the therapy that he was a young man who had poor judgment and little conflict-free individuality and who lived impulsively. He acted out in order to avoid recognizing his own painful negative feelings. He seemed to have needed more protection and understanding as a child than his parents were capable of giving him. Instead, he was physically abused by his mother.

He had been a breech delivery and had rheumatic fever at age 8. In school he often fought and was teased by the other children. He stated that if someone tried to pick on him, "I would punch him out." As a child he had suffered from hyperactivity and inability to concentrate on tasks, and was thus an academic underachiever. He was continually in trouble, and his mother would often slap him around. She reminded him often that he was a disappointment to the family. She continually compared him to his brother, who was "the good one." His father, an engineer and inventor, was a successful businessman. Richard believed that his parents' marriage was an unhappy one. Richard recalled that his parents "were always fighting about something." His father was demanding and critical. Richard was labeled the "family black sheep" and everyone's "cross to bear." Richard also remembered that his father would drink alcohol every time he had to speak in front of an audience. His only happy memory was of having been accepted by his classmates when he was 16 years old; he had his driver's license and was considered to be a lot of fun. Four months short of graduation, however, Richard impulsively quit high school.

Soon after, Richard enlisted in the navy, where he served as a corpsman stationed in North Carolina for one year. His duties consisted of handing out medication for the men on sick call. Richard stated he never felt as though he "fit in" in the navy. He did not feel comfortable with any of the other men. He was introduced to the use of drugs while in the service. Shortly thereafter, he offered Valium to a man sitting next to him at a bar. The man turned out to be a narcotics agent. Richard was charged with selling drugs, but the charge was eventually dismissed. With his parents' help, and the services of an attorney, Richard obtained a general discharge from the navy.

Richard left the navy and returned to live with his parents. He met and married a young woman, and they moved to Florida. He began to feel that his work as a respiratory therapist was depressing, and he found himself dwelling on existential issues of life and death. He began distancing himself from his wife; she felt rejected, and the relationship ended. Richard continued his cycles of drinking, depression, withdrawal and drinking.

Approximately five years before he entered treatment, he threatened a man in an automobile with a gun (which, according to him, was unloaded). He was intoxicated at the time and wanted the man to give him money for more alcohol. Following this incident, he once again moved back with his parents. He became increasingly depressed and began drinking more heavily- over a quart of vodka a day. He was also taking prescription drugs-analgesics and codeine. He resorted to self-medication whenever he felt unable to cope with his problems or fears. He also reported having seizures, which were directly related to his alcohol and drug intake.

Richard was eventually hospitalized in a Veterans Administration hospital for two months. His presenting complaints were that he suffered from racing thoughts and confused thinking. At that time, he was being medicated with two milligrams of chlorpromazine (Thorazine) daily.

After discharge from the hospital, Richard returned to the New York area. His parents arranged for him to live in an adult home for four months because they felt that he might benefit from a structured, supervised way of life. Richard resented this, feeling that they were intruding into his privacy and trying to control his life.

What Does Alcohol Abuse Look Like?

Roger was fired from his job. He did not want to go home so he went to the local bar instead. One drink became two drinks which wound up being six drinks. The bartender stopped serving him because he felt Roger had had enough to drink. Roger's speech was slurred and he was becoming aggressive towards the other bar patrons. He was unsteady as he tried to walk to the men's room.

Alcohol abuse affects many dimensions of behavior, including motivation, cognition, affect, motor skills and self-care capacity. Often, the alcoholic's sole motivation is alcohol; his life is dominated by an overwhelming interest in and desire for alcohol, to the exclusion of other activities and interests. Disrupted families and unemployment are often the result.

Cognitive changes are also common. Alcoholics often lack self-confidence and maintain a generally negative view of themselves. It is not clear whether negative self-esteem develops after the alcoholics begin to fail in their endeavors, or whether these views were present prior to the development of the alcoholic behavior. As previously noted, the advanced alcoholic may experience other cognitive problems, such as memory blackouts, hallucinations, and eventual intellectual deterioration.

Alcoholics undergo a number of affective changes. The most common affective reactions are depression, anxiety, guilt, anger, and hostility. These affective reactions are common in many patterns of maladaptive behavior and therefore cannot be used as precise criteria for identifying alcoholics.

Motor difficulty is also common. Loss of coordination and slurred speech during intoxication, and tremors and seizures during withdrawal are examples of alcohol-induced motor impairment. The alcoholic may lose the motor skills necessary for, as well as an interest in, self-care.

Deterioration in appearance, poor hygiene, malnutrition, and neglected health are common in the late stages of "true" dependence.

Substance abuse affects people from all walks of life. It affects people regardless of age, sex, ethnicity or socioeconomic status. In December of 2012, the Center for Disease Control and Prevention issued their report entitled *Summary Health Statistics for U.S. Adults: National Health Interview Survey 2011*. Part of the report was on alcohol drinking status. 52% of adults aged 18 and over were current regular drinkers. 60% of men were current regular drinkers compared with 44% of women. When results are considered by single race and ethnicity, 57% of Non-Hispanic white adults were current regular drinkers compared with 42% of Hispanic adults and 39% of non-Hispanic black adults. (Vital and Health Statistics Dec. 2012).

Chronic substance abuse can cause long lasting damage in brain function. The damage can affect thinking, problem solving, memory and physical dexterity. It also impairs verbal, visual, and spatial ability. The extent of damage to brain tissue depends on the extent of heavy alcohol abuse. When the drinking stops, a certain amount of healing is possible.

What Does Substance Abuse Feel Like?

Barbara's parents separated and filed for divorce. She was angry at her father for cheating on her mom and she was mad at her mother for giving her father a reason to cheat. Since then, Barbara had been hanging out with the "bad" kids at school, as her mother put it. Those kids had no curfew and did whatever they wanted when they wanted. She decided she wanted to be like them. She cut class with them and talked back to the teachers like they did. She wanted to distance herself from her parents and her feelings about them. One of her new friends suggested she try inhaling nail polish remover. She said she wouldn't feel anything but happy feelings and nobody would know what she was doing because it was just nail polish remover. When Barbara got home she inhaled the nail polish remover, so much that not only did she have feelings of euphoria, but she also experienced dizziness and slurred speech. When she tried to walk down the steps, she fell. Her mom heard her fall, and realized there was something wrong when she could not understand her speech, and called 911.

The Roman poet, Horace, in the first century BC, wrote about the effects of wine: "It discloses secrets; ratifies and confirms our hopes; thrusts the coward forth to battle; eases the anxious mind of its burthen; instructs in arts. Whom has not a cheerful glass made eloquent! Whom not quite free and easy from pinching poverty!"

Alcohol tends to depress activity in all living cells, and in that sense is a true depressant. The casual observer of a cocktail party or a college beer party might wonder just how depressing alcohol is as she notices the drinker's loquaciousness, laughter, and general expansiveness. The explanation is that alcohol, initially at least, selectively depresses those more recently evolved parts of the cerebral cortex that are concerned with self-evaluation and control, thus serving to release the emotional motivational centers from these control centers. There is evidence, however, that some metabolic products of alcohol may more directly produce stimulating effects, possibly increasing levels of certain neurotransmitters, such as norepinephrine (Lahti and Majchrowicz 1974). In addition, it is probably true that some of the uninhibited behavior associated with alcohol probably results from learned expectations about how to behave when intoxicated. After a certain level of alcohol accumulates in the blood, the well-known syndrome of drunkenness occurs, with increasing impairment of cognitive functioning and physical coordination. If consumption continues, the result is a state of total incoordination and incapacitation, leading to loss of consciousness.

Continued use of alcohol in large quantities has a variety of physical consequences, the least serious of which is the chronic irritation of the stomach lining, resulting in indigestion or ulceration. Extensive use also results in the accumulation of fat in the liver, reducing its functioning and eventuating, if continued in a marked impairment of this organ called *hepatic cirrhosis*. X-ray scanning procedures have shown that cerebral atrophy is associated with extensive and chronic alcohol abuse (Fox et al. 1976). A number of other debilitating and potentially lethal consequences can also follow chronic and extensive use, including damage to the cardiovascular system and the development of a life-style that renders the chronic abuser vulnerable to a variety of serious diseases. How much of these effects are due to the direct pharmacologic effects of alcohol and how much life-style that accompanies chronic and protracted use is not always clear, nor may the question be entirely relevant to the need to stop the destructive processes.

The Client's Dilemma

Tammy has had a history of drug and alcohol related problems. For her it is like a chronic disease that will not go away. It has been a rollercoaster ride with her substance abuse and her husband is ready to get off the ride. Tammy had stopped abusing drugs but continued drinking. She has been drinking heavily for the past 10 years. Her husband has said that she needs to get her act together for good this time or he is leaving her. Not wanting to lose her husband, Tammy decides to quit drinking. After the two days without a drink, she is experiencing anxiety and insomnia. She cannot hold a conversation with co-workers and is having trouble focusing at work. When eating dinner at home she notices her hand is shaking as she brings the fork to her mouth.

The disease concept of alcoholism can be explained as follows. Some people- the people who eventually become alcoholics- are born with a specific vulnerability to the physiological effects of alcohol. Because of this vulnerability, they react to alcohol more intensely than do others, and they develop a much greater need for alcohol- a need that becomes an obsession and ultimately leads to addiction.

The disease lies dormant until the susceptible individual begins to drink, at which time a predetermined, predictable process is initiated. It is not a sudden, all at once process; it is a gradual, progressive one. Its full development may take years, sometimes as many as 15. At first drinking is moderate and for pleasure. Later it becomes heavier as alcohol is used for relief from anxiety and escape from emotional and daily life problems. The drinker next finds that he needs alcohol not only for relief and escape, but also just to be able to perform the ordinary tasks of life and work. At this stage the drinker has become psychologically dependent on alcohol, but it is not yet an addiction; the drinker can still control his intake.

Along with behavioral progression, however, a crucial physical change had been taking place. As a result of prolonged exposure to high concentrations of alcohol, an alteration takes place in the body's tissues. Somehow the metabolic process of cells are altered to incorporate alcohol as an ingredient. Now the cells must have alcohol in order to carry on their normal functioning. If they are deprived- if the individual does not drink- the body reacts with severe disturbances, known as withdrawal. In its mildest state, this syndrome-or group of symptoms- takes the form of severe shakes. In its most extreme form, it is manifested in DTs.

According to the disease concept of alcoholism, the drinker has progressed from psychological dependency to physical dependency, or true addiction. Now not only does the psyche demand alcohol, but the body demands it as well. Since this craving is outside voluntary control, the drinker may be unable to resist it.

From a psychological point of view, people who become alcoholics are alcoholism prone, not because of physical disability, but because of psychological disabilities. These are people who, in childhood, went through disturbing emotional experiences, such as parental rejection, parental cruelty, inability to make friends, lack of success in school, lack of fulfillment and gratification, constant parental conflict, alcoholism in the family, a broken home, or other such difficulties. As a result of these distressing experiences, these children developed feelings of anxiety, depression, insecurity, loneliness, repressed anger, and low self-esteem- feelings they carry into their adolescence and adulthood.

In addition to this handicapping burden from childhood, these individuals are also hindered by a cluster of personality traits that limit their capacity to deal realistically with emotional problems and the daily problems of living. These traits include low tolerance for frustration and suffering, the need for immediate gratification, poor impulse control, and limited ego strength (the ability to cope with and overcome problems).

Persons so disposed have an urgent need for (1) relief from emotional distress; (2) an easy, instant source of pleasure, gratification, and self-esteem; and (3) a way to deal with a reality they cannot handle. Alcohol provides all of these. It anesthetizes emotional pain, produces euphoria, inflates the deflated ego, beautifies the ugly self-image, and modifies reality so that the drinker does not have to deal with it.

The condition becomes progressively worse, not because of some preexisting physical disease, but because of a step-by-step destruction of the person's psychological control over his own behavior and a step-by-step submission to an unreal, fantasy experience in which right and wrong, responsibility, goals, achievement, and societal acceptance no longer have any meaning. By then, escape and oblivion are all that matter from hour to hour, from day to day.

Theories and Explanations of Alcoholism/Substance Abuse

Alcoholism/substance abuse appears to be related to a variety of factors that can operate in different ways in different individuals. It appears that there is no single etiological agent that can be traced in all, or even most, cases. As with other types of abnormal behaviors, there are probably multiple factors underlying each case of alcoholism/substance abuse. It is also likely that the relative importance of factors will vary from individual to individual. In general, though, as in the case for schizophrenia, biological factors, such as genetic predisposition to alcoholism and psychological factors, such as social learning and high stress, appear to be major causes of alcoholism or substance abuse.

Psychoanalytic

Psychoanalytic theorists believe that alcoholism is the overt symptom of unconscious emotional problems. Some psychoanalytic theorists feel that alcoholism is a symptom of unsatisfied dependency needs. This dependence, in turn, is thought to stem from an oral fixation. It is proposed that the future alcoholic remains developmentally immature, fixated at the infantile oral stage. This fixation is thought to explain the dependency, low frustration tolerance, excessive ingestion of alcohol, and antisocial tendencies of adult alcoholics. Alcohol, these theorists feel, provides a substitute milk that nourishes and reduces fear (Menninger 1938). The substitute nourishment, while sustaining the individual, does not contribute to ego maturation and the development of good object relationships.

Another similar psychoanalytic view holds that as an infant, the male alcoholic was overly close to a mother who did not satisfy his oral needs. Turning to the father would then stir homosexual impulses, which would then be repressed. Unable to accept these impulses, the male alcoholic drinks to reduce both homosexual fears and hostility toward women. As alcohol fails to meet these needs, the person drinks more and more as a passive means of suicide (Fenichel 1945).

There is some evidence that alcoholics may in fact have more intense oral needs than other people. For example, alcoholics are much more likely than nonalcoholics to be heavy cigarette smokers (Maletzky and Klotter 1974). Other research has shown that boys with strong oral needs are more likely than others to become alcoholics.

As for the dependency of alcoholic, this theory is supported by a wealth of research data (McCord et al. 1960) and is likely to receive the hearty assent of anyone who has lived with an alcoholic. It is no secret that alcoholics are not self-sufficient people, willing to take responsibility for their actions. On the contrary, they tend to seek out anyone or anything (including the alcohol) on which to pin the blame for their troubles. It was not they who caused the accident or the divorce; it was the alcohol. It is important to note, however, that most evidence for the dependency theory is retrospective evidence, and it is therefore possible that the dependency of alcoholics develops out of their drinking problem rather than vice versa, or at least that the two problems feed each other in a vicious cycle.

Somewhat opposite of the dependency theory is the second major theory to develop out of current research-that alcoholics are power seekers who begin drinking in order to foster within themselves the comforting illusion that they are in control. McClelland and co-workers (1972) have built an entire treatment program around this theory. Despite the credible aspects of this theory, however, there is an absence of empirical data to support these psychoanalytic notions (Frank 1970).

Thus, early psychodynamic views theorized that the alcoholic was fixated at the oral stage of psychosexual development and had extreme dependency needs. Out of this traditional view came the search for the so-called alcoholic personality that was prone to the disorder. Although some studies have suggested that, relative to their non-drinking peers, young drinkers are more aggressive, impulsive, anxious, and depressed and have lower self-esteem (Braucht et al. 1973), there has been no solid evidence to support the basic notion of the alcoholic personality.

Freud believed that personality consists of the id, ego and superego. The id is instinctive, impulsive, and childlike. It wants immediate satisfaction of needs, urges, and cravings. In the case of the alcoholic, the id craves alcohol. The superego is sometimes thought of as the parent or conscience. It is the moral component of the personality. The superego knows "right" from "wrong" and its function is to control the impulses of the id. Finally, the ego is similar to the adult and it mediates the id and superego.

Anxiety is a driving force in psychoanalytic theory. Anxiety signals a threat but it can overwhelm the ego. When anxiety is overwhelming, a person relies on defense mechanisms such as denial, avoidance, rationalization, regression, projection, etc. Denial, especially, is common among substance abusers who frequently deny having a problem.

One contemporary psychoanalytic view of substance abuse is that it is a defense against anxiety. Addicts abuse alcohol or other substances to protect themselves against overwhelming anxiety and other painful emotions such as loneliness and depression. When alcohol is used to avoid anxiety evoking situations, the abuser never grows up. He/she never develops appropriate coping mechanisms. Instead, they just grab the bottle, which may be what early psychoanalytic theorists referred to as being fixated at the infantile oral stage. They believed that the substance abuse was a symptom of unsatisfied dependency needs (Gumbiner 2010).

Another contemporary view of substance abuse is from psychoanalyst Sandor Rado, MD. He said that "the study of the problem of addiction begins with the recognition of the fact that it is not the toxic agent, but the impulse to use it, that makes an addict of a given individual." Accordingly, much of the addiction field now acknowledges that the object of study should be the individual rather than the substance.

Psychoanalysts want to understand their clients as deeply as possible. In order for treatment to be successful, they must understand that each client is different. Clients have their own histories and come with a unique set of needs, desires and fears. Each of these must be addressed and understood (Rothschild 2013).

Social Learning

Since the 1960's, more attention has been given to a social-learning interpretation of alcoholism. According to this view, individuals learn to be alcoholics, even though biological predispositions may also play a role in the development of alcoholism and other addictive behaviors. The social-learning view focuses on four factors in the development and maintenance of excessive drinking: positive and negative reinforcement, tension reduction, modeling, and cognitive factors such as beliefs and expectations (Davidson 1974; Miller 1976).

The generally pleasant consequences of drinking tend to be reinforcing in themselves. These pleasant consequences include the immediate, relaxing physiological effects of the alcohol; the attention and approval of friends; and positive changes in behavior, like increased gregariousness and friendliness, which may lead to other reinforcers. Considerable research has, in fact, shown that alcohol is a powerful *positive reinforcer* which alcoholics will work very hard to obtain (Davidson 1974; Nathan and O'Brien 1971). Research has also shown that animals will consume sufficient quantities of alcohol to become intoxicated, but usually only if the alcohol has been mixed with more pleasant tasting substances, such as fruit juices, or if it has been substantially diluted with water. Interestingly, most human drinkers, including those who later develop drinking problems, have a history of initially drinking mixed drinks before they develop a taste for straight liquor (Davidson 1974).

According to the learning-theory position, the development of alcoholism is an operant-conditioning procedure based on negative reinforcement. Specifically, the dynamics are as follows. We all have our share of troubles- anxiety, self-doubt, depression, guilt, anger, and so forth. In the process of emitting different behaviors in an attempt to reduce our psychological discomfort, some of us will take a drink. And alcohol can definitely do the job. Acting as a depressant, it dulls or deadens entirely whatever psychological distress we are experiencing. Alcohol thus becomes associated with the alleviation of psychological pain. And because of this negative reinforcement, the drinking behavior is likely to be repeated.

Actually, learning theory views the development of alcoholism as a two-stage process. At first, persons may drink excessively only at times of psychological stress. In our society, however, regular heavy drinking is frowned upon. Individuals may therefore begin to feel guilty about their episodes of heavy drinking and about behaviors that accompany it. In short, the solution to stress (alcohol) becomes itself a source of stress. And what do these persons do in order to relieve this increasing stress? They resort to the behavior which they have learned is effective in reducing psychological stress: drinking. Hence, they drink to reduce the feelings of guilt and anxiety that have developed because they drink too much- a vicious cycle.

Negative reinforcement can also play a powerful role in alcoholism since drinking is also reinforced by the reduction or elimination of some unpleasant condition. If drinking helps to reduce anxiety, guilt, depression, pain, or other forms of discomfort, the individual is likely to increase or at least continue drinking. This basic principle emphasizes the following sequence: a stressful situation leads to an unpleasant feeling, which leads to excessive drinking, which results in relatively immediate tension reduction. As Miller (1976) has indicated, the more frequently this sequence occurs, the more likely it is that the person will drink excessively to cope with stress; the more stress, the more important the reinforcing properties of alcohol become. In the advanced stages of alcoholism, when the person is clearly addicted to the alcohol, reducing the discomfort of withdrawal symptoms is likely to be another important factor in maintaining the alcoholic pattern.

Although *tension reduction* properties are readily apparent, it is not entirely clear how important this factor is in maintaining drinking behavior. In the early 1960's, it was believed that tension reduction was the primary explanation for the development of alcoholism. In recent years, however, it has been found that alcohol does not always reduce anxiety, depression, and other unpleasant conditions (Cappell and Herman 1972). In some cases, alcohol may actually increase anxiety or depression, especially in chronic alcoholics (Nathan and O'Brien 1971). There may be, for example, a "kickback" effect. An individual feels tense. She has a drink to reduce the tension. It appears to work. As the alcohol wears off, the tension may reappear, only it's more uncomfortable than it was before. Now an even greater volume of alcohol is needed in order to reduce the tension.

This cycle is somewhat supported by a study by Williams (1966), which also suggests that the amount of alcohol consumed is an important variable in determining its effect on anxiety and depression. Moderate levels of alcohol reduce unpleasant emotions, but continued drinking will eventually begin to increase the anxiety and depression to near the levels that the person had prior to drinking. In summarizing the issue, Miller

(1976) suggests that the role of discomfort reduction for the alcoholic is quite complex. For example, certain stressors do appear to lead to increased drinking in alcoholics, whereas other stressors do not. Social stressors increase drinking rates (Miller et al. 1974), while threat of pain does not appear to have the same effect (Higgins and Marlatt 1974).

Modeling is the third learning factor that helps to explain alcoholism (Bandura 1969). Modeling theorists suggest that persons will imitate what others do, if the person being observed has a high reward value (is respected or has power) and is reinforced for his behavior. A number of studies (MacKay 1961; Wood and Duffy 1966) have shown that alcoholics are much more likely than non-alcoholics to have had an alcoholic parent. It is therefore possible that young people, when confronted with problems, and since they have been raised in a home with an alcoholic parent, their problems are likely to be substantial leading them to resort to the same coping mechanism they saw their parent resort to...drinking.

We have already noted that alcoholism tends to run in families. In addition to the genetic interpretation of this finding, it is possible that the child observes the parent's behavior and learns through modeling to engage in the same or similar drug-taking behavior. Later in life, the person is more likely to drink excessively around other drinking models-friends, relatives, or spouse. Marlatt (1974) showed in an experimental situation that heavy drinkers do consume significantly more alcohol when they are with someone who drinks at high rates than when they are with light drinkers.

Finally, the importance of *cognitive factors* is drinking behavior has recently received considerable attention (Marlatt 1978, Wilson 1978). These authors summarized several studies that show the powerful influence of cognitive factors on drinking behavior. One of the major factors studied was the influence of cognitive expectations about alcohol and its effects. Marlatt and colleagues (1973) found that alcohol consumption was influenced more by cognitive factors than by the actual presence of alcohol in drinks. In a study designed to test expectancy factors, they found that expectancy had a significant effect on how much beverage the subjects drank. Both the alcoholic and social drinkers drank more if they *believed* the beverages contained alcohol, regardless of whether the drinks actually contained alcohol. When subjects, including alcoholics, expected nonalcoholic drinks, they drank relatively little, even when an alcoholic drink was provided.

Other studies have shown that expectancy factors have a significant effect on the influence of alcohol on sexual and aggressive behavior (Marlatt et al. 1973), Wilson and Lawson 1976). Other studies have found similar effects of expectation on increasing aggression (Lang et al. 1975) and on increasing sexual arousal to deviant stimuli depicted in a tape of a simulated forcible rape (Briddell et al. 1978). These results clearly show that certain expectations about alcohol can powerfully influence behavior.

Social learning theory looks at the individual learning process, the formation of self, and the influence of society in socializing individuals. Behaviors and attitudes develop in response to reinforcement and encouragement from the people around us. It states that an individual's identity is not a product of the unconscious, but of modeling oneself in response to the expectations of others. In the case of a child, he or she observes the parent's behavior and learns through modeling to engage in the same or similar behavior. Later in life, the person is is more likely to drink excessively around other drinking models- friends, relatives, or spouse.

Social learning theorists believe that substance abuse represents a way of coping with difficult situations, positive and negative affects, and invitations by peers to use substances and so on. By the time substance abuse is severe enough for treatment, it may represent the individual's single, overgeneralized means of coping with a variety of situations, settings and states. Treatment has to help patients to see the high risk situations where they are most likely to use substances and develop different and more effective ways of coping with them. In an article from the Journal of Abnormal Psychology, *Coping, expectancies, and alcohol abuse: A test of social learning formulations,* it states that numerous studies have shown that reliance on alcohol as a coping mechanism is associated with heavy or abusive drinking (Farber, Khavari, & Douglass, 1980;Mulford, 1983; Parry, Cisin, Balter, Mellinger, & Manheimer, 1974). For example, 93% of a sample of diagnosed alcoholics were classified as escape drinkers, in contrast to the typically low rates of endorsement of drinking-to-cope items among non-problem drinkers (Farber et al., 1980). Moreover, drinking to cope has been shown to predict abuse status after controlling for level of consumption (Polich & Orvis, 1979), thereby suggesting that the adverse consequences of a reliance on alcohol to cope cannot be accounted for solely by increased alcohol consumption.

The use of alcohol to cope with stressful situations has also been implicated in post treatment relapse. Marlatt and Gordon (1979) found that over three-quarters of their sample of relapsed alcoholics reported taking their first drink in situations where they were faced with either unpleasant emotional states (e.g., anger and frustration stemming from an argument with someone) or social pressure to resume drinking. Collectively, these data provide clear support for the conceptualization of drinking as a coping response in stressful situations. Moreover, they suggest that individuals who rely on drinking to cope are likely to drink more heavily and to develop problems indicative of abuse syndromes.

Humanistic-Existential

The predominant humanistic theory is based on the work of psychiatrist Eric Berne, who developed an approach called *transactional analysis* (TA). This theory proposes that persons play circular games that produce no change or growth in their lives. A *game* is a program or set of principles that guides a person's life, the manner in which they live, and the decisions they make. Games are often based on early experiences, and decisions may thus be ill conceived, forced, and immature. Once persons decide to play a game, they develop a script in order to get others to cooperate with them.

Steiner (1969), using the TA model, talks about three games alcoholics play, called "Drunk and Proud," "Wini" and "Lush". The details of the game differ, but they share the same general existential position, which can be phrased as "I'm no good and you're OK (Ha! Ha!)." In each of these games, in order to obtain some attention and social reinforcement, alcoholics put themselves in a position in which others will disapprove of them. On the surface, those who disapprove of the alcoholic's behavior appear to be virtuous and blameless; however, they are soon put in a position in which they are made to feel foolish and guilty. This twist represents the "Ha! Ha!" part of the script. Each game has its own dynamics, aims, rules, and roles to be taken by family members and friends; also included are roles in the helping professions. Some of these roles include Patsy, Dummy, Rescuer, Persecutor, and Connection.

In "Drunk and Proud," the alcoholic says "You're good; I'm bad (and try and stop me). The alcoholic misbehaves while under the influence of alcohol and then apologizes. If you accept the behavior, you appear foolish and helpless (a patsy). If you reject the behavior, you appear to be the persecutor of a "sick person". No matter how noble your intentions are, sooner or later the alcoholic's behaviors provoke an angry outburst, which proves that you really do not care. In "Lush" the alcoholic says "I'm crazy or depressed and only you can make me feel better." Because of a lack of reinforcement, the alcoholic hurts himself and receives sympathy, attention and reinforcement (*strokes*, in TA terminology) from various rescuers. Therapists and social workers are quite often induced into playing the game.

In the game of "Wino," in which the alcoholic is saying, "I'm sick; you're OK (Ha! Ha!)," he drinks until physical deterioration has set in. In this case the alcoholic believes that services and goods are given out by people in power only to those who are helpless and crippled. This attitude probably results from severe deprivation in early childhood. A judge often becomes the patsy in this game by sentencing an alcoholic to jail or a hospital in the winter, where he gets exactly what he wants (food, clothing, shelter, sympathy and care). Unfortunately, the life plan or goal of these games is eventual self-destruction.

Richard, our previously described case, certainly liked to play the victim. He was the poor, unfortunate one who was under the control of others, an object of abuse. While there were times when he was also the recipient of help from others, he always defeated their efforts by starting to drink again, placing himself once again in the victim position; their efforts failed him.

He remembered a dream he had had as a child, in which he was forbidden by his mother to go to the store to buy candy. He rebelled, however, and went anyway. On his way to the store, he was hit by a car and his bicycle was mangled. He then witnessed his own funeral as a detached spirit, watching everybody cry over his death. If we see the death of a child as his true self, then the spirit is the detached and disowned part of himself who is only vaguely interested in what is happening. His mother is the inhibiting force, and the bicycle is the lost autonomy. He will never again do as he truly wishes.

The humanistic-existential perspective views the alcoholic as someone who has rejected, or indeed someone who has never located, a real identity. Instead of giving expression to their true selves and accepting the risks involved in such a choice, alcoholics attempt to cope with life's problems by playing roles that are unacceptable to themselves and that are not favored by, but are understandable to, society. In so doing, they give up their freedom to choose self-actualizing behaviors, behaviors that would be more congruent with their true selves. The longer they continue this self-defeating behavior, the more isolated they become from their true selves and from other human beings.

Family Environment

The disease model of drug abuse has led investigators to emphasize individual factors in the search for explanations of this phenomenon. Recently however, there has been a move to explore the role of small social groups, such as families and gangs, as well as the part played by the larger social system in the maintenance of drug use and abuse. One group that exerts a good deal of influence on behavior is the family. However, attempts to pinpoint a particular family constellation that produces drug abuse in its members have been as fruitless as the search for the "addict personality."

The contemporary family disease models emphasize codependency, alcoholism as a disease, and family members' learning to focus on changing themselves-all concepts deriving from disease models. At the same time, many disease model treatment programs that include the family also emphasize communication, dysfunctional family roles, and family equilibrium-concepts derived from family systems theory (Rotgers et al. 1996).

Initial family research on alcoholism focused on the wife of the male alcoholic. She was thought to be dependent and neurotic, and it was alleged that to prevent exposure of her own inability to be independent, she started her husband drinking and encouraged him to continue even when he seemed about to stop. Research has demonstrated, however, that many personality problems exhibited by the wives of alcoholics were consequences of their attempts to cope with the situation, rather than causes of their husbands' drinking (Kogan and Jackson 1965). In addition, the personalities of wives of alcoholics could not be distinguished from those of wives of nonalcoholics (Kogan and Jackson 1965).

Jackson (1968) has identified the stages through which a family proceeds in its attempts to cope with an alcoholic husband. These stages parallel Jellinek's in some respects. At first *excessive drinking* puts a strain only on the marital relationship. Drinking episodes eventually become more public, however, and the family suffers *social isolation*. The third stage begins when the *family gives up* efforts to control the excessive drinking and no longer supports the alcoholic member. Now the *wife takes control* of the family, reassigns herself and to capable children what used to be the husband's tasks. By *isolating the drinking member*, the family is then able to regain its equilibrium and reduce stress.

This stage may continue toward a physical separation between husband and wife, and lead to eventual divorce. At this point, however, the husband usually begins to seek treatment. If he maintains sobriety and attempts to reenter the family, he may find that he no longer has a "slot". The family may be unwilling to go through the stress of another reorganization. The husband's rejection and isolation may be a factor in his later resumption of excessive drinking.

More recent work on the possible role of the family in alcohol abuse views the family as a system in which the behavior of each member is interrelated and coordinated with the behavior of others. In this approach, developed by Steinglass and associates (1971), drinking it's either a signal of stress within the family system or an integral, adaptive part of family maintenance. In one of the families studied, the wife uses alcohol to increase assertiveness in coping with threats to the family from the outside world when her husband refused to assert himself.

Research support comes from Gorad (1971), who found that in families with an alcoholic, both the husband and wife were competitive, escalated conflicts, did not handle outside stress well, and did not work toward achieving joint goals. Alcohol was used by the partner who was unable to compete directly to maintain his or her position and the family equilibrium. Although the role of the family in maintenance of drug use is just beginning to be explored, it is clear that the family is a major factor in passing along drug-related behaviors and attitudes from one generation to the next.

Looking at the family as a whole system, a person who is abusing substances influences and is influenced by other systems such as extended family systems, work or school systems, not by one person. These systems interact with one another. They are dependent upon one another. The immediate family influences and feels the effects of substance abuse. This is transferred to the extended family who in turn may try to help. The substance abuser may go to work or school and affect those systems via the teachers, students or a supervisor. The people in those systems then contact a member of the immediate family and the circular pattern continues. The substance abuse affects every member of the family. As the substance abuser continues to drink or use, it causes a range of emotional, spiritual, and financial problems for almost everyone involved, including family, friends and coworkers.

Biological

Some evidence suggests that a biological predisposition, possibly controlled through genetic transmission, may be important in alcoholism. There is considerable evidence, for example, that alcoholism tends to run in families (Winokur et al. 1970). It is quite common to find that alcoholics had a parent, usually the father, who was also an alcoholic. However, this does not necessarily mean that genetic factors are involved in alcoholism. It may simply mean that the person learned the behavior while growing up with a parent modeling drinking behavior as a means of handling problems.

Early studies on adoption, in fact, suggested that adopted children of alcoholics were not more likely to become alcoholics themselves (Roe et al. 1945). However, more recent studies conducted in Denmark suggest that there is a genetic predisposition to alcoholism; Goodwin and colleagues (1973) compared a group of 55 male children who were adopted from alcoholic biological parents to a matched group of 78 control subjects who were also adopted but did not have an alcoholic biological parent. The children were adopted within 6 weeks of their birth and had no knowledge of or contact with their biological parents. They were interviewed when they were adults (average age 30) by a psychiatrist who did not know that the subject's biological parent was alcoholic. Ratings and information gathered by the psychiatrist pointed to several differences in the two groups of adoptees. Some 18 percent of those with alcoholic parents were themselves alcoholic, in contrast to a 5 percent alcoholism rate among the controls. In addition to being almost four times more likely to become alcoholic, the children of alcoholics had significantly more divorces, psychiatric hospitalizations, and treatment specifically for drinking problems. In general, the conclusions were that a biological predisposition might be relevant in alcoholism because of the comparatively high rates found in the adopted offspring of the alcoholic parents.

Goodwin and co-workers (1974) conducted a further investigation using some of these same experimental subjects who happened to have siblings who were raised by their alcoholic parents. This study found high rates of alcoholism in both the adoptees and those who were raised by their alcoholic parents. The groups did not differ significantly from each other. In other words, those who were raised by their alcoholic parents were no more likely to become alcoholic than those who were adopted and raised by nonalcoholic foster parents. Again, the evidence suggests the importance of a biological predisposition.

Miller (1976) and others have suggested that some individuals may inherit certain characteristics that will make them more or less likely to become alcoholic. For example, nonalcoholics may have a more immediate adverse reaction to alcohol because of gastrointestinal sensitivity or other physiological differences. There is some suggestion that Orientals, who have generally low rates of alcoholism, may have this type of sensitivity to alcohol (Ewing et al. 1974).

It is important to be aware of the complex nature of substance abuse and to be aware of its many faces in both the identified patient and his/her family members. It is rarely the case that only one family member is substance dependent. Family studies indicate that alcohol has a high rate of familial transmission. Bennett and Wolin (1990) have reported transmission of alcoholism is more probable if there is continuing interaction between alcoholic parents and their adult offspring. Also, adult males are more likely to develop alcoholism if there is continuing interaction between them and alcoholic parents of their spouses. This transmission can be attributed to an acceptance of alcohol as part of the "family culture" and an inculturation effect on the offspring (Rotgers et al. 1996). Studies done by Bennett and Wolin indicated that in 25 families with a history of alcoholism, those who kept family rituals (dinnertime or holiday celebrations) even during heavy drinking periods, showed less alcoholism among offspring. Among 68 adult married couples from a alcoholic family of origin, deliberate and planned family rituals seemed to protect against transmission of alcoholism into their own families. They were asked if the families most severely affected by alcohol were the ones with the most disrupted households and associated psychopathology, and whether the severity of the alcohol problem, not the "symptom" of disrupted family rituals, was responsible for increased transmission of alcoholism to the offspring. They found that the severity alcoholism in the family of origin of the transmitter vs. non-transmitter families was not different and concluded that transmission was not due to severity of the parental alcohol.

Therapy Techniques

Regardless of which theory or combination of theories prevails, alcoholics can be helped. The basic goal of treatment is to break the dependency on alcohol, to rid them of the compulsive need to drink. Various methods are used to achieve this goal- physical, psychological, and a combination of both.

The potential for recovery from alcoholism is greatly enhanced when treatment begins in the early stages-before the dependence has become firmly entrenched and before the drinker's entire life is alcohol centered. Alcoholics in late stages, especially those in whom physical and physiological deterioration is far advanced, have very poor prospects for recovery. Also, it is generally agreed that individuals whose alcoholism starts early and develops rapidly have a poor prognosis, a poor chance of being treated successfully. Patients whose alcoholism starts later in life and develops slowly are regarded as having a better prognosis, provided, of course, that they seek treatment. The prognosis is also good, in general, for those who have remained socially involved; have had good achievement in work, business, or raising a family; and have a capacity for warm, deep personal relationships.

Statistics on long-range outcomes of treatment for alcoholism vary considerably, depending on the population studied and on the treatment facilities and procedures employed. They range from low rates of success for long-term alcoholics to recoveries of 70 to 90 percent when up-to-date treatment and aftercare procedures are used. Although individual psychotherapy is sometimes effective, the focus of psychological measures in the treatment of alcoholism more often involves group therapy, behavior therapy, and the Alcoholics Anonymous (AA) approach.

Detoxification

Any treatment of alcoholism generally begins with a medical treatment called *detoxification-* that is, removing the alcohol from the alcoholic's system and seeing the alcoholic through the withdrawal symptoms. The patient is hospitalized, and a tranquilizer such as diazepam (Valium) or chlordiazepoxide (Librium) is substituted for the alcohol. Withdrawal to the substitute drug is usually completed in five to seven days. High levels of vitamins, especially the B complex, are administered daily to counter the nutritional deficiencies. Sunce Hydration is also common in withdrawal, a high liquid intake is maintained. Finally, depending on the severity of the alcoholism, an anticonvulsant such as phenytoin (Dilantin) may be administered to eliminate the possibility of seizures.

Once detoxification is completed, the difficult part of treatment begins-the effort to change the alcoholic from a drinking social dropout with disrupted interpersonal, family, and job relationships, to an integrated, self-sustaining, coping member of society. This is not an easy task, however. Since rehabilitation affects so many aspects of the alcoholic's life, the most effective alcohol rehabilitation programs are *multimodal* in nature. Within a supportive and nonthreatening environment, alcoholics are provided with occupational therapy to help them learn or relearn occupational skills; relaxation therapy to teach them how to reduce tension without alcohol; and group and individual therapy to help them learn something about themselves and to teach them how to relate to others without a drink in their hands. Family or marital therapy is then useful, to resolve some of the problems that have contributed to or resulted from the drinking; vocational counseling then helps get clients back to work, thus keeping them busy, boosting their self-esteem, and relieving their financial worries. Often included are lectures and films dealing with alcoholism, physiology, psychology, and human relations. These are designed to help the patient understand the disease, why the succumbed to it, how it affects them physically and psychologically, and how it affects their relationships with family members and others. These forms of treatment proceed concurrently, and most, if not all, clients participate in them daily.

For those classes of substance that produce substantial withdrawal syndromes (i.e. alcohol, opioids, and sedative-hypnotics), medications are frequently needed to reduce or control often dangerous symptoms associated with withdrawal. Agents such as methadone, clonidine, naltrexone (Charney et al., 1986) and more recently, buprenorphine (Kosten & Kleber, 1986), are typically used for management of opioid withdrawal. Alcohol withdrawal is treated with barbiturates or long-acting benzodiazepines when appropriate. Withdrawal from barbiturates and sedative-hypnotics usually involves closely monitored, gradual reductions of the substance or the substitution of a cross tolerant, longer-acting drug, often phenobarbital (Alling 1992). Because some of these agents, particularly barbiturates, are likely to be misused by some patients, detoxification is usually done in an inpatient or closely controlled setting. Furthermore, the role of psychotherapy during acute detoxification is typically extremely limited due to the level of discomfort, agitation, and confusion the patient may experience (Rotgers et al. 1996).

Psychodynamic Treatment

Psychodynamic treatment of the alcoholic aims not so much at the symptom-that is, the drinking-as at the underlying psychic cause, since according to psychodynamic theory there will be no symptom relief until there is relief of the unconscious conflict. However, psychodynamic therapy has a relatively low success rate with alcoholism and is generally not a common form of treatment for this disorder.

In treating families or couples with addiction problems, psychodynamic family therapists listen for evidence of unconscious processes in the family, such as unexpressed wishes and feelings and the support of other family member's defenses. Family members may have a difficult time recognizing and expressing their anger at or disappointment in the substance abuser. The therapist encourages family members to say what they are feeling and asks them to listen without criticizing.

Behavioral Treatment

Traditional psychodynamic psychotherapy attempts to deal with unconscious conflicts presumed to be at the bottom of a psychiatric illness. In the case of alcohol dependence, the assumption is that when the conflict is resolved, the alcoholism will be easier to overcome. Behavior therapy, on the other hand, which ignores the psychological dynamics of illness, concentrates on the excessive drinking itself. The drinking is regarded as inappropriate learned behavior that can be unlearned-eliminated-through a variety of behavioral techniques.

One of the most rapidly developing forms of treatment for alcohol abuse disorders is behavior therapy, of which several types exist. One is *averse conditioning*, involving a wide range of noxious stimuli. A noxious (offensive) stimulus-such as an emetic drug or an electric shock-is administered along with the taste, smell and sight of an alcoholic drink. The procedure is repeated daily for several weeks. Ultimately, the pain, revulsion, and discomfort produced by the shock or by vomiting become associated with alcohol in the drinker's mind. This negative association works to extinguish the drinker's desire for alcohol.

Today a variety of pharmacological and other deterrent measures can be employed after detoxification. In order for the alcoholic to unlearn the drinking response, this response must be either extinguished-that is, no longer reinforced by anxiety reduction-or made aversive through some kind of punishment. Since it is difficult to arrange things so that alcohol intake is not followed by a reduction in anxiety, most behavioral treatments of alcoholism rely on the use of aversive techniques.

One such aversive method involves the use of drug called disulfiram (Antabuse), a chemical that interferes with the normal processing of alcohol for about two days after it is taken. When Antabuse and alcohol are combined, a toxic agent accumulates in the bloodstream, causing an extremely unpleasant reaction. The individual flashes, his heart rate increases, he experiences extreme nausea, and he generally feels as though he is about to die. The pairing of this reaction with alcohol is, of course, a classic case of aversive conditioning. Furthermore, Antabuse treatment is also based on the assumption that it will help the alcoholic avoid impulsive drinking (Baekeland et al. 1971), since if he wants to take a drink without becoming violently ill, he has to stop taking Antabuse at least two days in advance. A drawback to Antabuse is that many patients, after taking the drug in the hospital, simply discontinue it once they are discharged. Consequently, treatment rarely relies on Antabuse alone. Instead, the drug is used as part of a more general rehabilitation program.

Another approach involves the intramuscular injection of emertine hydrochloride, an emetic. The client is given alcohol before experiencing the nausea that results from the injection, so that the sight, smell, and taste of the beverage becoming associated with severe retching and vomiting. With repetition, this classic conditioning procedure acts as a strong deterrent to further drinking-perhaps in part because it adds an immediate and unpleasant physiological consequence to the more general socially aversive consequences of excessive drinking.

Other aversive methods include the use of mild electrical stimulation, which presumably enables the therapist to maintain more exact control of the aversive stimulus, reduces possible negative side effects and medical complications, and can even be administered by means of a portable apparatus that can be used by the patient for self-reinforcement. Using a procedure which pairs electrical stimulation with drinking-associated stimuli, Claeson and Malm (1973) reported successful results-no relapses after 12 months-in 24 percent of a study group consisting mostly of advanced-staged alcoholics.

Aversive conditioning with emetic drugs has been in use for decades but on a small scale. Electric shock has come into use only during the past 15 years. Both methods are very complex, requiring hospitalization in special hospitals and the attention of specially trained professionals. Generally, psychotherapy is given along with aversive conditioning, so that the underlying conflict and the drinking habit itself are attacked simultaneously.

Another approach, called *overt sensitization*, involves extinguishing the drinking behavior by associating it with noxious mental images rather than chemical or electrical stimuli (Cautela 1967). Positive results have been reported, with the reduction of drinking for a time. However, the long-term effects of covert sensitization generally have not been impressive. To expect such stimuli as images to change a deeply ingrained life pattern is perhaps unrealistic. Covert sensitization procedures might be effectively used as an early step of alcohol rehabilitation, but other treatment procedures should later be used while the person remains abstinent. The most important effect of any type of aversion therapy with alcoholics, though, seems to be the temporary extinction of drinking behavior, making it possible for other psychosocial methods to be used effectively (Davidson 1974). Other behavioral techniques have also received a great deal of attention in recent years (see also Gottheil et al. 1982, Miller 1978, Nathan 1977, Sobell and Sobell 1973). However, Pendry, Maltzman, and West (1982) followed up on the subjects of the original Sobell study and found that only 1 out of 20 subjects was still successful in controlling drinking. Clearly, additional research will be needed to determine the success or failure of controlled drinking as a treatment approach.

Behavior therapy strongly emphasizes the importance of setting goals and practicing new ways of interacting during treatment sessions and at home between sessions. The therapist is active in the sessions. Assessments are used to guide the sessions and to help establish treatment goals. Homework assignments are given weekly. The families are given interventions to improve family relationships. These include increasing pleasing behaviors toward one another, shared recreational and leisure activities, and training in communication and problem-solving skills to help resolve conflicts and problems.

For children and adolescents as well as couples, behavioral contracts can be used. A behavioral contract involves identifying, defining and agreeing to a set of target behaviors. For children and adolescents, this would include completion of household chores, and complying with time schedules. Consequences for breaking the contract and rewards for complying with the contract are explicitly defined and used to positively modify the child or adolescent's behavior (Pagliaro, 2012, p. 351-352).

For a couple seeking treatment for alcohol, both the drinking of the alcoholic member and the overall health of the relationship must be addressed. The behavioral contract for couples defines the drinking goal for the alcoholic, for example, 6 months of no drinking, what steps the alcoholic is going to take to reach the goal, what will the consequences be if the alcoholic does not meet the drinking goal, what the spouse will do to facilitate recovery and what the spouse will do if the alcoholic begins to drink again (Rotgers et al., p. 150-151).

Humanistic Treatment

Humanistic treatment for alcohol, as for other disorders, emphasizes the need for individuals to look inside themselves and work hard to identify the real self, the self that they would truly choose to be. Equally important is the confrontation with the nonchosen self, the role that they have been playing. Through these therapeutic dialogues, individuals are helped to realize that they alone must make the choice between two different behavior patterns. This philosophy is actually quite close to the basic tenet of Alcoholics Anonymous. AA's position is simply that every day, alcoholics must decide anew whether they will escape from the self into alcohol or whether they will deal directly with the difficulties and anxieties they all must confront sooner or later.

The humanistic perspective views human nature as basically good, with an inherent potential to maintain healthy, meaningful relationships and to make choices that are in the interest of óneself and others. The humanistic therapist focuses on helping people free themselves from disabling assumptions and attitudes so they can live fuller lives. The therapist emphasizes growth and self-actualization rather than curing diseases or alleviating disorders. This perspective targets present conscious processes rather than unconscious processes and past causes, it holds that people have an inherent capacity for responsible self-direction. For the humanistic therapist, not being one's true self is the source of problems. The therapeutic relationship serves as a vehicle or context in which the process of psychological growth is fostered. The humanistic therapist tries to create a therapeutic relationship that is warm and accepting and that trusts that the client's inner drive is to actualize in a healthy direction.

Alcoholics Anonymous

The most successful of the regular nonprofessional meeting programs for alcoholics is AA. The AA program started in 1935, soon after the end of Prohibition, and has since spread throughout the world. The organization was started by two individuals, Dr. Bob and Bill W., in Akron, Ohio. Bill W. recovered from alcoholism through a "fundamental spiritual change" and immediately sought out Dr. Bob, another alcoholic, who, with Bill's assistance, achieved recovery. Both began to help other alcoholics. As a result, there are now over 10,000 group members in the United States alone. In addition, AA groups have been established all over the world. AA is not a panacea. Not all alcoholics benefit from, or can even tolerate, the group's approach. But it is an option to which every alcoholic should be exposed.

AA operates primarily as a nonprofessional counseling program in which both person-to-person and group relationships are emphasized. AA accepts both teenagers and adults with drinking problems. There are no dues or fees. The organization does not keep records or case histories, nor does it participate in political causes. It is not affiliated with any religious sect; however, spiritual development is a key aspect of its treatment approach. To ensure the anonymity of the alcoholic, only first names are used. Meetings are devoted partly to social activities, but consist primarily of discussions of individual problems with alcohol, often with testimonial from recovering alcoholics.

An important aspect of AA's rehabilitation program is that it lifts the burden of personal responsibility by helping alcoholics accept that alcoholism, like many other problems, is bigger than they are. Henceforth, they can see themselves not as weak-willed or lacking in moral strength, but rather as having a disease. They cannot drink. Just as other people may not be able to tolerate certain types of medication, the alcoholic cannot tolerate alcohol. With mutual help and reassurance through participation in a group composed of others who have shared similar experiences, alcoholics eventually acquire insight into their problems, a new sense of purpose, greater ego strength, and more effective coping techniques. And, of course, continued participation in the group helps prevent the crisis of relapse.

The encouragement and guidance received at meetings and through informal associations help alcoholics to strengthen their determination and to resist the urge to drink. On admission to AA, the new member is introduced to the AA guidelines, known as the "twelve steps." Each person is encouraged to follow them at his own pace. The twelve steps consist of a series of acknowledgements and resolutions but the alcoholic: that he is in the grip of a force over which he has no power; that he has turned over his will and life to God as we understand Him; that he has inventoried all his weaknesses and shortcomings and asks God to remove them; that he will make amends to those he has harmed; that he has had a spiritual awakening and will at all times practice the twelve-step principles and carry the message to other alcoholics.

The success of AA seems to be based on two tenets: (1) once an alcoholic, always an alcoholic; and (2) no one can stop drinking without help. AA believes that alcoholics are powerless in the face of forces greater than themselves and, unaided, will always remain alcoholics. The organization sees alcoholism as a lifelong problem from which individuals never recover. This model, by focusing on internal causes of alcohol addiction, leads alcoholics to believe that their excessive drinking is a matter of lack of internal control over their own drinking behavior. Consequently, they must completely abstain from alcohol and must rely on AA for comradeship and support in doing so.

Such support is provided not only through meetings, but also through AA's famous buddy system. When members feel that they cannot keep themselves from taking a drink, they are supposed to call AA. One or two members will then come as soon as possible to help the individual fight the urge/ In the process, it is believed, they will also be helping themselves. As alcoholics become more and more involved in AA groups and activities, they become like members of a secret society, carefully observing the organization's code of words and rituals, becoming very suspicious of all outsiders. Often the AA subgroup occupies so much of the members' time that they may neglect their families, thereby creating new problems.

The effectiveness of AA has been debated. Members claim a 50 percent cure rate, but they neglect to mention the high initial dropout rate. The results of independent studies show the actual cure rate to be about 30 to 33 percent (Ditman 1967), which is about equal to the cure rate produced by other treatments.

AA is neither a medical nor a psychological approach for treatment of alcoholism. It employs four factors widely shown to be effective in relapse prevention in addictions: (1) external supervision, (2) substitute dependency, (3) new caring relationships, and (4) increased spirituality. In conjunction with step 1, members learn to overcome their strong denial of their own drinking problem. At the meetings, members introduce themselves by saying "Hello, my name is _____ and I'm an alcoholic. AA gives alcoholics the social support necessary to maintain abstinence and an effective surrogate for their previously patterned drinking time or "familiar bar scene". The meetings serve as a place to go on evenings, weekends and holidays for socialization with friends who provide understanding and help to alleviate social isolation and loneliness.

Here are the Twelve steps of Alcoholics Anonymous:

1. We admitted we were powerless over alcohol—that our lives had become unmanageable.
2. We came to believe that a Power greater than ourselves could restore us to sanity.
3. We made a decision to turn our will and our lives over to the care of God as we understood Him.
4. We made a searching and fearless moral inventory of ourselves.
5. We admitted to God, to ourselves, and to another human being the exact nature of our wrongs.
6. We were entirely ready to have God remove all these defects of character.
7. We humbly asked Him to remove our shortcomings.
8. We made a list of all persons we had harmed, and became willing to make amends to them all.
9. We made direct amends to such people wherever possible, except when to do so would injure them or others.
10. We continued to take personal inventory and when we were wrong promptly admitted it.
11. We sought through prayer and meditation to improve our conscious contact with God, as we understood Him, praying only for knowledge of His will for us and the power to carry that out.
12. Having had a spiritual awakening as the result of these Steps, we tried to carry this message to alcoholics, and to practice these principles in all our affairs.

Copyright A.A. World Services, Inc. (Rev. 5/09/02)

Narcotics Anonymous

Narcotics Anonymous is a nonprofit fellowship or society of men and women for whom drugs had become a major problem. They meet regularly to help each other stay clean. They are not interested in what of how much you used, but only what you want to do now about your problem and how they can help. Membership is open to all drug addicts, regardless of the particular drug or combination of drugs used. NA provides a recovery process and a peer support network that are linked together. Members share their successes and challenges in overcoming active addiction and living drug free productive lives through the application of principles contained within the Twelve steps and Twelve Principles of NA.

The Steps

1. We admitted we were powerless over alcohol -- that our lives had become unmanageable.
2. Came to believe that a Power greater than ourselves could restore us to sanity.
3. Made a decision to turn our will and our lives over to the care of God as we understood Him.
4. Made a searching and fearless moral inventory of ourselves.
5. Admitted to God, to ourselves, and to another human being the exact nature of our wrongs.
6. Were entirely ready to have God remove all these defects of character.
7. Humbly asked Him to remove our shortcomings.
8. Made a list of all persons we had harmed, and became willing to make amends to them all.
9. Made direct amends to such people wherever possible, except when to do so would injure them or others.
10. Continued to take personal inventory and when we were wrong promptly admitted it.
11. Sought through prayer and meditation to improve our conscious contact with God as we understood Him, praying only for knowledge of His will for us and the power to carry that out.

12. Having had a spiritual awakening as the result of these Steps, we tried to carry this message to others, and to practice these principles in all our affairs.

The Traditions

1. Our common welfare should come first; personal recovery depends on AA unity.
2. For our group purpose there is but one authority -- a loving God as He may express Himself in our group conscience. Our leaders are but trusted servants; they do not govern.
3. The only requirement for AA membership is a desire to stop drinking.
4. Each group should be autonomous except in matters affecting other groups or AA as a whole.
5. Each group has but one primary purpose - to carry its message to the alcoholic who still suffers.
6. An AA group ought never endorse, finance, or lend the AA name to any related facility or outside enterprise, lest problems of money, property, and prestige divert us from our primary purpose.
7. Every group ought to be fully self-supporting, declining outside contributions.
8. Alcoholics Anonymous should remain forever nonprofessional, but our service centers may employ special workers.
9. AA, as such ought never be organized; but we may create service boards or committees directly responsible to those they serve.
10. Alcoholics Anonymous has no opinion on outside issues; hence the AA name ought never be drawn into controversy.
11. Our public relations policy is based on attraction rather than promotion; we need always maintain personal anonymity at the level of press, radio and films.
12. Anonymity is the spiritual foundation of all our Traditions, ever reminding us to place principles above personalities.

In NA, membership is based on the desire to stop using drugs including alcohol and has as a foundation the principle of complete abstinence. It has been the experience of NA members that complete and continuous abstinence provides the best foundation for recovery and growth.

Group Therapy

Group therapy attempts to force alcoholics to face their problem and recognize the possible disastrous consequences, but it also encourages them to begin to see possibilities for coping with it. Often, but by no means always, this double recognition paves the way for developing more effective coping skills and taking other positive steps toward dealing with drinking.

In some instances, the spouses of alcoholics and even their children may be invited to join group therapy meetings. In other situations, family treatment is itself the central focus of the therapeutic effort. In the latter case, the alcoholic is seen as a member of a disturbed family in which all the members have a responsibility for cooperating in treatment. Since family members are frequently the persons most victimized by the alcoholic's addiction, they often tend to be judgmental and punitive, and the alcoholic, who has already passed harsh judgment on himself, tolerates this further devaluation very poorly. In other instances, members of the family may unwittingly encourage an alcoholic to remain addicted, as, for example, when a wife with a need to dominate her husband finds that a continually drunken and remorseful spouse best meets that need.

Group therapy is becoming an increasingly accepted form of treatment for substance abusers due in part to the popularity of self-help groups like AA and NA. Although the goals of therapy and self-help groups differ in many ways, the self-help movement has demonstrated that groups of people coming together to work on a common problem can be helpful in terms of sharing and identifying with others who are going through similar problems, and also in terms of understanding the impact of alcohol and drugs on those who abuse these substances as well as on those who are closely connected to the substance abuser (Washton, 1995).

Group therapy can be conducted in inpatient, residential, and outpatient settings. They are directed by a professionally trained leader. An effective group leader involves members in the group process, links individual efforts, identifies themes and patterns of interaction, evaluates progress and terminates the group effort (Stevens & Smith, 2009).

There is psychoeducational group therapy for substance abusers as well as psychotherapeutic groups. Psychoeducational groups are structured and provide a planned framework that can be modified, replicated or adapted to fit different types of client groups. The interventions in this type of group are planned and focus on specific learning outcomes (Capuzzi & Stauffer, 2012). The group leader guides the group. In psychotherapeutic groups, there is no set agenda for each group session. Group members are encouraged to take an informal leadership role and develop their own goals, agendas and contracts which is opposite to the psychoeducational group.

Group therapy creates an opportunity for a positive interpersonal conversation that can replace isolated self-involvement. The group members can help each other in "confronting defense mechanisms and blind spots, resulting in accomplishment of treatment goals". It uses peer influence and motivation to enhance individual commitment to recovery (Capuzzi & Stauffer, 2012).

Family Therapy

Family therapy is based on the theory that stress and conflict in the family are capable of provoking emotional disorders in one or more vulnerable members of the family. Treating the patient individually might help to eliminate some of the symptoms, but this gain would be undone by the persistence of the strains within the family. The aim of family therapy is to treat the family members together in order to undo mutually destructive patterns operating within the family and to relieve pressures that are playing on the vulnerable individual's weakness. When there is alcoholism in the family, therapy is directed, in part, toward changing the family interactions that tend to reinforce the alcoholic's vulnerability. Efforts are made to enhance the alcoholic's psychological growth so that he will accept more constructive roles in the family and refrain from using alcohol as a coping device.

Substance abuse in either adults or adolescents can develop during periods in which the family as a whole is having difficulty with an important developmental issue, such as separation, or when the family is experiencing a crisis. During these periods, substance abuse can serve to distract family members from their central problem. A substance abuser's social systems such as family, peer network or co-workers can serve as both a risk factor and a protective factor for substance use. Important relationships tend to be negatively affected during active addiction. As a result, participation in couples or family therapy can help to repair relationships that have been damaged by chaos, broken trust, and financial strain that are common to addiction, and to increase the likelihood of sustained recovery. Family therapy may be particularly helpful when children are involved. Involvement of family members tends to increase the patient's involvement in and commitment to treatment (Brownwell, 2012).

What is important thing to observe is who comes to the first session with the substance abuser. "This is usually an unspoken statement on the part of the addict about important issues to be addressed during treatment" (Stanton, Todd et al., 1982). In this first session, information is gathered about the substance abuser's present substance abuse status, their history of substance abuse, previous treatment programs or therapy and any family issues surrounding the substance abuser.

It is important that a system for enabling the substance abuser to become sober be established so that family therapy can take place effectively. The severity of the abuse will determine what specific methods will be used to achieve abstinence of the substance. For example, mild or moderate abuse in a teen can be controlled if both parents agree on clear limits and expectations and how to enforce them. The family is encouraged to come up with some type of system that will allow the substance abuser to stay free of whatever substance is being abused. Therapy will be successful if all family members work toward abstinence.

Follow Up

One part of the most successful rehabilitation programs is a follow-up treatment component. The ex-patients usually meet one or more times a week for three to six months, or perhaps for the rest of their lives. This continued contact provides support for the individuals, reminding them once again that they are not the only alcoholics in the world and that people are there to help them. Furthermore, the follow-up meetings give alcoholics the opportunity to continue working on their problems and to learn additional interpersonal coping skills.

In their extensive four-year follow-up of a large group of treated alcoholics, Polich and colleagues (1980) found that the course of alcoholism after treatment was variable. In some respects the findings of this study were not encouraging and seemed to emphasize the treatment failures among alcoholics. Only 7 percent of the total sample (922 males) abstained from alcohol use throughout the four-year period; 54 percent continued to have alcohol-related problems. Some 36 percent of the sample demonstrated alcohol-dependency symptoms, and another 18 percent suffered adverse consequences (e.g. arrests while drinking).

On the positive side, the study can be viewed as demonstrating a clear beneficial effect of treatment for at least some individuals. Although 54 percent had drinking problems at follow-up, over 90 percent of the subjects had had serious drinking problems at the beginning of treatment-A significant reduction.

The outcome of treatment is most likely to be favorable when the drinking problem is discovered early, when the individual realizes the need for help, when adequate treatment facilities are available, and when alcohol-use reduction is an acceptable treatment goal (as opposed to strict abstinence). In their study of various treatments of chronic severe alcohol problems, Brandsma and colleagues (1980) found that direct treatment, whether professional or paraprofessional, insight-oriented or rational-behavior based, was more effective than an untreated control situation. One important finding was that professional treatment was more effective than nonprofessional treatment, although either of the two major therapeutic orientations (insight-oriented versus rational-behavior therapy) was equally effective. AA was the least effective, partly due to high dropout rate.

As with other serious maladaptive behaviors, the total alcoholic treatment program measures to alleviate the patient's often destructive life situation. As a result of their drinking, alcoholics often become estranged from family and friends, and their jobs are lost or jeopardized. Typically, the reaction of those around them is not as understanding or supportive as it would be if they had a physical illness of comparable magnitude. Simply helping them learn more effective coping techniques may not be enough if the social environment remains hostile and threatening. For alcoholics who have been hospitalized, halfway houses, designed to assist them in their return to family and community, are often an important adjunct to the total treatment program. The concept of a *community reinforcement approach* has been developed to focus on helping problem drinkers achieve more satisfactory adjustments in key areas of their lives, such as marriage, work, and social relationships. This approach seems to offer a promising conceptual basis for future treatment programs.

Follow up meetings are important to help the individual stay on a successful path to recovery and to prevent relapse. The rate of relapse following "successful" treatment of harmful patterns of drug and substance use among children and adolescents is quite high (Pagliaro 2012, p. 359-360). They state that the use of these three recommendations would help to minimize the potential for relapsed use: 1. Individualize treatment to the specific needs and characteristics of the child or adolescent; 2. Employ specific indicators or performance goals to objectively evaluate the success of treatment outcomes and subsequently the degree of relapse or efficacy of relapse prevention; and 3. Periodically, as individually indicated, prophylactically reassess children and adolescents and proactively intervene to prevent relapse. Once children and adolescents are abstinent, the frequency and length of their sessions are gradually decreased. This helps to maintain communication link and help line for the client. It shows continued concern and allows the therapist to detect problems early and allows the client to request assistance if necessary (Pagliaro 2012).

Pharmacotherapy

Pharmacological treatments have been evaluated for their ability to facilitate abstinence, restore homeostasis and prevent relapse. This chart shows FDA approved pharmacotherapies.

Medication	What It Treats	How It Works	Prescribing Notes
Disulfiram (Antabuse)	Treats Alcoholism	Interferes with elimination of alcohol from the body; build-up of acetaldehyde; causes an unpleasant reaction	Typical dose is 125–500 mg/day orally; Need to avoid all alcohol, including mouthwash, communion wine, and vanilla extract; Potentially dangerous for patients with psychotic disorders and general medical conditions
Naltrexone (ReVia, Vivitrol)	Alcoholism and opioid addiction	Blocks opioid receptors; in some patients this reduces alcohol related euphoria; may reduce opioid cravings	For alcoholism: Typical dose is 50 mg/day orally (ReVia) or 380 mg injected monthly (Vivitrol); Reduces heavy drinking; Some liver monitoring needed; For opioid addiction: Typical dose is 50 mg/day orally (ReVia) or 380 mg injected monthly (Vivitrol); Less effective than methadone or buprenorphine; Some liver monitoring needed

Acamprosate (Campral)	Alcoholism	Somewhat uncertain, but likely restores GABA-glutamate balance	Typical dose is 666 mg orally, three times daily; Promotes abstinence; Eliminated by the kidneys
Methadone (Dolophine)	Opioid addiction	Binds to opioid receptors; prevents withdrawal and cravings; and blocks the effects of other opioids	Dosing is individualized, but is generally 80–120 mg/day orally; Only available through federally licensed opioid treatment programs (methadone clinics); Potentially lethal if taken with benzodiazepines
Buprenorphine (Suboxone, Subutex) Note: Suboxone also contains naloxone	Opioid addiction	Binds to opioid receptors; prevents withdrawal and cravings; and blocks the effects of other opioids	Dosing is individualized, but is generally 12–16 mg/day sublingually; Available in office-based settings through specially licensed prescribers; Less abuse liability than methadone
Nicotine (Nicorette and others)	Nicotine addiction	Binds to nicotine receptors; prevents withdrawal and craving	Dosing is individualized and depends on formulation; Formulations can be combined to suppress

			cravings and symptoms of withdrawal; Nicotine toxicity is unlikely as patients self-titrate to their typical level of nicotine
Bupropion (Zyban)	Nicotine addiction	Increases dopamine levels by blocking presynaptic reuptake; reduces withdrawal and cravings	Typical dose is 150 mg orally, once or twice daily; May make cigarettes taste bad; Usual antidepressant side effects possible
Varenicline (Chantix)	Nicotine addiction	Binds to nicotine receptors; prevents withdrawal and craving; and blocks the effects of nicotine	Typical dose is 0.5–1 mg orally, once or twice daily; Dose reduction needed in chronic kidney disease; Recent concerns about depression, aggression, suicide, and nightmares

Pharmacotherapy is a mainstay of the medical management of both acute overdosages involving the various drugs and substance abuse and their respective withdrawal syndromes. It is often a necessary and integral part of the treatment of adolescents who may have dual diagnoses. Failure to treat the co-occurring disorder adequately may significantly contribute to relapsed use of the drug or substance of abuse (Pagliaro 2012).

Family Therapy Treatment

Structural Family Therapy is an effective way to help a family dealing with substance abuse. Structural therapy attempts to restructure the maladaptive family boundaries that separate family members from each other in destructive ways. When there are problems in a family, boundaries can become unclear and there is a breakdown in the family hierarchy. Structural therapy changes the family's behavior by opening alternative patterns of interaction that can modify family structure, not by creating new structures, but by activating dormant ones (Nichols 2010). Some of the techniques used in structural therapy are reframing, enactment and fixing the boundaries.

A family who identifies their 16 year old son as a substance abuser may say that he is doing it because he wants to disobey his parents. A structural therapist may reframe that saying the son's substance abuse may be his way of establishing his independence or that he is insecure at this time of his life (i.e. puberty). It gives the family an alternative view of the presenting problem. Using this same example to show an enactment, the therapist may say to the son, tell me what dinner time is like in your home. The son may say that dad eats in front of the TV and he and mom eats in the kitchen. The son says I want us to eat together and talk to each other. The therapist may say to the dad, do you hear what your son is saying? For the son, eating together and talking to each other may allow him to be able to talk to his parents about what is going on in his life. The substance abuse is away for him to get his parent's attention. Having the family eat a meal together can help to re-establish the hierarchical boundaries. Mom and dad's parental boundary comes together again and the son can see them as a unit, not separate entities. The therapist may suggest that the family try eating together one time and see how it goes. The number can gradually increase as therapy continues.

Solution-Focused Therapy is another type of family therapy treatment that can be used with substance abuse. With this model of therapy, what caused the problem does not need to be known. The person is not the problem. The problem is the problem. The focus is on the mindset which can be changed. The clients are helped to shift from negative thinking to positive thinking. When the thought process becomes positive, the language spoken can be changed. Language creates reality. The therapist wants the client to go from problem talk to solution talk. The techniques for Solution-Focused Therapy are constructed around two strategies, developing well-focused goals within the client's frame of reference and generating solutions based on exceptions (Nichols, 2010, p. 326). To develop goals for this type of therapy, the therapist will pose several questions to the client once he or she has heard the presenting problem. The client will be asked how will they know when the problem has been solved, how will they know when the therapist is no longer needed, what has to be different for that to happen, and what will others notice that will be different. Each family member will have a different answer for each question according to how it pertains to them.

To help a client with its goals and changes, specific types of questions are asked. The main one is the miracle question. To a family present with substance abuse, the therapist would say: Now I want to ask you a strange question. Suppose while you were sleeping tonight and the entire house is quiet, a miracle happens. The miracle is that the problem which brought you here is solved. However, because you are sleeping, you do not know the miracle has happened. So, when you wake up tomorrow morning, what will be different that will tell you that a miracle has happened and the problem which brought you here is solved?" (Nichols, 2010, p. 327)

The miracle question makes the family aware of goals that can be attained despite the problem. The family talks about the things that would be different when the miracle happens. For the son, he would know the miracle has happened because his father would tell him to have a great day at school and that he would see him at dinner time. The dad would know that the miracle has happened because his wife would ask him what he'd like to have for dinner. Mom would know that the miracle has occurred because her son would thank her for making breakfast and kiss her on the cheek as he left for school. The miracle question gets the family to think about what the future could be.

In addition to the miracle question, the therapist utilizes the exception question, scaling questions and compliments. The exception allows the family to explore a time when they did not have the problem. Addressing the son, the therapist would say, recently, when did you have the urge to drink, but didn't? What will make it possible for more of that to happen?

The son may answer "two days ago, when mom ruined dinner. I thought she was going to cook something else and we'd end up eating dinner at 9 PM, but she ordered a pizza. Next time I'll help with dinner to make sure it comes out okay." Scaling questions help the client and therapist to identify concrete behavioral changes and goals. The therapist may ask the dad, on a scale of 1 to 10, 1 being when you called and 10 being you not having to see me anymore, where are you right now? If the dad answers 3, the therapist then asks what it would take to make it go up. His answer might be his son talking to him without an attitude. Scaling questions allow the client and therapist to acknowledge small changes. When a therapist uses compliments, he or she is pointing out the positive aspects of what the client has done. When the son tells the therapist he helped his mom with dinner, the therapist says "Wow! No kidding! How did you do that?" The compliments allow the clients to discuss their successes and build up their self-confidence. Once the family has reached the goals it set out to achieve, they will tell the therapist that they no longer need therapy. They let the therapist know that they will call for a follow up appointment should they need it.

In Solution-Focused Therapy, the therapist "encourages the client to use his or her own previous exception behavior and/or test behaviors that are part of the client's description of his or her goal" (Terry S. Trepper, 2012). It takes the family from the present to the future. Solution-focused therapists do not teach clients what to do. They help them to remember what they already know how to do. He/she shows the client that they are the experts of their lives and they know what it is they want to change.

When to Refer

As has been already noted, the biological components of the disease of alcoholism (whether causative or a consequence of the illness) can be conducive to creating the need for sustained drinking behavior. Thorough medical assessment is therefore necessary for helping the alcoholic back to recovery.

Referral to AA meetings or to Alanon is also a necessary initial step in helping alcoholic clients back to feeling that others understand their plight. These meetings also allow alcoholics to realize that there are some constructive options for dealing with dysfunctional aspects of their lives.

The alcohol-free climate of these groups, together with positive steps toward accepting their behavior (which had previously induced more guilt, anxiety, depression, and hopelessness), now make it possible to confront and eventually put to rest old patterns on the road to recovery. These groups provide the environment for acceptance, caring and revitalization of aggressive or frustrated feelings which have been so typical of the alcoholic's way of life.

If during the treatment process, the problem drinking has given way to alcoholic alibis and rationalizations of drinking behavior so that the physical demands for drinking occur together with the loss of control, then referral to an alcohol counselor is necessary. These clients need to be educated about the fact that internal needs have substituted for the previous reactive drinking despite the periods of abstinence. Acceptance of help from a source outside of self is necessary.

During periods of prolonged drinking, the alcoholic client may need an alcohol-free environment and a source of an external structure, such as hospitalization, for detoxification. This may prevent physical problems and accidents while also providing time to convince the client to make a commitment to a new way of dealing with old problems.

Information about alcoholism and treatment resources may be obtained from the National Clearing House for Alcohol Information, P.O. Box 2345, Rockville, Maryland, 20852, or from the National Council on Alcoholism, 733 Third Avenue, New York, New York, 10017. The council can direct therapists to many helping resources in the United States. Information acan also be obtained from the Substance Abuse and Mental Health Services Administration, 1 Choke Cherry Road, Rockville, MD, 20857 or by calling 1-877-SAMHSA-7.

References

Alcoholics Anonymous. (n.d.). Retrieved June 4, 2014, from http:// www.aa.org

Alling, F. A. (1992). Detoxification and treatment of acute sequelae. In J. H. Lowinson, P. Ruiz, and R. B. Millman (Eds.), *Comprehensive Textbook of Substance Abuse*. New York: Williams & Wilkins.

American Psychiatric Association. (2013). *Diagnostic and statistical manual of mental disorders* (5th ed.). Washington, DC:

Atwood, J., & Chester, R. (1987). *Treatment Techniques for Common Mental Disorders.* New Jersey: Jason Aronson Inc.

Austin, G. A. (1978). *Perspectives on the History of Psychoactive Substance Abuse.* Washington, D.C.: U.S. Government Printing Office.

Baekland, F., Lundwall, L., Kisin, B., & Shanahan, T. (1971). Correlates of outcome in disulfiram treatment of alcoholism. *The Journal of Nervous and Mental Disease 11*, 365-382.

Bandura, A. (1969). *Principles of Behavior Modification.* New York: Holt, Rinehart & Winston.

Becker, S. J. (2013) Adolescent substance use, national trends, consequences and promising treatments. *The Brown University Child and Adolescent Behavior Letter,* 29(5).

Brandsma, J. M., Maultsby, M. C., & Welsh, R. J. (1980). *Outpatient Treatment of Alcoholism: A Review and Comparative Study.* Baltimore: University Press.

Braucht, G. N., Barkarsh, D., Follingstad, D., & Berry, K. L. (1973). Deviant drug use in adolescence: a review of psychological correlates. *Psychology Bulletin 79*(2), 92-106.

Bennett, L.A., & Wolin, S.J. (1990) "Family Culture and Alcoholism Transmission," in Alcohol and the Family. Collins, R.L., Leonard, K.E. and Searles, J.S. (eds.), 194-219. New York, Guilford Press.

Briddell, D.W., Rimm, D.C., Caddy, G.R., Krawitz, G., Sholis, D., & Wunderlin, R.J. (1978). The effects of alcohol and expectancy set on male sexual arousal. *Journal of Abnormal Psychology 2*, 31-40.

Brownwell, K. D., & Gold, M. S. (2012) *Food and Addiction: A Comprehensive Handbook,* New York: Oxford University Press.

Calahan, D. (1978). Subcultural differences in drinking behavior in U.S. National surveys and selected European studies. In *Alcoholism: New Directions in Behavioral Research and Treatment,* ed. P. E. Nathan, G. A. Marlatt, and T. Loberg. New York: Plenum.

Cappell, H., & Herman, C. P. (1972). Alcohol and tension reduction: a review. *Quarterly Journal of Studies on Alcohol 33*, 33-64.

Capuzzi, D., & Stauffer, M. D. (2012). *Foundations of Addictions Counseling.* New Jersey: Pearson.

Cautela, J. R. (1967). Covert sensitization. *Psychological Reports, 20*, 459-468.

Charney, D. S., Heninger, G. R., & Kleber, H. D. (1986). The combined use of clonidine and naltrexone as a rapid, safe and effective treatment of abrupt withdrawal from methadone. *American Journal of Psychiatry 143*, 831-837.

Claeson, L. E., & Malm, U. (1973). Electro-aversion therapy of chronic alcoholism. *Behavior Research and Therapy 11*(4), 663-665.

Cooper, M. L., Russell, M., & George, W. H. (1988). Coping, expectancies, and alcohol abuse: A test of social learning formulations. *Journal of Abnormal Psychology*, 97(2).

Davidson, W. S. (1974). Studies of aversive conditioning for alcoholics: a critical review of theory and research methodology. *Psychological Bulletin 81*(9), 571-581.

Ditman, K. S. (1967). Review and evaluation of current drug therapies in alcoholism. *International Journal of Psychiatry 3*(4), 248-266.

Ewing, J. A., Rouse, B. A., & Pellizzari, E. D. (1974). Alcohol sensitivity and ethnic background. *American Journal of Psychiatry 131*, 206-210.

Farber, P. D., Khavari, K. A., & Douglass IV, F. M. (1980). A factor analytic study of reasons for drinking: Empirical validation of positive and negative reinforcement dimensions. *Journal of Consulting and Clinical Psychology*, 48, 780–781.

Fenichel, O. (1945). *The Psychoanalytic Theory of Neurosis.* New York: Norton.

Fox, J. H., Ramsey, R. G., Huckman, M. S., & Proske, A. E. (1976). Cerebral ventricular enlargement: Chronic alcoholics examined by computerized tomography. *Journal of the American Medical Association 236*: 365-377.

Frank, G. H. (1970). On the nature of borderline personality: A review. *Journal of General Psychology 83*(1), 61-77.

Franklin, C., Trepper, T. S, McCollum, E. E., & Gingich, W. (2012) *Solution-Focused Brief Therapy: A Handbook of Evidence-Based Practice.* New York: Oxford University Press.

Gomberg, E. S. (1974). Women and alcoholism. In *Women and Therapy: New Psychotherapies for a Changing Society*, ed. V. Franks and V. Burtle. New York: Bruner/Mazel.

Goodwin, D. W., Schulsinger, F., Hermansen, L., Guze, S.B., & Winokur, G. (1973). Alcohol problems in adoptees raised apart from alcoholic biological parents. *Archives of General Psychiatry 28,* 238-243.

Goodwin, D. W., Schulsinger, F., Moller, N., Hermansen, L., Winokur, G., & Guze, S.B. (1974). Drinking problems in adopted and nonadopted sons of alcoholics. *Archives of General Psychiatry, 31*(2), 164-169.

Gorad, S. L. (1971). The alcoholic and his wife: Their personal styles of communication and interaction. *Dissertation Abstracts International, 32*(B-4), 2395-2396.

Gottheil, E., Thornton, C. C., Skoloda, T. E., & Alterman, A. I. (1982). Follow-up of abstinent and non-abstinent alcoholics. *American Journal of Psychiatry, 139*(5), 560-565.

Gross, M. M., and Lewis, C. (1973). Observations on the prevalence of the signs and symptoms associated with withdrawal during continuous observation of experimental intoxication and withdrawal in humans. In *Alcohol Intoxication and Withdrawal: Experimental Studies,* ed. M.M. Gross. New York: Plenum.

Gumbiner, J. (2010, January 12). What causes addiction? Psychoanalytic theories of addiction. Retrieved June 3, 2014, from http://www.psychologytoday.com

Higgins, R. L., & Marlatt, G. A. (1974). The effects of anxiety arousal upon the consumption of alcohol by alcoholics and social drinkers. *Journal of Consulting and Clinical Psychology, 41,* 426-433.

Ingalls, Z. (1978). On campus, the biggest drug problem is alcohol. *Chronicle of Higher Education,* 3-5.

Jellinek, E. M. (1952). Phases of alcohol addiction. *Quarterly Journal of Studies on Alcohol, 13,* 673.

Jellinek (1971). Phases of alcohol addiction. In *Studies of Abnormal Behavior,* ed. Chicago: Rand McNally.

Kaufman, E. (1985). *Substance Abuse and Family Therapy.* New York: Grune & Stratton.

Knupfer, G. (1972). Ex-problem drinkers. In *Life History Research in Psychopathology,* vol. 2, ed. M. Roff, L. N. Robins, and M. Pollack. Minneapolis: University of Minnesota Press.

Kogan, K. L., & Jackson, J. K. (1965). Stress personality and emotional disturbance in wives in alcoholics. *Quarterly Journal of Studies on Alcohol, 26*(3), 395-408.

Kosten, T. R., & Kleber, H. D. (1986). Buprenorphine detoxification from opioid dependence: A pilot study. *Life Sciences, 42*, 635-641.

Lahti, R. A., & Majchrowicz, E. (1974). Ethanol and acetaldehyde effects on metabolism and binding of biogenic amines. *Quarterly Journal of Studies on Alcohol, 35*, 1-14.

Lang, A. R., Goeckner, D. J., Adesso, V. G., & Marlatt, G. A. (1975). Effects of alcohol on aggression in male social drinkers. *Journal of Abnormal Psychology, 84*, 508-518.

MacKay, J. R. (1961). Clinical observations on adolescent problem drinkers. *Quarterly Journal of Studies in Alcoholism, 22*, 124-134.

Maletzky, B. M., & Klotter, J. (1974). Smoking and alcoholism. *American Journal of Psychiatry, 131*(4), 445-447.

Marlatt, G. A. (1974). Modeling influences in social drinking: An experimental analogue. Paper presented at the Association for Advancement of Behavior Therapy, Chicago.

Marlatt, G.A. (1978). Craving for alcohol, loss of control, and relapse: A cognitive-behavioral analysis. In *Alcoholism: New Directions in Behavioral Research and Treatment,* ed. New York: Plenum.

Marlatt, G. A., Demming, B., & Reid, J. B. (1973). Loss-of-control drinking in alcoholics: An experimental analogue. *Journal of Abnormal Psychology, 81*, 233-241.

Marlatt, G. A., & Gordon, J. R. (1979). Determinants of relapse: Implications for the maintenance of behavior change. In P. Davidson (Ed.) *Behavioral medicine: Changing health lifestyles.* New York: Brunner/Mazel.

McClelland, D. C., Davis, W. N., Kalin, R., & Wanner, E. (1972). *The Drinking Man.* New York: The Free Press.

McCollom, E. E., & Trepper, T. S. (2001). *Family Solutions for Substance Abuse, Clinical and Counseling Approaches.* New York: The Haworth Press.

McCord, W., McCord, J., & Gudeman, J. (1960). *Origins of Alcoholism.* Stanford, CA: Stanford University Press.

Mello, N. K., & Mendelson, J. H. (1979). Experimentally induced intoxication in alcoholics: A comparison between programmed and spontaneous drinking. *Journal of Pharmacology and Experimental Therapy, 173*, 101-105.

Menninger, K. (1938). *Man Against Himself.* New York: Harcourt Brace.

Miller P. M., Hersen M., Eisler R. M., & Hilsman G. (1974). Effects of social stress on operant drinking of alcoholics and social drinkers. *Behavior and Research Therapy, 12*, 67–72.

Miller, P. M. (1976). *Behavioral Treatment of Alcoholism.* New York: Pergamon.

Miller, W. R. (1978). Behavioral treatment of problem drinkers: A comparative outcome study of three controlled drinking therapies. *Journal of Consulting and Clinical Psychology, 50*,   491-498.

Mulford, H. (1983). Stress, alcohol intake and problem drinking in Iowa. In L. A. Pohorecky & J. Brick (Eds.) *Stress and Alcohol Use, Proceedings of the First International Symposium on Stress and Alcohol Use.* New York: Elsevier.

Nathan, P. E. (1977). An overview of behavioral treatment approaches. In *Behavioral Approaches to Alcoholism*, ed. G. A. Marlett and P. E. Nathan. New Brunswick, N.J.: Rutgers Center for Alcohol Studies.

Nathan, P. E., & O'Brien, J. S. (1971). An experimental analysis of the behavior of alcoholics and nonalcoholics during prolonged experimental drinking: A necessary precursor of behavior therapy? *Behavior Therapy 2*, 455-476.

NA. (n.d.). Retrieved June 4, 2014, from http://www.na.org

Nichols, M. P. (2010). *Family Therapy, Concepts and Methods.* Boston: Allyn & Bacon

Pagliaro, L. A., & Pagliaro, A. M. (2012). *Handbook of Child and Adolescent Drug and Substance Abuse: Pharmacological, Developmental, and Clinical Consideration.* New Jersey: John Wiley & Sons.

Parry, H. J., Cisin, I. H., Balter, M. B., Mellinger, G. D., & Manheimer, D. I. (1974). Increasing alcohol intake as a coping mechanism for psychic distress. In R. Cooperstock (Ed.) *Social aspects of the medical use of psychotropic drugs.* Toronto: Addiction Research Foundation of Ontario.

Pendery, M. L., Maltzman, I. M., & West, L. J. (1982). Controlled drinking by alcoholics? New findings and a reevaluation of a major affirmative study. *Science, 217*(9), 169-174.

Pihl, R. O., & Spiers, P. (1978). Individual characteristics in the etiology of drug abuse. In *Progress in Experimental Personality Research,* vol. 8, Ed. New York: Academic.

Polich, J.M., Armor, D. J., & Braiker, H. B. (1980). *The Course of Alcoholism: Four Years After Treatment.* Santa Monica: Rand Corporation.

Polich, J. M., & Orvis, B. R. (1979). *Alcohol problems: Patterns and prevalence in the U.S. Air Force.* Santa Monica, CA: Rand Corporation.

Roe, A., Burks, B. S., & Mittleman, B. (1945). Adult adjustment of foster children of alcoholic and psychotic parentage and influence of the foster home. *Memorial Section on Alcohol Studies.* New Haven: Yale University Press.

Rotgers, F., Keller, D., and Morgenstern, J. (1996) *Treating Substance Abuse, Theory and Technique,* New York: The Guilford Press.

Rothschild, D. (2013 May 29) Psychoanalysis is Addiction Treatment's Missing Piece. Retrieved June 4, 2014, from http://www.thefix.com/

Schuckit-Rorpes, M. A. (1979). Ethanol ingestion: differences in blood acetaldehyde concentrations in relatives of alcoholics and controls. *Science, 203,* 54-55.

Sellers, E. M., & Kalant, H. (1976). Drug therapy: alcohol intoxication and withdrawal. *New England Journal of Medicine 294*(4), 757-762.

Sobell, M. B. & Sobell, L. C. (1973). Individualized behavior therapy for alcoholics. *Behavior Therapy, 4,* 49-72.

Stanton, M. D., Todd, T. C. & Associates. (1982). *The Family Therapy of Drug Abuse and Addiction.* New York: The Guilford Press.

Steiner, C. M. (1969). The alcoholic game. *Quarterly Journal of Studies on Alcohol, 30,* 920-938.

Steinglass, P., Weiner, S., & Mendelson, J. (1971). A systems approach to alcoholism: A model and its clinical application. *Archives of General Psychiatry, 24*(5), 401-408.

Stevens, P., & Smith, R. L. (2009). *Substance Abuse Counseling, Theory and Practice.* **New Jersey: Pearson.**

Tavel, M E. (1962). **A new look at an old syndrome: Delirium tremens.** *Archives of Internal Medicine, 109,* **129-134.**

Victor, M., & Adams, R. (1953). **The effects of alcohol on the nervous system.** *Research Publication Association of Nervous Mental Disorders, 32,* **526-573.**

Washton, A. M. (1995). *Psychotherapy and Substance Abuse: A Practitioner's Handbook.* **New York: The Guilford Press.**

Williams, A. F. (1966). **Social drinking, anxiety, and depression.** *Journal of Personality.* **New York: Ronald.**

Wilsnack, S. (1973). **Femininity by the bottle.** *Psychology Today, 6,* **39-42.**

Wilson, G. T. (1978). **Booze, beliefs, and behavior: Cognitive process in alcohol use and abuse. In** *Alcoholism: New Directions in Behavioral Research and Treatment,* **ed. New York: Plenum.**

Wilson, G. T., & Lawson, D. M. (1976). **Expectancies, alcohol, and sexual arousal in male social drinkers.** *Journal of Abnormal Psychology, 85,* **587-594.**

Winokur, G., Reich, T., Rimmer, J., & Pitts, F. N. (1970). **Alcoholism III: Diagnosis and familial sychiatric illness in 259 alcoholic probands.** *Archives of General Psychiatry, 23,* **104-113.**

Wood, H., & Duffy, E. (1966). **Psychology factors in alcoholic women.** *American Journal of Psychiatry, 123*(3), **341-345.**

Chapter 12

Schizophrenia

(295.90) (F20.9)
Joan D. Atwood, Ph.D.

What is Schizophrenic Behavior and How Do You Recognize It?

"The author who undertakes to write a handbook chapter on the phenomena conventionally included under the rubric schizophrenia-- questions of his own sanity and proper intellectual humility aside- faces an enormously intimidating task" (Carson, 1983). A tremendous amount has been written about schizophrenia, and an equally overwhelming amount of research has been conducted on the topic. This chapter provides an overview of the topic.

The schizophrenias are a group of psychotic disorders which are characterized by gross distortions of reality. Schizophrenic behaviors are typified by withdrawal from social interaction and by distortion and fragmentation of perception, thought, and emotion. For the most part, schizophrenia has severe consequences for the affected person and their families. In addition, schizophrenia poses a serious problem to the mental health agencies whose main function it is to provide treatment and support. While fewer than 1 person in every 100 will at some time be diagnosed as schizophrenic, such persons do represent a significant proportion of the patients in inpatient and outpatient mental health facilities. The etiologies and treatment of the disorder, therefore, are matters of great concern.

Until the end of the nineteenth century, the several forms of what we now call psychosis were generally considered to be the result of a single disease. Historically, schizophrenic disorders were attributed to a type of mental deterioration beginning early in life. In 1860, Morel, a Belgian psychiatrist, described the case of a 13 year old boy who, over a period of time, lost interest in his studies, became increasingly withdrawn, seclusive, and taciturn, and appeared to have forgotten everything he learned. Morel believed the boy's functions had deteriorated as a result of a genetic abnormality and that they were therefore irrecoverable. He used the term dementia precoce (mental deterioration at an early age) to describe the condition and to distinguish it from disorders of old age.

One of the first persons to classify schizophrenia as a distinct disorder was Emil Kraeplin (1856-1926), the influential German psychiatrist. In the nineteenth century, he adopted the Latin form of the term. He called the disease dementia praecox. It was Kraeplin who first proposed the idea that there were three separate psychoses, representing three separate disease entities: hebephrenia, catatonia, and paranoia. Kraeplin believed that this apparent mental deterioration of the young was an organic disorder and that recovery from it was impossible.

In 1911, the term schizophrenia was suggested by the Swiss psychiatrist Eugene Bleuler, and it eventually replaced the earlier term. The word schizophrenia is derived from the Greek words meaning "split mind." Bleuler used the term schizophrenia because he thought the disorder was characterized primarily by disorganization of thought processes, lack of coherence between thought and emotion, and inward orientation, away from reality. For Bleuler, the splitting thus implied, not multiple personalities, but a splitting within the intellect and between intellect and emotion. Bleuler chose it to refer to the fragmentation of emotion, thought, and perception that characterized the disorder.

Bleuler also introduced a fourth classification of the disorder, the simple type. He believed that schizophrenia was characterized by a splintering of the psychic functions rather than by gradual deterioration, and he noted that while some schizophrenics did deteriorate, others remained unchanged, and some even improved. Thus, he was also the first to distinguish between chronic and acute schizophrenia. Like Kraeplin, Bleuler believed in an underlying organic trend toward schizophrenic deterioration. Yet he went considerably beyond Kraeplin by taking into account psychological explanations of schizophrenic behavior. Bleuler explained disordered thought in terms of attention deficits, association disturbances, and ego disintegration.

A completely different approach to the origins and cure of schizophrenia was then propounded by a contemporary of Kraeplin's and Bleuler's, Adolf Meyer (1866-1950). Meyer, an American neuropathologist, who was recognized as the dean of American psychiatry, believed that there were no fundamental differences between schizophrenics and normals and, further, that there were no differences in their respective psychological processes. Rather, he believed, that the cognitive, and behavioral disorganization that was associated with schizophrenia from inadequate early learning, and reflected "adjustive insufficiency" and habit deterioration. He felt that individual maladjustment, rather than biological malfunction, lay at the root of the disorder. Meyer's approach mandated research in an area wholly different from those of Bleuler or Kraeplin. While they strengthened the biological tradition of research in schizophrenia, Meyer gave impetus to a tradition that focused on learning and biopsychosocial processes.

Most theorists today agree that it is not clear that schizophrenia is a singular process. The existence of schizophrenia, does not in and of itself establish similarity of underlying organization in each case of schizophrenia any more than does a medical diagnosis of hypertension, which can be due to many different underlying conditions. Thus, many clinicians today believe that there may be several schizophrenias, each with a different etiological pattern and set of psychodynamics (Bellak, 1980).

Since Bleuler's (1911) description of schizophrenic persons who recovered after relatively short periods of disordered behavior, a great deal of research has been focused on identifying factors that are associated with a favorable prognosis. This line of research has led to the description of two patterns of schizophrenic disorders-- one associated with chronic, long-term disability and the other with shorter periods of disordered functioning. These are not considered subtypes of schizophrenia; rather, this distinction applies to all four types listed. The distinction basically refers to two different courses of the disorder. Sometimes schizophrenic disorders develop slowly and insidiously. Here the early clinical picture may be dominated by seclusiveness, gradual lack of interest in the surrounding world, excessive daydreaming, blunting of affect, and mildly inappropriate responses. This pattern is referred to as process schizophrenia; that is it develops gradually over a period of time and tends to be long-lasting. It is characterized by a gradual onset of maladaptive behavior early in life, considerable social withdrawal, and poor personal adjustment. The outcome or process schizophrenia is generally unfavorable, partly because the need for treatment is usually not recognized until the behavior pattern has become firmly entrenched. Poor premorbid personality features or chronic schizophrenia are alternative terms referring to this pattern and are approximately equivalent in meaning to process.

In other instances, however, the onset of the schizophrenic symptoms is quite sudden and dramatic and is marked by intense emotional turmoil and a nightmarish sense of confusion. This pattern, which is usually associated with identifiable precipitating stressors, is referred to as reactive schizophrenic (alternatively, good premorbid conditions or acute schizophrenia). In contract to process schizophrenia, reactive schizophrenia has a relatively sudden onset and is clearly associated with some precipitating event in the life of the individual who showed a relatively satisfactory adjustment earlier in life. The symptoms of reactive schizophrenia usually clear in a matter of weeks, although in some cases an acute episode is the prelude to a more chronic pattern.

Keep in mind that this process-reactive distinction should be viewed, not as a dichotomy, but rather as a continuum. The distribution of schizophrenic individuals can be envisioned in the familiar bell-shaped curve, with relatively few falling at either the process or reactive extremes and most falling somewhere in the middle.

Another distinction which has gained increased prominence in recent years is that between paranoid and non-paranoid symptom patterns among persons diagnosed as schizophrenic. In the paranoid pattern, delusions, particularly persecutory or grandiose ones, are a dominant feature. In the non-paranoid forms, such delusions, if present at all, tend to be rare and fleeting. Evidence is building that important differences exist between those who exhibit a predominantly paranoid symptom pattern and those who exhibit few, none, or inconsistent paranoid symptoms. In general, paranoid schizophrenic individuals tend to be more "reactive" than "process" in type and to have a more benign course and outcome (Ritzler, 1981). They may be genetically less vulnerable to schizophrenia than the non-paranoid types (Kendler and Davis, 1981). Adding to the confusion, is the finding that a substantial number of persons originally diagnosed as having paranoid schizophrenic symptoms are later diagnosed as having non-paranoid ones (Kendler and Tsuang, 1981).

Whether process, reactive, paranoid, or non-paranoid in the general sense of these terms, schizophrenia encompasses many symptoms that vary greatly from one individual to another. The basic experience in schizophrenia, however, seems to be one of disorganization in perception, thought, and emotion.

Clinicians have made the following general observations of schizophrenia. Sullivan (1962) believed that when persons experiencing a dramatic first-time psychotic break have a history of good social adjustment, they may be able to treat the psychotic break as useful, leading to reorganization of the personality. Mosher (1974), Laing (1960), Bowers

(1961), and others suggest a positive outcome of a first psychotic break if an individual receives proper treatment.

A few characteristics of schizophrenics are quite useful in predicting potential for improvement. For example, it is widely held that the more favorable the individual's prepsychotic adjustment, the better the prognosis. Also, the more sudden the onset, the more favorable the prognosis. One of the most consistent findings is that process schizophrenics have a much poorer prognosis than reactive schizophrenics. Approximately 55 percent of the process type will remain unimproved, compared with less than 10 percent of the reactive type (Stephens, 1970). This prognosis also carries over to the similar distinction on the chronic-acute dimension. Those who have an acute onset (that is, less than six months) have a much better recovery rate than those with a more gradual onset.

Stephens (1978) identifies several other factors related to a favorable prognosis:

1. married at one time, especially if there is an existing satisfactory marital relationship.
2. at least an average IQ.
3. a specific precipitating event.
4. period from onset of symptoms to hospitalization less than six months.
5. previous work history.
6. clear-cut depressive symptoms.
7. absence of emotional blunting.
8. absence of schizoid (severely withdrawn) personality.
9. confusion or perplexity about condition.

Stephens predicts the presence of at least five of the nine items were predictive of a favorable outcome.

Schizophrenia is indeed a strange and puzzling disorder, comprising a group of behaviors whose prominent common features include retreat from reality, emotional blunting, and disturbed thinking. These features vary in severity from client to client. It is a serious condition, often involving severe impairment of social, occupational, and personal functioning, loss of contact with reality, and great subjective discomfort.

The estimated incidence of schizophrenia is about 1 percent of the population, a figure that has been quite stable over time. The actual incidence of the disorder has been estimated at about 150 cases per 100,000 population per year (Crocetti and Lemkau, 1967). The number of new cases of schizophrenia is estimated to be between 100,000 and 200,000 persons every year in the United States (Babigan, 1975). There are approximately 1 million actively diagnosed schizophrenic persons in the United States at the present time (Berger, 1978) and probably 10 to 15 times more than that who are subject to schizophrenic episodes (Dohrenwend et al, 1980). However only 600,000 are treated in a typical year. Schizophrenics constitute the largest diagnostic group of patients in psychiatric hospitals. They occupy almost two thirds of the beds in psychiatric hospitals and one quarter of all hospital beds. About one fourth of the patients admitted each year to mental hospitals and clinics are diagnosed as schizophrenics, and since schizophrenic individuals often require prolonged or repeated hospitalization, they usually constitute about half the patient population for all available psychiatric hospital beds (President's Commission on Mental Health, 1978).

There appear to be substantial gender differences in the age of onset of schizophrenia: Men are at risk for schizophrenia before age 25, while women are at risk for schizophrenia after age 25 (Levine, 1981; Zigler and Levine, 1981). Although schizophrenic disorders sometimes occur during childhood or old age, about three fourths of all first admissions are between the ages 15 and 45, with a median age of just over 30. Most schizophrenics admitted to the hospital are between 20 and 40 years of age, and the hospitalization rate among persons in the age group 25 and 34 is strikingly higher than for any other age group (Yolles and Kramer, 1969). The incidence is about the same for males and females. First hospitalizations average four to five months and hospitalizations throughout the schizophrenic's life may last 10 years or longer.

It appears that schizophrenic disorders occur in all societies, from the aborigines of the western Australian desert and the remote interior jungles of Malaysia to the most technologically advanced societies. An interesting study is reported by Murphy (1978), however, who found that the prevalence rate of schizophrenia is markedly higher in the Irish Republic than in Northern Ireland. Numerous other studies identify areas of especially high or especially low prevalence rates of schizophrenia throughout the world. Thus, the oft-quoted 1 percent may be quite misleading (Torrey, 1980). Besides the Irish Republic, there are two other areas having well-documented rates of schizophrenia: a region of Croatia in Yugoslavia (Crocetti et al, 1971) and the northern reaches of Sweden (Book, 1979). Among the methodologically sound studies showing low prevalence rates of schizophrenia are Eaton and Weil's (1955) well-known survey of the Hutterite communities in the United States and the study by Torrey and colleagues (1974) of the highland dwellers in Papua, New Guinea. By and large, in the studies noted, the variations from expected rates of prevalence are far from trivial and cannot readily be accounted for along genetic or other biological bases. There is evidence, however, that certain cultural factors may operate in some cases to enhance and facilitate the risk of schizophrenia and in other cases to weaken its expression.

By far the most puzzling and unexpected of epidemiological findings on schizophrenia has been the recent discovery that births of schizophrenics persons tend to concentrate in certain months of the year. The findings reviewed by Torrey (1980) are so numerous and compelling that they cannot be dismissed. It appears that the births of persons who later become schizophrenic tend statistically to occur in the later winter or spring months.

Babigan (1975) summarized other factors related to the diagnosis of schizophrenia:

1. The incidence of schizophrenia is higher in lower socioeconomic groups.
2. Schizophrenia is more prevalent in nonwhites compared with whites; but the rate in men and women is approximately equal.
3. Schizophrenics are at a greater risk of early death than "normals."
4. The reproduction rate of schizophrenics' persons is lower than that of the general population.
5. The total direct and indirect cost of schizophrenia in our society is estimated at $14 billion a year.

Garmezy and Streitman (1974) outlined the antecedents of schizophrenia. The most powerful predictor of schizophrenia is a family history of the disorder. On the average, 10 percent of persons who have one schizophrenic parent will eventually be diagnosed as schizophrenic. For individuals who have two schizophrenic parents, the chances increase 35 to 40 percent (Hanson et al, 1977; Rosenthal (1970). Interestingly as will be discussed later, the unaffected children of schizophrenic parents often appear to be particularly talented and creative (Meehl, 1962).

Another predictor of schizophrenia is severe family conflict. Often this centers on extremely poor, disorganized relationships between family members. Marital disharmony and poor communication are quite common in these families (Jacobs, 1975; Robbins, 1966). A third general predictor is socioeconomic status (Dohrenwend and Dohrenwend, 1969; Faris and Dunham, 1939, Hollingshead and Redlich, 1958). Consistent findings have indicated that the incidence of schizophrenia is highest in the lowest socioeconomic groups.

The schizophrenics are considered the most serious of all psychotic disorders because of their complexity, high rate of incidence, especially during the most productive years of life, and their tendency to recur and/or become chronic.

Criteria

Before listing the diagnostic criteria for schizophrenia, it is important to note some important diagnostic and methodological considerations. Researchers are required to establish operational definitions of the terms that are incorporated in their diagnostic criteria for mental health. An operational definition specifies precisely what observable phenomena the term designates. It appears, however, that every researcher's operational definition of schizophrenia is simply a matter of his or her own way of diagnosing clients. There is not much diagnostic agreement among professionals when it comes to schizophrenia. Consider, for example, the finding, published in a recent cross-national study, that schizophrenia is more common in New York than in London, while the affective disorders are more common in London than in New York. A group of investigators (Cooper et al, 1972), guessing that this disparity might have more to do with national diagnosis "favorites" than with an actual difference in the psychic life of Londoners and New Yorkers, decided to test this hypothesis by showing groups of psychiatrists in New York and in London identical videotapes of doctor-patient interviews. The results confirmed the investigators' hypothesis. In cases involving both mood and thought, the American psychiatrists tended to attribute more weight to the thought disturbance and were consequently more likely to diagnose the patient as schizophrenic. The British psychiatrists, on the other hand, tended to see the mood disturbance as the primary symptom and therefore diagnosed the patient as either manic or depressed.

Such inconsistencies exist not only from one country to another, but also among professionals. A given patient who has received one diagnosis from one clinician might very well be given a different diagnosis by another. Both Beck and colleagues (1962) and Sandler and colleagues (1964) found that the percentage of agreement among professionals on a general diagnosis of schizophrenia ranged from only 53 percent to 74 percent. When attempts have been made to specify the subcategory of schizophrenia, the rate of agreement generally dropped to between 35 percent and 50 percent. This lack of agreement hinders any attempt to make meaningful comparisons between research findings.

The following are symptoms for a schizophrenic disorder: Delusions, hallucinations, disorganized speech (e.g. frequent derailment or incoherence), disorganized or catatonic behavior, negative Symptoms (i.e. diminished emotional expression or avolition). The individual's level of functioning in one or more major areas, such as work, interpersonal relations, or self care, is markedly below the level achieved prior to the onset (or when the onset is in childhood or adolescence, there is failure to achieve expected level of interpersonal, academic, or occupational functioning.

Case Description

Carrie Z was a 27 year old, single, Jewish, white woman who had successfully completed three years of college. However, she was functioning on minimal educational and vocational levels and had progressively deteriorated since her first hospitalization. She had a full head of dark hair streaked with gray, glasses, and an acne scarred complexion. She sobbed almost constantly, but the crying did not appear to be reactive to sad affect. The patient was referred by her counselor at the transitional living center, an after-care program for psychiatric patients, where she lived with a roommate.

Carrie stated that in order to remain in the transitional living center, she was required to participate in psychotherapy and that she was being forced to seek the services of the clinic. On the other hand, she also admitted through her tears that she hoped her future therapist would give her some motivation. During the intake interview, she avoided eye contact, used copious quantities of tissues, and alternated her tears with angry answers or self-pitying statements.

Carrie was born and raised on Long Island, New York, the youngest of three daughters. She described her mother as loving and strict and her father as domineering and controlling. The only significant childhood even that she recalled was was her father's business bankruptcy, which occurred when she was 8 years old. This event had severely limited the family's standard of living. It was later learned that because of his business failure, Mr. Z. had become peripheral to the family. As a result, Carrie no longer felt like the prized and cared for child. Her early schooling was uneventful, and she said that she did have some friends. She reported that she often "made new friends by crying." Her first year and a half of college was interrupted by the first of many "depressions." She began group psychotherapy at age 19 and experimented with sex and drugs. She dropped out of college by the end of her junior year, after cutting classes and not seriously studying. She spent the next year and a half at her parent's home, "doing nothing." The feeling induced during the interview was that Carrie was often out of touch with events and her surroundings. She also often indulged in fantasies that were either sexual or involved the reliving of angry moments with her family and her friends.

Her inpatient history began when she was 23 years old and was hospitalized for three months in a reputable private hospital. She then spent eight months in a day hospital program affiliated with that institution and eventually moved to her own apartment near the hospital. At that point she was being maintained on imipramine hydrochloride (Tofranil) and loxapine succinate (Loxitane). She then returned to college for a while and, believing herself to be well, stopped all medication. She was rehospitalized shortly thereafter, discharged, and rehospitalized later that year. Upon discharge, she moved into an apartment supervised by the transitional living program.

Carrie created so many problems for her roommate that she was moved to a smaller room. The residents were expected to do their own cooking and cleaning. Carrie insisted that she had been forced into the program by her psychiatrist and her parents, and it was characteristic of her to assume little responsibility for any of shopping, cooking, or cleaning unless it was insisted upon by the counselors. She started the intake interview by crying about having eaten her roommate's food, which she said she was unable to resist due to her lack of willpower. She seemed to have been compelled to do so by force beyond her control.

She was required to do volunteer secretarial work at a nearby hospital, but she often did not go, opting instead to stay in her apartment and sleep late. She reported that she was a chronic liar who often felt suicidal because of the hopelessness of her situation. Referring to all the "shit" that she had been through, Carrie asserted that she wanted the therapist to know nothing more about her. She then fell silent and did not resume talking until the interviewer did.

She was familiar with psychotherapeutic techniques and themes as the therapist was. She even recounted her diagnoses (schizophrenia, paranoid type; schizophrenia, chronic type; and schizoaffective disorder). She was being medicated with 50 milligrams of Elavil three times a day and 50 milligrams of Prolixin Decanoate, injected intramuscularly every other week.

Characteristically, Carrie indicated that her self-expectation was just to "shuffle along" in her therapy. She seemed quite taken aback by the therapist's statement that since all the therapists hard, they usually expected the same thing of their patients. Carrie was thoroughly socialized into the role of chronic psychiatric patient and received satisfaction from the hopelessness, pity, and low self-expectations often ascribed to such patients. While not denying the evident and serious pathology in this young woman, the clinic's review team felt that the therapist should avoid the traditional focus on symptoms and unconscious conflicts, and should instead focus on the "here and now" in her therapy sessions. She was a classic example of an intelligent, alert patient who could discuss her psychodynamics for hours while disowning all responsibility for her behavior.

Carrie experienced a thought disorder when overwhelmed with anxiety stimulated by interpersonal, vocational, and intrapsychic events. She was also subject to extreme variations in affect that often further disorganized her thinking to the point of loosening of associations and tangentiality of thought. Although she seemed intent on convincing the interviewer that she pulled "things together for herself," the opposite impression was created. Her only clean intention during the interview was to manipulate the interviewer into feeling that she was honest with herself, which her behavior during the remainder of the sessions then contradicted.

What Does Schizophrenic Behavior Look Like?

Bleuler chose the term schizophrenia because it described the disorder's central symptom: a lack of association (a split) either among ideas or between ideas and emotions. This lack of coherence in the individual's mind may result in the association of words, not on the basis of any logic whatsoever; but only, for example, because they rhyme. Such a series of rhyming or similar-sounding words is called a clang association. Cohen and co-workers (1974) have pointed out that schizophrenic speech is ordinarily quite competent syntactically--that is, subject, verb, predicate, modifiers, and so forth are usually present and in the proper order. Thus, it is not the sentence structure that is incorrect but the meaning of the words themselves.

According to Cohen and coworkers (1974), schizophrenia can make common primary associations to given stimuli about as easily as normal people can. It is the more subtle secondary associations which a schizophrenic cannot make--at least not without becoming confused and incoherent. Cromwell and Dukecki (1968) have suggested that the schizophrenic has difficulty "disattending to" a stimulus after having attending to it. This hypothesis is similar to that presented by Cameron (1938), who saw schizophrenic thought as an overinclusion of stimuli. Like normal persons, the schizophrenic forms many tangential associations to stimuli, including the stimulus of his or her own speech; unlike normal persons, however, the schizophrenic cannot filter out the irrelevant associations. In other words, the individual's behavior is filled with many irrelevant items and, as a result, it is difficult to make sense out of the stream of speech.

The elements of schizophrenic incoherence vary from case to case. The speech of some schizophrenics is permeated by neologisms, words that are formed by condensing and combining several words. Another common schizophrenic feature is echolalia, the constant parroting or repetition of certain words and phrases. Some schizophrenics display verbigeration, a senseless repetition of the same words or phrases. Mutism may typify schizophrenic language; it represents an extreme form of the schizophrenic's communication deficit and has been observed in some individuals for periods of many years. Part of the schizophrenic's communication deficit is a sharp reduction in the expression of appropriate emotional responses. S/he frequently appears to be indifferent and at times seems totally apathetic. The indifference and seeming apathy are part of his or her emotional blunting. The shallowness with which s/he expresses his or her feelings, and an apparently arbitrary dissociation of feeling and verbal expression. As stated earlier, the schizophrenias are characterized by delusional beliefs and disturbances in thought processes, sensations and perceptions, affect, and motor behavior.

Disorganized Thought Processes

One aspect of the schizophrenic's difficulty in thinking and speaking clearly is a tendency toward loose, disjointed expression. Bleuler (1950) referred to this process as derailment of associations, by which he meant that the schizophrenic becomes distracted by irrelevant associations, cannot suppress them, and as a consequence wanders farther and farther from the subject. The thinking and language of the schizophrenic is often loose, disjointed, disorganized, tangential, and illogical. This obvious and often bizarre characteristic has been referred to variously as derailment, loose associations or cognitive slippage (Meehl, 1962). Schizophrenic thought and language often appears to follow sound patterns rather than logic. A typical clang association might be, "I lack Jack, not black, stabbed in the back."

Schizophrenic speech aberrations range from only slight peculiarities to total disorganization. The combination of words and phrases in what appears to be a completely disorganized and idiosyncratic fashion is referred to as word salad. Unlike neologisms, word salad seems to have no communicative value whatsoever. Now does it appear to reflect thoughts that generalize on the basis of tangential associations? Seemingly devoid not only of logic and meaning but even of associational links, word salad is defined by its total inaccessibility to the listener.

In describing schizophrenic symptomatology, most specialists make little distinction between disorders of thought and disorders of language, reasoning that the confused speech of the schizophrenic is simply the result of confused thinking. However, some writers (Fish, 1957, Kleist, 1960) have suggested that schizophrenic language disturbances result not from disordered thought processes, but rather from disorganization an inaccessibility of verbal symbols. Thus the schizophrenic might know what word she wants but might simply be unable to find it. Schizophrenic speech often includes words and phrases not found in even the most comprehensive dictionary. These neologisms are often formed by combining parts of two or more regular words, or, they may simply involve the use of common words in a unique fashion. In either case, what is interesting about neologisms is that while they are sometimes unintelligible, they are at other times manage to communicate ideas quite clearly and vividly. In any case, the symptomatic speech must be severe enough to impair effective communication.

Delusional Beliefs and Hallucinations

A delusion is an irrational belief that an individual holds with great vigor despite overwhelming evidence that it has no basis in reality. A delusion, then, is a belief contrary to social reality that becomes fixed and resistant to change even in the face of strong evidence against it. Delusions are among the most common of the schizophrenic thought disorders. Approximately three quarters of all schizophrenics hold beliefs that others consider to be false or illogical (Lucas, 1962). In a sample of 405 schizophrenics, Lucas and colleagues (1962) found 71 percent to be delusional.

Several types of delusions are particularly common: grandeur, persecution, and reference; thought broadcasting, thought blocking, and withdrawal; and thought insertion and control.

The individual with ***delusions of grandeur*** believes that he is a famous or important person, usually a political, military, or religious leader. At the other end of the continuum is the ***self-deprecatory delusion***- the belief that one has done some horrible deed. Such beliefs may explain feelings of guilt and a need for punishment.

Delusions of Persecution

Delusion of persecution involve the belief that one is being plotted against, spied upon, threatened, interfered with, or otherwise mistreated. People with delusions of persecution believe that they are threatened and persecuted by various persons or groups, and they find confirmation for this delusion by misinterpreting everyday experiences; they might insist, for example, that a group of laughing persons are laughing at them.

Delusions of Control (also called delusions of influence)

Delusions of control lead one to believe that other persons, animals, or things are controlling their thoughts or actions, often by means of electronic devices which send signals directly to their brains.

Persons with ***delusions of influence*** believe that they are being controlled by some external agent. Thus, they might believe that a murderous impulse, a sexual fantasy, or an urge to commit suicide is imposed from the outside. The controlling agent may be God, the devil, or some vague "they." The critical difference between a neurotic obsession or compulsive urge as being implanted by an external agent. In contrast to the belief that external agents are inserting thoughts into one's head is the delusion that one's thoughts are being broadcast into the external world so that everyone can hear them.

Hypochondriacal Delusions

Hypochondriacal delusions are also common. These beliefs differ from neurotic hypochondriacal beliefs in the delusions are generally marked by a bizarre quality. For example, schizophrenics may believe that their insides are melting or that their brains are full of gelatin. Delusions of sin and guilt involve the unfounded belief that one has committed an unpardonable sin or has brought great harm to others. Theorists generally believe that as an extension of an egocentric and autistic orientation, many schizophrenic individuals at some point begin to see personal significance in everyday events, to "read" in intents and meanings that are not there. Personalizations of everyday experiences, or ideas of reference, provide a background against which more systematic delusions can develop. Other delusions, such as ***delusions of body change***, are beliefs about physical changes to the body; for example, a man may believe that his body is changing from male to female, that his or her insides are rotting, or that his or her head is filled with cement.

Disturbances in Sensations and Perception

There is considerable evidence that the schizophrenic's perception of the world is different from that of "normal" people. First, schizophrenics consistently report perceptual dysfunction. Second, these reports are confirmed by standard laboratory perceptual tests, which indicate that schizophrenics perform poorly on such perceptual tasks as size estimation (Straus et al, 1974), time estimation (Johnson and Petzel, 1971; Petzel and Johnson, 1972), and proprioceptive discrimination (Ritzler and Rosenbaum, 1974). Other tests have shown schizophrenics to be generally deficient in sensory sensitivity (Broen and Nakamura, 1972).

To the observer, the most dramatic type of schizophrenic perceptual disorder is the hallucination, a sensory perception which occurs in the absence of any appropriate external stimulus. Most of us are able, with varying degrees of vividness, to hear imagined voices, to form pictures "in the mind's eye," and even to recreate experiences of taste, touch, or smell in the absence of any primary stimulation. But we are usually aware that these sensory experiences are the byproducts of our imagination rather than responses to extreme stimuli. Furthermore, we probably feel that we have control over such experiences. Hallucinations differ from "normal" imaginings in two respects. First, they are not conjured up or created at will; they occur spontaneously. Second, while many schizophrenics do recognize that the voices they hear exist only in their minds, many others are not sure of whether their hallucinations are real or imagined, and a fair percentage--presumably the more severely psychotic (Buss, 1966)-- are convinced that their hallucinations are perceptions of objectively real events.

The common clinical observation is that auditory hallucinations are the most frequent, followed by hallucinations involving other senses. These frequencies have been confirmed by Malitz and colleagues (1962), who found that out of a random sample of 100 schizophrenics, 50 percent reported auditory hallucinations, while 9 percent reported visual hallucinations.

Disturbances in Affect

Schizophrenia is characterized by disturbances in affect. The affective abnormalities suffered by the schizophrenic differ from those that typify the affective psychoses in two important respects. First, the affective psychoses involve either deep depression or manic elation, or a combination of the two; in schizophrenia, on the other hand, what is generally seen is either a lack of affect or affect which is inappropriate for the immediate context. Second, the affective psychoses may involve sudden and extreme mood reversals. For example, the bipolar psychotic is capable of progressing rapidly from a state of expansive euphoria to a state of bleak despair. In contrast, the schizophrenic is unlikely to undergo such extreme mood shifts.

Three basic types of affective abnormality are common to schizophrenics. The first is the ambivalent affect. In this case, the schizophrenic may manifest both a strong positive reaction and a strong negative reaction at the same time, which leads to a state of confusion or blocked action. the second abnormality is a constricted emotional responsiveness, often described as flat affect. Nothing can elicit any emotional response whatsoever from the person; regardless of what is going on around him or her, s/he remains totally apathetic. Finally, many schizophrenics display inappropriate affect, that is, their emotional responses are entirely unsuitable to the immediate context. For example, a client may giggle upon hearing of his mother's death, or he may become very angry when given a present.

Disorders of Motor Behavior

The variety of unusual behaviors, including the absence of behavior, manifested by schizophrenics seems to be limited only by the boundaries of the behaviors themselves. In other words, in spite of the wide range of behaviors, both usual and unusual, taking place on a hospital ward, there is one behavior that is strikingly absent: interpersonal interaction and attraction. Rarely do these clients engage in small talk. Rarely do they address one another except to ask for a cigarette or a light. Indeed, one of the most salient characteristics of severely disturbed clients is withdrawal from interpersonal relationships. This is especially true of the chronic schizophrenic.

The question remains, though, is this social withdrawal a response to living year after year amid the unchanging drabness of the institutional ward? Or is it due specifically to an avoidance of interpersonal involvement on the part of schizophrenics? Duke and Mullins (1973). for example, found that chronic schizophrenics preferred greater interpersonal distances than either non-schizophrenic psychiatric clients or a group of "normal" people. They also found that although hospitalization did have some effect upon interpersonal distance, hospitalization alone did not account for the magnitude of interpersonal distance preferred by the schizophrenics. Furthermore, it has been found that schizophrenics tend to look at other people less than do "normal" people, and that they have a tendency to avoid the gaze of anyone looking directly at them (Harris, 1968).

What Does Schizophrenia Feel Like?

Paranoia is a term borrowed from ancient Greece, in which it means "beside or outside reason," a fitting description of the delusions of persecution that constitute the most prominent symptom of paranoid schizophrenia. The paranoid individual feels singles out and taken advantage of, mistreated, and plotted against, stolen from, spied upon, ignored, or otherwise mistreated by enemies. The delusional system usually centers around one major theme, such as financial matters, a job, or other life affairs. For example, a woman who is failing on the job, may insist that her fellow workers and supervisors have it in for her because they are jealous of her ability and efficiency. As a result, she may quit her job and go to work elsewhere, only to find a similar friction developing and her new job in jeopardy. Now she may become convinced that the first company has written to her present employer in the hope of turning everyone against her so that she would not be given a fair chance. With time, more and more of the environment is integrated into her delusional system as each additional experience is misconstrued and reinterpreted in light of her delusions.

Although the evidence advanced by paranoid persons to justify their claims may be extremely tenuous and inconclusive, they are unwilling to accept any alternative explanation and are impervious to reason. For example, a husband may be convinced of his spouse's unfaithfulness because when he answered the phone on two occasions, the party on the other end hung up. Argument and logic are futile; in fact, any questioning of the delusions only serves to convince the client that the investigator has sold out to his enemies.

Although ideas of persecution predominate, many paranoid individuals develop delusions of grandeur, in which they endow themselves with superior or unique ability. Such exalted ideas usually center on messianic missions, political or social reforms, or remarkable inventions. Paranoid persons who are religious may consider themselves appointed by God to save the world and may spend most of their time preaching and crusading. Threats of fire and brimstone, burning in hell, and similar persuasive devices are liberally employed. Many paranoid persons have become attached to extremist movements and are tireless and fanatical crusaders, although they often do their cause more harm than good with their self-righteousness and condemnation of others.

Some paranoid individuals develop remarkable inventions that they have endless trouble patenting or selling. They gradually become convinced that there is a plot against them to steal their invention, or that enemies of the United States are working against them to prevent the country from receiving the benefits of their remarkable talents. Aside from the delusional system, such individuals may appear perfectly normal in conversation, emotionality, and conduct. Hallucinations and other obvious signs of psychopathology are generally not found.

This normal appearance, together with the logical and coherent way in which the delusional ideas are presented, typically make paranoid individuals most convincing and they very often fool fledgling professionals. However, the delusional system is apt to be convincing only if one accepts the basic premise or premises upon which it is based. The defense of the premise or hypothesis is based on logically air-tight polarities of thought which defy testing or reasonable argumentation or reasoning. The paranoid premise is often a defense against severe confusion about both self-concept and relationships with others. If the usual derailment of ideas or loss of association of ideas are not present, one would diagnose the individual as having a paranoid psychosis--not paranoid schizophrenia.

Dependency

Schizophrenics have difficulty developing close relationships with other human beings. One probable reason is conflict over dependency. The dependence on parents, which most adolescents begin to resolve, is for the schizophrenic a repetition of the dependency struggle for infancy. The individual fears that closeness will result in a loss of identity--being engulfed o even, symbolically eaten up alive. On the other hand, he may fear that his own intense wish for closeness and need fulfillment will lead to his eating up his loved one. The schizophrenic wants to be independent but at the same time feels this to be dangerous to himself as well as the loved one. Therefore, wishes to be independent cannot be gratified, and closeness is impossible. Because of the pain of this conflict, the person falls out of contact with himself and into a state of no feelings and no felt wishes. He then feels that he has no "I" and no capacity to say "I want" in a relationship.

Rage

Another reason for the difficulty that schizophrenics experience in being close to other human beings is intense rage. Generally, the rage is caused by the injustices psychotic individuals believe have been foisted upon them and by their enormous envy of others for their ability to cope. The world of reality, the world of people, even the parts of the personality that wish to relate to reality are hated by the psychotic and are felt to be the enemy. The external world is perceived as depriving and persecutory. Their withdrawal from others expresses this rage and terror, and rage makes it difficult to satisfy any need. Attacks on people (in terms of their thoughts and fantasies) who are trying to help them are common.

Projection of this anger onto the world causes the individual to see others as hostile and hurtful. Denial of large aspects of reality and projection of negative feelings onto the outside world are common psychotic defense mechanisms. One of the authors interviewed a patient in a veterans' hospital who appeared to be making a stable adjustment and for whom the staff psychiatrist thought it appropriate to consider discharge. When his thoughts and plans were further assessed, however, it was ascertained that the patient had no intention of shopping for food, cooking, or eating. In fact, his refusal to attend to these aspects of his corporal life is what led to his hospitalization in the first place. The antipsychotic medication and structured life on the ward, where all his physical requirements were attended to, had not changed his thinking to the extent that he had learned that he had to take care of his own needs. He had simply gone along with the staff's instruction in routines of self-care. He assumed that returning to the world outside of the hospital meant that he no longer had to conform to the routine!

If the schizophrenic approaches any feeling of closeness to another, the result is often a breakdown in the relationship, a state of confusion, and massive anxiety. The desired closeness brings with it intense hatred and the wish to annihilate the loved one and destroy those parts of the personality that seek the closeness. Schizophrenics generally hate their own loving feelings and any person for whom they might experience those feelings. They experience this hate because, for them, interpersonal relationships lead only to overwhelming pain.

Rosenfeld (1965) describes this confused state in a young patient who was beginning to feel some closeness to her therapist. She finally admitted that she was madly in love with him and wanted to marry him. She wanted to approach him in a seductive manner and then strangle him. She stated that he had simultaneously saved her life and driven her mad. The fear of the aggressiveness that is experienced along with love, the intense rage, causes the psychotic patient to turn away from love objects and withdraw from people. Potential love objects are devalued and ridiculed. Contempt is often expressed for the behavior or possession of others. In fact, contempt is often felt for all reality, and the schizophrenic uses this contempt as a reason to avoid other people, asserting that "no one is good enough for me." Hostile rejection of others, arrogant, omnipotent egocentricity, and angry withdrawal mask enormous pain and the fear of loving.

Feelings of Deadness

Schizophrenics commonly complain of affective deadness. Clients often relate terrifying dreams or fantasies of dying. Some psychotic individuals report that they are really in the grave and that someone else s walking around in their bodies, leaving them with a feeling of nothingness.

Feelings of Terror

When the feelings of unreality become severe, the schizophrenic appears to experience terror. Often these individuals will do anything to regain some sense of reality or feeling of life, including performing self-destructive acts like cutting, hurting, or hitting themselves, screaming, or beating their own heads.

Feelings of Badness

Schizophrenics often feel that evil and badness are at the core of their beings. This extremely painful feeling of badness has been theoretically explained as the result of primitive, guilt-like, self-punitive feelings resulting from envy, greed, and aggressive wishes. The badness may also be seen as pure destructive rage that has not been tempered by loving, positive experiences. The schizophrenic experiences just being alive as bad.

A young man who was interviewed by one of the authors felt that he talked to and was directed by the devil. He tried to fight him off, but the devil succeeded in entering his body. After he had known the interviewer for some time (several sessions), he asked if the interviewer wanted to enter his body also. The therapist would thus be engulfed by the devil and/or the bad self, and then both would be helpless to the patient's rage and self-punitiveness.

Feelings of Pain

The schizophrenic's psychological death--the numbing of feelings and wishes to relate--is extremely painful. The pain, which has been described as grief over the loss of one's self, is made bearable only through the use of primitive defense mechanisms such as delusions, hallucinations, and loss of ego boundaries. Psychological death comes when all wishes for fulfillment of basic needs and all wishes for real intimacy are abandoned as futile. The real self, the feeling self, withdraws inside the fantasied womb, leaving a "false self," a dead self, to function and relate superficially to the world. The pain is locked up within the person, and enormous relief is experienced when it is touched on or shared with another, such as the therapist. The danger remains, however, that the pain can be externalized, displaced, or projected on the therapist and can be represented as a struggle from which the patient must escape or avoid by getting rid of the therapist.

Carrie, the "professional patient," was helped by her therapist to feel more alive during sessions. She eventually felt that waking up and getting up out of bed was desirable; however, this behavior also triggered feelings of guilt and conflict about giving up infantile satisfactions like staying in a safe, warm bed, and self-gratifying fantasies about how safe and comfortable she felt. By staying in bed, she also avoided all adult responsibilities. While rushing up the steps to her appointment, she had a self-punitive fantasy of throwing herself down the steps. Better yet, she thought, maybe she would throw the therapist down the steps; after all, wasn't it the therapist who was responsible for her present suffering and pain? Thus, the small degree of success produced by allowing reality to come through was quickly dissipated by displacing the strength onto the therapist, who was the intrusion into her false-comfortable existence. She continually returned to this false self whenever reality intruded too heavily upon her.

Feelings of Rebirth

Often the schizophrenic wishes for a rebirth--to feel, to become alive, to relate to a reality, to grow emotionally, to develop creative resources, and to enter into an interpersonal relationship in which she can separate and individuate to develop a unique identity. Although individuating is a crisis for most adolescents, for a schizophrenic, their common fantasy of dying and being reborn demonstrates the extreme of this need to grow.

Creativity

Any comprehensive treatment of schizophrenia must take into account the possible relationship between schizophrenia and and creativity. Being related to a schizophrenic may not be all that bad; in fact, it may have some distinct advantages. Reporting on a follow-up study of children born to schizophrenic mothers and placed in adoptive or foster homes shortly after birth, Heston and Denney note that the children who did not become schizophrenic were more "spontaneous," "had more colorful life histories," "held more creative jobs," and pursued more imaginative hobbies..." than normals (Heston and Denney, 1968, P. 371). Indeed, one study reports that the non-paranoid schizophrenics scored higher on a test of creativity than either the paranoid schizophrenics or non-paranoid controls (Keefe and Magaro, 1980; Magaro, 1981).

A study of genetics and schizophrenia in Iceland further supports the connection between creativity and schizophrenia. Karlson reports that the "genetic carriers" of schizophrenia often exhibit "unusual ability" and display a "superior capacity for associative thinking" (Karlson, 1966, p, 61). Fascinated by this finding, Karlson proposes that society may even depend upon "persons with a schizophrenic constitution" for its social and scientific progress. He remarks that a disproportionate number of the most creative people in philosophy, physics, music, literature, mathematics, and the fine arts often developed psychiatric disorders. "Superphrenic" is Karlson's term for these people, who are both related to schizophrenics and recognizably outstanding in politics, science, and the arts.

The Client's Dilemma

Carrie experienced an intense sense of failure in both early performance as a college student and later regression and deterioration of vocational and social skills. She consequently expected that others would reject and ultimately abandon her. She was thus unable to remain consistently involved in her work and in relationships. She was hypersensitive to others' responses, both verbal and nonverbal, and this influenced her to be ever vigilant, suspicious, and defensive. Her dependency was so well entrenched by her repeated failures over the three years since her last hospitalization that she had little hope that anything would change.

Despite a primary diagnosis of schizophrenia, she had a passive-aggressive personality structure and readily experienced narcissistic injury, which could seriously disorganize her thinking. Depressed affect, at times accompanied by suicidal ideation, was often experienced in response to injuries to self-esteem precipitated by performance difficulties or disappointments in interactions with others. Before she could allow herself to experience disappointment with her roommates, she would blame and verbally attack them or fail to do what was expected of her. This would result in her roommates' or counselors' deciding that she needed to be moved to another apartment or discharged from the program.

She often vacillated between guilt and self-disparaging preoccupations, which later turned to paranoid ideation that others were picking on her and wouldn't give her a chance. When faced with the possibility of rejection, her reality testing and judgment became impaired. Carrie's impulse control was poor, as she experienced a high degree of restlessness and had a need for immediate gratification. She relied heavily on others for validation and she often chose relationships based on their potential for providing self-indulgence and immediate need gratification. However, her fear of engulfment in these relationships overwhelmed her sense of boundaries and blurred her self-experienced. Only the ever-present role of the helpless, deprived, hopeless, patient have her a sense, if somewhat fragile, of herself.

When she was disturbed she experienced racing and flooding of thoughts, and her speech was pressured and tangential. Depression, especially, when accompanied by varying degrees of suicidal ideation, was frightening to her, as it heightened her sense of vulnerability and brought with it the possible need for another hospitalization. Although Carrie was of above-average intelligence, her emotional lability was so overwhelming at times that it interfered with her cognitive functioning. She was nevertheless able to enter into a therapeutic alliance with her therapist and to use the therapist as an auxiliary ego to sort out thoughts and feelings she experienced as confusing and disorganizing. Her self-esteem improved as she began to experience success in task-focused activities. All of these gains were reversed, however, when she stopped taking her medication. Indeed, consistent use of Loxitane and Imipramine was effective in enabling Carrie to compensate from an acute psychotic state and helped her to maintain a state of remission. When she took her medication, she was no longer troubled by ideas of reference, or suicidal ideation, or flooding by disorganized thoughts.

Theories, Explanations, and Interventions for Schizophrenic Behavior

The etiology of schizophrenia has been a puzzle of central concern to psychologists and psychiatrists for over a century. Behavioral extremes also seem to exert their own influence and fascination. Quite unlike most medical problems, which can be traced to a single microorganism or a single organ dysfunction, schizophrenia appears to be the result of a highly complex interaction of social, psychological, interpersonal, and biological factors, each of which has claimed the attention of a number of theoretical perspectives.

Research on schizophrenia has taken two divergent paths. On the one hand are the medically oriented researchers, who explore genetic heritage and physiological processes. These investigators have discovered many drugs that alleviate some of the symptoms of schizophrenia. The success of drug treatment has emptied many hospital wards and has promoted research into the biochemical roots of psychosis. The second path has been the search for psychological causes, beginning with psychoanalytic researchers working with hospitalized schizophrenics. Their theories initially focused on the internal, intrapsychic life of the schizophrenic; more recently, however, they have also examined the family environment for clues as to the reasons for the schizophrenic's lack of adaptation to reality. Most therapists now believe that the causes of schizophrenia are both biological and psychological. It has been suggested that biochemical weakness or predisposition, intrapsychic difficulties, and life stress resulting from a traumatic or maladaptive family situation probably combine to produce a schizophrenic break.

The Psychological Theories

Psychological theories of schizophrenia generally focus on the child's early family life and how specific types of parent-child relationships can lead to schizophrenia.

Psychoanalytic

According to the psychoanalytic theorists, there is no single psychodynamic formulation of schizophrenia; instead, there are a variety of positions, all of which are basically offshoots of Freud's theories. Orthodox Freudian theory speculated that excessively strong id impulses provoked regression to the earliest stage of development, in which no ego had yet been formed to interact with reality. Although Freud devoted his attention primarily to the neuroses, he did offer an interpretation of psychosis as well, and especially of paranoia. In his earliest psychoanalytic study of psychosis (1911), Freud viewed the development of the disorder as a two-stage process. The first stage involves a complete or partial withdrawal of cathexes (emotional investments) from the object world, the world of people and things. In the second phase, the restitution phase, the individual attempts to regain the lost object world by substituting imaginary events and relationships for the real ones that have been abandoned. Thus, hallucinations can be accounted for as remembered sensory events that the psychotic uses to replace lost object relations.

According to Freud, the schizophrenic's disturbed thinking can be seen as the result of a similar two-stage process. First there is the withdrawal of cathexes from internal forms of object representation -- that is, the individual's mental images of the object world. Then, in the restitution phase, the cathexes are redirected toward words that remain in the memory but that are no longer tied to appropriate objects. As a result, the words come out by they are no longer coherent, since they have lost their value as symbols of real things (Freud, 1915). Thus, the pre schizophrenic child, because of his deficient perceptual apparatus and learning capacity, does not internalize a stable sense of himself from his early experience with his parents. In times of stress, the fragile self does not endure, leaving the schizophrenic selfless and alone. The overwhelming experience leads to the schizophrenic to attempt to understand objects that have been distorted (object restitution) in ways that constitute familiar symptoms of schizophrenia (hallucinations and delusions, for example).

Thus, although Freud did not concentrate on schizophrenia, he did attempt to explain it. However, his theory was not a very helpful one. Freud believed that schizophrenics were narcissistic -- that they had withdrawn their energies from the outside world and turned inward upon themselves, unable to cathect with the world of objects.

After Freud's elaboration in 1926 of the structural concepts of ego and superego, the psychoanalytic interpretation of psychosis shifted from object decathexis to ego insufficiency or disintegration. According to the latter view, the schizophrenic is a person who, because of inability to cope with unacceptable id impulses, regresses to an early phase of the oral stage. In this phase of infancy, there is not yet a separate ego to exercise the basic cognitive functions of perception, memory, judgment, and so forth. Hence the psychotic's loss of contact with reality, since the phase to which he has regressed provides no developed cognitive apparatus for reality testing.

Whereas regression is the mechanism that has received theoretical emphasis in psychoanalytic accounts of schizophrenia, projection has been viewed as the basic mechanism of paranoia. In all his cases involving paranoia, Freud inferred a connection with repressed homosexuality (Jones, 1955). When the ego is threatened by these unacceptable id impulses, the projection mechanism presumable enables the individual to externalize them. That is, the source of the threat is no longer seen as within oneself, but rather as coming from someone else -- "It is not my own desires that are threatening me; it's that person over there who is threatening me." Hence the development of delusions of persecution.

Most psychoanalytic investigators feel that schizophrenia reflects an *impaired or defective ego structure*. There are those, such as Hartmann (1953) and Jacobson (1964), who attribute the defectiveness of the schizophrenic ego to constitutional defects and vulnerabilities and/ or environmental trauma. For the ego to develop properly -- that is, to develop a boundary between internal and external reality -- it is thought that there must first be a "good enough" self with no basic deficits and then what Winnicott (1958) has called "good-enough mothering." Normally the good-enough mothering becomes internalized, imparting a basic sense of trust and security. Without one or both of these factors, the probability of schizophrenia is increased.

Mahler (1975) and others see schizophrenia as difficulty with the early childhood phases of separation-individuation. Mahler stresses the central role of separation and individuation in normal and pathological development. She believes that parental unresponsiveness to the infant's needs, or withdrawal of emotional supplies when the baby initially attempts separation and individuation, leads to what is called a *developmental standstill*, or a retreat to an autistic and symbiotic phases in the infant's relationship to the mother. During such phases, the infant has a poor sense of herself as independent from the mother. It is only through a gradual process of separation that the formation of a stable sense of self is possible. This process is seen largely dependent upon the libidinal gratification available from the mother. Masterson (1972) suggests that when there is a problem, the difficulty is due to the lack of emotional supplies and support necessary for the unfolding of the individual's personality.

British psychoanalyst Melanie Klein (1946), who has influenced many American analysts, believes that the newborn's psyche is sufficiently organized to experience anxiety, to build defense mechanisms, and to make fantasy- as well as reality-based relations to people and things. In order to defend against overwhelming anxiety, the infant learns to introject (take in psychologically) and project (out outside of the self psychologically). During the first six months of life, she believes, the infant takes a paranoid-schizoid position, in which he feels persecutory anxiety because "bad parts of the self" are projected into the environment. In most cases, the infant then moves into the depressive position, in which the bad parts of the self are accepted as part of the self. If things do not proceed normally, however, the infant (who may become schizophrenic) remains or returns to the paranoid-schizoid position.

Grotstein (1977) feels that schizophrenia is the "result of a defective development of the eo caused by either heredity or early environmental circumstance. The resultant infantile maldevelopment is due to ever defensive attacks by one part of the psyche upon other aspects which can sense and perceive its needs." This attack on one's own sensations and thinking takes place to avoid the "nameless dread"-- being absolutely overwhelmed with internal and external stimuli. The child's infantile self is unable to cope and deadens itself as its only defense. Since the immature, vulnerable personality cannot perceive and integrate stressful stimuli, it attacks and deadens itself to protect itself. Such patients are thus literally and figuratively out of contact with themselves, unable to differentiate between external reality and sensory impressions which tell the of their own subjective needs. Schizophrenia, then, according to these theorists, is an undifferentiated process that results in the experience of a lack of boundaries between sensations and thought, which then results in feelings of psychological deadness.

Gunderson and Mosher (1975) describe schizophrenia as a disorder of ego functioning which is caused by negative parent-child experiences and possibly, too, by biological-constitutional elements. They suggest that the schizophrenic's inability to develop and maintain accurate internal representations of the outside world causes the production of restitutional symptoms such as delusions and hallucinations. These symptoms become prominent when the individual is confronted with the stresses of developing independent, mature, trusting relationships.

The neo-Freudians view schizophrenia as a developmental disorder (White and Watt, 1973). The child, having experienced relationships with others as painful and hostile, withdraws into a world of fantasy, a withdrawal which he expresses in behavior. Having withdrawn from others, the child never develops appropriate social behaviors, which results in further unpleasantness and consequently in further withdrawal. Such continually negative social experience severely damages the child's self-esteem. While young, the child may manage to cope with is world of unhappiness. At some point later in life, however, he may experience such negative social encounters that the resulting anxiety, pain, and withdrawal cause a general breakdown in functioning -- a schizophrenic break.

From a psychodynamic perspective, then, the irrational thoughts and bizarre behavior of the schizophrenic are caused by unconsciousness of urges and ideas that usually remain inaccessible. These thoughts break through to awareness when the individual undergoes a regression brought about by his/her generalized fear of the world. According to psychodynamic thought, the schizophrenic's fearfulness was originally created by profoundly frustrating interpersonal relationships in the early years of life, during which he had no expectation of support and warmth from the social environment. As a result, the infant regards others as not only uninterested in him, but dangerous and threatening as well. Especially dangerous are sexual, aggressive, and dependent relationships. These theorists feel that the onset of schizophrenic symptoms do not represent a new problem, but rather are signs of a life crisis in which previously controlled thoughts and fantasies are given overt expression. The maladaptive behavior generally becomes noticeable during the post-adolescent period, because it is then that the individual is expected to become independent and to cope successfully with the environment. Schizophrenic post-adolescents have no faith in their ability to accomplish anything of value in the social environment. Thus, they continue to live within themselves. As their terrible fear of people causes them to lose contact with the environment, schizophrenics struggle to provide a new environment to which they can adjust.

Cameron (1963) believes that the ***pseudo-community***, a device attributed to paranoia, is also applicable to most varieties of schizophrenic reactions. He defines a pseudo-community as a reconstruction of reality containing both real and imagined individuals. The purpose of the development of the schizophrenic's pseudo-community is not so much to achieve rapprochement with reality, but rather to establish a world that will minimize the experience of anxiety. According to Cameron, the premorbid schizophrenic, like all other pre-psychotic personalities with basic ego defects, seems especially vulnerable to five general situations: loss or threatened loss of basic security; upsurge of erotic or hostile impulses; sudden increase in guilt (conscious, preconscious, or unconscious); and reduced general effectiveness of ego adaptation or defense.

The schizophrenic person -- whose conscious and preconscious psyche is flooded with infantile impulses, fantasies, conflicts, and fears -- meets adult demands with archaic forms of defense, such as massive projection, introjection, or denial. The loss of reality adaption renders the person unable to control the environment or to negotiate the various aspects of daily living. Cameron then describes schizophrenic as a thought disorder that has two basic aspects: (1) the inability to think and communicate in conventional terms due to social isolation, and (2) the use of unrealistic thought as a defense against anxiety (and in the case of the schizophrenic, the development of a pseudo-community).

According to Arieti (1955, 1969), two cognitive principles are especially needed to interpret schizophrenic thought. One of them, the *principle of active concretization*, states that although the schizophrenic is capable of thinking in abstract terms, she is not able to sustain this process when the situation is too anxiety provoking. With an increase in anxiety, the schizophrenic immediately and unconsciously shifts to a concrete mode of thought. The Von Domarus principle states that while normal persons interpret events on the basis of their objective features, schizophrenics interpret on the basis of their objective features, schizophrenics interpret events in an idiosyncratic and unrealistic way (Von Domarus, 1944).

Interpersonal

The interpersonal perspective focuses primarily on the individual's interactions in an effort to determine what kind of interpersonal relationships could possibly bring about schizophrenia. According to Sullivan (1931), normal human beings have all sorts of skills that they are inclined to take very much for granted. They need these skills to function every day, and they continually monitor their behavior to guard against unfortunate mistakes. Sullivan called these "monitoring systems" or "supervisory patterns" and remarked that they are really like imaginary people who are always with one, carrying on a helpful dialogue.

With the schizophrenic, however, these supervisory patterns break down; Sullivan feels it very likely that they were not too firmly established in the first place. In any case, deprived of the capacity to monitor their own behavior and thoughts, schizophrenics have a great deal of difficulty determining what is appropriate and what is inappropriate. Indeed, what is left of their own supervisory patterns seems to have acquired an almost independent existence or dissociative phenomenon. Therefore, what most persons experience as a part of themselves become strange and alien to schizophrenics. They do not have imaginary listeners or spectators. They may actually hear voices correcting them or commenting on their behavior. They may actually see other people watching them (Linn, 1977).

Because schizophrenics cannot regulate their own behavior very effectively, their ability to communicate with others is likely to be severely impaired. They are thus increasingly thrown back into a strange, often frightening, world. It is a world populated by their own private symbols and words, concepts that cannot be readily shared with anyone else. Consequently, schizophrenics often sound as though they are speaking some exotic foreign language. Generally speaking, the more disturbed the client, the more unintelligible his speech and ideas (Sullivan, 1962).

Social Learning

A substantial and persuasive body of research indicates that schizophrenics have difficulty maintaining selective attention (Neucherlein, 1977), such as in reaction-time tasks, which require the person to respond as quickly as possible when cued to do so. The question, though, is what causes these deficits in the first place. They may be due to high distractibility (Chapman and McGhie, 1962), slow processing of sensory input (Yates, 1966), or interfering factors such as increased anxiety (Mednick, 1958). Ulman and Krasner (1975) have focused more on environmental controls over attention and believe that such deficits may be caused by a lack of reinforcement; attention, like any other response, requires sufficient reinforcement in order to be maintained.

If one stops attending to important social cues, one is likely to be defined as socially inappropriate or bizarre. This is likely to lead to a certain amount of isolation, since others tend to avoid contact with anyone who appears to be so "strange." This may lead to a loss of social relationships and further withdrawal from social situations. Stated somewhat simplistically, this is the basic premise of social learning perspective.

Mednick (1958) and Ullmann and Krasner (1975) have also proposed that schizophrenic behavior is caused and maintained from various sources.

Mednick's theory focuses on internal sources of reinforcement, whereas Ullmann and Krasner speak in terms of external sources.

Ullmann and Krasner (1975) believe that everyone is crazy to some extent, but that most of us either are not reinforced or are punished for our bizarre behavior. If individuals who otherwise received little attention from others were to act in a strange way, however, the attention they received might reinforce the behavior. This could lead to an increase in the frequency or magnitude of the behavior, such that, if it continued to be reinforced, it might be maintained from various sources, eventually causing the person to behave in a schizophrenic way.

Ullman and Krasner's interpretation of schizophrenia is within a behaviorist tradition. According to these investigators, the schizophrenic is subject to the same principles of learning and behavior as are "normal" people; however, because of a failure of reinforcement, the schizophrenic has ceased to attend to the social stimuli to which most of us respond. Instead, s/he attends to his or her own idiosyncratic cues, and as a result, his or her behavior seems odd or bizarre to the "normal" observer. As Ullmann and Krasner point out, "Attention responses require effort. When they do not pay off, they believe, they decrease in emission" (1975, p.357). And this, they believe, is what happened to the schizophrenic. Furthermore, the following behavioral cycle may be instituted: When an individual ceases responding to certain accepted social cues, s/he may become the target of disciplinary action and social rejection, leading to deeper feelings of alienation and adding to the belief that others are out to get him or her. Hence, his or her behavior becomes even stranger. In addition, other sources may begin providing reinforcement for his deviant behavior, in the form of either social attention or any of the other advantages one gains from being "sick." Once reinforced, these behaviors will, of course, increase in frequency.

In support of their argument that schizophrenia is a learned behavior, Ullman and Krasner cite two basic lines of evidence. First, there is good reason to believe that schizophrenics know what they are doing. For instance, their bizarre behaviors are not equally distributed across situations; rather, like other learned behaviors, they are often responses to specific stimuli. Schizophrenics have been found to engage in impression management--that is, they can look "healthy" or "sick." depending on the advantages or disadvantages of each. Moreover, schizophrenics appear to be much more socially sensitive than one would expect. Ullmann and Krasner (1975) believe, then, that the basic process involved in schizophrenia is the extinction of attending to typical social stimuli.

Humanistic-Existential

Most humanistic and existential theorists direct their attention primarily to the neuroses, but a few systematic attempts have been made to apply the humanistic-existential model of behavior to the problem of psychosis. The writer who has contributed the most in this area is R.D. Laing, a British existential psychiatrist. Laing's interpretation may be reduced to two central arguments. The first is that mental illness is largely a matter of perspective. His second point is that schizophrenic is simple "a special sort of strategy that a person invents in order to live in an unlivable situation" (1964, p. 187). Laing argues that a schizophrenic may be more sane than the society which labels him mad. According to his theory, schizophrenia is not insanity, but rather hypersanity, an exploration from our own insane reality into another reality in the existential search for autonomy and meaning.

One of the most extreme existential views put forth by Laing 1967, is that schizophrenia is a positive growth experience used by the person to cope with an insane world. He also believes that psychosis is caused by the parental definition of a child's being a certain way when he cannot possibly fulfill that definition psychiatrist, Laing argues, have no right to interfere with the schizophrenic's quest: "Can we not see that this voyage is not what we need to be cured of, but that it is in itself a natural way of healing our own appalling state of alienation called normality?" (1967, p. 116).

In his defense of the schizophrenic experience against the presumptions of conventional psychiatry, Laing is supported by a group of writers whose major contention is that the state called "insanity" is simply a label fabricated by society to justify the exploitation of persons so labeled. This group, which includes Thomas Szasz and a number of eminent writers, along with Laing, sees the schizophrenic virtually as a victim of an Establishment plot. These psychiatrists, psychologists and sociologists would like to do away with conventional psychiatry and to redefine psychosis as a disruption of social or interpersonal relationships. Szasz (1976) insists that the disorder is nothing more than a political label. He believes that schizophrenia is the result of a deficiency in introjected objects; the schizophrenic has so few internal objects that s/he has few models to use in living.

Mosher (1974) lists four major criticisms raised by this group of traditional views and treatment of the person's labeled schizophrenic. First, they argue that by classifying so-called schizophrenics as mentally ill or diseased, society justifies the detention of these individuals in distant, dehumanizing, impersonal institutions and also sanctions treatment methods that do no more than persuade deviant individuals to conform more closely to society's norms. Second, these critics point out the adverse social consequences of the labeling process; for example, a person who has at any time been labeled schizophrenic will probably have difficulty for the rest of his life both in establishing social relationships and in getting a job. Scheff (1970) in particular believes that the labeling process is the single most important cause of continuing deviance.

A third source of criticism is psychiatry's preoccupation with finding out what kind of "disease" the person has, to the neglect of the person him or herself. And fourth, these writers object to the traditional doctor-patient relationship, which, they feel, enables the physician to have unlimited power to manipulate--often for the satisfaction of his own needs--the submissive, dependent patient. By its very nature, they believe, this relationship destroys any possibility of patient's achieving the independence they are supposed to achieve.

Family Environment

The following family patterns have been theorized as recognizable for schizophrenia: problematic parenting, disturbed marital relationships, and communication problems. The schizophrenogenic parent--usually thought to be the mother-- has been described as domineering, rejecting, cold, and immature. Initially, the family environment theories focused on the over-controlling mother s responsible for the development of schizophrenia in the child. It was believed that the mother's behavior tended to foster dependency and in so doing made the child prone to schizophrenia.

The terms *symbiotic union* and *over-controlling mother* have also been applied to this parenting pattern. A number of studies have suggested that there is a high frequency of symbiotic unions between parents and children who later become schizophrenic. In symbiotic unions, mothers encourage their children to form extremely strong dependencies on them. Often the mother will continue to treat the child as if s/he were still an infant (for example, mothers may continue to bathe their adolescent sons).

The notion of symbiotic unions is quite similar to the over-controlling patterns see on the mothers of schizophrenics. McCord and co-workers (1962) found that 67 per cent of schizophrenics had what they determined to be over-controlling mothers, in contrast to only 8 percent of the mothers of matched control subjects.

In 1948, Frieda Fromm-Reichman coined the term *schizophrenogenic mother* to describe the type of mother who was capable of inducing schizophrenia in her children. Such mothers were characterized as cold, domineering, rejecting, and uet overprotective. The father, meanwhile, was faulted mainly for his passivity in not interfering in the pernicious mother-child relationship.

Bateson and colleagues (1956) believed that the communication patterns between the mother and child was a critical factor in the development of schizophrenia. This emphasis on the mother as the principal culprit in producing schizophrenia was not new when they wrote their now famous article. During the 1950s, Bateson and his associates advanced a rather specific hypothesis concerning the development of schizophrenia: the theory of the *double bind*. In the double bind situation, the mother gives the child mutually contradictory messages, meanwhile implicitly forbidding the child to point out the contradiction. The child is caught in the middle; no matter which alternative he chooses, he is the loser. In short, the child is in a double bind, a no-win situation.

Bateson and colleagues proposed that the type of mother most likely to engage in a double-bind communication is one who finds closeness with her child intolerable but who at the same time finds it intolerable to admit this to herself. In other words, she pushes the child away and her child senses this "push." but when the child withdraws, the mother accuses the child of not loving her. Bateson and co-workers suggested that people who become schizophrenic were repeatedly confronted with "impossible" situations during childhood. No matter how they behaved, their parents make them feel "damned if they did" and also "damned if they didn't."

Potential schizophrenics are, in short, consistently subjected to demands that are both arbitrary and contradictory. Bateson and colleagues propose that children who are continuously placed in such a situation will not be able to relate to others. The parent's incompatible messages to the child almost certainly evoke in the child a state of overwhelming anxiety and frustration--overwhelming enough to cause some people (especially those who had remained very dependent upon their parents) to break down.

Research on the role of the double-bind communication in the development of schizophrenia has been largely anecdotal and very scanty. Consequently, there does not seem to be much support for considering the double bind as a major factor in the etiology of schizophrenia. However, often more general communication problems, such as unclear and inaccurate communication, have been found more frequently in families of schizophrenics than in families of "normal" controls (Jacobs, 1975).

Lidz (1973) suggests that schizophrenia is related to difficulty in the establishment of preverbal mutuality between the mother and the child. Before the child can speak, or when he can say only single words, the mother must be able to fulfill his needs by intimately knowing the child and his behavior patterns. According to Lidz, the mothers of most schizophrenics are so profoundly egocentric that they respond to their own needs rather than the needs of the child. He has proposed the notion of schizophrenogenic families in which there is a delusion that pervades all family relationships. Recent investigations (e.g. Caputo, 1968), however, have suggested that the fathers are as responsible as the mothers for the hostile, aggressive atmosphere that seems to permeate the homes of many schizophrenic children. In fact, the trend of recent studies has been to focus attention on the communication patterns among all members fo the family (Mishler and Waxler, 1968).

The data on family systems suggest that there may be some factors--such as severe family conflict, or inaccurate or distorted communications--that are in some way related to schizophrenia. It is generally agreed that the family has a greater impact on the individual's psychosocial development than any other element in society.

Searles (1959) describes the following six ways in which parents can undermine their child's confidence to differentiate her own emotional reactions and perceptions of reality: (1) the parent repeatedly calls attention to areas of the child's personality that are different from the areas that the child feels are important to defining his or her identity. (2) The parent simultaneously exposes the child to stimulation and frustration or rapidly alternates stimulation and frustration. (3) The parent switches from one topic to the next while maintaining the same emotional feeling, so that matters of life and death are spoken of as if unimportant. (4) The parent switches emotions while discussing a single specific topic. (5) The parent stimulates the child sexually in areas in which it would be disastrous to find gratification. (6) The parent relates to the child simultaneously on different levels. Searles feels that these processes, which can literally drive a person insane, are unconscious, but are nonetheless the ingredients of the pathogenic relationships of psychotic families.

Bowen (1960) hypothesizes that one child may be selected as the focal point toward which both parents direct their emotional immaturity. This in turn helps them to achieve a fragile stabilization of their own relationship. In addition, Mosher, Pollin, and Stabenau (1971) suggest that such a focal child may be selected from among the others because s/he is weaker, less intelligent, or otherwise constitutionally inferior to his siblings. Similarly, Waring and Ricks (1965) found a higher frequency of what they termed emotional divorces in the parents of schizophrenics. Although the parents were not actually separated or divorced, they were living in their own separate worlds, with very few positive interactions taking place between them.

Lidz (1973) claims that a great number of schizophrenic children come from families that fall into one of two categories: *the schizmatic family*, in which parental discord has divided the family into opposing factions and *the skewed family*, which remains reasonably calm, but only because one spouse is totally dominated by the pathology of the other. In the marital schism, there is open conflict between the parents, who attempt to control each other's in various power plays. These parents are divided into two antagonistic and competing factions. Marital Skew describes the situation in which the dominant partner is seriously disturbed, and the spouse passively submits to the will of the disturbed partner. In both situations the child is denied the emotional support necessary for a sense of security and self-worth, the ingredients necessary for emotional growth.

Lidz, then, views schizophrenia as an outcome of disturbed family communication patterns which negate the "selfness" of the person that will eventually be labeled schizophrenic. In such a chaotic setting, the children have inevitably received very faulty training in reality testing and have grown up riddled with insecurities. It is therefore almost impossible for them to achieve a firm sense of identity, and at least some of them eventually break down and develop schizophrenia. Both patterns may have negative effects on the children who grow up with poor examples of how parents relate to one another.

He also believed that mothers of schizophrenics are so egocentric that they cannot respond to the child's preverbal needs. The mother can respond only to her own needs Arieti (1974b) sees the schizophrenic's family milieu as one in which the child is deprived of all security and is surrounded by anxiety and hostility in most, if not all, family interactions. In setting the tone of such interactions, the relationship of the parents is particularly decisive. although the data do indicate that disturbed marital and family relationships are associated with later schizophrenia, it is not clear that these conflicts are necessary or sufficient causes of schizophrenia.

Concern with specific forms of family deviance implicated by the earliest investigators, such as "double binding," "pseudomutuality," and the "transmission of irrationality," seems to have given way to broader concepts of overall communication deficiency. Thus, Singer and colleagues (1978) employed the concept of communication of deviance to refer to 32 categories of peculiarities in Rorschach responding found to differentiate between the parents of schizophrenic (including borderline) persons and those of neurotic or normal persons. Interestingly, the actively schizophrenic offspring turned out to have lower communication deviance scores than their parents, perhaps suggesting a parent-to-child directional effect.

Important work by these investigators has also shown to be possible to predict later development of schizophrenia from parental communication deviance measured at a point before breakdown but during serious adolescence disturbance (Goldstein et al, 1978). Vaughn and Leff's (1976, 1981) studies related relapse rates in schizophrenia to a certain pattern of noxious communication in families, termed "expressed emotion;" the study by Scott (1976) related outcome after a schizophrenic break to patterns of reciprocal perceptions of each other held by client and family members; and perceptions of each other had by partners and family members; and Waxler (1974) and Lion (1974) employed the strategy of "artificial families--triads consisting of a client and two (unrelated) parents. They found that the cognitive performance of schizophrenic persons improved when they communicated with normal parents, whereas Lion demonstrated a deterioration in the performance of normal parents when communicating with a schizophrenic son. She also found that parents communicated better with their own schizophrenic son than the strangers' schizophrenic sons. Evidence of circularity notwithstanding, it is probably fair to say that the available findings strongly implicate family communication patterns as having at least some etiological significance in schizophrenia.

It should be noted, however, that while many investigators accept the correlation between schizophrenia and disordered family relationships, drawing etiological conclusions from studies of the families of schizophrenic children is always hazardous. In the first place, there is the chicken-egg problem: it is not clear whether the family disruptions are causing the child's disorder or whether the presence of an abnormal child produces abnormal relationships among family members (Gunderson et al, 1974). Furthermore, there is the third variable problem. For example, it is possible that both child's disturbance and the abnormal family interactions are the result of yet another factor, such as a shared genetic defect (Reiss, 1974). In any case, studies of the families of schizophrenics are extremely difficult to conduct, both because of the ethical problems--for example the invasion of the family's privacy of the implication that the parents are to blame for the child's deviance. Nevertheless, recent developments in family study methodology, particularly the high-risk family studies, are making it increasingly possible for the investigators to address the critical questions in this area.

Biological Factors

The Diathesis-Stress Model

There remains a great deal of disagreement over the particular mode of genetic transmission. Early researchers tended to hold to the monogenetic biochemical theory: that a single gene--dominant, recessive, or intermediate--was responsible for a specific metabolic dysfunction which in turn then produced the behavioral manifestations of schizophrenia. Within the past few years, however, there has been a stronger movement toward a diathesis-stress position. According to this theory, what is inherited is a diathesis or predisposition, toward schizophrenia, and that the schizophrenia itself will develop only if certain life stresses are encountered.

The most widely known diathesis-stress model is that proposed by Meehl (1962). Meehl postulates that the phenotypic consequence of the genetic abnormality is a neural defect which he labels *schizotaxia*. The normal stresses and strains of any social learning environment produce in schizotaxic individuals a somewhat peculiar personality organization which Meehl calls schizotypy. If schizotypes have the good fortune to be reared in a favorable social milieu, then they will remain fairly normal, though perhaps slightly eccentric. But if their milieu is stressful--if, for example, the mother has engaged in double-bind communication--then it is more likely that they will develop clinical schizophrenia. Thus, as long as schizotypes do not encounter severe stress in their lives, they will not become schizophrenic, even though they may seem a bit odd. Under sufficient stress, however, they will not be able to cope adequately and might develop a full-blown schizophrenic behavior pattern. In contrast, whose who have not inherited the schizotaxia will be relatively immune to a schizophrenic pattern even under considerable stress.

The diathesis-stress model of Meehl seems to be a step in the right direction since it takes into account both genetic and environmental factors. Here, a predisposition, or diathesis, is inherited, but only if sufficient stress is encountered is the person likely to develop the disorder. This model implies that the primary predisposing factor is genetically determined, is permanent, and with sufficient stress will result in a relatively enduring schizophrenic behavior pattern.

The Vulnerability Model

The vulnerability model proposes that each individual has a certain degree of vulnerability that under certain circumstances will lead to a schizophrenic episode. Although this view is similar to the diathesis-stress model, some distinctions are made. First, the origins of vulnerability can be diverse and are not limited to genetic causation. Vulnerability could be due to a combination of biological and psychological factors. There will be debate as to how much is contributed by each factor, but the essential feature is that non-biological factors can also influence vulnerability. Thus, some of the components of vulnerability are inherited, but some are acquired. Zubin and Spring (1977) note that the potential stressors, which they refer to as "challenging events," will call for some forms of adaptation or coping. If the stress is above the person's threshold, there is likely to be an episode of maladaptive behavior, in this case a schizophrenic episode. However, if the stress can be reduced to a level below the threshold, the maladaptive behavior is likely to resolve.

Family Studies

If a disorder is genetically transmitted, then relatives of an affected individual are more likely to have the predisposing gene than are persons in the general population. If the incidence of the disorder among the relatives is significantly higher than among the general population, then a genetic contribution to the etiology is suspected. Thus, a disorder that shows a pattern of transmission from unaffected mothers to 50 percent of their sons suggests that an X-chromosome-linked mode of inheritance is involved. (Karon and Vandenbos, 1981). If both parents and children manifest a disorder, the gene suspected of causing the condition must be dominant. When 25 per cent of the children of unaffected parents manifest a disorder, the responsible gene is considered to be recessive. Schizophrenia, however, does not appear to fall into any of these categories (Kessler, 1980; Lidz, 1973).

Recent studies have found that for all siblings of a schizophrenic, the risk of schizophrenia is higher than for individuals in the general population. These rates vary from 2 to 46 times higher than the risk for schizophrenia in the average population (Rosenthal et al, 1975). Among first degree relatives of the patient, the average risk for schizophrenia is roughly 8 to 10 percent. The risk for relatives is graded, so that relatives who share comparatively few genes with an affected individual show a lower rate of schizophrenia than do those who have more genes in common.

Family studies of the genetics of schizophrenia clearly indicate that the more closely one is related to a schizophrenic, the more likely one is to develop schizophrenia. The child of a schizophrenic parent has a 16.4 percent chance of developing schizophrenia, and the child of two schizophrenic parents has a 68 percent chance of becoming schizophrenic, as compared to an incidence of less than 1 percent in the general population. However, because some families tend to share the same environment as well as the same genes, it is nearly impossible in family studies to determine whether correlations are the function of genetic or environmental influences.

Twin Studies

Many researchers have compared identical twins (monozygotic twins) with fraternal twins (dizygotic) on the concordance for diagnoses of schizophrenia. Higher concordance rates among monozygotic twins, who have the same genetic material, and dizygotic twins, who share roughly 50 percent of the same genes, as would any pair of siblings, provide strong evidence of genetic factors in the transmission of schizophrenia. Kallman (1941) conducted two important studies of the genetics of schizophrenia. The first was on brothers and sisters of 1,000 patients of a Berlin psychiatric hospital, and the second was on 953 twins from New York psychiatric hospitals. Kallman found full siblings of patients to have a higher expectancy for the disorder than half siblings. The highest concordance of schizophrenia was among children of schizophrenic parents and among monozygotic (identical) twins.

Book (1960) also showed that the incidence of schizophrenia was higher in the families of schizophrenics than in the general population. Slater (1968) showed that schizophrenia was present in 14 percent of schizophrenic dizygotic (fraternal) twins and 76 percent of monozygotic twins. Although many of the data on schizophrenia have been questioned on the basis of faulty statistical techniques, these studies appear to confirm the belief held for centuries that schizophrenia is likely to run in families. However, these early studies were not well controlled and tended to find higher concordance rates in identical twins than in fraternal twins. More recent and better controlled twin studies have found much lower concordance rates than the earlier studies, but they have consistently shown that identical twins are more concordant than fraternal twins

In the twin studies conducted over the past fifty years, then, the mean concordance rates for schizophrenia in monozygotic twins comes to 43.9 percent, approximately five times as great as the mean concordance rate of 8.8 per cent for dizygotic twins (ban, 1973; Rosenthal, 1970). As more recent studies have improved in research methodology, the concordance rates have tended to diminish for both monozygotic and dizygotic twins (Allen et al, 1972; Mosher and Gunderson, 1973). Nevertheless, the monozygotic and dizygotic concordance ratios found in these studies usually lie between 3:1 and 6:1.

Adoption Studies

The adoption studies come even closer to separating the influence of heredity and environment. Most adoption studies follow this procedure: A group of adopted children, preferably infants, who were born to schizophrenic parents are compared to a control group of adopted children born to non-schizophrenic, or "normal," parents. Assuming the adopting parents were "normal," certain findings would then be expected, depending upon how important the genetic influence was. If genetic transmission is occurring, adopted children of schizophrenics should be more likely to become schizophrenic than children of normal parents. And this is indeed what many adoption studies have found.

Heston (1966) completed one of the most methodologically sound adoption studies. He was able to gather very detailed information on 47 individuals who had been removed very shortly after birth from their schizophrenic mothers, who were hospitalized in psychiatric institutions. These infants had been placed either in foster homes or with relatives and were raised without any contact with their biological mothers. A control group included individuals who had been raised in the same foster or adoptive home settings in which the experimental subjects had been placed. Independent ratings by two psychiatrists were rendered on these individuals following interviews and testing. Heston found that 5 of the 47 children of the schizophrenic mothers (10,6 percent) were diagnosed as schizophrenic, whereas none of the control-group subjects were. When Heston made the age corrections, which means that he took into consideration the statistical chances of developing schizophrenia at a later age, the rate increased to 16.6 percent.

An important result of Heston's work is emphasized by those who favor a genetic model of schizophrenia (Gottesman and Shields, 1976). It should be pointed out that this 16.6 percent age corrected incidence of schizophrenia in adopted children is almost identical to Kallman's (1953) rate of 16.4 percent for children raised with one schizophrenic parent. From an environmental viewpoint, one would expect that children raised away from their schizophrenic parents should be less likely to develop schizophrenia behavior patterns than children raised with their parents.

Most of the adoption studies first identify a group of psychotic parents and then study the offspring. However, another approach would be to identify any adoptees who become schizophrenic and then study their biological and adoptive families. With this strategy in mind, Kety and colleagues (1975) used the Danish registry to find adopted individuals who had been diagnosed as schizophrenic and a matched control group. The biological and adoptive families were then compared. For the control group there were no differences in the rate of schizophrenia in biological and adoptive families. As would be expected from a genetic viewpoint, however, the biological families of adoptees who became schizophrenic had a much higher incidence of the disorder than did the adoptive families that raised these individuals.

Probably one of the most interesting studies that has attempted to sort out the influence of genetic and environmental factors was reported by Wender and colleagues (1974), who also used the Danish registry to obtain their subjects. In addition to the typical comparisons of adoptees born to schizophrenic parents and those born to normal parents, Wender and coworkers were also able to study a unique group of adoptees. Subjects in their group were born to normal parents but were adopted and raised by in which at least one of the adopting parents was eventually considered schizophrenic, or at least borderline schizophrenic. They found that adoptees born to normal parents but raised by a schizophrenic parent were no more likely to be considered disturbed than those raised by normal adoptive parents. Once again, the group most likely to be diagnosed schizophrenic were those who were born to schizophrenics.

It seems somewhat clear that genetics does have some influence on the development of schizophrenia. The real question is not whether there is an influence, but rather how much of an influence is contributed by genetics. The process-reactive distinction provides some clues in determining the relative degree of genetic involvement. Garmezy (1970) proposed that there is a greater genetic involvement in process schizophrenia than there is in reactive schizophrenia. Some support for this view was provided by Kringlen (1968) who found that the concordance rate for process schizophrenia in monozygotic twins was higher =than for reactive schizophrenia.

The adoption studies have not gone unchallenged. Sarbin and Mancuso (1980) have delivered a highly detailed critique of the findings and conclusions thus far reported. This, although the genetic case is impressive, it is not yet definitively settled.

Biochemical Theories

Protein Abnormalities

In the late 1950s, Heath isolated a factor in the blood serum of schizophrenics that he believed disturbed neural functioning in the brain, thus causing schizophrenia. This factor as a simple protein. Heath (1960) called the protein *taraxin,* from the Greek word meaning "to disturb." When Heath injected taraxin into monkeys, marked changes in behavior and in electroencephalogram (EEG) tracings were observed. In addition, prison volunteers who were injected with the substance showed a number of characteristically schizophrenic symptoms, such as severely disorganized thought processes, withdrawal, and feelings of depersonalization. These startling findings received a great deal of attention at the time of publication, but because some investigators found it difficult to replicate Heath's work (Seigel et al, 1959), further investigation is necessary before any firm conclusions can be drawn.

Other researchers are convinced that schizophrenia is due to biological changes in the brain, which may or may not have a hereditary link. Metabolic or allergic causes for some schizophrenias are based on the finding of an abnormal protein called *traxein* in the blood of schizophrenics. Kay (1972) showed that the serum of schizophrenics is toxic for tadpoles and rats. Other experimenters have demonstrated that extracts of the urine of schizophrenics change the behavior of rats and disturb spiders' ability to construct webs. Early researchers showed that schizophrenics have a deficiency in their ability to take in oxygen. Also, the carbohydrate metabolism of schizophrenics is different from that of "normal" people. Liver insufficiency is claimed by Buscaino (1952). Others report a high concentration of aromatic compounds in the urine of schizophrenics.

Schizophrenic patients are widely reported to exude an unusual odor and to have oily skin. Perhaps the odoriferous substance is a clue to the schizophrenic metabolism; however, the schizophrenics studied had been hospitalized for years, and hospital living plus poor personal habits may have accounted for the odor. Sines (1959) report that both trained rats and a human odor-testing panel were able to discriminate between the sweat of schizophrenics and normal controls. However, Kety, one of the foremost researchers in this area, argues that many biochemical studies have not been confirmed (Arieti, 1974a). Horwitt (1956) notes that the various biochemical theories of schizophrenia render the schizophrenic a sorry specimen, with his liver, brain, kidneys, and circulatory system impaired, deficiencies of every vitamin, and enzymes, and hormones out of balance.

It is important to note that emotional activity does require biochemical processes, which means that the emotions of schizophrenics may be correlated with, but not caused by, biochemical processes. Thus, one does not know whether disturbed thoughts cause disturbed biochemistry or whether disturbed biochemistry causes disturbed thoughts (or whether a third factor causes both). All that is known now is that biochemistry and thoughts may be statistically associated.

If there is a genetic factor in schizophrenia, the question becomes, what is the phenotypic mechanism that translates the genetic abnormality into behavioral abnormality? Many investigators today believe that this mechanism has to do with body chemicals, but for the reason mentioned earlier in this chapter--specifically, interference by third variables such as hospitalizations, drugs, diet, and exercise--the progress in biochemical research has been slow and has suffered setbacks.

Transmethylation

The transmission of nerve impulses in the brain is dependent upon several different neurotransmitters that chemically bridge the gaps between neural synapses. Interestingly, many of these transmitters are structurally similar to hallucinogenic substances that cause distorted perceptual experiences, such as LSD or mescaline. Osmond and Smythies (1952) suggested the transmethylation hypothesis, which holds that, through some metabolic error, the carbon-oxygen molecule methyl is added to the neurotransmitters, rendering them even more similar to hallucinogens. In other words, individuals predisposed to schizophrenia appear to have a built-in supply of substances that can dramatically alter their behavior.

The research supporting the transmethylation hypothesis has taken two different approaches. In one line of research, substances that increase the supply of methyl molecules were administered to schizophrenic individuals (Park et al, 1965). As predicted, these substances were found to exacerbate the schizophrenic's behavior problems. Conversely, Hoffer and Osmond (1962, 1968) showed that high doses of niacin (nicotinic acid or Vitamin B-3), which decreases methyl levels, resulted in improvements in the treated individuals. The transmethylation hypothesis has received some support; however, there have also been failures to replicate some of the positive findings.

What we are left with, then are some interesting hypotheses whose confirmation has proved extremely elusive. As a consequence, investigators seem to have turned much of their attention to other things.

Dopamine

Various lines of evidence have also suggested that one particular neurotransmitter, dopamine, may be related to schizophrenia (Meltzer and Stahl, 1976; Snyder, 1974). The first line of evidence is related to the action of the phenothiazines, which are a group of drugs that are relatively effective in decreasing schizophrenic symptoms such as disturbed thought processes and hallucinations. Research suggests that phenothiazines block the receptor sites of nerves that respond to dopamine in the dopamine tract. This tract of nerve fibers is located in the midbrain and limbic system and may be closely related to arousal and attention processes (Ungerstedt, 1971). Thus, the phenothiazines can be thought of as decreasing various symptoms by decreasing the activity of dopamine.

A related piece of evidence is that many schizophrenics who are treated with phenothiazines develop various Parkinsonian symptoms, which increases the supply of dopamine. Thus, the Parkinsonian symptoms in the schizophrenic on phenothiazines may be due to too much of a decrease in dopamine activity.

The dopamine hypothesis has also been supported by various findings with amphetamine drugs, a group of powerful stimulants. Many types of amphetamines are available. Some have been used by dieters because of the diminished appetite produced by these drugs, and others, like dextroamphetamine, or "speed," have been used extensively by drug abusers. It has been found that many individuals who used high doses of amphetamines for long periods of time develop what appears to be paranoid schizophrenia, or amphetamine psychosis (Griffith et al, 1972). Furthermore, small doses of amphetamines seem to aggravate the behavior problems of schizophrenic individuals. As a result, Snyder (1974) has argued that amphetamines produces a schizophrenic-like disorder. Supporting this view is the fact that phenothiazines seem to be the best treatment for amphetamine psychosis.

Davis (1978) has noted several temporal factors that do not fit. For example, dopamine receptors are blocked quite rapidly with the ingestion, in clinical doses, of a neuroleptic drug. However, the clinical effect in terms of a lessening of schizophrenia-like symptoms normally develops gradually over a period of weeks, during a time in which many patients are actually acquiring a tolerance to dopamine blockade. In response to these problems, Davis offers a two-factor theory of schizophrenia, in which dopamine plays a distinctly secondary role; the first factor (unspecific) actually gets the schizophrenia going, while the dopaminergic activity simply turns up the speed. What this amounts to, of course, is a rejection of dopamine's alleged etiological significance in schizophrenia.

The biochemical theories most popularly held today are all based on the hypothesis that schizophrenia is caused by substances known as methylated amines, which are produced by the body and and act as hallucinogens (like LSD or mescaline), causing hallucinations and disorganized thinking. In one line of research, a group of neurotransmitters known as indoleamines, principally serotonin and tryptamine, are believed to be chemically altered (Methylated) in an abnormal way to form hallucinogenic compounds. For example, Mandell and colleagues (1972) have reported that under certain circumstances, an enzyme in the brain known as indoleamine-N-methyltransferase can convert serotonin and tryptamine into a hallucinogenic compound.

Another group of neurotransmitters that has gained attention are the catecholamines, principally epinephrine, norepinephrine, and dopamine. It has been proposed that in the schizophrenic, these catecholamines are abnormally methylated into a mescaline-like compound. For example, Friedhoff (cited in Mosher and Gunderson, 1973) has demonstrated that the human organism is able to synthesize, from dopamine, compounds that are similar to the dimethoxy hallucinogens, of which mescaline is one.

Somewhat conversely to these positions, it has been suggested by other researchers that schizophrenia is caused not by the production of abnormal methylated amines, but rather by an inability to demethylate normally present hallucinogenic amines, and thus to prevent their accumulation.

The Physiological Approach

Studies in the physiological aspects of schizophrenia do not necessarily compete with genetic or biochemical views. Rather, by concentrating on the functions and processes of the body rather than on the qualitative biological differences between individuals, they tend to complement the other views, adding another side to what may be a many-faceted organically based condition. It should be kept in mind, however, that a physiological abnormality, similar to a biochemical abnormality, may well be the result, rather than the cause, of schizophrenia. Or, as in the earlier situation, both the abnormality and the schizophrenia may be the result of a third variable.

Neurophysiological Dysfunction

Studies show that autonomic arousal patterns among schizophrenics are different from those observed in normal people (Fenz and Velner, 1970). What researchers have discovered is that in resting states, the arousal level of schizophrenics is higher than normal, but in situations that call for a reaction to some stimulus, the arousal level of schizophrenics is lower than normal. In sum, the schizophrenic is over-reactive in situations that require a resting state and underactive in situations that call for an alert state (Buss, 1966). To account for this apparent contradiction, it has been suggested that faulty metabolism of neurotransmitters are what produces the autonomic overactivity of schizophrenics, and that the low level of reactivity is simply a normal reaction of the nervous system to high resting levels. For example, it has been shown in normal subjects that at extremely high resting levels of autonomic arousal, a stimulus will generally not elicit further arousal; rather, a paradoxical decrease in arousal may be affected (Lacey, 1956). Thus, the lower reactivity of schizophrenics may not be a primary characteristic but rather a secondary one, reflecting the "normal" functioning of a hyperactive nervous system (Buss, 1966)

Low Stress Tolerance

Investigators have also suggested that the schizophrenic does not have a store of adaptive energy that may be mobilized in order to cope with the stresses of everyday life. Such a deficiency, they feel, might be genetic. On the other hand, some researchers have suggested that it might be a physiological consequence of the strains imposed on the body by a prolonged schizophrenic condition (beck et al, 1963; Luby et al, 1962). One study has shown, for example, that during acute schizophrenic episodes, certain steroids are excreted at abnormally high levels (sachar et al, 1970). It is possible that a series of such episodes might eventually simply exhaust the adrenal glands, which would then cease to secrete the hormones necessary to deal with stress.

Sociological Theories

Rosenhan's (1973) well-known study provides little assurance that professional diagnosticians are routinely capable of detecting "malingering." In an article entitled, The Art of Being Schizophrenic, Haley was the first to take the suggestion explicitly. Braginsky and colleagues (1969) demonstrated that a group of hospitalized mental patients, most diagnosed schizophrenics, were actively engaged in impression management and in controlling the diagnoses and other assessments made of them by the professional staff. Shimkunas (1972), Ritchie (1975), and Levy (1976) presented experimental evidence that certain behaviors that are definable of schizophrenia (delusional verbalizations, for example) are variably emitted by persons diagnosed as schizophrenic. The chief value of these studies is in demonstrating that schizophrenia, viewed as a class of behaviors, seems to present itself and disappear according to the characteristics of the interpersonal situation confronting the patient. Drake and Wallace (1979) presented evidence that hospital stays of "functionally psychotic" patients are determined primarily by preferences for hospital versus community living, not by the severity of the disorder. Most of the severely disturbed patients were the ones who gained discharge from the hospital!

Sociological researchers have suggested that the passive apathetic, and bizarre behavior of long-term hospitalized schizophrenics may be the result not on any of the effects of their psychological difficulty, but also of their treatment within the hospital setting. Goffman (1961) spent a year observing patients in Large state hospital and found that their behavior was very similar to that of other inmates in what he called "total institutions"--jails, reform schools, and so on, which regulate every aspect of a person's life. Goffman feels that the behavior of mental patients is similar to that of prisoners, sanitorium inmates, prisoners of war, preparatory school students, and armed forces recruits. People in each of these groups are depersonalized by their environments. They lose their individuality and personality as they come under the total control of bureaucratic authorities who demand complete adherence to a rigid set of rules. Though the position somewhat oversimplifies the situation, Goffman feels that the passive, uninvolved behavior of chronic mental patients is a result of living in an environment that is dull and boring and makes no allowance for individualized behavior. In addition, hospital staff expect little of the chronic patients and do not get involved with them. Their expectations thus become a self-fulfilling prophesy.

Some attempts to alter the treatment patterns of chronic schizophrenics have been successful, and the behavior of certain individuals has changed. Allon and Azrin (1965) note that when hospital staff expect responsible behavior from their chronic patients, they do in fact get it. Some treatment programs for such patients have focused, not on the causes or treatment of their disorders, but on teaching socially useful, adaptive behavior and creating environments in which such behavior is rewarded. It has been theorized that people become chronic patients when they do not have the social skills to survive in the outside world. As Goffman notes, the hospital environment does little to foster such adaptive, socially appropriate behavior.

The High Risk Strategy

The high risk strategy in its usual form capitalizes on the actuarial fact that a substantial proportion of children born to schizophrenic parents will become schizophrenic. Pioneered by Fish (1957) and Sobel (1961), high risk research has proliferated at a very rapid rate in recent years. Mednick and Schulsinger (1973) found that the following were among the factors differentiating the schizophrenic form other high risk subjects: (1) Their (schizophrenic) mothers' disorders and first hospitalizations occurred at a younger age, suggesting greater severity. (2) Obstetrical complications, including long labor, occurred more often in their births. (3) Teachers judged their school behavior as erratic, disturbing, persistently upset, aggressive and violent. (4) In a more recent study, Mednick and colleagues (1973), employing path analysis, discovered that for males (but not for females), the age of the mothers' onset of the disorder apparently contributed to a schizophrenic outcome only indirectly, through enhancing the likelihood of parent-child separation. (5) This analysis also showed that for males (but not for females), schizophrenia was predicted by autonomic nervous anomaly, which was, in turn, well predicted by complications in the mother's pregMichelle or in the subject's birth.

Therapeutic Techniques

Members of the mental health professions are generally called upon to identify high risk populations and to identify high-risk populations and to offer preventative, as well as therapeutic and palliative, services. They generally participate as part of the hospital interdisciplinary team in treatment planning and implementation for the psychiatrically ill patient and are responsible for treatment planning and implementation in outpatient and community care facilities. They often see the patient or the patient's family, or both, in an outpatient facility, such as a halfway house or community mental health centers. Schizophrenic patients require ongoing support if they are to remain in the community and their families need help and education to adjust to the disorder. Mental health professionals can develop family and patient self-help groups, set up supervised residences and sheltered workshops, and make necessary referrals.

The administrative structure of community mental health agencies is unwieldy and does not facilitate care of the chronic patient. Responsibility for such patients is divided among state, county, and voluntary agencies. Mental health professionals can help to coordinate community facilities and evaluate both the need for care and the agencies' ability and willingness to meet the community's identified mental health needs. By initiating joint planning on the part of hospitals, public health facilities, welfare agencies, and voluntary agencies, mental health professionals can make efficient use of the now-fragmented mental health service system, much to the benefit of the mentally ill.

Equally important, mental health professionals must identify vulnerable persons and facilitate their entry into treatment before they develop an illness that overwhelms both the family and the patient. To this end, it is necessary to develop new resources, organize natural support networks, and establish linkages and networks between people and resources. It is also necessary to help patients overcome their resistance to utilizing these resources.

Until the mid-1950s, treatment of schizophrenia was primarily custodial. Patients were warehoused for long periods of time in environments that were both under stimulating and hopeless. The disorder and the hospital environment often interacted to bring about behavior that required physical restraint.

There are as many approaches to treating schizophrenic behavior as there are theories of its etiology. Nearly any form of therapy that one could imagine has been tried, sometimes to the dismay of the schizophrenic individuals being treated. Numerous biological forms of therapy have been used, including electroconvulsive shock, insulin shock, psychosurgery, numerous types of chemotherapy, and massive doses of vitamins (orthomolecular therapy), brain pacemakers, and kidney dialysis. Psychologically oriented approaches to therapy have included many types of individual, family, and group therapy from various theoretical orientations. Institutional approaches for dealing with schizophrenia have involved standard hospital care, milieu therapy, token economies, and halfway houses. The most recent endeavors have taken place in community based mental health centers which use a variety of therapeutic interventions to keep and treat the individuals in their own communities.

Since schizophrenics are so commonly treated with drugs, it is difficult to find research on drug-free individuals who receive only psychological treatment (May, 1975). Nevertheless, there are some general findings that are relatively consistent for the different forms of psychological therapy.

The treatment of schizophrenia depends on the stage of the disorder, the depth of the regression, the grasp on reality that remains, and the patient's desire for therapy and ability to establish a relationship with the therapist. It is necessary from the outset to help these patients move from their regressed state to a more integrated level of functioning.

1. First and foremost, establish a positive therapeutic alliance with the client.

In the case of Carrie, although her orientation to person, place, and time appeared inappropriate, her cathexis to reality was quite tenuous. Attending weekly sessions and talking at great length about her feelings and her past was not a sign of her motivation to help herself. In fact, the therapist could easily have assumed that her life outside the sessions was going quite well, since Carrie hardly ever mentioned it. However, frequent complaints from her counselors and roommates led the therapist to explore with her the reality of her life as she lived it outside the therapist's office. It then became clear that a hornet's nest of turmoil and problems in daily living existed for her.

Frequent bouts of hysterical crying with her counselors at the transitional-living quarters occurred daily, often with the client blaming her roommates for their lack of cooperation and hostility. She avoided caring for her room, cooking, and shopping for food. When she was confronted with this, she would temporarily conform and then feel entitled to eat her roommate's food without asking permission. Beneath the superficial surface of the conforming, compliant patient was an angry, negativistic, rebellious woman who felt entitled to be cared for by others and who was bent on coercing others to provide this care? Her attendance at weekly therapy sessions was not a sign of motivation; instead, it was a defense against revealing her feelings about what was happening and her adamant resistance to change.

Carrie viewed the therapist's attempt to establish a caring, supportive relationship with her as a hostile, exploitative act, no doubt a collusion on the part of the therapist and counselors to judge the efforts at cooperating with her roommate's inadequate behavior. She experienced the therapist's gentle inquiries into the events of her life as a hostile effort to deprive her of her right to lead her own life. The therapist's attempts to clarify the reality of the situation often led to carries' ruminating about her problems and bemoaning her fate as a hopeless, unwanted patient. It was therefore very important to the therapist to help Carrie distinguish between her own feelings and those of the therapist.

2. *Identity the hidden thoughts that evoke the client's emotional responses.*

Treatment of schizophrenics requires considerable patience and constant awareness of and reasonable response to their feelings. The client's emotional responses are appropriate to his inner experience, which he may successfully hide from the therapist. Schizophrenic clients tend to exhibit low frustration tolerance, suspiciousness of the therapist's motives, and projection onto the therapist of their own prejudices and fears.

After several sessions with her male therapist, Carrie asked her therapist if he had noticed that she sat with her legs crossed. When the therapist did not reply affirmatively, she stated that she did this because she did not want him to enter her through her vagina, which she knew was what he wanted to do. Interpretation of the desire for sexual fusion does not appear to be indicated for this client; instead, recognition of her anxiety and positive reinforcement of her desire for a firmer sense of self and clearer ego boundaries were more appropriate interventions.

Since these clients feel incapable of dealing with real life, they may resent the therapist's intrusion into their fantasy lives of withdrawal and safety from a turbulent existence. Although they are aware that the therapist's goal is to return them to the real world, this prospect holds untold terrors for them. Often, this anxiety may provoke a temporary regression that interrupts therapy. These clients may also erupt with hostile or violent reactions when they feel that their retreat is being threatened by the efficacy of treatment.

Fromm-Reichman (1959) explained that the therapist must be engaged in an ongoing sympathetic and understanding relationship with the schizophrenic client; intellectual comprehension of the illness is secondary. Wolberg (1954) emphasized that the therapist must continuously analyze his own reactions because his sense of frustration may arouse the client's aggression and interfere with treatment. Wolberg cautioned that the therapist must provide unlimited warmth, understanding, protection, and assistance.

Carrie was often troublesome, frustrating, belligerent, and overwhelming in her demands for instant attention and understanding. However, it was important for the therapist to guard against careless and impulsive expression of frustration. Instead, a reasonable and measured reaction to the client's confusion and poor reality testing often enable her to become more reasonable and self-contained.

"The chief emphasis in treatment must be on the creation of human relationship with the client that had pleasure value for him or her. Only by this means will s/he relinquish the safety and gratification of regression and, utilizing the therapist as a bridge, return to reality" (Wolberg, 1954, p, 63). In Carrie's dreams, a benevolent, bearded male figure (which were the physical characteristics of her therapist) appeared to carry her to a peaceful land. This dream occurred well before Carrie could express any pleasure or trust in her male therapist, who was, she felt, only out to use her.

Since the ego of schizophrenic clients is very immature, their reactions to people are unstable and ambivalent. Carrie often felt rejected and frustrated for insufficient reasons; her concept of reality was distorted and unreliable, so that her inner mental processes were often confused with external reality. Such clients may react with hostility if the therapist does not grant what they wish. On several occasions when Carrie was involved in group treatment with another therapist, she would storm out of the room spewing vulgar accusations if the group did not pay immediate attention to her demands or complaints.

3. *Pay imminent attention to client's strange gestures; they constitute important non-verbal information.*

The schizophrenic client may choose to remain silent throughout the therapy hour. When the client finally feels safe and trusting enough to communicate with the therapist, however, s/he will often reveal all that was absorbed during the silence. It is helpful to remember that symptoms express the client's feelings.

The first step in resolving schizophrenic symptoms, then, is to establish an emotional contact with the client. Making an accurate interpretation or spontaneous clarification of what the client is communicating may make him or her feel secure enough to relinquish some of his or her psychotic manifestations.

Identifying the major difficulties in coping with each developmental task are of critical importance to the therapist, whose task is to strengthen the client's capacity to deal with the exigencies of the environment. Clarifying the client's problem and identifying stressors related to certain events in the life-cycle are of essential value in therapy. The first manifestation of Carrie's problems appeared while she was away at school. Subsequent attempts to gain independence were often acted out by stopping her medication, running away from therapy treatment, and returning to the school when her problems first occurred in an attempt to recapture the freedom from anxiety she had felt as a student.

Individual Psychotherapy

In order to treat the schizophrenic client, the psychodynamically oriented therapist often has to combine the principles of psychoanalysis with principles from other schools of thought, such as the behaviorist's emphasis on reinforcement and the humanist's concern for personal autonomy. In treating the schizophrenic, psychodynamically oriented therapists proceed in many respects as they would with lesser disorders. With the schizophrenic, however, much more attention is given to creating a warm, nurturant therapeutic relationship (Arieti, 1974b). Through this relationship and through analysis of the transference, the therapist aims to heal the psychic wounds left over from childhood and to reorient the schizophrenic toward interpersonal relationships. In short, the therapist becomes a sort of second parent, providing the sympathy, support, and esteem that the patient needs in order to rediscover the sources of value and pleasure in himself and others.

Individual psychodynamic psychotherapy has not been found effective in treating schizophrenia, however (Feinsilver and Cunderson, 1972, May 1975). There are few well controlled studies of psychotherapy with schizophrenics (Feinsilver and Gunderson, 1972); in general, the results have not been impressive and suggest that psychodynamically oriented psychotherapy adds very little to pharmacology and hospital care.

Social countertransference issues arise in therapy with schizophrenics. Most notably, the basic dependency needs of the schizophrenic client have not been adequately gratified; hence the severity of the symptoms. If the therapist can gratify the patient's needs in a practical and realistic way, however, the results can be surprisingly positive.

Generally, patients suffering from severe forms of schizophrenia benefit most from learning basic trust and self-acceptance through the therapeutic alliance. The schizophrenic client fears experiencing warm and positive feelings, which, in any case, are sporadic. The therapist should utilize his or her own optimistic and encouraging approach to generate an effective relationship with the client.

While the schizophrenic has a fear of becoming close, there is also a wish to become a part of others in order to make himself or herself feel whole. Establishing and maintaining emotional support is of the utmost importance in the therapeutic relationship. It is only when the schizophrenic client is able to have a satisfying experience with someone who does not encompass and overwhelm him that he can begin to trust in and benefit from the relationship.

If the client is listless and withdrawn, the therapist should attempt to stimulate his or her interest in the environment. The client's withdrawal is and attempt to deal with frustration and hopelessness, and he needs great encouragement to give up his coping mechanisms. While often ambivalent about giving up his or her isolation and social withdrawal and attempting to cope with life, the schizophrenic also wishes that someone would care enough about him to help him do so. Withdrawal is also a way to prevent rejection, and the schizophrenic client may make it clear that s/he will accept pleasant experiences only on his own terms. The therapist should then accept the client's limitations while providing consistent interest. It is of great importance to follow the client's lead in maintaining an emotional distance with which he feels comfortable.

Even though schizophrenic clients are often preoccupied with fantasy material, it is best to postpone direct exploration of this material until they are better integrated. At the same time, MacKimmons (1969) suggests that therapists pay close attention to their own responses to the schizophrenic client's distorted thinking. If the therapist cannot understand the client, the therapist might say that s/he is having difficulty following what the client is saying. In this way, the therapist can both ascertain whether the client is able to present material in another way and learn what the client wishes to communicate. The schizophrenic client also needs the therapist's active assistance in defining problems and focusing on issues. The therapist should direct attention to the client's strengths (while not discounting problems), thereby furnishing positive feedback. Any bit of progress is very significant to these clients, so the therapist should be sure to acknowledge each one.

There is agreement that rage commonly underlies the schizophrenic client's inhibition. Schizophrenics withdraw from contact with the world for fear that if they expressed themselves, they might lose control of their aggressive, destructive impulses.

Family Therapy

A variety of techniques have been used to alter interactions in the families of schizophrenic individuals. Although it seems that family therapy would be useful because of the potential involvement of the family in the schizophrenic's behavior, relatively few adequate studies have examined this issue. In their review of recent types of family interventions, Massie and Beels (1972) concluded that even though some poorly designed studies indicate the potential effectiveness of family therapy, there remains a clear need for systematic evaluation.

Among the most interesting of the uncontrolled studies in this area is the one reported by Jackson and Weakland (1961). After periods of 3 to 4 months in treatment, 6 out of 7 hospitalized patient-members of treated families had returned to the community, and a comparable proportion of outpatients had also significantly benefitted in terms of similar criteria.These authors also reported the significant deterioration of some nonpatient members of the treated families, an observation that contributed to the idea of family homeostasis. Among the more controlled studies of family intervention is that of Ro-Trock and co-workers (1977), in which individual and family therapies were competitively compared. The outcome measures were complex and difficult to interpret, but in the important dimension of rehospitalization, family therapy was the winner by a substantial margin. It is obvious that family therapy is difficult to research on many dimensions, among them that of isolating what is therapeutic; what is normal, and what is destructive.

Family therapy with schizophrenics focuses on correcting family role relationships and skewed and schismatic family patterns. A popular treatment approach, it usually involves client, parents, and or/spouses. Other relative's central in the patient's life may also be included. Family therapy can help family members better understand each other's point of view. This can modify a family's attitude and behavior, which may be related to the development and maintenance of the patient's illness.

It is probably that the failure of parents to preserve appropriate age and sex boundaries between family members plays a role in the etiology of schizophrenia. Sometimes the parent turns to a child rather than the spouse to gratify emotional needs. Or, children are obliged to assume the parenting role. In some families, communication is distorted. Since researchers have produced the strongest and most consistent evidence for links between patterns of maladaptive interaction and schizophrenia, it is essential that both individual and family therapy be employed in the treatment of adolescents and young adults who are schizophrenic.

Lidz (1973) suggested that family pathology is often extensive and forms a pathogenic environment for the patient. Therefore, it is usually unwise for the patient to return to his environment. Although making alternate living arrangements usually requires considerable work with the parents and the patient, the outcome of treatment may depend on taking this step. The mental health professional working with schizophrenic clients should consider family therapy.

Family therapy was initiated early in the initial hospitalization of the Z. case. Mr. and Mrs. Z. both acknowledged a wish to work on their difficulties, as they had a long history of marital conflict. They needed help in dealing with their feelings of rage and guilt in relation to their daughter and her psychiatric illness. They insisted that they wanted her to function on an adult, responsible level and live apart from them; it was obvious, however, that her illness played a significant role in keeping them together. Both parents experienced frustration, disappointment, and a lack of support in not having their needs met by one another. With difficulty, they made efforts to change their interactions with Carrie so as not to infantilize her and to support differentiation and autonomous functioning.

Family sessions were held at one point in the treatment with the patient's individual hospital therapist, the parents, the client, and her sister. It emerged that dependency was of concern to all members, as was the client's illness and its impact on family interactions. These issues particularly concerned her parents, who devoted a great deal of energy to being with the patient and trying to help her, to the exclusion or minimization of interaction with other family members or friends. They needed help in dealing with their own fears around the unpredictability of their daughter's responses. The opportunity to deal with one another directly helped to diminish distortions.

It was important for family members to see that, in the course of a session Carrie could move from a depressed, angry position to one in which she was composed and able to express herself clearly and with relevance.

They began to trust that dealing directly with each other could enhance feelings of hopefulness and diminish their collective sense of helplessness, inadequacy, and incompetence.

Despite this gain, Mr. Z. withdrew from sessions in the autumn of his daughter's hospitalization, leaving the client and her mother in joint sessions. His absence was ostensibly related to work pressures, but his withdrawal came at a time when there was a beginning shift in family functioning as members took greater responsibility for themselves as separate individuals and began to move away from a hyper-vigilant response to Carrie. The father's behavior also resembled Carrie's first withdrawal and unavailability to the family when they had experienced financial difficulties. It was at that time that Carrie first felt that she was no longer special to her father. Thus, the semblance of family cooperation and strength soon evaporated into mistrust and turbulent anger.

Mr. Z. was concerned that confronting their marriage of accommodation would create stress for him and his wife. He was not prepared to deal openly with his extramarital relationship. Both Mr. and Mrs. Z. expressed a desire to maintain the avoidance pattern of dealing with their difficulties, recognizing that they could remain in a superficially caring relationship. It was agreed that each needed time for self-reflection before resuming joint treatment. Family therapy was then modified to focus on discharge planning and on the sibling relationship. Carrie and her sister found it difficult to examine their relationship because of long standing hurt, anger, and defensiveness, which characterized the entire family system. By the time of Carrie's discharge, Mr. and Mrs. Z. were able to express disappointment over the daughter's slow progress, but they had developed more realistic expectations and were less critical. Carrie was able to tolerate other family member's feelings about her without becoming defensive.

Carrie retained her wish to be pseudo-independent and autonomous, and she had had great difficulty accepting help from a hospital program that she felt stigmatized her. She also had minimal ability to adapt to separations and transitions; despite numerous hospitalizations, she had not been in any sustained treatment. She attempted to impress her therapists with abstractions and intellectualizations, presenting herself as a passive-aggressive individual who resented the dependent patient role. She was indecisive and lacked insight. At times loose and tangential, she could organize her thoughts and remain goal oriented when asked to do so.

Carrie sensed her parents' disappointment and embarrassment about their pathetic, strange child who was so obviously ill. As the youngest of several females, she was forced to compete for her father's attentions by being "cute, seductive, and smart." Failure was not tolerated in this materialistic, success-oriented family, whose central concern was the community's evaluation of them. Mr. and Mrs. Z. indeed offered scant nurturance or support. Mr. Z. was seductive and superficial, while Mrs. Z. was hysterical and labile. The patient's tendency to fall apart and become overwhelmed by small setbacks resembled the mother's behavior.

Group Therapy

Group therapy is widely used in the treatment of schizophrenia, especially following discharge from hospitals. More research is needed, but a number of studies have found posthospital group therapy to be somewhat effective (May, 1975). In general, the research comparing group and individual therapy has found group therapy to be more effective. For example, O'Brien and colleagues (1972) found that after 2 years, 40 per cent of individual therapy patients had to be rehospitalized, but only 24 percent of group patients had to return to the hospital. The efficacy of group therapy is not surprising, since group-oriented programs "force" a certain amount of social interaction and may thereby prevent social isolation common among schizophrenics.

In our experience in an outpatient setting, group modality, in conjunction with individual therapy and chemotherapy, is extremely effective in preventing further regressive behavior and rehospitalization. Clients were referred by their individual therapists for screening by the group therapist. Criteria were established for participation in the group. These criteria included: the absence of extremely interfering hallucinations or delusions, the absence of extreme paranoid trends that could be disruptive to the group, and willingness to participate in group activities.

The group initially focused on "safe topics" daily routine, preparation for holidays and the attendant increased contact with family members, and the discussion of psychotropic medication. Later, these "veterans of multiple hospitalizations" would recount their "battle experiences." The group established its own norms about the need for medication, increasing the probability that members would be medication compliant.

As the group became more cohesive and less deferential to the group leader, the members began to explore painful feelings around setting lower standards of functioning for themselves, "losing the dream" of finally getting well, and modifying their unrealistic ambitions and wishes. Finally, the group discussed adjusting to the prospect of limited achievement and the possibilities of feeling comfortable with their limitations. The group developed its own climate of support and nurturance and provided its own parenting and problem solving to help members through interpersonal conflicts.

The group members socialized with each other after group sessions, and planned and supported each other in attending community events that would have paralyzed them if they were to have attended on their own. Members who dropped out of the ongoing two year group were more apt to discontinue their medication, become socially isolated, regress, and finally, require hospitalization.

Several conclusions regarding group therapy for schizophrenics were also noted in O'Brien's (1975) review.

1. Group therapy may be advantageous for schizophrenic out-patients.
2. Group therapy is less effective and may be detrimental to acutely psychotic patients.
3. For withdrawn schizophrenics, the therapist's primary task is to promote social interaction among group members.
4. Group therapy can be effectively combined with other treatment modalities.

Thus, the primary aim of group psychotherapy is to facilitate the patient's awareness into personal and interpersonal problems and to provide a supportive environment in which patients can develop appropriate social skills. Group treatment helps schizophrenic clients develop social skills and establish supportive friendships.

Social Learning Therapy

The utility of therapeutic efforts based on learning theory principles has been demonstrated n a number of large studies (O'Leary and Wilson, 1975). Rather than trying to change the whole schizophrenic syndrome, social learning techniques usually focus on target behaviors that are interfering with the client's functioning. Various techniques have been successfully used to increase appropriate behaviors and to improve interpersonal skills (hersen and Bellak, 1976). Other interventions have been successful in eliminating or decreasing inappropriate behaviors such as delusional speech, reported hallucinations, mutism, bizarre verbalizations, destructiveness, noncompliance, and apathy (Lieberman et al, 1974).

Individually tailored behavior therapy involves considerable therapist time costs. Thus, the more comprehensive behavioral treatment programs are usually established in institutional settings, where many problem behaviors can be treated simultaneously. This has been found to be more feasible and effective and less expensive than standard hospital care.

Many of these programs systematically build in reinforcement contingencies that will teach new adaptive skills, rather than merely provide custodial care. Such programs are often termed *token economies* (Atthowe and Krasner, 1968; Ayllon and Azrin, 1963). The basic components of a token economy include the following:

1. Delineation of the adaptive behaviors that are to be reinforced.
2. Specification of a number of back-up reinforcers that clients can work for. (These reinforcers might include either tangible items, such as food or cigarettes, or privileges, such as going on a pass, watching a movie, or extra television time).
3. A specific medium of exchange (that is, the actual tokens--perhaps poker chips or paper money) which would be used like "real money" to purchase the available reinforcers.
4. A set of exchange rules which indicate how many tokens each reinforcer will cost.

The token economy is structured so that the behaviors to be learned will be reinforced with tokens that can in turn be spent in any way the client wishes. Behaviors that are considered maladaptive might be "fined" in order to extinguish them. When a hospital discharge is a possibility, it is often assumed that a long-term client will have to first learn how to function in the hospital's artificial token economy in order to function successfully within the monetary system of our society.

One of the most impressive studies comparing comprehensive token economy methods with other procedures was carried out by Paul and Lentz (1977). The results of this complex and important study have important implications for the treatment of chronic psychiatric clients. In this project, which took over six years to complete, Paul and Lentz compared two psychological approaches to standard hospital care-a social learning program which included a token economy and a l=milieu therapy program. Milieu therapy attempts to incorporate all staff members and clients into a total therapeutic community. The two methods shared similar comprehensive objectives, which included the following:

1. resocialization (teaching self-care, interpersonal, and communication skills).
2. teaching vocational and housekeeping skills.
3. reduction in bizarre behavior.
4. provision of aftercare support in the community.

The Milieu training program emphasized communication of expectations, group support and cohesiveness, group pressure, and group problem-solving efforts. This was consistent with most Milieu approaches, which generally maintain a democratic philosophy in which the client is more of an equal participant than a dependent patient.

The social learning program used a token economy with a heavy emphasis on reinforcement for appropriate behavior, modeling of correct behavior, extinction of undesirable behavior, and skills training groups. The standard hospital program was primarily a maintenance program, providing physical care, medication, and routine patient activities.

The subjects included in this study were the most severely disturbed schizophrenics with the least chance of recovery--they had been hospitalized for an average of over 14 years. The findings indicated that although both psychological programs were more effective than standard care on most measures of treatment success, the social learning approach was consistently the most effective method. Probably the most impressive finding was that over 90 percent of the released social learning patients were able to remain continuously in the community in some type of treatment setting through the final 18 month follow-up evaluation.

Community-Based Programs

Over the past twenty years, there has been a steady decline in the number of schizophrenic persons treated in residential psychiatric institutions and a decline in the average stay in such facilities. These declines have come about for four basic reasons: the advent of major tranquilizers; the belief, generally based on fact, that psychiatric hospitals are a bad place for anyone to live; the belief that clients can more appropriately and effectively be treated in their own communities; and perhaps, more importantly, the fact that outpatient treatment facilities are simply less expensive than long-term inpatient care. Collectively, this movement has been referred to as ***deinstitutionalization***. Since the 1960s, therefore, federal and local governments have funded two kinds of community facilities: Community mental health centers, designed to provide local treatment, and halfway houses or group homes, designed to ease the transition from psychiatric hospitals back to the community.

Psychiatric hospitals, or psychiatric units of general hospitals provide a temporary protective environment in which the client can be helped through the initial period of acute disturbance. S/he can then be transferred to an outpatient community facility. However, long term hospitalization may offer the best therapeutic result in some cases and should be available as a referral source.

After clients emerge from the initial crisis, they need help adjusting to life in the community. Occupational therapy, vocational counseling, job training, art therapy, and social clubs are appropriate supportive services. Community-centered treatment of schizophrenic clients can provide them with the social and vocational skills they need to lead productive and meaningful lives outside the hospital.

Chemotherapy

Before this section ends, a word must be said about the various antipsychotic drugs that are prescribed to modify the effects of the supposed biological abnormalities that have been discussed in this chapter. Lehman (1974) lists three principal uses of these drugs: (1) to bring the client out of an acute schizophrenic crisis; (2) to facilitate management and control of clients; (3) to prevent the reoccurrence of schizophrenic symptoms. The chemotherapy makes it possible to realize these goals in large number of cases is beyond dispute. The question that remains, however, is whether such effects are due to the chemicals themselves or to the expectations of clients and staff.

The drug chlorpromazine (Thorazine) revolutionized the treatment of schizophrenia. In 1955, there were about 560,000 patient in American psychiatric hospitals, and 1 out of every 2 hospital beds was devoted to psychiatric care. It was then estimated that by 1971, some 750,000 beds would be required to care for the growing psychiatric population. In fact, there were only 308,000 patients in psychiatric hospitals in 1971, less than half the projected estimate, and about 40 percent fewer than were hospitalized in 1955. By 1977, the patient census had declined to less than 160,000. Such is the power of the major tranquilizers.

Of the major tranquilizers, chlorpromazine (Thorazine) and haloperidol (Haldol) are two of the most commonly used. Their most striking effect is the degree to which they "tranquilize," make peaceful, even sedate. Could it be that these drugs are no different from barbiturates, whose sedative action produces no greater improvements for schizophrenics than a placebo? Some evidence suggests that this is not the case (Klein, 1968). The major psychotropic medications including phenothiazines, chlorpromazines and haloperidol seem to have specific ameliorating effects on schizophrenic symptoms, beyond their sedative effects and even beyond their impact on anxiety. Thought disorder, hallucinations, flattened affect, and withdrawal-- all of these are affected by these drugs. Equally important, these drugs have virtually no effect on psychiatric symptoms that are not associated with schizophrenia (Casey et al, 1960; Klein, 1968). Subjective emotional experiences, such as guilt and depression, continue unabated despite a course of drug treatment.

Just how the phenothiazines achieve their effects on schizophrenic symptoms is not yet clear. Nevertheless, the average hospital stay for a schizophrenic client has declined to fewer than 13 days, whereas it formerly was months, years, even a lifetime. Phenothiazines have, nearly single-handedly, been responsible for a revolution in psychiatric care.

Unfortunately the antipsychotic drugs have a variety of unpleasant side effects that often lead clients to discontinue using them. Side effects of chlorpromazine, for example, frequently include dryness of the mouth and throat, drowsiness, visual disturbances, weight gain or loss, menstrual disturbances, constipation, and depression. for most patients these are relatively minor problems; for others, however, they are annoying enough to induce them to discontinue medications after discharge.

One class of more serious side effects, called extrapyramidal, or Parkinson-like, effects, appears to arise because, as previously noted, antipsychotic medications affect the dopamine receptors, which are implicated in Parkinson's disease. These drugs do not cause Parkinson's disease, but they do induce analogous symptoms, including stiffness of muscles and consequent difficulty moving; freezing of facial muscles, which results n a glum or sour look as well as an inability to smile; tremors of the extremities as well as spasms of limbs and body; and akathisia, a peculiar "itchiness" in the muscles which results in an inability to sit still and an urge to pace continuously and energetically (Snyder, 1974). Other drugs can control these side effects, but no phenothiazine has yet been produced which avoids them.

Even more serious is the neurological disorder called tardive dyskinesia. Its symptoms consists of sucking, lip-smacking, and vermicular tongue movements. Tardive Dyskinesia is not reversible. Conservative estimates are that it affects 18 percent of hospitalized schizophrenics, and the figure rises with clients' age and length of time on antipsychotic medication (Klein, 1968)/

In sum, schizophrenia can at this time be neither prevented nor cured. Nevertheless, substantial numbers of clients recover sufficiently to lead rewarding and functional lives in the community. Schizophrenics are treatable by a combination of medication, therapy, and other modalities. However, it is critical to identify the person in psychological trouble before personality change, withdrawal, and interpersonal difficulties become pronounced. Effective treatments cannot be provided if necessary resources do not exist or remain underutilized by various social and ethnic groups. Mental health professionals have an invaluable role to play in comprehensive treatment of the schizophrenic client.

When to Refer

1. Clients diagnosed with Schizophrenia should be referred if they are showing increased signs of psychotic defenses such as hallucinations or delusions or anxiety despite the therapist's efforts to help them contain it. Schizophrenic clients should be referred to a psychiatrist if their medication is ineffective. The need psychiatric evaluation in order to determine whether increasing the dosage of the present medication or changing the medication is advisable. Schizophrenic clients should also be referred if, along with the anxiety, the initial symptoms of the illness reappear.

2. If, despite every effort to help the client, s/he is unable to reality test or to control destructive impulses, then a psychiatric emergency exists. The client's judgment is impaired. Immersion in his or her delusional system adds to his feeling of being out of control. Most state hospitals and general hospitals have psychiatric emergency units in which the client's need for hospitalization can be evaluated. Alternatively, an attempt to tranquilize the client can be made in the emergency unit.

3. Referral to a day hospital is appropriate if the family environment seems to exacerbate the client's symptoms.

4. For clients who are able to return to their stable functioning, vocational evaluation and socialization groups are necessary referrals. At this point in treatment, the client will need additional stimulation and positive reinforcement in order to remain actively engaged in the external social environment. Many mental health centers and hospital outpatient departments provide groups for previously hospitalized clients where friendships can be formed, social skills can be practiced, and feelings can be shared. A transitional living referral may be necessary in order to remove

the client from the isolated, dependency-inducing environment of the psychiatric hospital.

5. If the therapist should become the personification of the bad parent to the client, the malevolent force in the client's life, then termination of treatment or referral to another therapist is necessary. This decision can be discussed with the client and, if appropriate, the family, and it can be explained that the continuation of treatment under this circumstance would be unproductive and perhaps dangerous. It should be noted that some degree of transference to the therapist as a malevolent parent can be helpful for working through the client's negative attitudes about him or herself, but a therapeutic alliance needs to be formed if this is to occur. The client would then be able to recognize that her reactions and feelings are being induced by the treatment process and that she is not just a victim of the therapist's neglect, abuse, or evil intent.

References

Allen, M.G., Cohen, S., and Pollin, W. (1972). Schizophrenia in veteran twins: a diagnostic review. *American Journal of Psychiatry* *128:939-947.*

Arieti, S. (1955). *Interpretation of Schizophrenia.* New York: Brunner/ Mazel.

Arieti, S. (1969). The meeting of the inner and the external world: in schizophrenia, everyday life and creativity. *American Journal of Psychoanalysis, 29*:115-130

Arieti, S. (1974a). An overview of schizophrenia from a predominantly psychological approach. *The American Journal of Psychiatry, 131(3)*:241-249.

Arieti, S. (1974b). *Interpretation of Schizophrenia.* rev. ed. New York: Basic Books.

Atthowe, J.M., and Krasner, L. (1968). Preliminary report on the application of contingent reinforcement procedures (token economy) on a "chronic" psychiatric ward. *Journal of Abnormal Psychology* 73:37-43.

Ayllon, T., and Azrin, N.H. (1965). The measurement and reinforcement of behavior or psychotics. *Journal of Experimental Analysis of Behavior* 8:357-384.

Babigan, H.M. (1975). Schizophrenia: epidemiology. In *Comprehensive Textbook of Psychiatry, vol. 2,* ed. A.M. Freedman, H.I. Kaplan and J.J. Saddock, 2ⁿᵈ ed. Baltimore: Williams and Wilkins.

Ban, T. (1973). *Recent Advances in the Biology of Schizophrenia.* Springfield, Ill.: Charles C. Thomas.

Bateson, G. Jackson, D., and Weakland, J. (1956). Toward a theory of schizophrenia. *Behavioral Science* 1:251-264.

Bellak, L. (1980). Introduction: an idiosyncratic overview. In *Disorders of the Schizophrenic Syndrome,* ed. L. Bellak. New York: Basic Books.

Blueler, E. (1950). *Dementia Praecox, or the Group of Schizophrenias.* New York: International Universities Press (original work published 1911).

Book, J.A. (1960). Genetical aspects of schizophrenic psychosis. In The *Etiology of Schizophrenia,* ed. D.D. Jackson. New York: Basic Books.

Bowen, M.A. (1960). A family concept of schizophrenia. In The *Etiology of Schizophrenia,* ed. D.D. Jackson. New York: Basic Books.

Bowers, M.K. (1961). Theoretical considerations in the use of hypnosis in the treatment of schizophrenia. *International Journal of Clinical and Experimental Hypnosis* 9:39-46.

Braginsky, B.M., Braginsky, D.D. and Ring, K. (1969). *Methods of Madness: the Mental Hospital as a Last Resort.* New York: Holt, Rinehart, & Winston.

Brandsma, J.M., Maultsby, M.C., and Welsh, R.J. (1980). *Outpatient Treatment of Alcholism: A Review and Comparative Study.* Baltimore: University Park Press.

Broen, W.E., Jr., and Nakamura, C.Y. (1972) Reduced range of sensory sensitivity in chronic nonparanoid schizophrenics. *Journal of Abnormal Psychology* 79(1):106-111.

Busciano, V.M. (1952). Extraneural pathology of schizophrenia (liver, digestive tract, reticuloendothelial system). In *Proceeding of the First*

International Congress of Neuropathology. Turin, Italy: Rosenberg & Sellier.

Buss, A.A. (1966). *Psychopathology.* New York: Wiley.

Cameron, N. (1938). Reasoning, regression and communication in schizophrenia. *Psychological Monographs 50,* (221).

Cameron, N. (1963). *Personality Development of Psychopathology: A Dynamic Approach.* Boston: Houghton Mifflin.

Caputo, D.V. (1968). The parents of the schizophrenic. In *Family Processes and Schizophrenia, ed.* E.G. Mishler and N.E. Waxler. New York: Science House.

Casey, J.F., Bennett, I.F., Lindley, C.J., et al. (1960). Drug therapy and schizophrenia: a controlled study of the effectiveness of chlorpromazine, promazine, phenobarbitol and placebo. *Archives of General Psychiatry 2*:210-220.

Chapman, L.J., and McGhie, A. (1962). A comparative study of disordered attention of schizophrenia. *Journal of Mental Science 108*:487-500.

Cohen, B.D., Nachmani, G., and Rosenberg, S. (1974). Referent communication disturbances in acute schizophrenia. *Journal of Abnormal Psychology 83*(1):1-13.

Crocetti, G.M., and Lemaku, P.V. (1967). Schizophrenia:epidemiology. In *Comprehensive Textbook of Psychiatry,* ed. A.M. Freeman, H.I. Kaplan, and J.J. Saddock, pp. 599-603. Baltimore: Williams and Wilkins.

Cromwell, R.L. and Dokecki, P.R. (1968). Schizophrenia language: disattention interpretation. In *Developments in Applied Psycholingusitics Research,* ed. S. Rosenberg and J.H. Koplin. New York: Macmillan.

Davis, J.M. (1978). Dopamine theory of schizophrenia: a two-factor theory. In *The Nature of Schizophrenia: New Approaches to Research and Treatment,* ed. L.C. Wynne R.L. Cromell, and S. Matthysse. New York: Wiley.

Dohrenwend, B.S., and Dohrenwend, B.P. (1969). *Social Status and Psychological Disorder.* New York: Wiley.

Drake, R.E. and Wallach, M.A. (1979). Will mental patients stay in the community? A social psychological perspective. *Journal of Clinical and Consulting Psychology* 47(2):285-294.

Duke. M.P., and Mullins, M.C. (1973). Preferred interpersonal distance as a function of locus of control orientation in chronic schizophrenics, nonschizophrenic patients and normals. *Journal of Consulting and Clinical Psychology* 41(2):230-234.

Farris, E.L., and Dunham, H.W. (1939). *Mental Disorders in Urban Areas: An Ecological Study of Schizophrenia and Other Psychoses.* Chicago: University of Chicago Press.

Feinsilver, D., and Gunderson, J. (1972). Psychotherapy for schizophrenics: is it indicated? A review of relevant literature. *Schizophrenia Bulletin* 6:11-23.

Fenz, W.D., and Velner, J. (1970). Psychological concomitants of behavioral indexes in schizophrenia. *Journal of Abnormal Psychology* 76(1):27-35.

Fish, J.F., Ramsey, R.G., Huckman, M.S. and Proske, A.E. (1976). *Journal of the American Medical Association.* 236:365-377.

Fromm-Reichmann, F. (1948). Notes on the development of treatment of schizophrenia by psychoanalytic psychotherapy. *Psychiatry11:*263-273.

Fromm-Reichmann, F. (1959). Loneliness. *Psychiatry* 22:1-15.

Garmezy, N. (1970). Process and reactive schizophrenia: some conceptions and issues. *Schizophrenia Bulletin* 2:30-67.

Garmezy, N., and Streitman, S. (1974). Children at risk the search for the antecedents of schizophrenia. Part 1: conceptual models and research methods. *Schizophrenia Bulletin* 8:14-90.

Goffman, E. (1961). *Asylums.* New York: Anchor Books.

Goldstein, M.J., Rodnick, E.H., Jones, J.E., et al. (1978). Familial precursors of schizophrenia: spectrum disorders. In *The Nature of Schizophrenia: New Approaches to Research and Treatment,* ed. L.C. Wynne, R.L. Cromwell, and S. Matthyse. New York: Wiley.

Gottesman, I.I., and Shields, J. (1976). A critical reviews of recent adoption twin, and family studies of schizophrenia: behavioral genetics and perspectives. *Schizophrenia Bulletin* 3:360-378.

Griffith, J.D., Cavanaugh, J., Held, N.N., and Oates, J.A. (1972). Dexatroamphetamine: evaluation of psychomimetic properties in man. *Archives in General Psychiatry 15*:240-244.

Grostein, J.S. (1972). A theoretical rationale for psychoanalytic treatment of schizophrenia. In *Psychotherapy of Schizophrenia,* ed. J. Gunderson and L. Mosher. New York: Jason Aronson.

Gunderson, J.G., Autry, J.H., and Mosher, L.R. (1974). Special report: schizophrenia. *Schizophrenia Bulletin 9*:15-54.

Gunderson, J.G., and Mosher, L. (1975). *Psychotherapy of Schizophrenia.* New York: Jason Aronson.

Hanson, D.R., Gottesman, I.I., and Meehl, P.E. (1977). Genetic theories and the validation of psychiatric diagnoses: implications for the study of children of schizophrenics. *Journal of Abnormal Psychology 86*(6):575-588.

Harris S.E. (1968). Schizophrenics' mutual glance patterns. *Dissertation Abstracts 298*:2202-2203.

Hartmann, H. (1953). Contributions to the metapsychology of schizophrenia. In *Psychoanalytic Study of the Child,* vol. 8, pp. 177-198. New York: International Universities Press.

Heath, R.G. (1960). A biochemical hypothesis on the etiology of schizophrenia. In *The Etiology of Schizophrenia,* ed. D.D. Jackson, pp. 146-156. New York: Basic Books.

Hersen M., and Bellack, A.S. (1976). Social skills training for chronic psychiatric patients: rationale, research findings, and future directions. *Comprehensive Psychiatry 17*:559-580.

Heston, L.L. (1966). Psychiatric disorders in foster home reared children of schizophrenic mothers. *British Journal of Psychiatry 112*:819-825.

Heston, L.L. and Denny, D. (1968). Interactors between early life experience and the biological factors in schizophrenia. In *The Transmission of Schizophrenia,* ed. D. Rosenthal and S.S. Kety. Elmsford, N.Y.: Pergamon.

Hoffer, A., and Osmond, H. (1962). Nicotinamide adenine dinucleotide in the treatment of chronic schizophrenic patients. *British Journal of Psychiatry 114*:915-917.

Hoffer, A., and Osmond, H. (1968). *Diseases of the Nervous System* 23:204-210.

Horwittm M.K. (1956). Fact and artifact in the biology of schizophrenia. *Science 124*:429-433.

Jackson, D.D. and Weakland, J.H. (1961). Conjoint family therapy: some considerations on theory, technique, and results. *Psychiatry* 24(2):30-45.

Jacobs, T. (1975). Family interaction in disturbed and normal families: a methodological and substantive review, *Psychological Bulletin* 82:33-65.

Jacobson, E. (1964). *The Self and the Object World.* New York: International Universities Press.

Johnson, J.E., and Petzel, T.P. (1971) Temporal orientation and time estimation in chronic schizophrenics. *Journal of Clinical Psychology* 27(2):194-196.

Jones, M. (1955). Social Psychiatry. *Digest of Neurological Psychiatry* 23:245-253.

Kallman, F.J. (1941). Knowledge about the significance of psychopathology in family relations. *Marriage and Family Living* 3:81-82.

Kallman, F.J. (1953). *Heredity in Health and Mental Disorder.* New York: W.W. Norton.

Karlson, J.L. (1966). *The Biological Basis for Schizophrenia.* Springfield, Ill.: Charles C Thomas.

Karon, B.P. and Vandenbos, G.R. (1981).*Psychotherapy of Schizophrenia Treatment of Choice.* New York: Jason Aronson.

Keefe, J.A., and Magaro, P.A. (1980). Creativity and schizophrenia: an equivalence of cognitive processing. *Journal of Abnormal Psychology* 89(3):390-398.

Kendler K.S. and Davis, K.L. (1981). The genetics and biochemistry of paranoid schizophrenia and other paranoid psychoses. *Schizophrenia Bulletin1*:689-709.

Kendler, K.S. and Tsuang, M.T. (1981). Nosology of paranoid schizophrenia and other paranoid psychoses. *Schizophrenia Bulletin* 7:594-610.

Kessler, S. (1980).The genetics of schizophrenia: a review *Schizophrenia Bulletin* 6(3):404-416.

Kety, S.S., Rosenthal, D., Wender, P.H., et al. (1975). Mental illness in the biological and adoptive families of adopted individuals who have become schizophrenic. In *Genetic Research in Psychiatry*, ed. R.R. Fieve, D. Rosenthal and H. Brill. Baltimore: Johns Hopkins University Press.

Klein, D.F. (1968). Psychiatric diagnosis and a typology of chemical drug effects. *Psychopharmacologia.13*(5):359-386.

Klein, M. (1946). Notes on some schizoid mechanisms. In *Development in Psychoanalysis,* ed. J. Riviere. London: Hogarth Press.

Kleist, K. (1960). Schizophrenic symptoms and cerebral pathology. *Journal of Mental Schience.* 106:246-253.

Kraeplin, E. (1919). *Demetia Praecox and Paraphrenia.* Trans. R.M. Barclay, ed. G.M. Robertson. Edinburgh: E.S. Livingstone.

Kringlen, E. (1968). An epidemiological clinical twin study of schizophrenia. In *The Transmission of Schizophrenia*, ed. D. Rosenthal, and S.S. Kety. New York: Pregamon.

Lacey, J.I. (1956). The evaluation of autonomic responses: toward a general solution. *Annals of the New York Academy of Science* 67:123-164.

Laing, R.D. (1960). *The Divided Self.* London: Tavistock.

Laing, R.D. (1964). Is schizophrenia a disease? *International Journal of Social Psychiatry* 10:184-193.

Laing, R.D. (1967). *The Politics of Experience.* New York: Pantheon.

Lehmann, H.E. (1974). The somatic and pharmacological treatments of schizophrenia. *Schizophrenia Bulletin 13*:27-45.

Levy, S.M. (1976). Schizophrenic symptomology: reaction or strategy? A study of contextual antecedents. *Journal of Abnormal Psychology* 85:435-445.

Lewine, R.R. (1981). Sex differences in schizophrena: timing or subtypes? *Psychological Bulletin 90*(3):432-444.

Liberman, R.P., Wallace, C., Teigan, J., and Davis, J. (1974). Interventions with psychotic behaviors. In *Innovative Treatment Methods in Psychopathology,* ed. K.S. Calhoun, H.E. Adams, and K.M. Michell. New York: Wiley.

Lidz, T. (1973). *The Origin and Treatment of Schizophrenic Disorders*. New York: Basic Books.

Liem, J.H. (1974). Effects of verbal communications of parents and children: a comparison of normal and schizophrenic families. *Journal of Consulting and Clinical Psychology 42:*438-450.

Linn, E.L. (1977).Verbal auditory hallucinations: mind, self and society. *Journal of Nervous and Mental Disease 164*:8-10.

Luby, E.D., Grisell, J.L. Frohman, C.E., et al. (1962). Biochemical, psychological and behavioral responses to sleep deprivation. *Annals of the New York Academy of Science 96*:71-78.

Lucas, C., Sansbury, P., and Collins, J.G. (1962). A social and clinical study of delusions in schizophrenia. *Journal of Mental Health 108:*747-758.

MacKinnon, P.C. (1969). The palmar anhidrotic response to stress in schizophrenic patients and control groups. *Journal of Psychiatric Research* 7(1):1-7.

Magaro, P.A. (1981). The paranoid and the schizophrenic: The case for distinct cognitive style. *Schizophrenia Bulletin 7*:632-661.

Mahler, M.S. (1975). *The Psychological Birth of a Human Infant*. New York: Basic Books.

Maltiz, S., Wikens, B., and Esecover, H. (1962). A comparison of drug induced hallucinations with those seen in spontaneously occurring psychoses. In *Hallucinations,* ed. L.J. West. New York: Grune & Stratton.

Mandell, A.J., Segal, D.S., Kuczenski, R.T., and Krapp, S. (1972). The search for the schizococcus. *Psychology Today 6*(5):68-72.

Massive, H.N. and Beels, C.C. (1972). The outcome of the family treatment of schizophrenia. *Schizophrenia Bulletin 6*:24-36.

Masterson, J.F. (1972). *Treatment of the Borderline Adolescent*. New York: Wiley.

May, P. R.A. (1975). Schizophrenia: Evaluation of treatment methods. In *Comprehensive Textbook of Psychiatry* ed. A.M. Freedman, H.I. Kaplan, and B.J. Saddock. Baltimore: Williams and Wilkins.

McCord, W., Porta, J., and McCord, J. (1962). The familial genesis of psychoses. *Psychiatry 25*:60-71.

Mednick, S.A. (1958). A learning theory approach to research in schizophrenia. *Psychological Bulletin 70*:681-693.

Mednick, S.A., and Schulsinger, F. (1973). A learning theory of schizophrenia. In *Psychopathology: Contributions from the Social Behavioral and Biological Sciences,* ed. M. Hammer, K. Salzinger, and S. Sutton. New York: Wiley.

Meehl, P.E. (1962). Schizotaxia, schizotypy, schizophrenia. *American Psychologist 17*:827-838.

Meltzer, H.Y., and Stahl, S.M. (1976). The dopamine hypothesis of schizophrenia: a review. *Schizophrenia Bulletin 2*:19-76.

Mishler, E and Waxler, N. (1968). *Interaction in Families: An Experimental Study of Family Processes and Schizophrenia.* New York: Wiley.

Mosher, L.R. (1974). Psychiatric heretics and extra-medical treatment of schizophrenia. In *Strategic Intervention in Schizophrenia: Current Developments in Treatment,* ed. R.Cancro, N. Fox, and L. Shapiro. New York: Behavioral.

Mosher, L.R., and Gunderson, J.G. (1973). Special report: schizophrenia. *Schizophrenia Bulletin 1*:7-9.

Mosher, L.R., Pollin, W., and Stabenau, J.R. (1971). Identical twins discordant for schizophrenia: neurologic findings. *Archives of General Psychiatry 24*:422-430.

Neucherlin, K.H. (1977). Reaction time and attention in schizophrenia: critical evaluation of the data and theories. *Schizophrenia Bulletin 3*:373-428.

O'Brien, C.P. (1975). Group therapy for schizophrenia: a practical approach. *Schizophrenia Bulletin 13*:119-130.

O'Brien, C.P., Hamm, K.B., Ray, B.A., et al. (1972). Group vs. individual psychotherapy with schizophrenics: a controlled outcome study. *Archives of General Psychiatry 27*:474-485.

O'Leary, K.D., and Wilson, G.T. (1975). *Behavior Therapy: Application and Outcome.* Englewood Cliffs, N.J.: Prentice-Hall.

Osmond, H., and Smythies, J. (1952). Schizophrenia: a new approach. *Journal of Mental Science 98*:309-315.

Park, L.C., Baldessarini, R.J. an Ketty, S.S. (1965). Methionine effects on chronic schizophrenics: patients treated with monomine oxidase inhibitors. *Archives of General Psychiatry 12*:346-351.

Paul, G.L., and Lentz, R.J. (1977). *Psychosocial Treatment of Chronic Mental Patients: Milieu versus Social-Learning Programs*. Cambridge: Harvard University Press.

Reiss, D. (1974). Competing hypotheses and warring factions: applying knowledge of schizophrenia. *Schizophrenia Bulletin 8*:7-11.

Ritchie, P.L. (1975). The effect of the interviewer's presentation on some schizophrenic symptomology. Unpublished Doctoral Dissertation, Duke University.

Ritzler, B.A. (1981). Paranoia: prognosis and treatment: A review. *Schizophrenia Bulletin 7*:710-728.

Ritzler, B.A., and Rosenbaum, G. (1974). Propioception in schizophrenics and normals: effects of stimulus and interstimulus interval. *Journal of Abnormal Psychology 83*(2):106-111.

Robbins, L.N. (1966). *Deviant Children Grown Up*. Baltimore: Williams and Wilkins.

Rosenfeld, H.A. (1965). *Psychotic States: A Psychoanalytic Approach*. New York: International Universities Press.

Rosenhan, D.L. (1973) On being sane in insane places. *Science179*:250-258.

Rosenthal, D. (1970). *Genetic Theory and Abnormal Behavior*. New York: McGraw-Hill.

Rosenthal, D., Wender, P.H., Kety, S.S., et al. (1975). Parent-child relationships and psychopathological disorder in the child. *Archives of General Psychiatry 32*:466-476.

Ro-Trock, G.K., Wellisch, D.K., and Schodar, J.C. (1977). A family therapy outcome study in an inpatient setting. *American Journal of Orthopsychiatry 47*:514-522.

Sachar, E.J., Kanter, S., Buie, D., et al. (1970). Psycho-endocrinology of ego disintegration. *American Journal of Psychiatry 126*(8):1067-1078.

Sarbin, T.R., and Mancuso, J.C. (1980). *Schizophrenia: Medical Diagnosis or Moral Verdict*. New York: Pergamon.

Scheff, T.J. (1970). Schizophrenia as ideology. *Schizophrenia Bulletin 2*:15-19.

Scott, C.L. (1976). Life events and schizophrenia: comparison of schizophrenics with a community sample. *Archives of General Psychiatry 34*(1238-1241).

Searles, H. (1959). The effort to drive the other person crazy: an element in etiology and psychotherapy of schizophrenia. *British Journal of Medical Psychology 32*:1-19/

Shimkunas, A.M. (1972). Demand for intimate self-disclosure and pathological verbalizations in schizophrenia. *Journal of Abnormal Psychology 80*:197-205.

Siegel, M., Niswander, G.D., Sachs, E., and Stravos, D. (1959). Taraxein: fact or artifact? *American Journal of Psychiatry 115*:819-820.

Sines, O.J. (1959). Reserpine, adrenaline, and avoidance learning. *Pyschological Reports 5:*321-324.

Singer M.T., Wynne, L.C., and Toohey, M.I., (1978). Communication disorders and the families of schizophrenics. In *The Nature of Schizophrenia: New Approaches to Research and Treatment,* ed. L.C. Wynne, R.L. Cromwell, and S. Matthyse, pp. 499-511. New York: Wiley.

Slater, E. (1968). A review of earlier evidence of genetic factors in schizophrenia. In *The Transmission of Schizophrenia,* ed. D. Rosenthal and S.S. Kety. London: Pergamon.

Snyder, S.H. (1974). *Madness and the Brain.* New York: McGraw-Hill.

Sobel, P.E. (1961). Infant mortality and malformation in children of schizophrenic women. *Psychiatric Quaterly 35*:60-65.

Stephens, J.H. (1970). Long-term course and prognosis in schizophrenia. *Seminars in Psychiatry 2*:464-485.

Stephens, J.A. (1978). *Schizophrenia Bulletin 4*(1)25-47.

Sullivan, H.S. (1931). The modified psychoanalytic treatment of schizophrenia. *American Journal of Psychiatry 11:*519-527.

Sullivan, H.S. (1962). *Schizophrenia as a Human Process.* New York: Norton.

Szasz, T.S. (1976). *Schizophrenia: The Sacred Symbol of Psychiatry.* New York: Basic Books.

Torrey, E.F. (1980). Epidemiology. In *Disorders of the Schizophrenic Syndrome,* ed. L. Bellak. New York: Basic Books.

Ullman, L.P., and Kransner, L. (1975). *Psychological Approach to Abnormal Behavior* 2nd ed. Englewood Cliffs, N.J.: Prentice-Hills.

Ungerstedt, U. (1971). Stereotaxic mapping of the monoamine pathways in the rat brain. *Acta Physiologica Scandinavica 367:*1-48.

Vaughn, C.E., and Leff, J.P. (1976). The influence of family and social factors on the course of psychiatric illness: a comparison of schizophrenic and depressed neurotic patients. *British Journal of Psychiatry 129*:125-137.

Vaughn, C.E., and Leff, J.P. (1981). Patterns of emotional response in relatives of schizophrenic patients. *Schizophrenia Bulletin 7*:43-44.

Von Domarus, E. (1944). The specific laws of logic in schizophrenia. In *Language and Thought in Schizophrenia: Collected Papers,* ed. J.S. Kasanin, pp. 104-114. Berkeley: University of California Press.

Waring, M., and Ricks, D.F. (1965). Family patterns of children who became adult schizophrenics. *Journal of Nervous and Mental Disease 140*:351-364.

Waxler, N.E. (1974). Culture and mental illness: a social labeling perspective. *Journal of Nervous and Mental Disease 159*(6):379-395.

Wender, P.H., Rosenthal D., Kety, S.S., et al. (1974). Cross-fostering: a research strategy for clarifying the role of genetic and experiential factors in the etiology of schizophrenia. *Archives of General Psychiatry 30*(1)121-128.

White, R.W., and Watt, N.F. (1973). *The Abnormal Personality.* New York: Ronald.

Winnicott, D.W. (1958). *Collected Papers.* London: Travistock.

Wolberg, L.R. (1954). *The Technique of Psychotherapy.* New York: Grune & Stratton.

Yates, A.J. (1966). Psychological deficit. In *Annual Review of Psychology,* ed. P.R. Farnsworth. Palo Alto, Calif.: Annual Review.

Yolles, S.F., and Kramer, M. (1969). Vital statistics of schizophrenia. In *The Schizophrenia Syndrome,* ed. L. Bellak and L. Loeb, pp. 66-113. New York: Grune and Stratton.

Zigler, E., and Levine, J. (1981). Premorbid competence in schizophrenia: what is being measured? *Journal of Consulting and Clinical Psychology 49*(1):96-105.

Zubin, J., and Spring, B. (1977). Vulnerability: a new view of schizophrenia. *Journal of Abnormal Psychology 86*:103-126.

Chapter 13

Psychopharmacology for Mental Disorders

Svetlana Popova, M.A., MFT

Medications are often prescribed to treat the symptoms of the emotional or mental problems that clients report. They are seldom used together with psychotherapy. However, it is important for the clinician to be familiar with the most common medications and to also be knowledgeable about the side effects and effectiveness of these medications (Kessler et al, 2005). Medications are prescribed to make people feel better so that they are able to function and participate in daily activities. Many of the mental illnesses can be treated without medications or with a combination of drugs and psychotherapy. However, in severe cases of individuals with illnesses such as depression or bipolar disorder, it is better to take medication to avoid possible complications and to recover enough for daily functioning.

Medication does not cure a disorder, but it may alleviate or reduce the symptoms. Some of the medications are prescribed for a short period of time and then the person is weaned off; others need to be taken for longer periods (Barlow & Durand, 2009). The same medication may have different effects on different individuals. There is also a different time-frame for when the medication starts working. For some medications, it may take several weeks for the effects to be noticed. Sometimes medications will be changed if the client reports that it is not working or if the client has an adverse reaction. Individuals, who do not improve with the first drug, may improve with a different one. Sometimes a second medication may be prescribed in order to enhance the effects of the first drug. It is also important for the client to not stop taking the medication abruptly because of the withdrawal symptoms and possible relapse. The medication should be gradually decreased with a doctor's recommendation (Zuvekas, 2005).

It is important to know that medications used for mental illnesses can have many unpleasant side effects, some of which may be irreversible. A side effect is an undesirable secondary effect of medication (Wooley & Shaw, 1954). Side effects can occur when the dosage is increased/decreased or an individual is ending the treatment. When side effects from taking medication are severe, an individual may be prescribed another drug to reduce the symptoms. Medications for mental illnesses are widely used nowadays. There are different types of medications available, such as narcoleptics, stimulants, antidepressants, and antianxiety medications. These medications typically have an effect on central nervous system, focusing on neurotransmitters and their receptors.

Below is a description of the medications used for the more common mental disorders:

Mood Disorders and Medications

Medications generally used for mood disorders are called antidepressants. They work by stabilizing some of the natural chemicals or neurotransmitters in the brain. Antidepressants are known to balance serotonin, norepinephrine, and dopamine. Antidepressants typically start working after 3 or 4 weeks, and may need to be continued for a long time depending on the severity of a disorder. There are three basic types of medication used to treat mood disorders: SSRIs (Serotonin-Specific Reuptake Inhibitors), MAO (Monoamine Oxidase) inhibitors, and tricyclic antidepressants. Tricyclic antidepressants (Tofranil, Elavil) are used for severe depression and may promote new nerve growth in the brain. When an individual starts antidepressants, he or she may feel worse in the beginning of the treatment. There are known cases when antidepressants lead to suicidal ideation especially in children and adolescents. Other side effects include dry mouth, constipation, difficulty urinating, drowsiness, sexual dysfunction, and weight gain (Pacher & Kecskemeti, 2004). Many side effects are said to disappear eventually.

MAO inhibitors work by breaking down serotonin and norepinephrine. MAO inhibitors appear to boost mood by progressing brain cell communication. They tend to be more effective and have fewer side effects. However, an individual taking those drugs needs to be very careful with diet because of the drug's interaction with tyramine, which can be commonly found in beer, red wine, or cheese. MAO inhibitors are also dangerous if taken with cold medicine. Common side effects include dry mouth, drowsiness, insomnia, dizziness, headache, involuntary muscle jerks, weight gain, and muscle aches. MAO inhibitors are usually prescribed when tricyclics are unsuccessful (Williams et al, 2002).

As the name implies, SSRIs (Prozac, Celexa, Lexapro, Paxil, Pexeva, Zoloft) work by blocking the reuptake of serotonin. The most frequently prescribed antidepressants, SSRIs alleviate depression by having an effect on neurotransmitters, which are used to correspond between brain cells. Changing the steadiness of serotonin appears to help brain cells send and receive chemical messages, which in turn boosts the individual's mood. Side effects may include but are not limited to: nausea, nervousness, dry mouth, vomiting, diarrhea, insomnia, suicidal ideation, and sexual dysfunction. SSRIs may also be used to treat conditions other than depression, such as anxiety.

St. John's wort is a natural herb medicine used for treatment of mood disorders. It is known to have few side effects and can be found in health food stores. However, a desired effect can be only achieved with the proper components. St. John's wort can dangerously interact with other medications and appears to interfere with some medications used to treat heart disease, depression, seizures, certain cancers, and oral contraceptives (Unutzer et al, 2000).

Another effective antidepressant drug is lithium. Side effects of lithium are potentially more serious and may result in fatigue, weight gain, or poisoning. Lithium is typically used for bipolar disorder because it seems to be effective in putting off manic episodes (Leahy et al, 2011).

Bipolar Disorder

Bipolar Disorder may be treated with mood stabilizers, antipsychotics, and antidepressants. Individuals who are prescribed mood stabilizers usually need to continue treatment for years. Anticonvulsant medications (Depakote, Tegretol, Lamictal, Trileptal) are also used as mood stabilizers. Antipsychotics used to treat people with bipolar disorder symptoms include Zyprexa, Abilify, Risperdal, Geodon, and Clozaril. Antidepressants such as Prozac, Paxil, and Zoloft are a few that are used for individuals diagnosed with bipolar disorder (Tschoner et al, 2007). People with bipolar disorder should not take an antidepressant on its own because depression can be quickly switched to mania which can be dangerous. There is no cure for bipolar disorder, but treatment works for many people (Sachs et al, 2000). It may be helpful for family members to keep a daily chart of mood symptoms, treatments, sleep patterns, and life events.

Anxiety Medications

Anxiety disorders are typically treated with antidepressants, anti-anxiety medication (benzodiazepines), and beta-blockers. Beta-blockers (Sectral, Tenormin, Zebeta, Metoprolol, Corgard, Bystolic) are used to treat a variety of conditions such as irregular heart rhythm, heart attacks, heart failure, migraines, and glaucoma. They work to reduce high blood pressure. Beta-blockers appear to manage some of the physical symptoms of anxiety, such as trembling and sweating. Many people who take beta-blockers do not have side effects such as fatigue, headache, cold hands, diarrhea, and constipation.

SSRIs such as Prozac, Zoloft, Lexapro, Paxil, and Celexa are commonly prescribed for panic disorder, OCD, PTSD, and social phobia. SSRIs are presently the indicated drug for panic disorder, although many side effects such as sexual dysfunction are possible to occur. SSRIs are effective for anxiety disorders in general and are useful for PTSD because they tend to alleviate severe anxiety and panic attacks that are so prominent in this disorder.

The anti-anxiety medications include Klonopin (for social phobia), Ativan (for panic disorder), and Xanax (for panic disorder and GAD). Benzodiazepines may make it difficult for some people to stop taking them because of psychological and physical dependence on the drug. Their most favorable use is for a short-term relief of anxiety. Approximately 60% of people benefit when on medication for anxiety, but the relapse rates are high as soon as the medication is stopped (Ashton, 1994).

Sexual Issues and Medications

A variety of drugs such as Viagra, Levitra, and Cialis have been developed to treat sexual dysfunctions, particularly Erectile Disorder. These drugs work by increasing nitric oxide, a chemical naturally produced in the body. Nitric oxide releases and loosens up blood vessels in the penis, assisting in getting and maintaining an erection. These drugs have no influence on the sex drive. They may be not safe to use if an individual has health problems such as eye problems, heart problems, liver disease, kidney disease, or a history of stroke. Side effects may include but are not limited to: headache, indigestion, runny nose, temporary vision changes, and dizziness. Some men may experience more serious side effects such as hearing or vision loss and a persistent erection.

Female sexual dysfunctions may be treated with hormonal medications depending on the disorder. Estrogen or androgen therapy may be used if a female sexual dysfunction has a hormonal cause.

There are some drugs such as cyproterone acetate and Depo-Provera that are used to treat paraphilia. These drugs may be beneficial for sexual offenders and work by decreasing sexual desire or reducing testosterone levels, but are not always successful.

Schizophrenia Medications

Neuroleptics (meaning "taking hold of the nerves") are the antipsychotic medications used for psychotic disorders. Neuroleptics are dopamine antagonists. These drugs work by alleviating positive symptoms such as delusions and hallucinations. They may be also helpful in reducing negative symptoms such as social deficits but to a lesser extent (Anderson et al, 1986). There are typical antipsychotics such as Thorazine, Prolixin, Serentil, Trilafon, Mellaril, Stelazine, Haldol, Loxitane, Moban, and Navane. These drugs may have potential neurological side effects such as Tardive Dyskinesia, which may be irreversible (Davidhizar & McBride, 1985). Side effects may also include dry mouth, blurred vision, and fatigue which may be a reason for some people to stop taking it. Each of these drugs may be effective for some people and not for others. Some people may be prescribed atypical antipsychotics such as Risperdal or Zyprexa. It may take several weeks before the antipsychotic medication takes effect.

Personality Disorders and Medication

For the personality disorders such as Borderline Personality Disorder-Compulsive Personality Disorder, Narcissistic Personality Disorder, Antisocial Personality Disorder and others, there are several drugs available. They include antidepressants, mood-stabilizing medication, anti-anxiety medication, and antipsychotic medications. Antidepressants may be prescribed for depressed mood, irritability, anger, or hopelessness.

Mood stabilizers can be helpful with mood swings, aggression, and impulsivity. Anti-anxiety medication may help with insomnia or agitation. Antipsychotic medication may be helpful for individuals with psychosis symptoms like losing touch with reality or odd communication (Bender et al, 2001).

Substance Abuse and Medication

First of all, substance abuse problem may be a sign of serious underlying issue. It is important to find out the reason for abusing alcohol which may include marital distress, anxiety, depression, and many other issues. Secondly, there are medications for withdrawal and for recovery. There are anti-anxiety medications (benzodiazepines) and seizure drugs used in the treatment of withdrawal symptoms.

There are different medications used for recovery when an individual practices sobriety. Antagonist drugs block or work against the effects of psychoactive drugs. Antagonists can be useful as an addition to psychotherapy. Medicines used for recovery include Antabuse, Revia, Vivitrol, Campral, and Topamax. Antabuse is typically used as an aversive treatment for individuals with alcohol dependence. This drug averts the breakdown of acetaldehyde (a by-product of alcohol) and the resultant buildup of acetaldehyde can make an individual feel sick. People who attempt to drink alcohol with Antabuse experience nausea, vomiting, elevated heart rate and respiration. Revia and Vivitrol can help with alcohol and opioid drug dependence. This antagonist works by blocking the part of the brain involved in generating pleasure from drinking alcohol or taking other drugs. Side effects of Revia and Vivitrol include nausea, low energy, and dizziness. Campral works by restoring the natural balance of neurotransmitters and may diminish alcohol cravings. Campral side effects include nausea, diarrhea, fatigue, change in sexual desire, and weight loss/gain. Topamax may be helpful with alcohol dependence and is known as an anticonvulsant drug. Some of the Topamax side effects contain fatigue, drowsiness, dizziness, trouble concentrating, confusion, diarrhea, and weight loss.

Methadone is another medication for drug abuse. Methadone is a narcotic analgesic or pain reliever. Methadone is typically used to treat addiction created by opiates or for other medical purposes like pain relief. This drug shares many characteristics of morphine and has similar side effects of other narcotic medications (Goodnough & Zezima, 2001). Methadone works by targeting parts of the brain and spinal cord to block the "high" caused by drugs such as heroin and by preventing the powerful euphoric rush of the drug. It is taken once a day and can ease the withdrawal symptoms for 24 to 36 hours, reducing the chance of relapse. In severe cases of opiate addiction, methadone needs to be taken for years. Some of the side effects include fatigue, drowsiness, dry mouth, difficulty breathing, difficulty urinating, and constipation. Each dose of Methadone stays in the body for a long time. That is why there is a possibility to become addicted to the drug. Also, some addicts may use it as the primary drug of choice (Goodnough & Zezima, 2001). Methadone relieves pain and can be used as part of a treatment program for detoxification or drug addiction.

Suboxone is a combination of buprenorphine and naloxone. It is an opioid medication similar to heroin, morphine, and codeine. It is commonly used to treat opiate addiction and its withdrawal symptoms. Sometimes it becomes a drug of choice. Suboxone works by blocking the effects of opiates while decreasing cravings and alleviating withdrawal symptoms. This drug is not recommended for children as it may cause potential death. Possible side effects include headache, sweating, nausea; sleep problems, flu-like symptoms, and difficulty breathing. Respiratory depression is a side effect that is prominent to other medications for opioid addiction. Suboxone is less dangerous than methadone because it is easier to stop taking but is habit-forming as well. Alcohol avoidance is recommended as with other opioid drugs as alcohol use may increase or interfere with the possible side effects.

Developmental Disorders and Medications

Medications commonly used to treat ADHD are stimulants. Stimulants tend to enhance and balance neurotransmitters. They include Ritalin, Metadate, and Concerta. They seem to be effective in reducing major symptoms of the disorder such as hyperactivity, impulsivity, and lack of concentration. Adderall is a longer-acting version but has similar effects. All these drugs appear to improve compliance and diminish negative behaviors in many children, and their effects do not generally last when the drugs are discontinued (Shea et al, 2004). Some children with ADHD do not respond to medications, and those children who do respond show progress in ability to focus their attention but do not usually show improvements in the areas of academics and social skills (Safren et al, 2005). The medication may cause unpleasant side effects, such as insomnia, drowsiness, irritability, and suicidal thinking.

People with mental disorders are able to live satisfying lives with the help of medications. Some mental disorders may be serious and long lasting while some mental disorders are mild. The best treatment option may be a combination of medication with psychotherapy. Medications may also help individuals to get better results in psychotherapy. Some individuals with severe cases of mental disorders such as depression are not able to function without medication. Because some medications work better for some people than for others; individuals may have to try several drugs before finding the one that works. It is important to know what kind of medication the individual is taking and for how long to be able to provide better treatment. Marriage and family therapists should be familiar with the possible medications clients take in order to help them to discontinue the medication or watch for side effects. Marriage and family therapists need to be able to consult with psychiatrists if medications should be changed or discontinued. It is also important to recognize how current medications fit in the overall treatment plan.

List of medications used for treatment of mental disorders and possible side effects:

Type	Medication	Use	Side effects
SSRIs	Prozac	OCD, depression, panic, social anxiety, PTSD, generalized anxiety	Headache, dry mouth, nausea, sleeplessness or drowsiness, agitation, suicidal thinking, sexual problems for both men and women
	Luvox	OCD, depression, panic, social anxiety, PTSD, generalized anxiety	
	Zoloft	OCD, depression, panic, social anxiety, PTSD, generalized anxiety	
	Paxil	OCD, depression, panic, social anxiety, PTSD, generalized anxiety	
	Lexapro	OCD, depression, panic, social anxiety, PTSD, generalized anxiety	

	Celexa		
SNRIs	Effexor	OCD, depression, panic, social anxiety, PTSD, generalized anxiety	Headache, loss of appetite, sexual problems, insomnia, nausea, dry mouth, dizziness, excessive sweating, fatigue, agitation, constipation
	Effexor XR	Panic, OCD, depression, social anxiety, generalized anxiety	
	Cymbalta	Generalized anxiety, social anxiety, panic, OCD	
	Pristiq	Depression	
BENZO-DIAZEPINES	Xanax	Panic, generalized anxiety, phobias, social anxiety, OCD	A risk of addiction, drowsiness, poor concentration, irritability, sedation, dizziness, weakness, unsteadiness,
	Klonopin	Panic, generalized anxiety, phobias, social anxiety	feeling of depression, loss of orientation
	Valium	Generalized anxiety, panic, phobias	

	Ativan	Generalized anxiety, panic, phobias	
	Serax	Generalized anxiety, panic, phobias	
	Librium	Generalized anxiety, panic, phobias	
Beta Blockers	Inderal	Social anxiety	Fatigue, cold hands, headache, upset stomach, constipation, diarrhea, dizziness.
	Tenormin	Social anxiety	
Tricyclic Anti-depressants	Tofranil	Panic, depression, generalized anxiety, PTSD	Dry mouth, constipation, bladder problems, sexual problems for men and women, blurred vision, drowsiness.
	Norpramin	Panic, depression, generalized anxiety, PTSD	
	Aventyl	Panic, depression, generalized anxiety, PTSD	
	Elavil	Panic, depression, generalized anxiety, PTSD	

	Adapin	Panic, depression	
	Anafranil	Panic, depression, OCD	
MAOIs (monoamine oxidase inhibitors)	Nardil	Panic, OCD, social anxiety, depression, generalized anxiety, PTSD	Not to take with food containing tyramine, dry mouth, nausea, diarrhea or constipation, headache, drowsiness, insomnia
	Parnate	Panic, OCD, depression, generalized anxiety, PTSD	
Typical Antipsychotics	Thorazine	Schizophrenia	Rigidity, persistent muscle spasm, tremors, restlessness, tardive dyskinesia
	Haldol	Schizophrenia	
Atypical Antipsychotics	Clozaril	Schizophrenia	Dry mouth, blurred vision, constipation, dizziness, weight gain, problems sleeping, tardive dyskinesia
	Risperdal	Schizophrenia	
	Zyprexa	Schizophrenia	
	Seroquel	Schizophrenia	
	Geodon	Schizophrenia	

	Abilify	Schizophrenia	
	Invega	Schizophrenia	
	Latuda	Schizophrenia	
Mood Stabilizers	Lithium	Bipolar Disorder	Nausea, vomiting, diarrhea, trembling, increased thirst and need to urinate, weight gain, drowsiness, a metallic taste in the mouth, abnormalities in kidney and thyroid function, blacking out, slurred speech, changes in heart rhythm or heart block, and increase in the number of white blood cells.
	Equetro	Bipolar Disorder	Weight gain, drowsiness, low energy, upset stomach, changes in liver function, thrombocytopenia, Stevens-Johnson syndrome, vomiting, blurred vision.
	Depakote	Bipolar Disorder	
	Lamictal	Bipolar Disorder	

Herbal Medicine	St. John's wort	Mild depression, anxiety, SAD, OCD	Can dangerously interact with other medication, upset stomach, skin rashes, fatigue, restlessness, headache, dry mouth, feelings of dizziness or mental confusion.
Medication for sexual Dysfunctions	Viagra	Erectile Dysfunction	Sudden vision loss, facial flushing, headache, stomach pain, nasal congestion, nausea, diarrhea, loss of hearing, dizziness,
	Levitra	Erectile Dysfunction	allergic reaction, nausea, tingling sensations, indigestion, back pain, muscle aches, flushing, runny nose.
	Cialis	Erectile Dysfunction	
Alcohol and drug abuse and dependence medications	Antabuse	Alcohol abuse	Blurred vision, numbness or tingling, stomach pain, skin rash or itching, yellow eyes or skin.

	Revia	Drug and alcohol addiction	Allergic reaction, blurred vision, fast heartbeat, mood changes, hallucinations, confusion, nausea, stomach pain, dark urine, yellow skin and eyes.
	Campral	Alcohol dependence	Diarrhea, nausea, vomiting, gas, stomach pain, loss of appetite, headache, drowsiness, dizziness, constipation, fatigue, weight gain/ loss, changes in sexual desire.
	Topamax	Prevention and control of seizures and migraines, habit of drinking too much alcohol	Tiredness, drowsiness, dizziness, loss of coordination, tingling, loss of appetite, diarrhea, weight loss, confusion, slowed thinking, trouble concentrating, nervousness, and memory problems.
	Methadose	Severe pain, heroin addiction	Low blood pressure, drowsiness, breathing problems, dizziness, fainting, nausea, vomiting.

	Suboxone	Opiate addiction	Cough, dizziness, fever or chills, flushing, headache, lower back or side pain, painful or difficult urination, sweating.
Stimulant medications	Ritalin	ADHD, narcolepsy	Fast heartbeat, feeling like you might pass out, fever, sore throat, headache, skin rash, aggression, restlessness, hallucinations, muscle twitches, easy bruising, high blood pressure.
	Metadate	ADD, ADHD, narcolepsy	Headache, stomach pain, loss of appetite, trouble sleeping, dizziness, nausea, vomiting, irritability, nervousness, blurred vision, dry mouth, constipation.
	Concerta	ADHD	Abdominal pain, decreased appetite, headache, dry mouth, nausea, insomnia, anxiety, dizziness, weight loss, irritability, hyperhidrosis. May lead to dependency.

	Adderall	ADHD, narcolepsy	Nervousness, restlessness, excitability, dizziness, headache, fear, anxiety, tremor, high blood pressure and heart rate. Habit forming.

References

Anderson, C. M., Reiss, D. J., & Hogarty, G. E. (1986). *Schizophrenia and the Family*. New York: Guilford Press.

American Psychiatric Association (2013). *Diagnostic and Statistical Manual of Mental Disorders* (5th ed). Arlington, VA: American Psychiatric Publishing.

Ashton, H. (1994). Guidelines for the Rational Use of Benzodiazepines. *Drugs*, 48(1), 25-40.

Barlow, D., & Durand, V., M. (2009). *Abnormal Psychology: An Integrative Approach*, 5th Ed.

Bender, D. S., Dolan, R. T., Skodol, A. E., Sanislow, C. A., Dyck, I. R., McGlashan, T. H., & Davidhizar, R., & McBride, A. (1985). Teaching the client with schizophrenia about medication. *Patient Education and Counseling*, 7(2), 137-145.

Depression and How Psychotherapy and other Treatments Help People Recover. (n.d.). *www.apa.org*. Retrieved from http://apa.org/topics/depress/recover.aspx#

Depression Medications. (n.d.). *Drugs.com | Prescription Drug Information, Interactions & Side Effects*. Retrieved from http://www.drugs.com/

Goodnough, A., & Zezima, K. (2011). When Children's Scribbles hide a Prison Drug. *www.nytimes.com*. Retrieved from http://www.nytimes.com/2011/05/27/us/27smuggle.html?pagewanted=all&_r=0

Gunderson, J. G. (2001). Treatment utilization by patients with personality disorders. *American Journal of Psychiatry*, 158(2), 295-302.

Information about Drug Side Effects. (n.d.). *Www.drugs.com.* Retrieved from http://www.drugs.com/sfx/

Kessler, R., C., Demler, O., Frank, R., G., Olfson, M., Pincus, H., A., Walters, E., E., Wang, P., Wells, K., B., & Zaslavsky, A., M. (2005) Prevalence and Treatment of Mental Disorders: 1990 to 2003. *The New England Journal of Medicine*, 352:2515-2523.

Leahy, R., Holland, S., J. & McGinn, L., K. (2011). *Treatment Plan and Interventions for Anxiety Disorders.* The Guilford Press. 2nd ed.

(n.d.). Retrieved March 5, 2015, from http://www.cdc.gov

(n.d.). Retrieved March 5, 2015, from http://www.levitra.com

(n.d.). Retrieved March 5, 2015, from http://www.mayoclinic.com

(n.d.). Retrieved March 6, 2015, from http://www.methadone.com

(n.d.). Retrieved March 7, 2015, from http://www.nami.org

(n.d.). Retrieved March 7, 2015, from http://www.nimh.gov

(n.d.). Retrieved March 8, 2015, from http://www.webmd.com

(n.d.). Retrieved March 11, 2015, from http://www.viagra.com

(n.d.). Retrieved March 15, 2015, from http://www.suboxine.com

(n.d.). Retrieved March 15, 2015, from http://www.topamax.com

(n.d.). Retrieved March 18, 2015, from http://www.psychcentral.com

(n.d.). Retrieved March 22, 2015, from http://www.rxlist.com

(n.d.). Retrieved March 22, 2015, from http://www.revia.com

(n.d.). Retrieved March 25, 2015, from http://www.fda.gov

(n.d.). Retrieved March 25, 2015, from http://www.howstuffworks.com

(n.d.). Retrieved March 25, 2015, from http://www.cesar.umd.edu

(n.d.). Retrieved March 25, 2015, from http://www.cialis.com

Pacher, P., & Kecskemeti, V. (2004). Cardiovascular Side Effects of New Antidepressants and Antipsychotics: New Drugs, Old Concerns? *Current Pharmaceutical Design*, 10(20), 2463.

Prescription Drugs and the Changing Patterns of Treatment for Mental Disorders, 1996-2001. *Health Affairs*, 24(1), 195-205.

Sachs, G. S., Printz, D. J., Kahn, D. A., Carpenter, D., & Docherty, J. P. (2000). The expert consensus guideline series: medication treatment of bipolar disorder. *Postgrad Med*, 1, 1-104.

Safren, S. A., Otto, M. W., Sprich, S., Winett, C. L., Wilens, T. E., & Biederman, J. (2005).

Cognitive-behavioral therapy for ADHD in medication-treated adults with continued symptoms. *Behavior research and therapy*, *43*(7), 831-842.

Shea, S., Turgay, A., Carroll, A., Schulz, M., Orlik, H., Smith, I., & Dunbar, F. (2004). Risperidone in the treatment of disruptive behavioral symptoms in children with autistic and other pervasive developmental disorders. *Pediatrics*, *114*(5), e634-e641.

Tschoner, A., Engl, J., Laimer, M., Kaser, S., Rettenbacher, M., Fleischhacker, W. W. & Ebenbichler, C. F. (2007). Metabolic side effects of antipsychotic medication. *International journal of clinical practice*, *61*(8), 1356-1370.

Understanding the Ritalin debate. (n.d.). Retrieved March 5, 2014, from http://apa.org/topics/adhd/ritalin-debate.aspx

Unutzer, J., Klap, R., Sturm, R., Young, A., S., Marmon, T., Shatkin, J., & Wells, K. B. (2000). Mental Disorders and the Use of Alternative Medicine: Results from a National Survey. *American Journal of Psychiatry*, 157(11), 1851-1857.Wang, S., S. (2014). Medications Cut Violence Among Mentally Ill In Study. *The Wall Street Journal*. www.wsj.com

Williams, R. S., Cheng, L., Mudge, A. W., & Harwood, A. J. (2002). A common mechanism of action for three mood-stabilizing drugs. *Nature*, *417*(6886), 292-295.

Wooley, D., W., & Shaw, E. (1954). A biochemical and pharmacological suggestion about certain mental disorders. *Proceedings of the National Academy of Sciences of the United States of America*, *40*(4), 228.Zuvekas, S. H. (2005).

Printed in the United States
By Bookmasters